Including Children with Special Needs

Including Children with Special Needs

A Handbook for Educators and Parents

EDITED BY
Diane Schwartz

Foreword by Susan Semel

HANDBOOKS FOR EDUCATORS AND PARENTS
James T. Sears, Series Editor

GREENWOOD PRESS
Westport, Connecticut • London

Library of Congress Cataloging-in-Publication Data

Including children with special needs : a handbook for educators and parents /
    edited by Diane Schwartz ; foreword by Susan Semel.
        p.   cm.—(Handbooks for Educators and Parents, ISSN 1554-6039)
    Includes bibliographical references and index.
    ISBN 0–313-33377–7 (alk. paper)
    1. Children with disabilities—Education—United States—Handbooks,
manuals, etc.   2. Mainstreaming in education—United States—Handbooks,
manuals, etc.   3. Special education—Parent participation—United States—
Handbooks, manuals, etc.   I. Schwartz, Diane.
LC3981.I62   2005
371.9'046—dc22   2005009649

British Library Cataloguing in Publication Data is available.

Library of Congress Catalog Card Number: 2005009649
ISBN: 0–313-33377–7
ISSN: 1554-6039

First published in 2005

Greenwood Press, 88 Post Road West, Westport, CT 06881
An imprint of Greenwood Publishing Group, Inc.
www.greenwood.com

Printed in the United States of America

The paper used in this book complies with the
Permanent Paper Standard issued by the National
Information Standards Organization (Z39.48–1984).

10 9 8 7 6 5 4 3 2 1

Every reasonable effort has been made to trace the owners of copyright materials in
this book, but in some instances this has proven impossible. The author and publisher
will be glad to receive information leading to more complete acknowledgments in
subsequent printings of the book and in the meantime extend their apologies for any
omissions.

For my children, Anna, Sarah, Laura, and Ben, whose work helping others is a constant source of inspiration.

Contents

Series Foreword

How can I advocate for my child? What are the best-school practices in teaching diverse learners? What programs are most effective in enhancing learning? These simple but profoundly important questions are the heart of this book series.

This handbook is a practical guide for parents/families and a standard reference resource for educators and libraries. The entire series provides an overview of contemporary research, theories, practices, policy issues, and instructional approaches on a variety of timely and important educational topics. It also gives straightforward recommendations for evaluating curriculum and advocating for children in schools.

Written in clear language, each handbook is divided into three major parts. An overview in Part I provides a framework for understanding the topic in terms of research and policy, and summarizes popular approaches, programs, and curricula. The next two parts go into greater depth in a manner most appropriate either for educators or parents, including an annotated bibliography of useful print, audio/video, and electronic resources and the end of each part. Part II is written for teachers, administrators, allied professionals, and those who are studying for such professions. It gives a concise overview of current and cutting-edge research and scholarship, details on research-based effective programs and best practices, and a guide for evaluating and implementing such programs and practices. Part III is written directly for parents and families. It provides an overview of specific issues of concern to parents, implications from research for everyday family life, and strategies for supporting their (and others') children through involvement in schools and civic life.

Schooling is one of the most essential institutions within a democratic society and education the single most important family investment. For citizens and parents, though, there are few "owner's manuals" to determine the quality of their investment. Too often we rely on others' judgments and standardized tests to infer value. But, just as quantity does equal quality, the judgment of others is no substitute for our own. Handbooks for Educators and Parents is the manual for a new millennium of learning and teaching.

Foreword

When Diane Schwartz initially conceived this book and discussed it with me, I was excited about the project, particularly because it was for a wide range of audiences engaged in the education of special needs children. I use the word "education" widely, to include those individuals both inside and outside of schools: parents, social workers, therapists, teacher educators, and teacher practitioners. This book has not disappointed me.

As I read the book in order to write this foreword, I was overwhelmed with the immense amount of knowledge that is contained within this volume both theoretical and practical—no mean feat. I was also struck by the realization of how far the field of special education has come and how far we have come as a society understanding and providing for children with special needs.

When my daughter Mags, a child with special needs, was born in 1969, this certainly was not the case. Because she was my first child, I had no frame of reference for normal child development. At best, I had my Psych 101 textbook, which had a brief chapter on the subject. I knew that something was amiss when her eyes did not set but continued to wander, and when she did not sit up at the appointed time the text said she should. When she crawled, she did so by dragging her legs, and her speech came late in the game. She was treated symptomatically, beginning with an orthopedist, then an audiologist and a speech therapist, and finally, a neurologist. I remember my pediatrician, new to the profession, telling me not to worry—that "even the most severely retarded children learn how to talk." I often wonder, if roles were reversed, how he would have felt if I had given that pronouncement to him. Clearly, I have not forgotten his words.

This scenario occurred at the beginning of 1970 when children and adults were still labeled retarded and worse, and warehoused in facilities such as Willowbrook, not much of an improvement from the conditions nineteenth-century social reformer Dorothea Dix fought against in Massachusetts. Willowbrook, however, became infamous after Geraldo Rivera exposed the inhumane and shocking treatment of its clients on national television, and serves as an important turning point in reforming the diagnosis and treatment of special needs populations.

A lot has happened in the last thirty-five years, as this book so importantly indicates. The passage of PL 94-142 in 1975 and that of IDEA two decades later have provided legal protections for children with special needs and contributed to the maturation of special education as a professional subject and academic discourse. Yet, as a society, we still do not deal as well as we should with disability, and mislabeling and overseparation of children are sometimes the result of zealous assessment regimes. Today, issues of special versus regular placement, mainstreaming and inclusion, medication and medicalization continue to be hotly debated. Nevertheless, we have made significant progress and continue to do so. Today, my daughter lives in a group home in New York State and has a job washing dishes. She can read, write, and speak, but she cannot as yet live unsupervised and cannot travel on her own. However, thanks to educated, caring professionals, she is reaching her potential and is a delightful if exhausting individual. It is my hope that this book will have a wide readership and be of service to those who care for and educate children like my daughter, Mags. I only wish that I had had this book when my daughter was born.

Susan Semel, Ed.D.
City College of New York and
CUNY Graduate Center, New York City

Preface

In 1997 the Individuals with Disabilities Act (IDEA) was reauthorized, establishing the view that the best way to educate students with special needs is in the general education classroom. This dramatic shift in the interpretation of "least restrictive environment" from a continuum of settings to a more inclusive one presents many policy changes for teachers and schools. Specifically, it requires school districts, to the maximum extent appropriate, to enable students with disabilities to be educated with their nondisabled classmates. If more restrictive environments, such as separate classes, are employed, this is acceptable only if the nature or severity of the disability is such that education in a regular class with aids and services cannot be achieved. Students with disabilities are now expected to participate in the same general curriculum taught to all the other children in their school and are held to the same standards as their nondisabled peers. In addition, the law requires general education teachers and parents to take a greater role in the Individualized Education Plan (IEP) process.

To meet the challenges these mandates present, we must help prepare all students of teaching to develop the necessary knowledge, skills, and values to serve children with special needs in general education classrooms. There is a significant need for current, straightforward, and user-friendly material to address the concerns of parents and inservice practitioners who have not been prepared for the changes they are now facing in their classrooms. We must also prepare the preservice general education student who may not be required to study special education but must work with classified students in their fieldwork and in their future professional life as teachers in inclusive programs.

FOCUS OF THE BOOK

Including Children with Special Needs: A Handbook for Educators and Parents is designed to meet the needs of parents and general educators in their newly defined role. The content is drawn from the many questions heard from parents who are trying to understand how inclusion affects the education of their children with special needs; from the experiences of teachers in the field who for the first time have students with disabilities in their classes; and from the many requests of administrators seeking information for their staffs. In fact, this book could have been titled *What Every Parent and Teacher Should Know About Inclusion: Responses to Educators' and Parents' Questions from the Field.*

The authors of this book take a comprehensive view of inclusion that encompasses all students with diverse learning needs. This includes students from different cultural and linguistic backgrounds and family structures, and students with varying personal interests, learning styles, and intelligences. While the inclusive school movement has focused on educating students with disabilities alongside their nondisabled peers, in a broader sense inclusion is about bringing equity and access to learning for all students. It is our hope that this reference book will provide parents and teachers with knowledge and insight into the many ways they can make their homes and classrooms more supportive and inclusive.

The editor wishes to acknowledge all the steadfast inclusive educators associated with the New York Task Force for Quality Inclusive Schooling, many of whom have served as contributing authors. This volume is an outgrowth of the shared vision of educators who strive to bring equity and justice into all classrooms.

The book is divided into three parts and thirteen chapters. The chapters feature Tips for Educators or Tips for Parents, as well as other resources to help parents and teachers develop an understanding of inclusive practices. Each part concludes with a bibliography. Finally, a glossary clarifies terms used in special education and inclusive education.

PART I: GENERAL INFORMATION ON INCLUSION FOR EDUCATORS AND PARENTS

Part I presents the foundations and fundamentals of inclusion. It introduces the paradigm shift in the education of students with disabilities from a segregated model to one of integration. The disability rights movement and the philosophical underpinnings of inclusive schooling are discussed, and an overview of the children being served by special education legislation is presented. Part I also explains how students with disabilities are identified, gives an in-depth look at the nondiscriminatory evaluation process, and shows how services are provided in the least restrictive environment as required by IDEA. A thorough examination of eligibility requirements and the Individualized Education Plan (IEP) process is also presented.

PART II: RESEARCH, THEORY, AND PRACTICE FOR TEACHERS

Part II examines the diverse needs of special learners and how teachers can address these needs in the general education classroom. Strategies are presented to help teachers collaborate with related services providers such as speech pathologists and physical therapists by inviting these professionals to be part of the classroom team. Similarly, suggestions for working with bilingual/ESL teachers to deliver instruction to students who are culturally and linguistically diverse and ideas on how to plan culturally responsive curriculum and instruction are also examined.

Additional techniques and strategies for accommodating students with special needs in the general education classroom are presented. These include a discussion of grouping for instruction, cooperative learning models, and classroom management supports. A focus on how to create supportive and positive classroom environments is stressed.

PART III: FOR PARENTS AND FAMILIES

The chapters in Part III examine ways for parents to become knowledgeable participants in the educational process. Part III also explores ways to promote effective advocacy for both parents and students, with an emphasis on building students' strengths, competencies, and independence.

Educational possibilities offered by innovative models, as well as assistive technology that has proven effective in helping students with disabilities learn, are described. Web sites and other dynamic resources are noted. Part III concludes with a discussion about how to change and transform our schools so that all learners have an opportunity to reach their full potential.

PART I

General Information on Inclusion for Educators and Parents

CHAPTER 1

Inclusion

Diane Schwartz

Sammy sits in the back of his third grade classroom with his one-on-one aide, working with math manipulatives to complete single-digit addition problems. The rest of his classmates sit at their desks working on their multiplication tables.

In a neighboring school district's third grade classroom, all the "inclusion kids" sit at the round table closest to the door, so that when they go to the resource room and to other therapists for related services, the other students in their class won't be disturbed.

In another school in the same district, Ms. Brown, a special educator, and Ms. Jones, a general education teacher, co-teach twenty-eight third graders. Visitors would have a difficult time identifying which students are classified as special needs children because both teachers work with all the students in the class.

Described above are three very different interpretations of inclusion. Each school principal takes great pride in describing his or her third grade programs as positive inclusive environments. Some educators may or may not agree.

The purpose of this book is to give the reader a wealth of information about inclusion—its philosophy, the laws that govern it, and its practice. You may find it interesting to return to these examples after reading the book, and ask yourself if these are positive inclusive environments.

INCLUSION: A PHILOSOPHY, NOT A PLACE

There is much debate about the precise operational definition of inclusion. In fact, if you were to visit several "inclusive educational settings" you might be surprised to find that inclusive school programs differ markedly. Most educators, however, would agree that inclusive education promotes the practice of educating students with disabilities alongside their nondisabled peers. This means that students with disabilities attend the same school and general education classes as their age-appropriate peers, as if they did not have a disability. Unlike the concept of mainstreaming, in which students with disabilities have to earn the right to be in general education settings by demonstrating proficiency in a particular area, the underlying assumption of inclusive education is that all students have the right to be educated in general education classrooms.

Inclusive education seeks to create a unified educational system, one that is able to accommodate the needs of all children. Inclusion is about many things: social justice, respect for university, professional collaboration. Inclusion is not about "dumping" children with disabilities into general education classrooms and hoping that it will work out.[1]

As a philosophy, inclusion means making a commitment to do whatever it takes to enable every child to belong[2] regardless of the child's ability to achieve.[3] For inclusion to succeed, all teachers must believe that all children can learn to high standards of achievement, be willing to work collaboratively with other professionals and parents, and, most importantly, respect and appreciate diversity.

The concept of inclusion is derived from special education law, first passed in 1975 as the Education for All Handicapped Children Act (EHA) or Public Law 94-142. Over the years, EHA has been modified in response to increased recognition of and debate over the needs of people with disabilities. In 1990 the first version of the Individuals with Disabilities Education Act was enacted. It was amended in 1997 and again in 2004, resulting in IDEA (as the law is commonly known). IDEA is the most recent special education law. Although the word "inclusion" is not specifically used in the law itself, IDEA requires school districts to educate students with disabilities in the "least restrictive environment" or LRE. The legal principle of LRE is aimed at fostering acceptance of diversity by ensuring that each child has access to learning in the general education community. This is accomplished by meeting the educational needs of all students through individualized instruction and collaboration with other professionals and parents. The law requires:

> To the maximum extent appropriate, students with disabilities . . . [will be] educated with students who are not disabled, and special classes, separate schooling or removal of students with disabilities from regular educational environment [can occur] only when the nature or severity of the disability of a child is such that education in regular classes with the use of supplementary aids and services cannot be achieved satisfactorily for the student.[4]

In 1991, Sailor identified the following critical components of inclusive schooling as necessary for enabling students with exceptionalities to become authentic members of their school communities:

- All students must have home school placements where they are part of chronologically age-appropriate general education classrooms in their neighborhood school or whatever school they would have attended had they not had a disability.

- There should be a natural proportion of students with disabilities in each school and each class so that each classroom contains the same proportion of students with disabilities found in the general community. This means that in a community with 12 percent disabilities among the population, an inclusive classroom would contain no more than 12 percent students with disabilities, or two to three in a class of twenty to thirty students.

- Every school must serve all children within its district. This philosophy of "zero reject" means that no student will be excluded on the basis of the degree or type of disability. Inclusion of all children is critical for developing a sense of community.

- School and general education placements must be age and grade appropriate so that no self-contained special education class will exist, no cascade of services; a continuum of placements for students with disabilities or other placement variations will exist.

- Cooperative learning and peer instruction should replace traditional methods as the preferred methods for inclusion.

- Special education resources are integrated into the general education environment so that they can be redistributed and used by all students.

Full Inclusion

Sailor's concept of inclusive schooling has sometimes been referred to as "full inclusion." Professionals who support full inclusion, or the belief that the general education classroom can and will be able to accommodate all students with disabilities, contend that even students with severe and multiple disabilities can benefit from general education placement. Proponents of this perspective argue that any restrictive environment is inherently flawed because it is a form of segregation.

"Full inclusionists" seek special education reforms that would, in effect, abolish special education as we have known it for the past twenty-five years. Advocates for reform[5] argue that a segregated system of special education has been around too long, resulting in the inability of general education teachers to know how to adapt and modify curriculum for diverse learners. They further point out that traditional segregated models of special education have been ineffective in preparing students with disabilities to become independent members of society when they reach adulthood. For example, the Rehabilitation, Research and Training Center for Economic Research on Employment Policy for People with Disabilities, at Cornell University, published a report stating that while unemployment in the United States from 1994 to 1998 was only 5 percent in the general population, among individuals with disabilities it was as high as 63 percent.

Perhaps this view of inclusion is best summarized by Lipsky and Gartner, who define inclusive education as "a provision of services for students with disabilities, including those with severe impairments, in the neighborhood school, in age-appropriate general education classes, with the necessary support services and supplementary aids both to assure the child's academic, behavioral and social success to prepare the child to participate as a full and contributing member of society."[6]

Other Views of Inclusion

Not all inclusion advocates believe in full inclusion. Many inclusionists do not believe that 100 percent placement in general education settings is required. These inclusion advocates believe that one type of placement may not meet the needs of all children[7] and are proponents of "choice in placement." They support the idea of a continuum of services from least restrictive to most restrictive.

Unlike the philosophy of full inclusion, this model offers a continuum of placements for children with varying special needs. These educators or "inclusionists" (as opposed to "full inclusionists") believe that the abolition of a continuum of placements (see Figure 1.1) is problematic because it reduces choice for students and their families. In fact, Jim Kauffman argues that it is inappropriate to characterize separate special education programs as segregation if the placement is chosen freely, made on a case-by-case basis, and chosen as the most appropriate setting for a student with a disability.[8] The Council for Exceptional Children (CEC), the largest and oldest professional organization for special educators, also endorses the continuum of services, stating:

> All children, youth and young adults with disabilities are entitled to a free and appropriate education that leads to an adult life characterized by satisfying relations with others, independent living, productive engagement in the community, and participation in the society at large. To achieve such outcomes, there must exist for all . . . options and access to a variety of programs and experiences based on individual educational need and desired outcomes.[9]

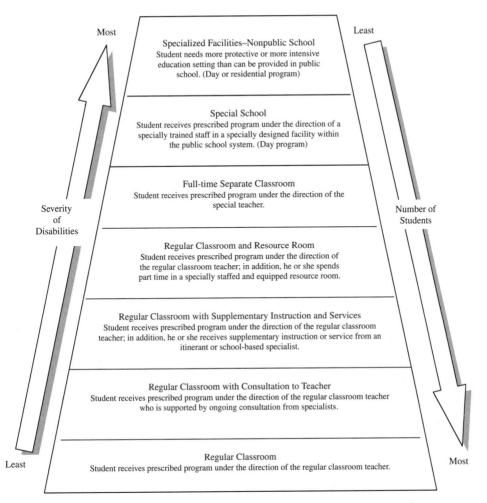

Figure 1.1. Continuum of Educational Services for Students with Disabilities

Source: From Heward, W. L. (2000). *Exceptional children: An introduction to special education.* Upper Saddle River, NJ: Merrill Prentice Hall. © 2000. Reprinted by permission of Pearson Education, Inc., Upper Saddle River, NJ.

While it is CEC's position that a continuum of services must be available, the organization strongly supports inclusion as a meaningful goal to be achieved in our communities and our schools. Advocates who believe in full inclusion and those who support a continuum of services share many of the same goals. They both seek to change the separate systems of education that have existed for students with disabilities and to accommodate the needs of diverse learners so that they can be educated in the general education classroom.

THE INDIVIDUALS WITH DISABILITIES EDUCATION ACT

In 1997, IDEA was reauthorized by Congress, resulting in several key changes, particularly in the definition of least restrictive environment. These changes further promoted the move to a more inclusive education based on making the classroom environment more enabling. Prior to 1997, LRE was interpreted to mean a variety of placements depending upon the nature and needs of the individual student. Today the presumption is that the least restrictive environment for children with disabilities is the general education classroom and that removal from that classroom has to be justified. (Figure 1.2 shows how the percentage of students with disabilities in the general education classroom has grown.) To further support the inclusion of students with disabilities, IDEA has redefined the relationship between special educators and general educators.[10] Whereas in the past general education teachers had minimal interaction with students with disabilities or special educators, IDEA requires general education teachers, in collaboration with support professionals, to share responsibility and accountability for the child with disabilities. The general education teacher has newly defined duties as a member of the special education team because IDEA requires that individualized educational plans (IEPs) for students with disabilities be linked to the general education curriculum. So, to an extent, a general education teacher must participate in the development of the IEP for the child. This includes helping the team determine what supplementary aids, services, and program modifications are needed by the student and what supports the general and special educators need to help benefit the child's participation in the general education program.

IDEA emphasizes the need for schools and teachers to make whatever adjustments or accommodations are necessary so that children with disabilities can participate in general education curriculum and assessment programs. This is further encouraged by new methods of financial support. Funding for students with disabilities, no longer limited to the child with special needs, can now support services provided in the general education classroom to the benefit of all children, disabled as well as nondisabled. By bringing special services into the general education classroom it is hoped that all teachers will become responsible for the education of all children. There is a compelling need for general education teachers and special education teachers to work closely together to meet this goal.

Now, a decade and a half after Sailor put forth his components of inclusive education, we can see many of his ideas in place. Models for inclusive schooling will continue to evolve and change over time; however, there are basic tenets of an inclusive philosophy of education that will re-

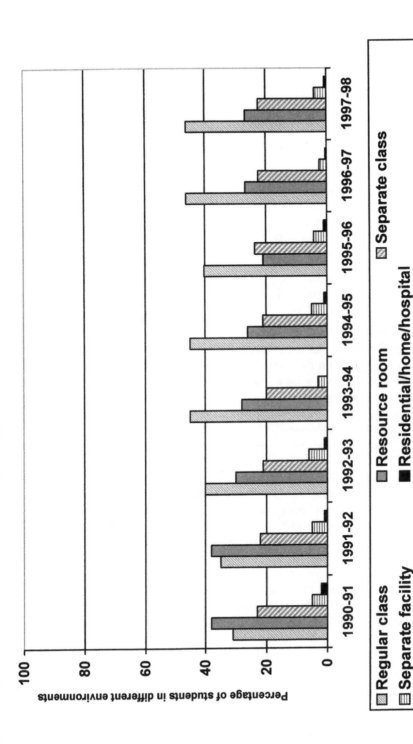

Figure 1.2. Percentage of Students with Disabilities Ages 6 to 21 Served in Each Educational Environment, 1990–91 to 1997–98

Source: U.S. Department of Education. (1993–1999). *Fourteenth–twenty-first annual reports to Congress on the implementation of the Individuals with Disabilities Act.* Washington, DC: U.S. Department of Education.

main constant. Inclusion once again is about many things: social justice, respect for diversity, professional collaboration. Inclusion is not about "dumping" children with disabilities into general education classrooms and hoping that it will work out.[11]

For an expanded list of what inclusion is and is not, see Table 1.1.

For more than twenty years, special education has been regarded as a place where children with disabilities were sent. The underlying assumption was that the general education classroom could not accommodate students with disabilities. With IDEA '97, a new era has begun in which special education is viewed as a service that students receive, for the most part, in general education classrooms. One of the most important aspects of the inclusive school movement is that all students, disabled and nondisabled, will have an opportunity to see each other's worth and be prepared for full participation in our very diverse society.

HISTORICAL BACKGROUND

The history of the treatment of individuals with disabilities in the United States from the mid-1800s to the 1970s is one of separate institutions for the disabled. Earlier, during colonial times, people with disabilities were able to function within the agrarian society while being cared for by their families. However, following the Industrial Revolution and the growth of cities, people with disabilities were less able to meet the greater demands of daily life. Asylums were initially built with humanistic intent to serve these populations. Reformers like Dorothea Dix, seeking better treatment for the dependent members of society, encouraged the development of institutions that were typically segregated into categories of disability such as mental retardation and insanity.

The institutional idea expanded rapidly, and with time, the original concern for helping disabled people was replaced by an attempt to protect society from them.[12] By the early 1900s, institutions served as a place to put individuals unwanted by the mainstream society. As the populations in these asylums soared, conditions deteriorated to the point that the institutions became human warehouses: places filled with despair, disease, and, often, death. This institutional model for serving persons with disabilities went unchallenged for over 100 years. It was not until the 1960s and 1970s that significant changes occurred. A new era of normalization, first developed in Sweden, promoted the idea that people with disabilities could lead lives as close to "normal" as the mainstream population. At the same time, exposés such as Geraldo Rivera's examination of Willowbrook revealed the shameful and horrifying conditions in such institutions to the American public.

The landmark Supreme Court decision *Brown v. Board of Education* (1954), which outlawed racial separation in public schools, served as the basis for a series of major class action lawsuits brought against state insti-

Table 1.1.
What Inclusion Is and Is Not

Inclusion Is:	Inclusion Is Not:
All children learning together in the same schools and the same classrooms, with the services and supports necessary so that they can be successful there	"Dumping" all children with disabilities into general education classes without the supports and services they need to be successful there
All children having their unique needs met in the same setting they would attend if they had no disability	Trading of the quality of a child's education or the intensive support services the child may need for inclusion
All children participating in all facets of school life	Doing away with or cutting back on special education service
Children with and without disabilities having opportunities (and support when needed) to interact and develop friendships with each other	Ignoring each child's unique needs
	All children having to learn the same thing, at the same time, in the same way
Children who have disabilities attending their neighborhood school (the same school they would attend if they did not have a labeled disability)	Expecting regular education teachers to teach children who have disabilities without the support they need to teach all children effectively
A method of schooling which emphasizes collaboration by melding special and regular education resources (staff, materials, energy, etc.)	Sacrificing the education of typical children so that children with disabilities can be included
Supporting regular education teachers who have children with disabilities in their classrooms	Serving students with disabilities in separate schools or exclusively in self-contained classes, based solely upon their categorical label
Children learning side by side though they may have different educational goals	Scheduling students with disabilities for lunch and other activities at different times than students without disabilities are scheduled
Regular education teachers using innovative strategies for varied learning styles of children in the class	Placing students with disabilities into regular classes without the planning, supports, and services needed [for] successful and meaningful participation
Integrating related services (such as speech, physical therapy, occupa-	Providing separate staff develop-

Table 1.1.
(continued)

Inclusion Is:	Inclusion Is Not:
tional therapy, etc.) in the regular classroom	ment for regular teachers and special education teachers, thus reinforcing notions of separate systems
Unconditional acceptance of all children as children	
Unconditional commitment to providing as much support as the child needs to be successful in general education environments	Denying students with disabilities services in general education classrooms because the staff is not willing or hasn't been given direction in how to adapt instruction to meet the needs of diverse learners
A focus on the parents' dreams and goals for their child's future	
A team approach which includes parents as equal members and emphasizes creativity and a problem solving attitude	Referring to special education students in stigmatizing terms such as "the handicapped class" or the "retarded kids"
An understanding of the fact that students don't need to have the same educational goals in order to learn together in regular classes	Making precipitous placement decisions for students with disabilities without their prior preparation
Strong leadership by school principals and other administrators	Locating special education classes in separate wings at a school
Encouraging and implementing activities that promote the development of friendships and relationships between students with and without disabilities	Exposing students to unnecessary hazards or risks
	Ignoring parents' concerns
	Placing older students with disabilities in schools for younger children
Providing the planning, support, and services necessary to meaningful and successful participation of students with disabilities in general education programs	Requiring students or their parents to waive their legal rights under IDEA for the "privilege" of being placed into a general education classroom
Having a school and district mission that is comprehensive and sets high expectations for all students, including those with disabilities	Limiting the opportunities for students with disabilities to participate in general education classes by doing all scheduling first for students with disabilities to participate only where space is available
Providing professional development and support for all personnel regarding effective practices for	

Table 1.1.
(continued)

Inclusion Is:	Inclusion Is Not:
inclusion of students with disabilities	Maintaining separate daily schedules for students with and without disabilities
Scheduling classes for all school activities in a way that maximizes opportunities for participation by students with disabilities	Serving students with disabilities in age-inappropriate settings by placing older students in primary settings or younger students in secondary settings
Assuming that all school and grade-level placements are age-appropriate	
Having all people on the staff understand and support the notion that students with disabilities can be served appropriately in general education classes and that this sometimes requires the staff to meet the learning needs that differ from those of most students	
Providing needed services within regular schools, regardless of the intensity or frequency	
Using "person first" language ("students with disabilities" instead of "disabled students") and teaching all students to understand and value human differences	
Teaching all children to understand and accept individual differences	
Allowing students who are not able to fully participate in an activity to partially participate, rather than be excluded entirely. Arranging for students with disabilities to receive their job training in mainstream community environments	

Source: Courtesy of the Pisces Full Inclusion Project, Maryland State Department of Education.

tutions on behalf of children with disabilities. In the 1970s, following the holding in *Brown* that separate education is inherently unequal and thus unlawful, federal courts in Pennsylvania (*Pennsylvania Association for Retarded Citizens [PARC] v. Commonwealth of Pennsylvania*) and the District of Columbia (*Mills v. Washington, D.C. Board of Education*) ordered school authorities to educate students with disabilities in the same schools and programs as students without disabilities.[13]

The *PARC* and *Mills* decisions were catalysts for many subsequent lawsuits on behalf of people with disabilities and provided the foundation for Public Law 94-142, the Education for All Handicapped Children Act, passed by Congress in 1975. Specifically, the federal judges called for "free and suitable publicly supported education" (*Mills*) for all children with disabilities in the "least restrictive" (*PARC*) setting possible. These requirements for a free and appropriate education for all children in the least restrictive environment are the heart of what became the Individuals with Disabilities Education Act.

Other key legislation, while not specifically focused on education, has helped protect the rights of children and adults with disabilities. The Vocational Rehabilitation Act of 1973 offered funding for rehabilitation and, more important, contained Section 504, the civil rights bill for the disabled. Section 504 prohibits discrimination against individuals with disabilities and provides for many educational accommodations that enable children with disabilities to participate fully in our schools. The Americans with Disabilities Act (ADA) of 1990 expands these rights from the educational environment to all public places, transportation, and employment.

Hahn argues that the growth of the disability rights movement and the accompanying move toward inclusion of students with disabilities into general education emerged from a fundamental philosophical shift away from a "functional limitations" view of disability toward a "minority group" model.[14] He believes that special education was historically viewed from a medical or deficit perspective in which the disabled had to be "fixed" with therapies and rehabilitation. Over time, educators have moved to a more sociopolitical view of special education in which disability is no longer a personal defect but rather the result of a disabling environment. In this new model of disability, it is the society's responsibility to provide services so that children with disabilities can be included in the general community of learners. From this civil rights perspective, the full inclusion of all children in the educational mainstream is a matter of social justice and a fundamental right.

SPECIAL EDUCATION TODAY

Each year the U.S. Department of Education publishes a report to Congress that presents data on the number of students served in special education as well as other key information, including graduation rates of students with disabilities, statistics on teacher shortages, and policy changes. The Twenty-Fourth Annual Report to Congress on the Implementation of the Individuals with Disabilities Education Act covers the 2000–2001 school year, during which 5,775,722 children aged six to twenty-one, 599,678 children aged three to six, and 230,853 infants and toddlers received services under IDEA, Parts B and C.

Close to 70 percent of all those receiving special education services are classified as either students with specific learning disabilities (over 50 percent) or students with speech or language impairments (19 percent). These two categories of disability, along with mental retardation (10.6 percent) and emotional disturbance (8.2 percent), represent close to 90 percent of all children receiving special education services and are classified as "high-incidence" disabilities. Low-incidence categories of disability represent about 10 percent of all students with disabilities and include multiple disabilities, hearing impairments, orthopedic impairments, other health impairments, visual impairments, deaf-blindness, autism, and traumatic brain injury. The twenty-fourth report to Congress can be found in its entirety online at www.ed.gov/offices/OSERS/OSEP.

Prior to the 1997 reauthorization of IDEA, the U.S. Department of Education required states to count students in special education according to their disability classification. Important reasons given for defining categories of disabilities are evaluating the prevalence of specific problems, beginning to develop a diagnosis and treatment plan, and providing the basis for future research and funding. Some educators argue that labels can restrict opportunities for students because labels cause teachers and other professionals to have low expectations for the student. Assigning a child to a category can have a negative effect by creating a self-fulfilling prophecy for the child. This has not been borne out by the research literature, nor has there been definitive research that demonstrates that the negative effects of labeling outweigh the positive effects of identifying students with disabilities for the purpose of providing services.[15] For the present, classification of disabilities under the law continues to serve as "an admission ticket to alternative educational services."[16] Table 1.2 lists the categories of special education identified by IDEA. Please note that people-first language is required. For example, referring to a child as "a girl with a learning disability" is preferable to referring to her as "a learning disabled girl." A people-first model conveys the view that the individual student is recognized first rather than his or her disability.

Classification schemes and definitions, as well as where students with disabilities are being served, have varied over the years. A review of class placement from 1990 to 1998 demonstrates a significant move toward placement of students with disabilities into the general education classroom (see Figure 1.2). In 1999–2000, 95 percent of students with disabilities were served in regular school buildings. While this trend toward inclusion is sig-

Table 1.2.
Classification Definitions

Disability	Definitions	Number of students served	Percentage of students with disabilities
Specific learning disabilities	IDEA Definition: The term "specific learning disability" means a disorder of one or more of the *basic psychological processes* involved in understanding or in using language, spoken or written, which disorder may manifest itself in imperfect ability to listen, think, speak, read, write, spell or do mathematical calculations. Such term includes such conditions as perceptual disabilities, brain injury, minimal brain dysfunction, dyslexia and developmental aphasia. Such term *does not include* a learning problem that is primarily the result of visual, hearing, or motor disabilities, of mental retardation, of emotional disturbance, or of environmental, cultural, or economic disadvantage. National Joint Committee on Learning Disabilities Definitions: Learning disabilities is a general term that refers to a heterogeneous group of disorders manifested by significant difficulties in the acquisition and use of listening, speaking, reading, writing, reasoning, or mathematical abilities. These disorders are intrinsic to the individual and presumed to be due to central nervous system dysfunction, and may appear across the life span. Problems in self-regulatory behaviors, social perception, and social interaction may exist with learning disabilities but do not them	2,887,217	50.0

selves constitute a learning disability. Although learning disabilities may occur concomitantly with other handicapping conditions (for example, sensory impairment, mental retardation, serious emotional disturbance) or with extrinsic influences (such as cultural differences in sufficient or inappropriate instruction), they are not the result of those conditions or influences.

| Speech or language impairments | A speech disorder reflects problems in delivering messages orally, such as when repeating words, mispronouncing sounds, or speaking with inadequate breath. A language disorder is a problem in receiving, understanding, and formulating ideas and information. Both types of communications disorders are addressed in the Individuals with Disabilities Education Act (IDEA) as being disorders that adversely affect a student's educational performance. | 1,093,808 | 19.0 |

| Mental retardation | American Association on Mental Retardation Definition: Mental retardation refers to substantial limitations in present functioning. It is characterized by significantly subaverage intellectual functioning, existing concurrently with related limitations in two or more of the following applicable adaptive skill areas: communication, self-care, home living, social skills, community use, self-direction, health and safety, functional academics, leisure, and work. Mental retardation manifests before age 18. | 612,978 | 10.7 |

| Emotional disturbance | IDEA Definition:
(i) The term means a condition exhibiting one or more of the following characteristics over a long time and to a marked degree that adversely affects a student's educational performance:
• An inability to learn cannot be explained by intellectual, sensory, or other health factors
• An inability to build or maintain satisfactory interpersonal relationships with peers and teachers | 473,663 | 8.2 |

Table 1.2.
(continued)

Disability	Definitions	Number of students served	Percentage of students with disabilities

	• Inappropriate types of behavior or feelings under normal circumstances
	• A general pervasive mood of unhappiness or depression
	• A tendency to develop physical symptoms or fears associated with personal or school problems
	(ii) The term includes schizophrenia. The term does not apply to children who are socially maladjusted, unless it is determined that they have an emotional disturbance.
	
	Mental Health and Special Education Coalition Definition:
	(A) The term emotional or behavioral disorder means a disability that is . . .
	   (i) characterized by behavioral or emotional responses in school programs so different from appropriate age, cultural, or ethnic norms that the responses adversely affect educational performance, including academic, social, vocational or personal skills;
	   (ii) more than a temporary, expected response to stressful events in the environment;
	   (iii) consistently exhibited in two different settings, at least one of which is school-related; and unresponsive to direct intervention applied in general education, or the
	   (iv) condition of a child such that general education interventions would be insufficient.		

18

(B) The term includes such a disability that co-exists with other disabilities.
(C) The term includes a schizophrenic disorder, affective disorder, anxiety disorder, or other sustained disorder of conduct or adjustment, affecting a child if the disorder affects educational performance as described in paragraph (I). (quoted in McIntyre & Forness, 1996, p. 5)

Multiple disabilities	122,559	2.1

IDEA Definition:
Multiple disabilities means concomitant impairments (such as mental retardation–blindness, mental retardation–orthopedic impairment, etc.), the combination of which causes such severe educational problems that they cannot be accommodated in special education programs solely for one of the impairments. The term does not include deaf-blindness.

Hearing impairments	70,767	1.2

IDEA Definition:
Hearing impairment that is so severe that the child is impaired in processing linguistic information through hearing, with or without amplification, that adversely affects a child's educational performance. IDEA's definition of hearing impairment is: An impairment in hearing, whether permanent or fluctuating, that adversely affects a child's educational performance but which is not included under the definition of deafness in this section.

Orthopedic impairments	73,057	1.3

IDEA Definition:
"Orthopedic impairment" means a severe orthopedic impairment that adversely affects a child's educational performance. The term includes impairments caused by congenital anomaly (e.g., clubfoot, absence of some member, etc.), and impairments caused by disease (e.g., poliomyelitis, bone tuberculosis, etc.), and impairments from other causes (e.g., cerebral palsy, amputations, and fractures or burns that cause contractures).

Table 1.2.
(continued)

Disability	Definitions	Number of students served	Percentage of students with disabilities
Other health impairments	IDEA Definition: Having limited strength, vitality, or alertness due to chronic or acute health problems such as a heart condition, tuberculosis, rheumatic fever, nephritis, asthma, sickle cell anemia, hemophilia, epilepsy, lead poisoning, leukemia, or diabetes that adversely affect a child's educational performance.	291,850	5.1
Visual impairments	IDEA Definition: An impairment in vision that, even with correction, adversely affects a child's educational performance.	25,975	0.4
Deaf-blindness	IDEA Definition: Individuals defined as deaf-blind may experience diverse combinations of vision and hearing impairments with normal or gifted intelligence or they may have additional mental, physical, and behavioral disabilities. . . . Because these individuals do not receive clear and consistent information from either sensory modality, a tendency exists to turn inward to obtain the desired level of stimulation. The individual may appear passive, nonresponsive, and/or noncompliant. Students with dual sensory impairments may not respond to or initiate appropriate interactions with others and often exhibit behavior that is considered socially inappropriate.	1,320	0.02

Autism	IDEA Definition: Autism means a developmental disability significantly affecting verbal and non-verbal communication and social interaction, generally evident before age 3, that adversely affects educational performance. Other characteristics often associated with autism are engagement in repetitive activities and stereotyped movements, resistance to environmental change or changes in daily routines, and unusual responses to sensory experiences. The term does not apply if a child's educational performance is adversely affected primarily because the child has a serious emotional disturbance.	78,749	1.4
Traumatic brain injury	IDEA Definition: An acquired injury of the brain caused by an external physical force, resulting in total or partial functional disability or psychosocial impairment, or both, that adversely affects a child's educational performance. The term applies to open or closed head injuries resulting in impairments in one or more areas, such as cognition; language; memory; attention; reasoning; abstract thinking; judgment; problem-solving; sensory, perceptual, and motor abilities; psychosocial behavior; physical functions; information processing; and speech. The term does not apply to brain injuries that are congenital or degenerative, or brain injuries induced by birth trauma.	14,844	0.3
Total		5,746,787	

Sources: Definitions and statistics from U.S. Department of Education. (2001). *Twenty-fourth annual report to Congress on the implementation of the Individuals with Disabilities Act*. Washington, DC: U.S. Department of Education. Additional definitions from Turnbull, A., Turnbull, R., Shank, M., & Leal, D. (2000). *Exceptional lives: Special education in today's schools*. Upper Saddle River, NJ: Merrill/Prentice Hall.

Table 1.3.
Percentage of Students Ages 6 Through 21 with Disabilities Served in
Different Educational Environments, 1999–2000

		Served outside the regular class			
Disabilities	All students with disabilities	<21% of the day	21–60% of the day	>60% of the day	Public separate facility
Specific learning disabilities	50.4	48.3	67.4	39.2	9.9
Speech or language impairments	19.2	35.5	4.6	5.0	2.5
Mental retardation	10.8	3.2	11.3	26.9	23.3
Emotional disturbance	8.2	4.5	6.8	13.3	32.9
Multiple disabilities	2.1	0.5	1.4	4.5	16.8
Hearing impairments	1.3	1.1	0.9	1.5	3.6
Orthopedic impairments	1.3	1.2	1.0	1.7	2.3
Other health impairments	4.5	4.2	5.2	3.8	2.1
Visual impairments	0.5	0.5	0.3	0.4	1.1
Autism	1.2	0.5	0.6	2.9	4.9
Deaf-blindness	0.02	0.01	0.01	0.05	0.2
Traumatic brain injury	0.2	0.2	0.2	0.4	0.3

Source: U.S. Department of Education, Office of Special Education Programs, Data Analysis System (DANS).

nificant, the number of students placed in various educational settings continues to be influenced by the category of disability. Students with learning disabilities and speech and language disabilities are usually served in inclusive classrooms, while students with low-incidence disabilities are more often in segregated settings. In 1999–2000, 87.5 percent of students with speech or language impairments, 45.3 percent of students with specific learning disabilities, 25.8 percent of students with emotional disturbance, 14.1 percent of students with mental retardation, and 11.2 percent of students with multiple disabilities were served outside the regular classroom less than 21 percent of the school day (see Table 1.3).

The greatest numbers of special education students come from low-income families living in urban areas (19 percent), as poverty and disability are highly correlated.[17] Perhaps this accounts for the disproportionate number of culturally and linguistically diverse students in special education, particularly African American and Hispanic students. A close examination of the *Annual Report to Congress* provides critical data about who the students in special education are and where they are being educated.

SUMMARY

The discussion of inclusion is the discussion of the current state of the American educational system. It is an examination of how we are teaching all the children in our schools regardless of disability. As a philosophy, it fosters a unified educational system that promotes social justice.

Inclusive education asks that special education become a service, not a place, and that children with disabilities are educated with their nondisabled peers as much as is possible. To accomplish this major educational paradigm shift, federal legislation, most recently IDEA '04, set out regulations and financial support to ensure the education of all children in the least restrictive environment. The inclusive class has been the most common response to this mandate.

Presently there is no definitive model of inclusion or the inclusive class. Variability exists in the implementation of inclusion, and educators range from full inclusionists to those who prefer a choice in placement with a continuum of services. Educators need to explore and share strategies and techniques that enable them to successfully move to inclusion. Change brings questions. Many of the questions about inclusive education, however, lack specific solutions or have multiple answers. What is definite is that inclusion does offer a viable response to the need for equity in our schools.

Tips for Educators

✎ Nationwide, 9–10 percent of school-aged children are classified for special education services. That means that a teacher in a typical classroom of twenty-five to thirty students should expect that two or three will have a disability or need to receive special services.

✎ Close to 70 percent of all students classified experience specific learning disabilities and/or speech and language disabilities. The majority of students with special needs will need help processing information.

✎ While the United States has adopted specific definitions for each classification of disability, it is important for classroom teachers and parents to realize that many students with diverse learning needs can benefit from similar interventions and adaptations.

NOTES

1. Corbett, J. (2001). *Supporting inclusive education: A connective pedagogy.* London: Falmer Press.

2. Villa, R. A., & Thousand, J. S. (Eds.). (1995). *Creating an inclusive school.* Alexandria, VA: Association for Supervision and Curriculum Development.

3. Friend, M., & Bursuck, W. D. (1999). *Including students with special needs: A practice guide for classroom teachers.* Boston: Allyn & Bacon.

4. IDEA, Section 1412(a)(5).

5. Stainback, S., & Stainback, W. (1992). *Curriculum considerations in inclusive classrooms: Facilitating learning for all students.* Baltimore: Paul H. Brookes Publishing Co.

6. Lipsky, D. K., & Gartner, A. (1996). Inclusion, school restructuring, and the remaking of American society. *Harvard Educational Review, 66*(4), 762–796.

7. Kochhar, C. A., West, L. L., & Taymans, J. A. (2000). *Successful inclusion: Practical strategies for a shared responsibility.* Upper Saddle River, NJ: Prentice-Hall.

8. O'Neil, J. (1995). Can inclusion work? A conversation with Jim Kauffman and Mara Sapon-Shevin. *Educational Leadership 52*(4): 7–11.

9. Council for Exceptional Children, (CEC). (1993). CEC policy on inclusive schools and community settings. *Teaching Exceptional Children, 25*(4), Supplement.

10. Kochhar, West, & Taymans (2000).

11. Corbett (2001).

12. Taylor, S. J., & Searl, S. J., Jr. (1987). The disabled in America: History, policy and trends. In P. Knoblock (Ed.), *Understanding exceptional children and youth* (pp. 5–64). Boston: Little, Brown.

13. Turnbull, A., Turnbull, R., Shank, M., & Leal, D. (1999). *Exceptional lives: Special education in today's schools.* Upper Saddle River, NJ: Merrill/Prentice Hall.

14. Hahn, J. (1989). The politics of special education. In D. K. Lipsky & A. Gartner (Eds.), *Beyond separate education: Quality education for all* (pp. 225–241). Baltimore: Paul H. Brookes Publishing Co.

15. Turnbull, A., Turnbull, R., Shank, M., & Leal, D. (1999).

16. Ysseldyke, J. E., Algozzine, B., & Thurlow, M. L. (2000). *Critical issues in special education.* Boston: Houghton Mifflin.

17. Turnbull, A., Turnbull, R., Shank, M., & Leal, D. (1999).

CHAPTER 2

The Special Education Process
Services and Accommodations

Waverlyn L. J. Peters

At a recent special education law conference, a scenario was presented after a two-hour lecture. Participants were asked to resolve the issue presented consistent with state and federal laws. The room was filled with lawyers, advocates, school board members, and administrators of special education programs. After a long pause a single participant volunteered. The correct response was given: "It depends."

Special education is a labyrinth of laws, regulations, and litigation. Laws outline the rules. Regulations explain how laws are implemented. Litigation clarifies the "it depends." This chapter will outline the key rules that govern the special education process. Each law or regulation has extensive rules and much nuance, but we will focus mainly on the major provisions and highlight some of the "it depends" issues in special education. Additional resources are listed at the end of the chapter.

Three major pieces of federal legislation govern the definition and provision of services to children and youth with disabilities: (1) the Individuals with Disabilities Education Act (IDEA); (2) Section 504 of the Vocational Rehabilitation Act; and (3) the Americans with Disabilities Act (ADA). These laws were enacted in response to the efforts of parents and advocates of children with disabilities.

The Individuals with Disabilities Education Act is an education entitlement law originally passed in 1975. It was then known as the Education for All Handicapped Children Act (EHA) or Public Law (PL) 94-142, and after revision in 1997 it was referred to as IDEA'97. In November 2004, IDEA assumed its current form. It is the driving force for the education of infants, toddlers, children, and youth with disabilities.

Section 504 of the Vocational Rehabilitation Act (PL 93-112) was passed in 1973 and was the first civil rights law that protected the rights of individuals with disabilities.[1] It mandates nondiscrimination in employment, housing, and access to public programs and facilities in programs receiving federal funding assistance.

In 1990 the Americans with Disabilities Act extended the nondiscrimination protections of Section 504 to public and private entities that provide public accommodations, transportation, telecommunications, and employment. This act greatly expanded the number of institutions that had to comply with legislation protecting the rights of those with disabilities, and likewise increased the number of people who could benefit from the act. The act applies without regard to the receipt of federal funds, meaning that even if an institution or business does not receive federal funding, it still has to comply.

ADA has no specific special education requirements. The Office of Civil Rights interprets ADA as incorporating all of the Section 504 protections.[2] These laws ensure the rights of students with disabilities to receive a free and appropriate public education, in the least restrictive environment, and to participate in the extracurricular activities of their public school district.

The word "inclusion" does not appear in IDEA, Section 504, or ADA.[3] The procedures required to identify and serve eligible students stated by these laws, however, are congruent with the philosophy of inclusion.[4] This chapter reviews IDEA and Section 504 and includes discussion of major provisions, eligibility criteria, service or program options, and service implementation.

IDEA REQUIREMENTS

The United States Constitution reserves all areas of responsibility not specifically given to the federal government to the states or to the people. Education is one of those state responsibilities. Prior to 1975, individual states developed diverse rules and policies regarding the education of children with disabilities. Educational opportunity for individuals with disabilities was limited in many states. The exclusion of children and youth from public education in the United States of America is well documented. Before the enactment of the Education for All Handicapped Children Act in 1975, Congress found that

- the special education needs of children with disabilities were not being fully met;

- more than one-half of the children with disabilities in the United States did not receive appropriate educational services that would enable them to have full equality of opportunity;

- 1 million children with disabilities in the United States were excluded entirely from the public school system and did not go through the educational process with their peers;

- many children with undetected disabilities were participating in regular programs without success; and

- because of the lack of adequate services within the public school system, families were often forced to find services outside the public school system, often at great distance from their residence and at their own expense.[5]

IDEA, as a federal education law, established minimum standards for special education and provides funding. The United States Congress initially promised to fund 40 percent of the additional education costs to the states. To date, the funding has fallen far short of these expectations,[6] with state and local school districts responsible for well over 60 percent of the additional costs. To receive IDEA funds, each state must develop laws and regulations that comply with the federal statute. The federal law is a minimum standard. State laws may include additional requirements. For example, New York State requires more participants in the evaluation process. IDEA has six central requirements: procedural safeguards; individualized educational programs; free and appropriate public education; least restrictive environment; zero reject; and nondiscriminatory assessment.

Procedural Safeguards

IDEA ensures an extensive list of procedural safeguards, or due process rights. These safeguards ensure parental participation in all aspects of the decision-making process. Research has shown that educational success is correlated with parental participation and involvement, particularly for children with disabilities.[7] Additionally, procedural safeguards ensure that children with disabilities receive nondiscriminatory treatment. Seven of the safeguards outlined in IDEA follow:

1. *Consent.* Parents have the right to give or withhold consent for the special education process.
2. *Access to educational records.* Parents have the right to examine and obtain a copy of all educational records and evaluations. Parents have additional rights to confidentiality as outlined in the Family Educational Rights and Privacy Act (FERPA).[8] FERPA denies federal funds to any school or college that fails to allow students and their parents access to records. Parents also have the right to refuse the disclosure of directory information (personally identifying information such as names, addresses, and disability information).
3. *Prior written notice.* Parents have the right to be notified of meetings or any act that may result in a change of educational placement or service. This notice must be in their primary language or their primary mode of communication (e.g., sign language).

4. *Independent evaluation.* If parents disagree with the evaluation results, they may obtain an independent evaluation. This may be at district expense if the district's evaluation is found to be inadequate. (Evaluations will be discussed in more detail under district responsibilities.)

5. *Impartial hearing.* Parents have a right to a hearing if they disagree with the recommendations or services delivered. At the hearing, an impartial third party (hearing officer) will listen to and examine evidence from both sides, and will render a decision. This decision is binding on both parties unless it is appealed. In some states, there is a state-level appeal process hearing. In other states, the parents or the district will proceed to the courts. A hearing and the exhaustion of all appeals may take several school years. Some appeals have reached the United States Supreme Court.

6. *Pendency.* During a hearing, mediation, independent evaluation, or litigation in court, the child's educational placement must remain the same unless the parties agree on an alternative or a hearing officer has so directed. This has also been referred to as the "stay put provision." For example, George is in a third grade general education class. The district is recommending that he be placed in a special education program in another school. The parents initiate a due process hearing. During the hearing George must remain in the general education class ("stay put").

7. *Attorneys' fees.* If the parent prevails in litigation, the district must reimburse the parent for attorneys' fees.

Individualized Educational Program (IEP)

An IEP is a major requirement of IDEA. It is a written document that lists the unique needs that make a student eligible for special education and related services. It specifies long- and short-term educational goals. The IEP, which is reviewed and revised periodically, also identifies the individually designed services that will help the student to meet his or her goals.

Free and Appropriate Public Education (FAPE)

IDEA defines FAPE as special education and related services that

(A) have been provided at public expense, under public supervision and direction, and without charge to parents;

(B) meet the standards of the State education agency;

(C) include an appropriate preschool, elementary or secondary school education in the State involved; and

(D) are provided in conformity with the individual education program required under section 614 (d).[9]

The concept of a free and appropriate public education has caused many disagreements between parents and districts. Clearly, special education services provided by the district must be free, appropriate, and public, and conform to the IEP. What are appropriate services? "It depends." It is in this situation that litigation provides some guidance.

Mary has been classified as having a specific disability in reading. The district recommends remedial reading provided by a special education teacher one period each day in a small group. The parents want a specialized reading approach provided individually for three hours per week.[10] Assuming that either service would be paid for and provided by the district, what is appropriate? A hearing officer or a court would decide. In making this decision they would look at landmark cases for guidance.

Landmark Cases. In *Board of Education v. Rowley* (1982), Amy Rowley was an elementary student who had minimal residual hearing and was identified as deaf. She had excellent lip-reading skills and was enrolled in regular classes with supplemental services. A sign language interpreter was used for a trial period and discontinued. Amy was making educational progress and moving from grade to grade. She had good grades although she was missing a portion of the instruction. Her parents alleged that Amy would not reach her full potential without a full-time sign language interpreter. The New York State school district was thereby denying Amy a free and appropriate public education.

The parents' request for a due process hearing was eventually granted by the United States Supreme Court. The court ruled that under EHA (Education for All Handicapped Children)/IDEA, a free and appropriate public education consists of "educational instruction specially designed to meet the unique needs of the [disabled] child, supported by such services as are necessary to permit the child to 'benefit' from instruction." According to the Court, "the law does not require a state or school district to maximize the potential of each disabled child commensurate with the opportunity provided to non-disabled children." If individualized instruction is being provided with sufficient support services to permit the child to learn and move from grade to grade, the child is receiving a "free appropriate public education" as defined by law. In *Polk v. Central Susquehanna Intermediate Unit,* the courts made a further clarification by ruling that more than a minimal benefit is required for a program to be considered appropriate.[11]

Mary's IEP would be evaluated to determine if it was designed to meet her unique needs and calculated to provide educational benefit. Information regarding Mary's current reading level and previous interventions would form a basis for the deliberation. Districts are not required to provide the best programs and services. A one-to-one service is not necessary for a recommendation to be appropriate. In Mary's case, however, the "it depends" aspect helped Mary's parents win the case. Mary's father and grandfather were both illiterate, with previously undiagnosed disabilities. Therefore, the court decided that Mary was entitled to the specialized reading approach.

Least Restrictive Environment (LRE) and Inclusion

Many parents and advocates believe that IDEA requires inclusion, although the term "inclusion" is not found in IDEA.[12] The act does not require that all students with disabilities be placed in the general education classroom 100 percent of the day. IDEA mandates that all students with disabilities be placed in the least restrictive environment. Specifically, IDEA states:

> To the maximum extent appropriate, children with disabilities, including children in public or private institutions or other care facilities, are educated with children who are not disabled, and special classes, separate schooling, or other removal of children with disabilities from the regular education environment occurs only when the nature or severity of the disability of the child is such that education in regular classes with the use of supplemental aids and services cannot be achieved.[13]

IDEA therefore does require that the general education classroom with supplemental aids and services be considered first. Supplemental aids and services could include the use of adaptive equipment and technology; the addition of support staff such as teacher aides; modification of instructional techniques; and modification of curriculum.

The general education classroom may not always be the least restrictive environment for students with disabilities. For example:

- Zachary is a secondary student who has had several psychiatric hospitalizations for suicidal ideation. He is classified as a child with a serious emotional disability. He attends regular classes and is currently on medication. He has panic attacks. He receives crisis counseling and general counseling weekly.
- Mary is ten and classified as having mental retardation. She is totally dependent in all areas of self-help (feeding, toileting). If left unattended, she will bang her head (self-abuse). She has limited readiness skills. She is in a small special class with nonacademic mainstreaming.

"It depends." Since the reinactment of IDEA in 1990, a growing body of court cases has provided guidance in determining the least restrictive environment.

Landmark Case. Rachel Holland was an elementary school student with a development disability. Her IQ was reportedly 44. The parents wanted a general education class placement. The district offered part-time regular class placement for nonacademic subjects. Part of the parents' objection was that the partial placement required her to change classrooms six times a day. During the litigation Rachel attended a private school. She was enrolled in a regular class with the support of a teacher aide. The parents' position was upheld.

The Rachel Holland case specifies four criteria for determining the LRE. The United States Court of Appeals ruled that before removing a student with disabilities from a general education environment, a school must consider:

- the educational benefit to the student from the general education class, particularly with respect to socialization, communication, and friendships;
- the disruptive effect on the general education class from the presence of the student with a disability;
- the amount of time the classroom teacher must spend with the disabled student; and
- the cost involved in including the student and its impact on the education of other students.

In *Poolaw v. Bishop* (1994), the court used the same criteria to recommend a more restrictive setting. In this case a thirteen-year-old profoundly deaf student moved into a new district. In his prior district he had remained in general education classes with the support of resource room, individual and small group instruction, a full-time interpreter, and weekly instruction in American Sign Language (ASL). He had limited communication skills. His level of performance in ASL had not improved. The new district was recommending a residential school with intensive ASL instruction. The parents disagreed and began litigation. The courts determined that the student's need for intensive instruction in ASL outweighed the nonacademic benefits of the general education classroom. The courts also ruled that the new school district was under no obligation to try the supplemental aides and services, which previously failed.[14]

In a review of the early LRE cases, Melinda Murphy, an attorney, listed the following factors as helpful in determining if the general education classroom was not the LRE:

- With the provision of appropriate supplementary aids and services (teacher support and training, equipment, use of teacher aides) the child cannot achieve satisfactorily, or obtain some educational benefit. (Note: Nonacademic benefits can outweigh strict academic benefits.)

- With the provision of supplementary aids and services, the other children in the general education classroom are being deprived of the educational benefits due to the time and efforts directed by the teacher toward the child with disabilities.
- The amount of curriculum modification necessary to support the child with disabilities in the general education classroom will result, in essence, in two separate classes in one room.
- The amount of curricular and instructional modification necessary to support the child with disabilities in the general education classroom will result in that child being deprived of a sense of belonging to the regular class.

Perry Zirkel conducted a factor analysis of court cases in the 1990s specific to inclusion.[15] The review did not focus on the larger concept of LRE. It looked only at cases for which "education in the general education classroom for a major portion of the day" was the central issue and the operational definition of inclusion. The purpose of the research was to determine if factors such as the year of the case or the analytic approach or "test" were associated with the outcomes.

Landmark Judicial Test Cases. Two test cases associated with LRE and inclusion are *Daniel R. R. v. State Board of Education* (1989) and *Roncker v. Walter* (1983). Daniel R. R. was a student with Down syndrome. Parents requested regular class placement. Daniel was placed a half-day in a special education program and a half-day in a general education program. After three months, the general education teacher found that she spent an inordinate amount of time with Daniel. In addition, she was modifying the curriculum almost beyond recognition. The district recommended discontinuation of the general education placement. The district was upheld. A two-pronged test used:

- Can the child receive some educational benefit from the placement in a regular class, with or without supplemental aids and services?
- If not, has the school district provided other opportunities for contact with normally developing peers (such as lunch, recess, gym, trips, other nonacademic activities)?

The courts considered the academic and nonacademic benefits but determined, however, that placement in a general education class was pointless if the curriculum was modified beyond recognition. The child would essentially be receiving special education; the only advantage Daniel would reap would be his position next to a normally developing student. In

Roncker v. Walter, a school that was exclusively for special education students was found to be superior placement.

Zirkel analyzed cases from 1990 to 1999[16] and reached the following conclusions:

- specifically relevant court decisions are relatively limited;
- no single factor was predictive of the court decision;
- court decisions were based on one or both landmark judicial tests listed above;
- of the factors analyzed, the age/grade of the child was most closely related to the outcome for an inclusive educational setting; and
- inclusion, in terms of modern case law, defies stereotypes.

Determination of LRE

Decisions regarding least restrictive environment always depend on the individual issues and circumstances. In making decisions, the multidisciplinary team (MDT) must keep a myriad of factors in mind. Zirkel developed a checklist to assist districts in identifying the LRE.[17]

Eligibility

Infants, toddlers, children, and youth with disabilities are eligible to receive special education under the law from birth to age twenty-one. The term "disability" is defined as having mental retardation, hearing impairments (including deafness), speech or language impairments, visual impairments (including blindness), serious emotional disturbance (hereinafter referred to as emotional disturbance), orthopedic impairments, autism, traumatic brain injury, other health impairments, or specific learning disabilities, and therefore requiring specially designed instruction and related services.[18]

Federal regulations provide specific criteria for each disability. "Developmentally delayed" is a classification that can be used for children ages three to nine or as a subset of that age group (ages three to five). Individual states may add to the list of disabilities. For example, New York State has added deaf/blind and multiple disabilities. New York also lists deaf and hearing impairments as separate disability categories. Only children who meet federal and state criteria are eligible for services and procedural safeguards.

Responsibilities of the School District

Many responsibilities are placed on the school district as a result of IDEA. For each responsibility the district must establish policies and procedures. The major responsibilities are child find; evaluations; a provision of special education and related services; and provision of qualified staff.

Child Find. School districts must "find" students with disabilities. This responsibility includes infants, toddlers, and students attending private or parochial school. A variety of procedures are used to locate students with disabilities. A primary method is to conduct a census that includes questions about students with disabilities. Districts may also advertise in local papers, community centers, childcare centers, libraries and places of worship.

Evaluations. Evaluations are conducted by a group of professionals alternatively known as a multidisciplinary team (MDT), an individualized educational program (IEP) team, or a committee on special education (CSE). This team conducts a nondiscriminatory individual evaluation of the student. The composition of the MDT varies. IDEA'97 mandates that the MDT must be comprised of

- the child's parents;
- at least one general education teacher of the child (if the child is, or may be, participating in the general education environment);
- at least one special education teacher, or, where appropriate, at least one special education provider of such child;
- a representative of the local education agency who
  - (a) is qualified to provide, or supervise the provision of, specially designed instruction to meet the unique needs of children with disabilities;
  - (b) is knowledgeable about the general curriculum; and
  - (c) is knowledgeable about the availability of resources of the local education agency;
- an individual who can interpret the instructional implications of evaluation results;
- at the discretion of the parent or the agency, other individuals who have knowledge or special expertise regarding the child, including related services personnel as appropriate (school psychologist, guidance counselor, social worker); and
- if appropriate, the child.[19]

The evaluation should consist of multiple measures, including standardized evaluations, observations, and other educational records. Evaluations address every area of suspected disability. Students must also be reevaluated periodically. Every three years a comprehensive reevaluation must be completed or at least considered with parent input. A reevaluation is not necessary if there is sufficient data to support the present level of service.

Provision of Special Education and Related Services. The district must provide the program and services. Districts are expected to provide a "continuum of alternate placements to meet the needs of children with disabilities for special education and related services."[20] Table 2.1 describes the placements specified in the regulations. In addition, the district must ensure that children with disabilities have a variety of programs and options provided to nondisabled children, including art, music, vocational education, and homemaking education.[21]

Qualified Staff. Districts must provide teachers and other support staff who are qualified to provide special education and related services. Districts must also have staff development plans to ensure that general education teachers become knowledgeable, and that special education teachers maintain and expand their skills.

Emily's Case. Emily is almost 5 years old and will begin kindergarten in the fall. She is currently enrolled in a private preschool program for children with Down syndrome. Emily's parents have referred her to the public schools in the town where they reside. They are seeking a public school placement with her older siblings who do not have disabilities. The MDT will conduct a comprehensive evaluation in all areas of suspected disability. The team members will use their knowledge about Down syndrome and information regarding Emily's unique characteristics to determine what will constitute a comprehensive evaluation.

A clinically sound protocol would involve obtaining anecdotal information from a number of sources including the parents and the current service providers in the current placement. Past evaluations conducted by the school or others authorized by the parent should also be reviewed. An individualized assessment would be designed to address all the areas discussed above. The assessment design might be a standard protocol of tests, with the clinical leader or MDT chairperson identifying the needs for specialized tests. A standard protocol would include at least an observation of the child in the current educational setting, as well as a psychological evaluation, medical evaluation, educational evaluation, and social history. The comprehensive evaluation must identify the student's strengths as well as weaknesses. For Emily, the comprehensive evaluation included the components in Table 2.2.

Based on the results of the evaluations, the MDT will determine whether Emily qualifies for special education and related services.

The actual activities of the MDT may vary by state, local district, and suspected disability. Each state has procedures or policies regarding the activities of the MDT. It is not uncommon for the MDT to conduct a standard battery of assessments. These assessments will also vary based on the child's suspected disability.

Table 2.1.
Continuum of Services

General Education	Classes that conform to the class size and instructional standards of the state and district.
Related Services	Part-time services provided by specialists that allow students to benefit from instruction. This includes counseling, occupational therapy, physical therapy, travel training, vocational counseling, nursing services, and others.
Consultant Teacher	Special education teacher who provides services in the regular education classroom to the student or to the classroom teacher. This includes curriculum modification, instruction, etc.
Resource Room	Part-time special education program. Instruction is usually provided by a teacher certified in special education and is given in small groups. Developmental instruction and remediation, as well as study and organizational skills, may be included. Areas addressed are determined by the IEP. This service is for part of the school day, usually between 20 and 50 percent.
Special Class	Class that includes only students with disabilities. The class size may vary, but in most states it is significantly smaller than the general education class. A teacher aide or assistant may be present.
Special School	A day school that serves only students with disabilities.
Residential	Residential schools for children with disabilities. Historically, many states have had residential schools for the blind and the deaf. The nature and type of residential programs will vary greatly from state to state.
Home/Hospital	Special education services provided at the student's home or hospital.

Table 2.2.
Student Evaluation

Type of Evaluation	Professional	Purpose
Psychological	Psychologist	Cognitive Function Behavior Management ADL Processing Observation in the current setting
Educational	Educational Evaluator	Pre-academic readiness Academic achievement
Social History	Social Worker	Developmental History Family functioning Interests and current functioning (ADL)
Medical	Medical Doctor	Physical status Screen vision and hearing
Occupational Therapy	Occupational Therapist	Fine motor skills, ADL
Physical Therapy	Physical Therapist	Gross motor, strength, endurance, balance
Speech/Language	Speech Language Pathologist	Communication—receptive and expressive language

Determination of Services

Services are determined at a meeting in which the MDT reviews the comprehensive evaluation results and any data presented by the parents and teachers. The evaluations are considered individually and in combination. Each clinician will be able to identify strengths, weaknesses, and the educational implications of the results. The participants will examine the data to look for congruent and inconsistent findings. Inconsistencies might be attributed to student factors such as fatigue, inattention, or inability to relate to the evaluators. Other inconsistencies may be related to the differences in the kind of student response required. For example, was Emily required to point to, say, or write the response? Each method requires a different type or level of skill.

The MDT must determine if the evaluation points to an educational disability as defined in IDEA and/or a specific state's definitions. If a disability is identified, an individualized education plan (IEP) will be developed. If the child is not considered eligible, a written notice is sent to the parents. The notice will indicate the decision of the MDT and the data on which this decision was made. If the parents agree with the recommendation, the process ends. If the parents disagree with the recommendation, they can exercise the due process right discussed earlier. They could ask for an independent evaluation or an impartial hearing.

If there is an educational disability, the MDT must develop an IEP. The IEP must include programs and/or supplemental aids and related services that ensure free and appropriate public education (FAPE) in the least restrictive environment (LRE). The IEP should identify present levels of performance, needs, and goals. Services should then be determined.[22] The following example provides excerpts from the evaluation of Emily and identifies the services the MDT considered.

The comprehensive evaluation of Emily determined that:

1. Emily functioned in the mentally retarded range of cognitive functioning and had significant delays in communication, self-help skills, and health and safety. The MDT decided she met the criteria for the classification of mentally retarded.

2. Emily had significant delays with fine motor activities such as writing, cutting, and snapping. The MDT decided she met the criteria for occupational therapy.

3. Emily's receptive language was delayed. She could, however, follow simple two-step commands. She had significant delays in expressive language. She had articulation problems, which made her difficult to understand out of context. The MDT decided she needed speech/language therapy.

4. Pre-readiness skills were emerging. She was able to recognize her first name, some letters of the alphabet, and colors. She could rote count from 1 to 10 but could not consistently count ten objects.

5. Emily had poor balance and weak muscle tone. This had a negative impact on her general coordination and ability to negotiate stairs. The MDT decided that she needed physical therapy (PT).

6. Social skills were emerging. Emily enjoyed interacting with other children. She had difficulty sharing and waiting for her turn in cooperative activities. Her expressive language problems made it difficult to understand her out of context. At times this led to displays of frustration that included crying and/or pushing.

An IEP was developed with goals and objectives. Placement recommendations varied:

- The school district administrator recommended a full-day special class placement to address Emily's academic, language, and social needs, and part-time regular class placement for nonacademic areas and related services of occupational therapy (OT) and speech.

- The current special education teacher recommended a half-day special class and a half-day of regular class related services.

- One evaluator recommended placement in the general education program with supplementary services.

The parents wanted their daughter to be in the same school as her siblings. The special education classes were not located in that building. What is the appropriate placement for Emily? Using the concepts discussed under LRE, the MDT determined that placement in the general education program would be appropriate at this time. In this case the meeting was adjourned to assess the general education program and environment to determine what supplemental services would be needed. Ultimately Emily was placed in the general education school environment with speech/language services (both in the regular classroom and in a special location), consultant teacher services, occupational therapy, and physical therapy. IDEA requires that the MDT recommendations be reviewed at least annually. The MDT decided to review Emily's progress after two months. Based on additional data (work samples, observations, reports, and anecdotal records), the MDT recommended an individual teacher aide.

Implementation of Services

Special education providers and general education teachers implement the IEP. In Emily's case, a case manager or leader would be assigned. This professional would be responsible for coordinating the services. This could be one of the teachers or a building principal. A meeting would be held with all involved to review the components of the IEP and its goals and objectives. Schedules would be established to reduce interference with instruction. The IEP should specify whether the services are provided in the classroom or in a separate room. The consultant special education teacher and related service providers are responsible for implementing specialized instruction; they serve as a technical resource for the general education teacher, and may answer questions regarding disability issues and offer strategies and approaches to address learning problems. This includes, but is not limited to, small group instruction and curriculum modification. The classroom teacher, as the primary education provider, will integrate Emily into the classroom by setting the tone of acceptance and providing accommodations and modifications throughout the school day.

Inclusion already exists in the diversity of needs in many general education classrooms across the country. Almost half of students with disabil-

ities spend 80 percent of the school day in the general education classroom.[23] Children with disabilities have their IEPs implemented daily by
regular and special education teachers. Sometimes these efforts are coordinated. Other times the professionals work in isolation. Best practice would
allow for collaboration. Examples of collaboration include common planning and preparation time; scheduled team meetings to discuss student
progress; team teaching; and concurrent professional development activities. Methods used must be systematic and reciprocal. They need to focus
on problem solving and foster respect:

- *Systematic.* Planned and scheduled opportunities are uniformly available for all practitioners.
- *Reciprocal.* The regular educator and the special educator grow professionally but learn from each other.
- *Focus on shared problem-solving.* The professionals jointly or by consensus identify problems or student needs and suggest solutions.
- *Foster mutual respect.* The behaviors and attitudes of the professional
  involved are also a factor. The professionals must have mutual respect
  and credibility. Without this critical element collaboration cannot be
  initiated.[24]

SECTION 504

Section 504 of the Vocational Rehabilitation Act of 1973 was the first
civil rights law protecting the rights of individuals with disabilities.[25] The
major thrust of the law is nondiscrimination in employment. The impact
of Section 504 of the Rehabilitation Act on schools was ignored or forgotten until the late 1980s.[26] Crafted in the political atmosphere of the
original version of IDEA passed in 1975, the requirements for public
school districts are familiar. Section 504 mandates a free and appropriate public education (FAPE), least restrictive environment (LRE), and procedural safeguards.

There are major differences between Section 504 and IDEA in three
areas.

- Funding—Section 504 does not provide specific funding.[27]
- Eligibility—Persons who are eligible for protection and services under
  Section 504 include adults and children with disabilities. The definition of disability is different.
- Procedures—Section 504's procedures or rules for evaluation and due
  process are not as prescriptive as IDEA's. A district may use IDEA
  procedures to handle their 504 obligations. This is not, however, required.

Eligibility for 504 Services

Eligible students are referred to as having a disability. For the purposes of 504, a disability is defined as "any person who (i) has a physical or mental impairment which substantially limits one or more of such person's major life activities, (ii) has a record of such impairment, or (iii) is regarded as having such impairment."[28]

A physical or mental impairment is defined as

(A) any physiological disorder or condition, cosmetic disfigurement, or anatomical loss affecting one or more of the following body systems: neurological; musculoskeletal; special sense organs; respiratory, including speech organs; cardiovascular; reproductive; digestive; genito-urinary; hermic and lymphatic; skin; and endrocrine; or (B) any mental or psychological disorder, such as mental retardation, organic brain syndrome, emotional or mental illness, and specific learning disabilities."[29]

Section 504's more comprehensive definition of disability results in more persons being eligible for special services in the schools, such as students with asthma, chronic diseases, HIV, or ADHD. There may be situations where students who have a handicap under Section 504 will not be considered disabled under IDEA. Children who are eligible under IDEA, however, are also eligible under Section 504. Table 2.3 helps to visualize this relationship.

Procedural Safeguards Under Section 504

Procedural safeguards under section 504 are less detailed than those under IDEA. Safeguards outlined in Section 504 include the following:

1. *Consent.* Parental consent is sought for initial evaluation only.
2. *Prior notice.* Parents have the right to be notified of anything that may result in a significant change of educational placement. There is no requirement that this notice be in writing, although written notice is recommended.
3. *Impartial hearing.* Parents have right to have a hearing if they disagree with the evaluations, recommendations, or services developed. The hearing procedures are left to the discretion of the local district. IDEA procedures could be utilized.

District Responsibilities Under Section 504

Many district responsibilities are outlined in the statute and regulations. For the purposes of this chapter, those regarding students and their parents will be highlighted.

Table 2.3.
Differences Between IDEA and Section 504

	IDEA	Section 504
Identification	• All school-aged children who fall within one or more qualifying conditions (i.e, autism, specific learning disability, speech or language impairment, emotional disturbance, traumatic brain injury, visual impairment, hearing impairment, deafness, mental retardation, deaf-blindness, multiple disabilities, orthopedic impairment, and other health impairments) • Requires that child's disability adversely affect educational performance	• Individuals who meet the definition of qualified "handicapped" person—i.e., has or has had a physical or mental impairment that substantially limits a major life activity or is regarded as handicapped by others (major life activities include: walking, seeing, hearing, speaking, breathing, learning, working, caring for oneself, and performing manual tasks) • Does not require that the student needs special education to qualify
Evaluation	• Full comprehensive evaluation required by multidisciplinary team • Requires informed and written consent • Requires reevaluation of each child, if conditions warrant a reevaluation, or if the child's parent or teacher requests a reevaluation, at least every 3 years • Provides for independent evaluation at district expense if parents disagree with first evaluation • Reevaluation not required before significant change in placement	• Evaluation draws on information from a variety of sources and is documented • Decision made by knowledgeable group. • Does not require consent of parents, only notice • Periodic reevaluation required • No provision for independent evaluation at school's expense • Reevaluation required before a significant change in placement

	IDEA	Section 504
Responsibilities to Provide Free Appropriate Public Education (FAPE)	• Requires an individualized education program (IEP) • Appropriate education means a program designed to provide "educational benefit" for a person with disabilities • Placement may be any combination of special education and general educations • Related services, if required	• Does not require an IEP, but does require a plan • "Appropriate" means an education comparable to the education provided to those students who are not disabled • Placement usually in general education classroom • Related services, if needed
Due Process	• Must provide impartial hearings for parents who disagree with the identification, evaluation, or placement of the student • Requires written consent • Delineates specific procedures • Hearing Officer appointed by impartial appointee • Provides "stay-put" provision until all proceedings are resolved • Parents must receive 10 days notice prior to any change in placement • Enforced by U.S. Department of Education, Office of Special Education	• Must provide impartial hearings for parents who disagree with the identification, evaluation, or placement of the student • No consent required • Requires that parent have the opportunity to participate and be represented by counsel—other details left to the discretion of the school • Hearing officer usually is appointed by the school • No "stay-put" provisions • No requirement of day's notice prior to change of placement • Enforced by U.S. Department of Education, Office of Civil Rights

Source: From deBettencourt, L. U. (2002). *Understanding the difference between IDEA and Section 504.* Pages 19–22. Copyright 2002 by The Council for Exceptional Children. Reprinted with permission.

- *Child find.* School districts must identify students with disabilities living within their jurisdiction. Districts must also notify these individuals or their parents of the district's FAPE obligations.

- *Evaluations.* A district must conduct a nondiscriminatory assessment in the student's native language. Evaluations may draw information from a variety of sources and should be conducted by a group of professionals knowledgeable about the student, evaluation data, and placement options. In contrast to IDEA's MDT specifications, no specific list of participants is required by Section 504. For example: Marisol has cancer and will be taking chemotherapy. She is exhausted and too ill to attend school. Prior to the diagnosis of cancer she had no school-related problems. A comprehensive evaluation might include a medical report and a review of school records. Finally, periodic reevaluation must also be conducted. No specific timelines are identified, however.

- *Nondiscriminatory program access.* The district must establish policies and procedures that ensure that no otherwise qualified individual is denied the benefits of the program or subjected to discrimination under the program solely because of his or her disability. Program access also includes physical access to the buildings and programs. This includes education programs, vocational services, and extracurricular programs. For example: A school district offers music instruction for talented elementary school students during a zero period (before the school day) at a central location. All parents provide transportation to the central site. The districts provide return transportation to home schools. Paula is a student with a physical disability and qualifies for specialized transportation (wheelchair accessible bus). She also qualifies for the special music program. Paula's parents work. They can transport her to the centralized location but cannot transport her to school. Must the district provide specialized transportation? Yes. Section 504 mandates that the district provide the transportation. Paula is a student with a physical disability and qualifies for the enrichment program. She cannot be denied access because of her disability (transportation needs).

- *Grievance procedures.* All school districts or local education agencies (LEAs) with more than fifteen employees must appoint a 504 compliance officer and establish internal grievance procedures. This requirement was developed primarily for employees with disabilities. The procedures must outline how discrimination complaints will reach a quick and equitable resolution. Parents may also access this process to discuss issues involving their children. Finally, this statute protects the rights of parents with disabilities. Parents may use this process when they believe they have been denied access to any programs or services. For example: Mr. and Mrs. Mc Elroy have a significant hearing loss. Their primary mode of communication is American Sign Language. They wanted to participate in parent-teacher conferences. The school failed to provide a sign language interpreter despite prior notification. Mr. and Mrs. Elroy could initiate a district-level grievance.

- *Self-evaluation.* Districts must conduct a self-evaluation. The purpose of the study is to identify and correct discriminatory policies and practices.

Services Available Under Section 504

Section 504 requires "the provision of general or special education and related aids and services that "(i) Are designed to meet individual education needs of handicapped persons as adequately as the needs of non-handicapped persons are met."[30] Special education is one option that is not frequently used, for two reasons. First, students with significant disabilities who require special education usually receive those services under IDEA. Second, as there is no supplemental funding, this does not encourage the provision of expensive services. Litigation has suggested, however, that any service listed in Table 2.1 could be appropriately recommended and provided.

The primary Section 504 service model is to provide accommodations and adaptations. The accommodations can be instructional and/or environmental. Deschenes, Ebeling, and Sprague[31] have identified nine categories of instructional adaptations that can be made in the general education classroom. These include adapting the amount of work completed, extending the amount of time allotted for tests and assignments, and changing the response modality (writing vs. speaking). Extended test time is used frequently as an accommodation. Part of the push for this accommodation is related to student-specific disabilities. Much of the overuse of this accommodation is related to the high stakes state-level tests and college entrance examinations.

Counseling by psychologists and social workers is another example of a related service provided under Section 504. These services might be utilized by students with behavioral, attention, and/or socialization issues related to such disabilities as ADHD.

Sample Accommodations Under Section 504. Three types of accommodations are environmental changes, provision of services in the home, and nursing services.

Environment Adaptation: Marisa is ten and has been identified as having an attention deficit hyperactivity disorder. She becomes easily distracted. Preferential seating (near the teacher, away from the window, in the front of the classroom) would be one appropriate accommodation.

Homebound Services: Marisol has cancer and is eligible for 504 protection because of a physical disability. Marisol's parents are requesting homebound services on an intermittent basis due to chemotherapy. The district's policy requires homebound services only for students who are expected to be out for twenty consecutive school days. Modifying the homebound instruction requirement would be an appropriate accommodation.

Intermittent Nursing Services: Nudis, a seven-year-old with diabetes, needs insulin injections during the school day. He has not learned to self-administer the medication. A reasonable accommodation is that the school nurse gives the injection.

Deciding on Appropriate Section 504 Services

A multidisciplinary team decides which services are appropriate. As noted earlier, the MDT members are chosen at the discretion of the district and should be outlined in its 504 procedures. Ideally, the current general education teacher should be a member of the team. The evaluation could be a review of existing data and medical information, and/or comprehensive evaluation consistent with IDEA. After considering the data, the team determines what the student needs in order to access the district programs. An accommodation plan must be developed. A written plan is recommended, though not required. The plan is reviewed periodically and prior to any major change in the program.

Implementation of 504 Services

The general education teacher will be the primary service delivery person for most 504 students. The general education teacher may be responsible for the instructional accommodation and implementation of environmental accommodations such as seating. Nurses and other support personnel will be responsible for services like the provision of medication and counseling. Best practice indicates that the teacher should be involved in the plan's development and have ready access to the plan. The services would be reviewed periodically.

SUMMARY

IDEA is the seminal federal legislation regarding the provision of special education services. It establishes the perimeters and sets minimum standards. IDEA requires that students with disabilities receive a free and appropriate public education (FAPE) in the least restrictive environment (LRE). Parents and children are protected by a number of due process rights that ensure parental consent and involvement. Districts are required to establish policies and procedures, to appoint a multidisciplinary team (MDT), to conduct a nondiscriminatory evaluation, and to offer a continuum of special education services. Services are determined by the MDT, of which parents (and, if appropriate, the child) are members. Litigation also plays an important role in the special education process. Parents may request an impartial hearing if they disagree with aspects of the process. This procedure may be resolved at the local level or may involve state or federal courts. Court decisions then establish how the special education laws and requirements are interpreted in the future.

Section 504 of the Vocational Rehabilitation Act of 1973 is a civil rights law. It provides no additional funding. It requires that all recipients of federal funds, including schools, comply with its provisions. An eligible person may be a child, an employee of the district, or a parent with a disability. A disability is defined as any physical or mental condition that significantly limits a life function such as learning, breathing, or walking. The students are eligible for general education, special education, and related services. For a number of reasons, related services and program accommodation are frequently used. To receive these services the parents must consent to a nondiscriminatory evaluation conducted by a 504 MDT. The team must have knowledge about the student's needs and the programs and services in the district. The recommendations of the team are referred to as an accommodation plan. This plan is implemented and periodically reviewed.

Tips for Parents

✎ FAPE is an acronym for "free and appropriate public education." The school is required to give each student an appropriate education. The school is not required to provide the best possible education.

✎ IDEA mandates that parents be equal partners in the special education process.

✎ Because IDEA is reauthorized and updated periodically, it is important to become familiar with the many resources available for parents.

RESOURCES FOR IDEA 2004

Analysis from NASDSE. www.nasdse.org/
NASDSE (National Association of State Directors of Special Education) offers a 200-page side-by-side that compares current law to the amended law signed by President Bush on December 3, 2004.
CEC's Summary of IDEA '04. www.cec.sped.org/pp/IDEA_120204.pdf
Courtesy of the Council for Exceptional Children.

Frequently Asked Questions About IDEA. http://edworkforce.house.gov/issues/109th/education/idea/ideafaq.pdf

Let's Go Section by Section. www.copaa.org/news/idea04.html
Courtesy of the Council of Parent Attorneys and Advocates (COPAA), take a look at the Comparison of H.R. 1350 (Individuals with Disabilities Education Improvement Act of 2004) and IDEA '97.

Mandlawitz, M. (2006). *What Every Teacher Should Know About IDEA 2004.* Boston: Pearson/Allyn & Bacon.
This booklet compares elements of IDEA '97 to IDEA '04.

A Side-by-Side Analysis of Transition Requirements. ncset.org/publications/related /ideatransition.asp
Courtesy of the National Center on Secondary Education and Transition (NCSET). This side-by-side analysis identifies major changes between IDEA 1997 and H.R. 1350 (IDEA 2004) concerning transition services for youth with disabilities.

Summary of the New IDEA Provisions. www.OCLB.info/pdf/NAPAS_IDEA2004 _Summary.pdf
Courtesy of the National Association of Protection and Advocacy Systems, Inc. (NAPAS).

Summary of the New Law. www.nichcy.org/reauth/2004IDEASUMMARY -12.04.doc
Courtesy of the National Committee of Parents and Advocates Organized to Protect IDEA.

Summary of the 2004 IDEA. www.ndsccenter.org/events.asp#summary
Courtesy of the National Down Syndrome Congress (NDSC), this summary looks at the IEP process, due process, and discipline.

NOTES

1. Sheehan, V. (2000, June). Section 504 and the Americans with Disabilities Act—An update. Paper presented at New York State School Boards Association Conference, Melville, New York.

2. CASE. (1999). *Section 504 and the ADA: Promoting student access—a resource guide.* (2nd ed.). Arlington, VA: Council of Administrators of Special Education.

3. Zirkel, P. (1999, August). Legal workshop on inclusion. Paper presented at Nassau BOCES Sliver Grant Inclusion Training, Rockville Centre, New York.

4. Zirkel (1999, August).

5. Individuals with Disabilities Act Amendments, 20 U.S.C. 1400 et seq. (1997).

6. Turnbull, A., & Turnbull, R. (1997). *Families, professionals and exceptionality: A special partnership.* Upper Saddle River, NJ: Merrill.

7. Turnbull, A., Turnbull, R., Shank, M. & Leal, D. (1999). *Exceptional lives: Special education in today's schools.* Upper Saddle River, NJ: Merrill.

8. FERPA is also known as the Buckley Amendment, 20 U.S.C. 1232g; 34 C.F.R. § 99.

9. Individuals with Disabilities Education Act Amendments (1997).

10. The Orton-Gillingham Method (International Dyslexia Association, Philadelphia, Pennsylvania).

11. Worona, J., & Sokol, P. (2000, June). Educating children with disabilities: Legal overview and update. Paper presented at New York State School Boards Association Conference, Melville, New York.

12. Zirkel (1999, August).

13. Individuals with Disabilities Education Act Amendments (1997).

14. Worona & Sokol (2000, June).

15. Zirkel (1999, August).

16. Zirkel (1999, August).

17. Zirkel (1999, August).

18. Individuals with Disabilities Education Act Amendments (1997).

19. 34 C.F.R. § 300.344.

20. 34 C.F.R. § 300.551.

21. 34 C.F.R. § 300.305.

22. Feldman, J. (2000, June). How to draft a legally defensible IEP: Legal overview and update. Paper presented at New York State School Boards Association Conference, Melville, New York; Individuals with Disabilities Act Amendments (1997).

23. Office of Special Education (OSEP). (2002). Twenty-fourth annual report to Congress on the Implementation of the Individuals with Disabilities Education Ad.

24. Heron, T., & Harris, K. (1993). *The educational consultant: Helping professionals, parents and mainstream students.* (3rd ed.). Austin, TX: Pro-ed.

25. Sheehan (2000, June).

26. CASE (1999); Zirkel (1999, August).

27. Sheehan (2000, June).

28. 29 U.S.C § 705 (20)(B).

29. 34 C.F.R. § 104.3.

30. 34 C.F.R. § 104.33 (b)(1).

31. Deschenes, C., Ebeling, D., & Sprague, J. (1994). *Adapting curriculum and instruction in inclusive classrooms: A teacher's desk reference.* Bloomington, IN: Center for School and Community Integration.

CHAPTER 3

Evaluating Students
for Eligibility

Ralph Zalma and Gloria Lodato Wilson

Tommy's teacher suspected that he had a disability based on her observations of his behavior, his work, and his lack of academic progress. As the educator who spends the most time with the student, the classroom teacher's observations and input are valuable. If you have a student who is having difficulties, and you suspect the student has a disability, document your observations and talk to the learning specialist, school psychologist, or special education administrator. They may decide to do a pre-referral investigation and intervention, or proceed directly to a formal referral. Table 3.1 provides helpful information on signs to look for under IDEA disability classifications.

THE ELIGIBILITY PROCESS

At times, the entire special education process can seem confusing. Why are some students classified and given services when others who seem to have the same difficulties are not? How can Tommy be in fifth grade, have such academic and behavioral difficulties, and not be receiving services? Why do some students in your class receive services who do not seem to need the support as much as Tommy? If you talk to friends in other schools or districts, why do the criteria for services seem to vary among school districts?

While the eligibility mandates for special education services put forth by IDEA are quite detailed, the information compiled is subject to considerable interpretation. Understanding the evaluation process can help make sense of ultimate decisions regarding a particular student's eligibility for services. For a determination of eligibility to be made, Tommy must participate in a nondiscriminatory evaluation with a multidisciplinary team (MDT) of professionals. The evaluation determines whether he has a dis-

Table 3.1.
Characteristics of IDEA Classifications

Disability	Signs
Autism	• Challenged by social conversations • Does not play with others • Frequently unresponsive to voices • May exhibit echolalia (repeats words or phrases) or other unusual speech patterns • Usually has language development delays • Disrupted by changes in daily routine • Difficulty sleeping • Engages in stereotypical behaviors[1]
Hearing impairment	• Speech may be difficult to understand • Student misunderstands others • Might turn head to one side trying to hear • Asks for information to be repeated • Looks at other students to determine instructions[2]
Emotional disturbance	• Difficulty with appropriate social adjustments • May be unable to build and maintain satisfactory interpersonal relationships • May engage in aggressive behaviors • May have pervasive mood of unhappiness or depression • May act out or withdraw during classroom instruction and independent activities • Problematic behavior occurs in more than one setting[3]
Mental retardation	• Does not attain appropriate developmental milestones • Does not learn as quickly as peers • Has difficulty retaining and generalizing learned skills • Has more limitations in adaptive behaviors than peers • Difficulty in academic areas in the general classroom • Limited reading comprehension and mathematical reasoning and application[4]

Table 3.1.
(continued)

Disability	Signs
Orthopedic impairment	• Difficulty moving in an organized and efficient way • Difficulty with fine motor activities • Difficulty with activities of daily living such as dressing, postural control, speaking, comprehending, or organizing • Not meeting developmental milestones[5]
Other health impairment	Specific: Attention Deficit/Hyperactivity Disorder (ADHD) • Careless mistakes; difficulty sustaining attention; doesn't seem to be listening; fails to follow through on tasks; difficulty organizing; often loses things; easily distracted; forgetful • Fidgety; leaves seat when expected to be seated; runs or climbs excessively or inappropriately; has difficulty playing quietly; talks excessively; blurts out answers or comments; has difficulty taking turns; acts as if always on the go • Work is consistently or generally poor • Work may be incomplete or completed haphazardly[6]
Specific learning disability	• Appears frustrated with academic tasks • May have stopped trying • Work is inconsistent or generally poor • Ineffective instruction is eliminated as the cause for academic difficulty[7]
Speech or language disorders	• Difficulty understanding and/or using language • Not achieving developmental milestones related to communication skills • May be hesitant to participate in verbal classroom work • Written classroom projects may reflect errors of verbal communication or be a preferred avenue of expression • Tests do not differentiate the student from others in many cases[8]

Table 3.1.
(continued)

Disability	Signs
Visual impairment	• Squints or seems to be bothered by light • Eyes water or are red • Holds books too close • Bumps into objects • Poor ability to learn incidentally from the environment[9]

Notes
1. Turnbull, A., Turnbull, R., Shank, M., & Leal, D. (2002). *Exceptional lives: Special education in today's schools*. (3rd ed.). Upper Saddle River, NJ: Prentice Hall, p. 349.
2. Turnbull, Turnbull, Shank, & Leal (2002), p. 534.
3. Turnbull, Turnbull, Shank, & Leal (2002), p. 160.
4. Turnbull, Turnbull, Shank, & Leal (2002), p. 279.
5. Turnbull, Turnbull, Shank, & Leal (2002), p. 416.
6. Turnbull, Turnbull, Shank, & Leal (2002), p. 386.
7. Turnbull, Turnbull, Shank, & Leal (2002), p. 119.
8. Turnbull, Turnbull, Shank, & Leal (2002), p. 502.
9. Turnbull, Turnbull, Shank, & Leal (2002), p. 569.

ability as defined by the federal government, and if the disability creates a need for special education services. As Tommy's general education classroom teacher, Ms. Smith will be called upon to offer information pertaining to Tommy's classroom performance and behavioral and social interactions.

Nondiscriminatory Evaluation

IDEA requires that once a referral is made and parental permission is given, the student participates in a nondiscriminatory assessment process. There are numerous safeguards in place to preclude arbitrary and discriminatory decisions. The assessment must include a sufficient number and variety of standardized tests to get a clear picture of a student's cognitive, behavioral, and physical skills. These assessment instruments must have strong psychometric properties, be culturally and racially unbiased, be administered by qualified professionals in appropriate settings, and be in a student's native language. The overall assessment must ultimately be interpreted by a group of professionals and parents.

Standardized Tests: Norm-Referenced and Criterion-Referenced Tests

Standardized or norm-referenced tests form the foundation of the assessment process. Norm-referenced tests are those that compare the student's performance to that of other students in the country and provide standard administration procedures. Because these tests are administered in exactly the same way to each student, it is possible to compare results from a particular student with those of a group of students of the same age and grade. These comparisons are then used to determine how far ahead or behind a particular student is compared to the normed sample. The norming sample that is used should resemble the student being tested. The question answered by a norm-referenced test is, How does this student compare to others like him/her? Table 3.2 lists commonly used norm-referenced tests. The results of a norm-referenced test are usually communicated by means such as standard scores, scaled scores, stanines, percentiles, and age and grade equivalents and are important in determining whether a student is eligible for services.

While norm-referenced tests primarily use raw scores, or total number of items answered correctly, to yield the ultimate score for comparisons, and typically cover a wide range of items, criterion-referenced tests rate a student's performance to a particular standard or criterion and address a narrow band of items. The basic questions answered in a criterion-referenced test are, Can this student do this particular task or meet this specific standard? Has this student mastered this skill? These results are usually skill-specific and yield important information for teachers to use in their classroom. So while norm-referenced tests compare student performance, criterion-based tests grade a student on his or her mastery of a skill or body of knowledge.

Informal and Formal Evaluation

Complete and thorough assessments use both informal and formal instruments. Generally, norm-referenced and published criterion-referenced tests are considered formal measures, while observations, checklists, and teacher-made tests are considered informal instruments. As a student's teacher you will normally not be responsible for administering individual formal assessments, but will likely be asked to contribute observational information as well as data on classroom performance (see Figures 3.1 and 3.2 and Table 3.4).

A multidisciplinary team (Table 3.3) is established to ensure that a student is not classified based on one person's opinion or on one test. This team is usually made up of a psychologist, special education teacher, gen-

Table 3.2.
Norm-Referenced Tests

Area	Test	Age/Grade	Skills Assessed
Intelligence	Wechsler Intelligence Scale for Children, Third Edition	6–16 yrs.	Overall intelligence Verbal intelligence Performance intelligence
	Stanford-Binet Intelligence Scale, Fourth Edition	2 yrs.–adulthood	General intelligence Analytic abilities Memory Reasoning
	Kaufman Assessment Battery for Children	2.5–12.5 yrs.	Intellectual functioning Achievement
Achievement	Woodcock-Johnson Psychoeducational Battery, Third Edition	Preschool–adulthood	Reading Mathematics Writing Knowledge
	Weschler Individual Achievement Test	5–19 yrs.	Reading Mathematics Writing Listening Oral communication
	Kaufman Test of Educational Achievement	1st–12th grade	Mathematics Reading Spelling
	Peabody Individual Achievement Tests—Revised	K–12th grade	General information Reading Mathematics Writing
	Wide-Range Achievement Tests—3	5–75 yrs.	Reading Arithmetic Spelling
Language	Peabody Picture Vocabulary Test-III	25–90+ yrs.	Receptive vocabulary
	Test of Written Language—3	7 yrs., 6 mos.–17 yrs., 11 mos.	Vocabulary Spelling Style and sentences Contextual conventions and language Story construction

Table 3.2.
(continued)

Area	Test	Age/Grade	Skills Assessed
Adaptive Behavior	AAMR Adaptive Behavior Scale, Second Edition: School Edition	6–21 yrs.	Adaptive behavior Maladaptive behavior
	Vineland Adaptive Behavior Scales	birth–18 yrs.	Communication Daily living Socialization Motor skills Maladaptive behavior

eral education teacher, parent, school district representative, student, and others. Each person on the team contributes in some essential way to the understanding of the student's abilities and difficulties and generally uses a variety of approaches that include both formal and informal measures. Information from current standardized tests is linked to observations, interviews, and previous performance on group or individual tests and past academic performance. The roles and particular tests used by each member of the team vary, and there is no mandated set of assessment instruments that must be uniformly used. This flexibility allows professionals freedom to choose instruments that are most appropriate for individual students.

For the most part, professionals in this process have traditionally been concerned with one overriding concern: Does this student have a disability and, if so, does it affect school performance? However, this narrow view has made it difficult to translate assessment results into useful teaching strategies. Waterman offers a more comprehensive series of questions that expand the assessment and can yield important information for teaching.[1] Some of the questions Waterman asks include:

- How can we manage the child's behavior, or teach the child to manage his or her own behavior?
- How can we help the child be neater, faster, quieter, more motivated?
- In what physical environment does the child learn best?
- What is useful, debilitating, or neutral about the way the child approaches the task?

Table 3.3.
Multidisciplinary Team Members and Their Roles

Team Member	Responsibilities
School nurse	• Initial vision and hearing screens • Checks medical records • Refers health problems to other medical professionals
Special education	• Consultant to regular classroom teacher during pre-referral process
Teacher	• Administers educational tests • Observes in other classrooms • Helps with screening • Recommends IEP goals, writes objectives, and suggests educational interventions
General education teacher	• Works with the special education team, student, and parents • Develops a learning environment for all students to learn • Implements pre-referral intervention strategies
Parent	• Informs school of family, medical, and educational history of student • Works with other team members to develop appropriate educational goals • Implements home academic and behavioral strategies
Special education supervisor	• May advise special education teacher on all activities • Guides placement decisions • Recommends services
Educational diagnostician	• Administers norm-referenced and criterion-referenced tests • Observes student in educational setting • Makes suggestions for IEP goals and objectives
School psychologist	• Administers individual intelligence tests • Observes student in classroom • Administers projective instruments and personality inventories

Table 3.3.
(continued)

Team Member	Responsibilities
Occupational therapist	• Evaluates fine motor and self-help skills • Recommends therapies • May provide direct services or consultant services • May help obtain equipment for student needs
Physical therapist	• Evaluates gross motor functioning and self-help skills, living skills, and job-related skills necessary for optimum achievement of student • May provide direct services or consultant services
School counselor	• May serve as objective observer in pre-referral stage • May provide direct group or individual counseling • May schedule students and help with planning of student school schedules
Speech/language therapist	• Evaluates speech/language development • May refer for hearing problems • May provide direct therapy or consultant services for classroom teachers
Audiologist	• Evaluates hearing for possible impairments • May refer students for medical problems • May help obtain hearing aids
School social worker	• Works directly with family • May hold conferences, conduct interviews, and administer adaptive behavior scales based on parent interviews • May serve as case manager

Source: Overton, T. (2002). *Assessment in special education: An applied approach.* Upper Saddle River, NJ: Prentice Hall.

- Can the student hold multiple pieces of information in memory and then act upon them?
- How does increasing or slowing the speed of instruction impact upon the child's accuracy?
- What processing mechanisms are being taxed in any given task?
- With whom has the child been successful? What about the person seems to have contributed to the child's success?
- What is encouraging to the child? What is discouraging?
- How does manipulating the mode of teaching affect the child's performance?

The psychologist generally conducts a wide array of tests, the most important being an intelligence test, which is a norm-referenced test used to determine a student's learning potential. While a student cannot be classified based solely on an IQ score, the information from an intelligence test usually forms the backdrop for interpretation of other assessment results. For example, by definition, a student who has a learning disability usually has average or above average intelligence, while a student considered to have mental retardation would have an IQ score below 70 and have adaptive skill deficiencies. A psychologist might also choose to administer "projectives" such as the Rorschach or Draw a Person Test that help determine the emotional state of a student. In addition, information from attention scales and depression scales can complete a picture of a student and offer information on why a student is performing in a certain manner.

The special educator is usually responsible for what is called a psychoeducational assessment. He/she will administer a series of tests to determine the skill level of the student in academic and process areas such as reading, writing, mathematics, listening comprehension, and oral expression. The special education teacher also looks at how a student learns, notes the strategies the student uses, and determines the points at which abilities break down. There is always some overlap between the information gathered by the psychologist and the special education teacher.

The general education teacher is asked to contribute samples of the student's work and brief reports based on observation of behavior and academic performance in the classroom. See Figures 3.1 and 3.2 for formats for observations and reports. This information is particularly helpful to the team in its efforts to understand the actual level of day-to-day functioning that is not measured with many more formal evaluation tools. Teacher reports give insight into how a student is using the skills he or she has, what the functional strengths and weaknesses are, where abilities break down, what strategies the student uses, what frustrates

Area	Time/Activity	Observations/Work Samples
Seatwork		
Groupwork		
Transitions		
Lunchtime and Recess		
Specials		
After school activities		

Figure 3.1. Format for Student Observation by a Classroom Teacher Including Work Samples

the student, what teaching strategies were used, and what contributes to success.

When making observations of a student in a classroom, some general guidelines are helpful. Decide to focus on the student for one day or a series of days and keep a record of your observations. Your write-up will be more complete if you touch on each area at least twice and within a variety of activities and settings. Both strengths and weaknesses should be addressed. Refer to Table 3.4 for questions to guide your observations.

Continuous and systematic observations of behavior in context can provide the necessary information to restructure the context, that is, modify the ecology of the classroom, rearrange schedules, rethink approaches to individual and group instruction, reflect on communication styles, and reevaluate how student performance is to be measured.

The parent is an important participant in the evaluation process and is the chief informant for the social history taken by a social worker or guid-

Name of Student:
Grade:
Teacher:
Date:

Classroom Behavior:

Classroom Task Performance:

Lecture:

Test Performance (quizzes, tests):

Homework Performance:

Relationships with Classmates and Adults:

Present Concerns:

Figure 3.2. General Teacher Report for a Student Referred for an Assessment

Table 3.4.
Questions to Focus Teacher Observations

Area	Questions
Physical	• Does s/he seem to be average in height and weight for her or his age? • Is s/he well groomed or does s/he look disheveled with shirttails hanging out and shoelaces untied? • Describe her/his gait and movement around the classroom; does s/he appear to be well coordinated? • Does your student use her/his eyes effectively to scan and search the environment or does s/he appear disoriented? • How carefully does s/he use his/her hands and fingers to explore objects, put things together, use writing implements, and express her/himself through gestures? • Is s/he aware of what is going on around her/him or is s/he somewhat confused and overwhelmed? • Is your student interested in the other children and what they are doing? • Does s/he want to join them and participate in activities or is s/he rather cautious, shying away from any contact with others?
Receptive and expressive language	• Does your student understand what you are talking about and what you are asking of her or him during your lesson presentations? • Is s/he able to effectively express her/himself and make known her/his needs to you and to other children? • Is her/his language age and grade appropriate? In your conversations with her/him and listening to her/his verbal interactions with others you will need to appraise the level of listening and oral vocabulary, pronunciation, use of syntactic grammatical forms and the fluidity of ideas as expressed in speech. • Is s/he an inquisitive child who is engaging in spontaneous verbalization or one who is reticent and responds only on demand?
Cognitive abilities	• Can s/he focus attention on what is happening during a lesson and can s/he listen carefully to what you are saying, or is s/he so distractible and hyperactive or so withdrawn and sedate that s/he becomes easily disoriented and confused? Chronic disorientation can lead to a variety of phobias and high states of anxiety that can result in increasing amounts of anger and acting-out behavior.

Table 3.4.
(continued)

Area	Questions
	• How well organized does your student seem to you?
	• Does s/he come to school with the necessary books and materials and completed homework assignments?
	• Can s/he anticipate what will happen during the current school day?
	• Is her/his desk neat and clean or is everything so disorganized that s/he becomes quickly overwhelmed and confused?
	• Is her/his approach to school tasks planned out or haphazard?
	• Is s/he calm and thoughtful in responses to the teacher, task demands, and interaction with peers, or typically impulsive in her/his approach to problem solving?
Metacognitive behavior skills	• Can the child remember what is expected of her/him?
	• Can s/he reason and be reasoned with?
	• Can s/he monitor her/his own behavior and use inner speech to regulate her/his actions?
Social interaction	• To what extent is your student aware of the verbal and gestured cues from others?
	• Is s/he sensitive to their facial expressions and the space between them?
	• What is the nature of their communication—is it give-and-take or dominated by one or the other?
	• Can your student reflect on what friends say?
	• Can you detect a sense of empathy between students or is dialogue between them primarily egocentric?
	• Does your student interact readily with others during group activities in class as well as extracurricular programs?
	• Are your student's attitudes and interests compatible with those of peers?
Additional information	• How frequent are the behaviors displayed?
	• How long do the behaviors last?
	• How long does it take for a student to respond to a request?

ance counselor. Through this history, parents relate important aspects regarding developmental milestones in the areas of language, physical growth and movement, educational history, family history (including the constellation of the family), and any academic or behavioral difficulties the parent or siblings experienced.

Provisions in IDEA underscore the importance placed on the parent in the special education process. Although some parents are quite vocal, many others rely on professionals to know what is best for their child and become intimidated by the formal proceedings of special education. Listening to the concerns, worries, dreams, and attitudes of parents can lead to powerful insights into the needs of the student.

The school district representative in the multidisciplinary team is usually a special education administrator whose responsibilities include safeguarding the rights of the students, conducting the meetings, and securing the recommended services. This administrator has the broadest view in the process and must balance the needs of the student with the availability of resources while ensuring that the student's rights are always protected. This is not an easy position to be in, and there are often disagreements surrounding the extent of services that will be provided. Understandably, all the participants want what is best for the student, but what form that takes is subject to debate.

Just as IDEA stresses parent participation, students are also encouraged to be active, vocal members of the team. Simply having a student attend a meeting and asking what he/she wants is insufficient. Teachers are encouraged to train students in self-advocacy skills to strengthen their voices and help them develop an understanding of their strengths and weaknesses as well as the impact of their disability on their lives, and to build techniques for expression of needs and desires.

The evaluation must be comprehensive and investigate all areas related to the suspected disability. Further assessments may be conducted by speech and language therapists, occupational and physical therapists, neuropsychologists, psychiatrists, and medical doctors.

Determination of Eligibility

For students to be declared eligible for special education services, it must be determined that they have a disability *and* that this disability negatively impacts their ability to progress in school. In other words, having a disability is in itself not enough to warrant special services. For instance, a student with diabetes certainly has a disability, yet this condition might not impact the student in school. Therefore, specific services might not be warranted. IDEA delineates disabilities by classification categories (see Table 3.5). The criteria used to establish a disability vary according to the classi-

Table 3.5.
IDEA Classification Categories of Disabilities

Classification	General Findings
Autism	• Qualitative impairment in social interaction and communication • Repetitive patterns of behavior • Many students with autism have IQs below 75; others attain average or above-average scores • Variation on achievement tests • Below-average adaptive behavior scores in areas such as communication, daily living, socialization • Limited interactions with peers and adults • Usually normal physical health[1]
Emotional disturbance	• Intelligence is usually, but not always, in the low average to slow learner range • The assessment results reflect ability rather than cultural difference • Emotional and behavioral disorders can sometimes be indicated by performance on subtests of the intelligence measure • Usually the student scores below average across academic areas • The student may act out or withdraw during evaluation • Student scores in the significant range on behavior rating scales • Student's performance on tests of self-esteem, personality and adjustment scales is below the norm • Student is experiencing difficulty in one or more areas of the curriculum • Student is experiencing difficulty relating to peers or adults and in adjusting to school or classroom structure or routine
Hearing impairment	• Recent scores with audiograms may indicate that the student's hearing loss is stabilized or worsening • Student may score significantly lower than peers on achievement tests if hearing loss has not been corrected before starting school or if academic program has not used alternative or augmentative communication • The student may have significant problems with receptive and expressive language • The student's speech is usually affected

Table 3.5.
(continued)

Classification	General Findings
	• The student may be performing below peers in one or more areas of the curriculum because of reading and/or language difficulties
Specific learning disability	• Student has average or above-average intelligence • Significant difference exists between what the student is capable of learning (as measured by intelligence test) and what the student has actually learned (as measured by the achievement test) • Differences exist in one or more of the following areas: listening, thinking, reading, written language, mathematics • Learning problems cannot be explained by the presence of emotional or behavioral problems • Vision and hearing are within average range • Learning problems have been apparent throughout time in school • The student's environment does not cause the learning difficulty[2]
Mental retardation	• The student has significantly subaverage intellectual functioning (falls in bottom 2 to 3 percent of population with IQ score of approximately 70 to 75 or below) • The student scores significantly below average in two or more adaptive skill domains, indicating deficits in skill areas such as communication, home living, self-direction, and leisure • The student experiences difficulty and frustration in one or more areas of the curriculum
Other health impairment	Included under "Other Health Impairment": Attention Deficit/Hyperactivity Disorder (ADHD) • Psychiatrist or psychologist determines that student meets DSM-IV criteria for ADHD: The behaviors have been present in more than one setting, were first observed before age seven, and have lasted more than six months • Student's intelligence may range from below average to gifted • Educational performance has been adversely affected • Student scores in the significant range on measures of attention or hyperactivity-impulsivity

Table 3.5.
(continued)

Classification	General Findings
	• The student's educational performance has been adversely affected by the condition • The student is experiencing difficulty in one or more areas of the curriculum, and the behaviors have caused the student to miss important skills
Orthopedic impairment	• Standardization of IQ tests may be violated because the student's physical disabilities interfere with the ability to perform some tasks • The student may be average, above average, or below average in intelligence and achievement • The student's differences in range of motion, motor patterns, gaits, and postures may present learning problems • The student may be unable to or have difficulty integrating visual and auditory input and motor output in skills such as cutting and carrying out verbal instructions in an organized manner • The student may have difficulty in self-care, household, community, and communication skills • The student may require extra time or assistance in mobility, self-help, positioning, and use of adaptive equipment
Speech or language impairment	• The student may be average, above average, or below average in intelligence • Language-related subtest scores may be lower than scores on subtests such as mathematics that do not require language skills • The student performs significantly below average in one or more speech or language areas • The student may avoid oral tasks and/or appears confused during conversations, and others may have difficulty understanding the student's speech
Visual impairment including blindness	• Standardization of IQ tests may need to be violated because the student's visual impairment interferes with the ability to perform some tasks • Student may be average, above average, or below average in intelligence

Table 3.5.
(continued)

Classification	General Findings
	• The student may not achieve in concept development and academic areas at levels of peers • The student may have difficulty in self-care, household, and community skills because of vision and mobility problems • The student may not participate in age-appropriate self-help, social, and recreational activities in home, community, or school • The student may not possess age-appropriate knowledge or skills in areas of communication, daily living, career awareness, sensory and fine motor, social, and self-advocacy • The student is unable or has difficulty in responding to print media without use of magnification or alternative strategies • The student cannot sustain reading in texts for long periods of time
Traumatic brain injury	• Student often shows extreme peaks and valleys on subtests and retains some skills but not others • Scores often look very different than scores received on tests taken before the injury • The student often has holding skills in some areas while other skills are affected adversely by the injury • Student may have difficulty in social, self-care, household, and community skills as a result of the injury • Student may have difficulty in areas of attention, memory, concentration, motivation, and perceptual integration • Student may demonstrate difficulty relating to others and behaving in socially appropriate ways • Student may appear frustrated, have limited attention span, fatigue easily, or lack motivation to perform academic tasks[3]

1. Turnbull, Turnbull, Shank, & Leal (2002), p. 349.
2. Turnbull, Turnbull, Shank, & Leal (2002), p. 119.
3. Turnbull, Turnbull, Shank, & Leal (2002), p. 456.

fication, as do the specific instruments used to uncover a suspected disability. Generally, all students assessed for eligibility for special education services will be given an individualized intelligence test and individualized achievement tests. They will be directly observed, and past records will be reviewed.

Difference of Opinion on Classification

There may be times that you, as a general education teacher, look at the assessment results, reflect on the student's functioning and behavior in your class, listen to other professionals at the meeting, and come to a different conclusion. You might think the student has a different disability or perhaps no disability. If you are a member of the IEP team and disagree with the findings of the committee, you can submit a separate statement to the committee that presents your conclusions. Tommy's teacher suspected a learning disability and was very interested to learn if the multidisciplinary team found evidence for this classification.

Making Sense of the Assessment Results

A useful psychoeducational evaluation report often begins with a reason for the initial referral, specific questions the evaluator will try to answer as a result of testing, and a short summary of background information on the student as a backdrop for the student's presenting academic and behavioral difficulties. This usually is followed by observations made during the evaluation and a statement regarding the validity of the present testing. Ethically, an evaluator must conduct the evaluation under sound conditions and must report that the results gathered are a good representation of the student's abilities. An evaluator would not, for instance, begin to test a student if the student was obviously sick or in the midst of a personal crisis. Following the observations, the evaluator reports the testing instruments used, an interpretation of the results, and then a brief summary with possible recommendations.

The following is the educational report on Tommy. In usual circumstances, there would be a series of reports, but for ease of presentation and reading, only an abridged educational assessment is presented here.

Comprehensive Assessment Report

Name: Tommy
Chronological Age at Time of Testing: 11 years, 1 month
Current Grade Placement: 5.3
Evaluator: Learning Specialist

Reason for Referral

Tommy was referred for an evaluation by his parents and his current fifth grade teacher, Ms. Smith, because of academic and behavior concerns. Despite pre-referral interventions, Tommy continues to experience frustrations in academic areas and has made little progress in the areas of reading and writing. Tommy also exhibits a poor ability to sustain attention, is often fidgety and disorganized, and can disrupt classroom routines.

Background Information

According to Tommy's parents, Tommy was the product of a normal pregnancy and birth, and he attained developmental milestones in motor and language areas within the expected time frames. Tommy's family moved from an urban area to this suburban community last year. Tommy resides in a private home with his parents and siblings. Tommy is the oldest of three children and has a brother who is ten years old and a sister who is seven. His brother is currently experiencing some academic difficulties, but his sister is reportedly doing very well in school. A review of Tommy's educational records indicates difficulties throughout his school life. Tommy was retained in first grade, and he received remedial services in reading in second grade. Tommy reportedly made enough progress for services to be suspended at the end of third grade. He and his family moved in the middle of fourth grade, and Tommy has not received any support services while in his present school.

Presently, Tommy is doing poorly in language arts, social studies, and science. He is doing well in math and is grasping new topics. A review of previous records indicates similar performance throughout his academic life. When interviewed, Tommy stated that he learned best when he listened to his teacher and that he generally disliked school. He noted that his only academic strength was mathematics and that his outside interests included baseball and soccer.

Behavioral Observations During Testing

Tommy was cooperative throughout the testing procedure, and rapport was easily established. He sustained attention and persisted on tasks. Although he appeared slightly distracted by noise, he was able to regain his focus. Tommy worked slowly and needed extensive time to process information and complete tasks; he became flustered during timed tests. Occasionally Tommy appeared confused with task directions, but when the format remained constant he worked with some confidence.

Tests Administered and Summary of Results

Woodcock-Johnson Tests of Achievement—Revised

	Standard Score	Percentile
Reading		
Letter-Word Identification	90	25
Passage Comprehension	85	16
Mathematics		
Calculation	103	58
Application Problems	98	46
Writing		
Dictation	80	09
Writing Sample	86	18
Information		
Science	78	07
Social Studies	84	15
Humanities	73	04

Wechsler Individual Achievement Test—II

Reading		
Basic Reading	88	20
Reading Comprehension	86	18
Mathematics		
Mathematics Reasoning	111	77
Numerical Operations	94	34
Language		
Listening Comprehension	96	40
Oral Expression	106	66
Writing		
Written Expression	88	20
Spelling	86	13

SUMMARY

The results of this evaluation reveal that Tommy is a student with skills that are within the average range for tasks involving math, listening, and oral expression, yet far below expectations in the areas of reading recognition and comprehension and all areas of written expression. A separate report of the testing completed by the school psychologist (Wechsler Intelligence Scale for Children—III) indicates that Tommy's intelligence is within the average range with a Verbal IQ of 110, a Performance IQ of 95, and a Full Scale IQ of 96.

Tommy used a combination of sight recognition and phonic skills to decipher words presented in isolation. Initially, he read in a quick and sure manner and spontaneously self-corrected. However, Tommy's performance soon broke down when the difficulty level of the words increased, and he achieved low average ratings (25th and 20th percentile) on tests of reading recognition. His skills in phonics are not imbedded in a firm foundation, and he does not appear to have a strong sight word repertoire. Tommy intently approached short reading passages, and he required a very long time to read, process, and respond. In fact, reading these short segments appeared to be an excruciating process. Longer passages were obviously even more difficult for Tommy, and he became visibly frustrated with these reading tasks. Tommy soon began to respond to questions regarding the readings by stating, "I don't know," and he continuously asked how many more of the reading questions he would have to endure. Errors in comprehension included recognizing stated and implied cause and effect, stated detail, and sequencing.

Tommy could not adequately communicate his thoughts through writing. Once again, his style of approaching the task, at least initially, was one of intent concentration. He was given fifteen minutes and directions for writing a descriptive letter. Tommy wrote, erased, wrote, reread, erased, wrote, until he finally put his head down and said, "Take this—I can't do it." What he did write showed that he had a fair use of words with little variety in vocabulary or style. Tommy's sentences were simply constructed, with many errors in grammar, punctuation, and capitalization. Tommy also had difficulty spelling words given in a traditional manner and consistently scored well below average on spelling subtests (9th and 13th percentile). An inspection of errors shows some consonant substitutions and omissions and vowel confusions, lack of application of spelling rules, and confusions with homonyms.

Tommy's mathematical skills were considered to be his strength (34th–77th percentile), and he approached all math tasks in a sure and confident manner. He correctly added, subtracted, multiplied, and divided whole numbers, and added and subtracted like fractions. Tommy used pencil and paper to solve application problems. He had some difficulty with multistep problems and exhibited some confusion with directions.

Tommy's acquisition of basic knowledge was evaluated in the areas of humanities, social studies, and science. Tommy demonstrated extremely poor knowledge of what is thought to be our "cultural literacy" and has a poor foundation for future acquisition of knowledge.

This summary delineated Tommy's performance in the areas of reading, writing, math, language, and knowledge. Tommy's manner of approaching all reading and writing tasks was slow and laborious. He required extensive time to arrive at answers, and he soon became frustrated with the process. It is probably accurate to surmise that in a situation in which Tommy needs to work alone, as opposed to the testing format where he is given encouragement by the evaluator, Tommy's persistence and performance will break down even sooner. In this sense, this evaluation can give us a glimpse into what might increase Tommy's scholastic performance. In the past, Tommy has been given extended time to complete tasks. However, this has not measurably increased his performance. The results of the present evaluation indicate that Tommy has marked and severe discrepancies in the areas of basic reading and writing, and that remediation in these areas is essential. In addition, Tommy, through persistent academic failure, has not learned efficient and effective study and learning strategies. Tommy needs to learn how to approach and complete assignments, how to break up tasks into manageable units, and how to break this cycle of failure.

Reading an assessment report such as Tommy's can be a daunting task. While professionals should write such reports so that parents and teachers can understand and interpret the results of the testing, this sometimes does not happen. When standardized tests are used, the results are reported through a series of standard and developmental scores. Understanding these numbers is an important way to ensure that you can come to your own conclusions. Table 3.6, Table 3.7, and Figure 3.3 list the types of scores you might find on common assessment reports, with definitions and implications for each. The definitions were adapted from the glossary provided by McLoughlin and Lewis.[2]

When you are given a report to read, it is advisable to review the test scores first to get an idea of the student's performance. Then look at the evaluator's report for the following:

- An indication of the student's general level of performance
- A discussion on how the test scores reveal the child's strengths and weaknesses
- Comments on how the child's test behavior may have influenced scores
- Evidence of observed "disabling condition" which may have affected the scores, such as sensory, perceptual-motor, language and emotional difficulties, level of attention, rate of response, etc.
- A discussion of how the student's level of performance and behavior may alter classroom learning and interpersonal relationships
- Comments on possible implications for instruction
- Recommendations for placement, instructional accommodations, and modification in curriculum materials as well as suggestions for additional referrals and testing when appropriate

Table 3.6.
Definition of Common Assessment Terms

Score	Definition	Implication
Percentile	A score that translates student test performance into the percentage of the norm group that performed as well as or poorer than the student on the same test.	Useful and easy score to use for interpretation. A percentile below 16 indicates below-average abilities.
Stanine	A derived score equivalent to a range of standard scores; stanines divide the distribution into nine ranges.	Often used to determine placements in gifted programs. Stanines of 8 and 9 are considered exceptionally high; stanines of 1, 2, or 3 are below average range.
Standard score	A derived score with a set mean and standard deviation; examples are IQ scores and T-scores.	Usually based on a mean of 100 and a standard deviation of 15 or 16. A standard score between 85 and 115 would be within the average limits.
Scaled scores	A derived score with a set mean and standard deviation.	Usually based on a mean of 10 and a standard deviation of 3. A scaled score between 7 and 13 would be within the average limits.
Age equivalents	A score that translates test performance into an estimated age; reported in years and months.	Age and grade equivalents should *not* be used for any educational purpose. These scores are very easy to misinterpret, are misused, and do not provide useful educational information.

Table 3.6.
(continued)

Score	Definition	Implication
Grade equivalents	A score that translates test performance into an estimated grade; expressed in grades and tenths of grades.	Age and grade equivalents should *not* be used for any educational purpose. These scores are very easy to misinterpret, are misused, and do not provide useful educational information.
Raw scores	The first test score calculated usually indicates the number of correct responses plus the number of items assumed correct.	This score is not useful for interpretation, but the scores that are derived from it are useful (percentiles, standard scores, stanines).
Z scores	Indicates where a score is in terms of standard deviations.	A z score between -1 indicates that it is 1 standard deviation below the mean, and z score of $+1$ indicates a score 1 standard deviation above the mean. A score between -1 and $+1$ is within average limits.
T scores	Describes data based on a normal distribution.	Based on a mean of 50 and a standard deviation of 10. A T score between 40 and 60 is within the average limits.
Standard deviation	A descriptive statistic that expresses the amount of variability within a set of scores.	Expressed in terms of the mean; scores between 1 standard deviation above and 1 standard deviation below the mean are within the average limits.

Source: The definitions were adapted from the glossary provided by McLoughlin, J. A., & Lewis, R. B. (2001). *Assessing students with special needs*. Upper Saddle River, NJ: Merrill Prentice Hall.

Table 3.7.
Examples of Testing Modifications

New York State lists examples of testing modifications that vividly portray the scope of possible accommodations:

Flexible Scheduling	• Extended time to complete tests (e.g., double time) • Administer tests over several sessions (e.g., sessions not to exceed 40 minutes) • Administer tests in several sessions over several days
Flexible Setting	• Administer tests individually in separate location • Administer tests to a small group in separate location • Provide special lighting (e.g., 75 Watt incandescent light on desk)
Revised Test Format	• Braille editions of tests • Large-print editions of tests • Increase spacing between test items • Increase size of answer blocks • Reduce number of test items per page • Increase size of answer bubbles • Arrange multiple choice test items in vertical format with answer bubble to the right of each possible choice • Omit questions which cannot be revised, prorate credit
Revised Test Directions	• Read directions to student • Reread directions for each page of questions • Simplify language in directions • Highlight (or underline) verbs in instructions • Provide cues (e.g., arrows and stop signs) on answer form • Provide additional examples
Use of Aids	• Amanuensis (scribe) • Tape recorder • Typewriter • Spell check device • Grammar check • Word processor

Table 3.7.
(continued)

	• Calculator (specify type/functions) • Abacus • Arithmetic tables • Visual magnification devices; specify type • Auditory amplification devices; specify type (e.g., FM system) • Auditory tape of questions • Repeat oral comprehension items more than specified in standard administration (e.g., repeat oral comprehension test items four times) • Masks (or markers) to maintain place • Passages read to student • Test passages, questions, items, and multiple choice responses read to student • Test passages, questions, items, and multiple choice responses signed to student
Other Accommodations	• Record answers in test booklet • Delete requirements to provide punctuation, paragraphing, and spelling

Source: University of the State of New York. (1995). *Test access and modification for individuals with disabilities*. New York: University of the State of New York.

Using Assessment to Inform Instruction

An effective psychoeducational evaluation should reflect a comprehensive understanding of the cognitive and psychosocial variables affecting problems in academic learning and classroom adjustment so that you can plan specific instructional approaches that will facilitate the child's learning. Often, these psychoeducational evaluations focus on the clinical appraisal of the differences between the atypical learner and the average learner. It is also very important to remember, however, to gather information from these evaluations about the talents and relative strengths that each student brings to your classroom. If this student with special needs is going to be part of the general learning community, then you as the classroom teacher are going to have to match her/his strengths with the performance expectancies of all the children in your class. Therefore, an appreciation of the student's multiple intelligences and unique coping behaviors needs to be noted in a well-conducted psychoeducational evaluation.

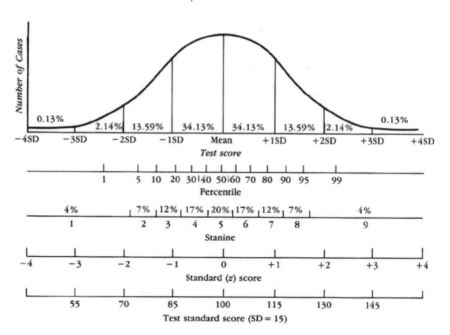

Figure 3.3. Relationships Among Different Types of Scores in a Normal Distribution

Source: McLoughlin, J. A., & Lewis, R. B. (2001). *Assessing students with special needs*. Upper Saddle River, NJ: Merrill Prentice Hall.

Although you should primarily attend to the strengths of a student, it is always important to remember that the student's unique barriers to learning cannot and must not be ignored. To do otherwise would be a major disservice to ensuring the child's academic achievement and psychosocial adjustment. A useful psychoeducational evaluation, therefore, is a comprehensive and integrated report describing current perceptual, linguistic, cognitive, and psychosocial behaviors in the context of the past developmental history of your student. The evaluation should answer its initial referral questions, illuminate how the child is learning, and recommend guidelines to you for enhancing her/his learning in an inclusive setting.

Test Accommodations and Modifications

Coming under the common rubric of "a level playing field," once a student is deemed eligible for special education services, the need for testing accommodations and modifications is discussed. These accommodations become part of the individualized educational program and are considered essential for fair and adequate evaluation of knowledge. The intent of the accommodations is to allow a student to demonstrate competence and to ensure that a student with a disability participates on an equal basis. Accommodations and modifications are needed so that the test in itself is not a measure of the disability.

Adaptations made on the basis of physical disabilities are the easiest to understand. Most can see the need, for instance, for a student with low vision to be given a large-print version of a test or an auditory tape of the questions. Somewhat harder to understand is the need for a student with attention deficit disorder to have tests administered individually in a separate location, or to have questions that are designed to measure reading ability actually read to a student with a learning disability. Each of these situations can be a valid application of accommodations. Questions of trust and fairness often surround the granting and understanding of testing accommodations and modifications.

A student is eligible for test modifications under certain circumstances. A student who is eligible for special education services may have an individualized education program that specifies the need for test modifications. A student who was once classified but is now declassified may also receive modifications if the Committee on Special Education determines that testing accommodations given before declassification continue to be needed by the student. Section 504 of the Vocational Rehabilitation Act covers students with disabilities who do not need special education services but may be entitled to testing accommodations. A regular education student who acquires a disability such as a broken arm before the administration of a test may also be granted accommodations. Table 3.7 provides a list of possible testing modifications and accommodations.

As a general education teacher of students with special needs, you will need to become aware of the testing modifications that are required for a particular student, and will be called upon to implement these modifications. General education teachers "must fully and consistently implement test modifications as specified in each student's IEP or 504 Plan, and refer students to the CSE or 504 Team when it is suspected that test modifications should be added, revised, or discontinued."[3]

Statewide Assessments

According to IDEA, children with disabilities are to be included in general state and district-wide assessment programs and must be given appropriate accommodations and modifications in order to ensure participation. Under some circumstances, alternative assessments are developed for students who cannot participate.

The area of high-stakes testing for students with disabilities is open to considerable debate. Advocates state that without the testing and subsequent analysis, students with disabilities are invisible. Without the public exposure, students with special needs will not be given consideration in general education decisions and reforms. Proponents also reason that without expectations there can be little progress, and that in the past special education services lost sight of normed behavior and functions to the detriment of the student. However, there is increasing resistance to high-stakes testing in general, and many parents and teachers of students with special needs are expressing concern regarding the stress generated and the high-stakes decisions that can negatively impact the student.

You may wish to take note of changing behavioral patterns during high-stakes testing situations in your classroom and interpret the effect of these testing conditions on the response levels of the students. In some instances, children will put their best foot forward and often excel—their performance can be notably different as compared to their usual classroom behavior. For other students, the formal testing situation is just too overwhelming and their performance declines, rapidly revealing proficiency levels far below what you would otherwise expect on the basis of typical classroom observations. This has led many teachers to question the validity of formal tests as true measures of students' capabilities, especially of students who are more vulnerable.

Each student will respond differently under varying conditions of the testing situation, and you might wish to systematically observe the student's behavior during test administration. This might include observations of the following:

- The student's sustained attention and concentration
- How organized the student is in her/his approach to answering test items
- The extent to which the student is confused as to what is expected
- The student's tolerance for frustration as demonstrated by how easily s/he may give up or persist, stick to the task, and complete it successfully
- How negative and resistant the student is to the entire testing process
- How reflective the student is or how impulsively s/he responds to questions
- The student's need for assurance and emotional support

Each of these behaviors will have a distinct effect on the outcome of testing and needs to be considered. You always will need to ask yourself, "Are these test results an indication of the true level of my student's level of knowledge and understanding?"

Alternative Testing

Although participation of students with special needs in district and statewide assessments is mandated under IDEA, there are circumstances where students' disabilities prohibit the reasonableness of the general mandate. Some students with severe disabilities (e.g., mental retardation, autism, multiple disabilities) can be exempted from the established assessments by the Committee on Special Education, but their skills must be assessed in an alternate manner. Performance, authentic, and portfolio assessments that stress functional skills offer alternatives for students with severe disabilities. Performance assessment looks at students performing tasks and assesses their relative mastery of the task; authentic assessment is done in real-life settings with actual materials; and portfolio assessment is a collection of the work that best typifies the student's skills.

SUMMARY

Assessment issues as they relate to students with special needs are quite complex. This chapter introduces the reader to the many dimensions of the assessment process, from identifying students who might warrant formal assessments to understanding and interpreting assessment reports. Signs of a possible disability are introduced, and teachers are guided through the characteristics of a range of disabilities as well as given structures for observing and reporting on student behaviors. The differences between norm-referenced and criterion-referenced tests are explained. A listing of commonly used norm-referenced instruments is presented, giving teachers an idea of the scope of possible assessment tools. One of the hallmarks of the assessment process is the integration of information from a multidisciplinary team, and information regarding the specific roles of team members is delineated. In addition, the intricate interpretations of testing data are reviewed through a case study. Issues of eligibility based on classification and need requirements are discussed as well as the possible accommodations that students might require based on need. Finally, the very pressing issues of statewide testing and alternative assessments and the ramifications for students with special needs are discussed.

Tips for Educators

✎ If a student in your class is having difficulties, take the time to focus your observations on the behaviors you feel are problematic. Use the format in Table 3.4 to record student performance and gather work samples.

✎ When we concentrate on a student's needs, it is very easy to overlook the many strengths of the child. Spend time looking for areas of competency that the student exhibits and relate this important information to members of the multidisciplinary team and to the student.

✎ When presented with the results of formal assessments, interpret the findings for yourself before you read the evaluator's summary of the findings.

✎ Continually evaluate the need for and usefulness of testing accommodations and modifications, making sure they are supporting the student's need for both success and independence.

Tips for Parents

✎ Be observant of your child. Share concerns about your child's development with his or her teachers.

✎ Keep records of conversations, meetings, observations, concerns, and so on, in a notebook so that you can refer back to dates and mark progress.

✎ Keep informed by speaking to other parents, reading, and accessing the Internet.

✎ Don't be fearful of asking questions or of being persistent. You know your child's needs, and you are your child's best advocate.

✎ Make sure that your child's strengths are valued and that his or her talents developed.

NOTES

1. Waterman, B. (1994). Assessing children for the presence of a disability. *NICHCY News Digest, 4*, 1–27.

2. McLoughlin, J. A., & Lewis, R. B. (2001). *Assessing students with special needs*. Upper Saddle River, NJ: Merrill Prentice Hall.

3. University of the State of New York. (1995). *Test access and modification for individuals with disabilities*. New York: University of the State of New York.

CHAPTER 4

Individualized Education Plan (IEP)

Laura G. Dorow and Lois A. Fisch

It was the end of her first week of teaching. Exhausted, Je'ne was ready to go home. Unfortunately, she still had to prepare for the IEP team meeting scheduled for early Monday morning. "What a nightmare," she thought. "I wish they would just put A.J. into a special ed classroom. Why do I have to be on this team? I don't know much about A.J.'s disability and I certainly don't know anything about IEPs. Sure, we talked about them in our methods classes. We even filled out a few examples for practice, but this isn't the same thing. I'm teaching twenty kids, and every one of them seems to have a special need of some sort. How am I supposed to teach nineteen other kids and, at the same time, prepare lessons especially for A.J.? It's impossible!"

Je'ne wasn't about to give up. She had worked too hard to give up her dream career because of one meeting. "I know what I'll do. My methods class teacher always said, 'When in doubt, make a list of questions and then find the answers.'"

In the past, it was all too common to discover the Individualized Education Plan (IEP) filed in the back of an administrative office, never to be seen by any classroom teacher. The IEP writing process was considered difficult and mysterious and was usually the professional responsibility of the special education teacher. Often, general education teachers felt that they had neither the expertise nor the authority to read and interpret an IEP for regular classroom use. With the advent of contemporary school reform efforts bolstered by federal and state mandates, inclusive classrooms are becoming the norm rather than the exception. Now, the general education teacher, as a member of a multidisciplinary planning team (MDT), must take an active role in the planning process.

This chapter provides an overview of the IEP planning process, familiarizes the reader with IEP terminology, and answers some of the most frequently asked questions about IEP writing.

EXPLANATION OF THE IEP

Most people believe that an IEP is essentially a written document outlining a specific educational plan for a student with disabilities. An IEP, however, is much more than that; it is the paper manifestation of the "dynamic, living process of problem solving among all IEP partners for determining the special education and related service supports needed for students with disabilities. . . . It is a process that has shared ownership among general and special educators, parents, students and other agency partners; a process focused on short- and long-range positive student results."[1]

Federal Law Requirement

The Individuals with Disabilities Education Act of 2004 states that the IEP must be developed by a team; be based on individual evaluation; address unique needs; promote progress in general education curriculum; reflect recommendations in the least restrictive environment (LRE); and be reviewed at least annually. A carefully thought out, well-written IEP plan allows everybody to go about the business of educating the student. It provides a clear sense of direction, a vision of the goals, and a plan for achieving them. The IEP identifies everyone's roles and responsibilities. Since it is a consensus plan, a well-written IEP prevents future misunderstandings among team members. The major ideas in IEP planning are as follows:

- Know how the student performs today.
- Think about dreams and goals for the future.
- Identify what the student will learn and do this year.
- Identify the supports and services the student needs for success.
- Stay as close as appropriate to what the student's peers are learning and doing.[2]

Issues Considered in the IEP Process

The IEP process must result in a plan that reflects and includes the following: Present level of performance; annual goals; recommended programs and services; participation in a regular education program; supports/modifications; school personnel; transition services; informing parents of student progress; location; and consideration of special factors.[3]

Participation of General Education
Teachers in the IEP Process

General education teachers are part of the IEP process for two primary reasons. First, it's the law (IDEA). Second, it makes sense. As education becomes more inclusive for all students, it is essential for the general education teacher to participate in the planning process. Involving all of the different constituents who are responsible for the student's education throughout the process makes it more likely that all of the student's needs will be met. In addition, the needs of each constituent can be addressed within the context of the larger educational environment. The consensus process makes it possible to create a plan that is efficient, sensible, and realistic. It also helps avoid unnecessary waste of time and resources.

One of the past criticisms of the IEP process has been that the IEP did not address the needs of the student or the teacher in the general education classroom. It was not uncommon for the general educator to have no input into the development of the IEP. In fact, in many schools the IEPs were not easily accessible to teachers and had little influence on the student's daily education. This should not be the model for developing and using IEPs. They should be developed by consensus, with the understanding that they will truly influence the student's education.

MDT Roles: A Review

General Educator. The general educator is the content specialist who knows what should be covered in the general education curriculum, and knows the type of learning experiences that occur in the student's classroom. The content specialist is also familiar with age- and grade-appropriate socialization skills and opportunities available to the student. The general educator is the MDT member most knowledgeable about the grade-level expectations, including minimum and mastery level for standards and competencies such as those required by state learning standards, standardized achievement tests, and content area standards.

The general education teacher collaborates with the special education teacher, who provides diagnostic and specialized teaching expertise. Together they can focus on the student's strengths to identify the accommodations and adaptations that will result in the student's maximum learning. Perhaps most importantly, the general education teacher provides information on the student's performance in the regular classroom. This information may range from informal observations to formal test results.

Special Education Educator. The special education teacher can provide insight into the findings of diagnostic evaluations, suggest teaching strategies appropriate for a specific disability, and share an understanding of the unique social and emotional needs of the student. The special education teacher has worked one-on-one with the student and can really talk about the student as a unique individual.

Related Service Providers and Administrators. Related service providers such as school psychologists, social workers, and guidance counselors bring their highly specialized knowledge to help identify and provide the support students need to meet their educational goals. The specialists at the IEP meeting will vary according to individual students' needs.

These professionals work with the students and their parents to problem solve, to make short- and long-term education and life plans, and to advocate for the supports and services that will help the students meet their goals. These professionals have expertise in realistically assessing students' strengths and weaknesses within the context of their dreams and goals for the future.

All members of the IEP team are responsible for ensuring that the student receives an appropriate free public education. Each team participant brings a unique perspective that will assure due process, financially responsible plans, and effective implementation of the IEP.

Parent Member. The parent member is appointed to serve on the team as an advocate for families and students. S/he shares knowledge of the school system and the IEP process from the viewpoint of a parent of a student with a disability. The parent member can especially help to make other parents feel comfortable during the IEP process so that they gain the confidence to participate fully in the decision making process.

Student's Parents. The student's parents bring valuable information to the IEP process. They know the student's capabilities outside the education setting. They are extremely knowledgeable about the student's likes and dislikes, past and present needs, and fears and dreams about the future. Many people work with a student and his or her family during the student's education career. Teachers, psychologists, social workers, and speech therapists come and go; however, only the student's parents are there through the years. Usually the parents are the only people at the IEP table who have this valuable perspective. While everyone else on the team is an expert about children, the parents are the experts concerning their child.

Student. Whenever possible, the student should participate in the IEP process as the decisions and planning directly affect him or her. The student is an advocate for her/his present needs and future goals. Through this process, the student can also become committed to the implementation of the IEP plan. Participation creates ownership, and ownership is directly related to motivation.

MDT Process

Resolving Differences Concerning Assessment Results. The consensus process serves to interpret all of the information in a way that most accurately describes a particular student. Everyone should feel comfortable in sharing assessment data gathered in a variety of settings and should not hesitate to ask for additional assessment information or for clarification.

Running the IEP Meeting. Usually the Committee on Special Education (CSE) chairperson runs the meeting, but the decisions are made by the consensus of the committee. It is important to make decisions by consensus rather than by majority vote, because when a team makes decisions using a democratic model there are winners and losers. In the democratic model, team members vote and agree to implement the ideas that receive the majority vote. This method puts into place a plan of action that may not be agreed upon in concept by all of the team members. In contrast, everyone on the team agrees with IEP decisions that are made through the consensus model. Therefore, the implementation of the plan will receive commitment and support from all of the team members.

- Everyone is responsible for ensuring that the student receives an appropriate education.
- No one should be advocating for his or her individual agendas.
- Everyone should be thinking about how the student will achieve maximum learning and socialization.

Meeting Standards. It is important to know that the IEP process is not about changing standards. Regardless of where standards come from, they apply to all students. They are created to identify what people should know and be able to do after studying a discipline. You must meet the requirements of the standard, though not necessarily in a standard way. Standards are about concepts. They do not identify small bits of content. Parallel goals that reflect the integrity of the standard can be used to teach a student with disabilities.

Matching a Student's Needs with the Standards

Let's look at a New York State standard: "Abstraction and symbolic representation are used to communicate mathematically." The concept is that we can represent mathematical ideas with symbols. In a high school math class, one of the goals is to learn to use algebraic and geometric representations to describe and compare data. A parallel goal based on the priority needs of a student with severe disabilities in this class could be to use math manipulatives to represent equalities. Regardless of the student's current level of performance, the goal is reaching the same standard. For example, if you teach a student to play basketball, the standards are the rules, how to shoot a basketball, how to dribble or pass the ball, and so on. Regardless of what skills or knowledge the player brings to the game, he/she is still required to meet the same standards. If a student wants to play basketball, we don't say that we will teach him or her to bounce the ball against the wall. However, we can make some accommodations or adaptations to begin to teach the game. We can lower the basket, use a larger ball, play one-on-one, or use a wheelchair; but the game of basketball ultimately remains the same. We do not take away the basics of the game. The ball must go through the basket. The same principle applies with standards. The basic concepts of the body of knowledge remain the same.

Higher-Level Learning Concepts. Consider critical thinking as another example. Teaching a toddler critical thinking could involve problem solving—for example, how to share a toy with other children. For a high school class, it might be exploring the causes of war and developing a peace strategy for the future. In each case the standard has been met because the student has performed the basic elements of critical thinking, such as identifying options, establishing criteria, weighing the benefits of each, and making a decision based on the evidence.

Teacher Use of the IEP to Inform Instruction

The IEP process gives the team a structure for instructional decisions regarding each individual student. The IEP presents an opportunity to collaboratively identify strategies and methods that will help the student advance from his or her current level of performance. It forces the team to think not only about immediate educational needs but also about how to meet future life goals of the student. Each member of the team brings specialized expertise, including knowledge about standards, curriculum content, teaching strategies, assistive technology, and other considerations. Together this powerful combination of advocates can design a learning plan that will really challenge the student and help the student achieve more than minimal goals.

Linkage of the Student's Individual IEP Goals and Objectives to State and District Standards. The IEP identifies accommodations, adaptations, and specific educational and behavioral goals and objectives that will help the student make progress toward achieving the standards. In a well-planned IEP, the connection between a student's written goals and objectives and the state and district standards should be obvious. When the student has met the specified goals and objectives, it will be clear that he or she has also met a component of the standards.

GOALS

Annual Goals

At the beginning, an annual goal is a realistic and reasonable statement of what the student will accomplish in one year. Annual goals should be student-centered, focusing on the student's age, present level of performance, rate of learning, interests, and abilities. All goals must be measurable. An annual goal designed to meet a writing standard might be, for example, "Susie will contribute written sentences to cooperative learning projects."

Short-Term Objectives

Short-term objectives are also referred to as benchmarks, instructional or learning objectives, and behavioral objectives. Whatever the terminology, these objectives are the small, measurable steps between the student's present level of performance and the goals. For example: Given a cooperative learning research project in social studies, Mary will correctly answer, in writing, using complete sentences, ten "why and what" questions related to the project. The project will be completed by the end of the semester. As of IDEA 2004, benchmarks and short-term objectives will only be used with students who take alternative assessments to meet alternative achievement standards.

IEP and Curriculum

The student is expected to learn and participate in the general education classroom to the same extent as everyone else in the classroom, whether or not a particular aspect is included in the student's IEP. Each student should be encouraged to learn as much as possible. Table 4.1 displays examples of how organizational learning skills are presented on an IEP across five developmental levels. Table 4.2 provides similar exemplars for improving math skills. It is critical to remember that the IEP is a bridge, not a roadblock. The IEP identifies only the areas where special support will be needed.

Meeting the IEP Goals

If the student does not meet the goals, the entire team, including the parents, should determine what went wrong in the instructional process and make appropriate changes. The IEP should be a clear plan that has been created by and agreed upon by consensus. If the proper IEP process was followed, there should not be any surprises leading to an adversarial relationship. The team, including the parents, works together to assess the student's progress throughout the school year and provides support as necessary. On the other hand, if the student achieves the goal halfway through the school year, celebrate and keep right on going! Set a new, higher goal.

Guiding Principles Regarding Programs, Supplementary Aids and Services, Accommodations, and Modifications

Once the team has agreed on the annual goals and objectives for the student's education plan, it must then identify the supports and services that will be needed to assist the student in attaining them. The team must also determine where, when, and how often the supports and services will be provided. Three guiding principles should focus the team's discussion regarding supports and services. The decisions must (1) focus on the student; (2) provide access to the general education curriculum; and (3) conceptualize special education as a service, not a place.

Supplemental aids and services make it possible for the student with disabilities to be an equal participant and make learning progress in the gen-

Table 4.1.
IEP Exemplars for Improving Organizational Skills Across Five Developmental Levels

	Preschool	K–3	4–6	7–12	Transition
Objective 1	Hangs up own coat	Puts notebooks and other required materials in book bag at end of day	Maintains daily homework assignment notebook	Maintains personal organizer showing assignment due dates, appointments, meetings, etc.	Maintains personal planner/PDA showing assignment due dates, appointments, meetings, medical appointments, etc.
Evaluation method	Observation	Observation	Checklist	Checklist	Checklist
Person responsible	Teacher's aide	Teacher's aide	Teacher	Teacher	Job coach
Evaluation schedule	Daily	Daily	Daily	Daily	Weekly
Special materials	Cubby or labeled coat hook	Book bag with name or ID tag	Assignment notebook	Personal organizer, computer, or PDA	Personal organizer, computer, or PDA

Objective 2

	Returns blanket to cubby after rest time	Puts worksheets into an assignment folder	Maintains subject specific folders	Maintains subject specific folders for each class. Folders are subdivided into categories	Maintains personal records: grocery list, bills, checkbook, etc.
Evaluation method	Observation	Observation	Checklist	Checklist	Checklist
Person responsible	Teacher's aide	Teacher's aide	Teacher	Teacher	Job coach
Evaluation schedule	Daily	Daily	Daily	Daily	Weekly
Special materials	Cubby or labeled storage area	Assignment folder	Subject folders in various colors	Three-ring binders with dividers and subject folders	Notebook, checkbook, folders, computer, PDA, as appropriate

91

Table 4.2.
IEP Exemplars for Improving Math Skills Across Five Developmental Levels

	Preschool	K–3	4–6	7–12	Transition
Objective 1					
	Counts aloud 1–10 independently	Uses manipulatives to solve single-digit addition problems	Uses manipulatives and calculator to solve simple word problems	Uses calculator to solve multistep word problems	Uses calculator to balance checkbook
Evaluation method	Observation	Observation and test	Observation and test	Observation and test	Observation and examination of checkbook
Person responsible	Teacher	Teacher, occupational therapist	Teacher, occupational therapist	Teacher	Job coach
Evaluation schedule	Daily until attained	Weekly until attained	Weekly until attained	Biweekly until attained	Monthly
Special materials	None	Math manipulatives	Math manipulatives and calculator	Calculator	Calculator and checkbook

Objective 2

	Places symbols of objects on bar graph	Draws bar graph using symbols or bars	Draws bar and line graphs of simple data	Interprets data from bar, line, and pie graphs	Uses graphs found in *Consumer Reports* Magazine to make purchase decision
Evaluation method	Observation	Performance task	Performance task or test	Performance task or test	Performance task
Person responsible	Teacher, occupational therapist	Teacher	Teacher	Teacher	Job coach
Evaluation schedule	Weekly	Biweekly	Biweekly	Monthly	Bimonthly
Special materials	Graph, symbols, or objects	Graph paper, ruler, tracing symbols, or computer	Graph paper, ruler, tracing symbols, or computer	Various graphs	*Consumer Reports* magazine or Web site

eral education classroom. Such aids may include accommodations and/or additional services for language and communication needs, vision or hearing needs, motor difficulties, behavioral and emotional needs, and learning assessment. Supplemental aids and services should, to the fullest possible extent, be integrated within the general education classroom.

Je'ne was feeling much better. She was ready for anything: ready to be an advocate for A.J. and his parents; ready to be a resource for his special service providers; and ready to plan lessons that would be appropriate for all of the children in her classroom, A.J. included.

SUMMARY

The IEP process consists of a series of collaborative MDT meetings that result in an education plan for a student with disabilities. Federal law mandates that all IEPs must be developed by a team, be based on individual evaluation, address unique needs, promote progress in the general education curriculum, and reflect recommendations in the least restrictive environment. Members of an IEP team include a special educator, related service providers, the school psychologist, the school social worker, the guidance counselor, a general education teacher, a parent, a parent advocate, and the child when age-appropriate. The individualized education program is a roadmap for lesson planning as well as for long-term goal setting. It should enhance, not impede, the education process for both the student and the teacher. An example of a comprehensive IEP is shown in Figure 4.1.

Tips for Educators

- ✎ Focus on the child, not the disability. Every child has his or her special strengths and talents. Capitalize on them. Don't let yourself be blinded by the generic, and often negative, description of the disability.

- ✎ Focus on the educational goals first, then identify or design activities that will most effectively help you achieve your goals.

- ✎ Work with the parents, not against them. You are the expert on children, but they are the experts on this child. Use their knowledge and insights to inform your planning.

- ✎ Remember that a consensus decision must meet the needs of everyone involved. It is better to spend a few more minutes at the planning table than to spend a year trying to implement an IEP you don't agree with.

CONFERENCE SUMMARY REPORT

Date

PURPOSE OF CONFERENCE *(Check all that apply)*		
☐ Initial evaluation	☐ Reevaluation	☐ Review of Existing Data
☐ IEP review/revision	☐ Transition	☐ Termination of Placement

☐ Manifestation Determination   ☐ Initial IEP
☐ Graduation   ☐ Other _____

STUDENT IDENTIFICATION INFORMATION

STUDENT'S NAME	☐ Yes ☐ No **Educational Surrogate Parent Required**
STUDENT'S ADDRESS (Street, City, State, Zip Code)	PARENT'S NAME
STUDENT'S DATE OF BIRTH (Mo./Day/Yr.)	PARENT'S ADDRESS (Street, City, State, Zip Code)
STUDENT'S GENDER	PARENT'S TELEPHONE NUMBER (Include Area Code)
LANGUAGE/MODE OF COMMUNICATION USED BY STUDENT	LANGUAGE/MODE OF COMMUNICATION USED BY PARENT(S)
STUDENT'S ANTICIPATED DATE OF HIGH SCHOOL GRADUATION	RESIDENT DISTRICT
STUDENT'S ID NUMBER	SERVING DISTRICT
MEDICAID NUMBER	HOME SCHOOL
DISABILITY(S)	PLACEMENT (To be completed after placement determination)
	☐ Yes ☐ No **Placement is in home school**

PARTICIPANTS

Signature indicates attendance. Check appropriate boxes to indicate which meetings were attended. Anyone serving in a dual role should indicate so on the following lines:

ELIG. REVIEW	IEP		ELIG. REVIEW	IEP	
☐	☐	_Parent_	☐	☐	_School Psychologist_
☐	☐	_Parent_	☐	☐	_Bilingual Specialist_
☐	☐	_Student_	☐	☐	_Interpreter_
☐	☐	_Regular Education Teacher_	☐	☐	_LEA Representative_
☐	☐	_Special Education Teacher_	☐	☐	_Other (specify)_
☐	☐	_Speech-Language Pathologist_	☐	☐	_Other (specify)_
☐	☐	_School Social Worker_	☐	☐	_Other (specify)_

☐ Yes ☐ NA   Explanation of Procedural Safeguards was provided to the parent(s) with the notice of conference.
☐ Yes ☐ NA   Parent(s) given a copy of the IEP.
☐ Yes ☐ NA   Parent(s) given a copy of the evaluation report and eligibility determination.
☐ Yes ☐ NA   Parent(s) given a copy of the district's behavioral intervention policies.
☐ Yes ☐ NA   Parent(s) given a copy of the district's behavioral intervention procedures (initial IEP only).
If the parent(s) did not attend the IEP meeting, document the attempts to contact the parent(s) prior to the IEP meeting.

SPECIAL EDUCATION FUNDING AND CHILD TRACKING SYSTEM (FACTS) (For District Reporting Purposes)															
FUND	PRIVATE FACILITY CODE	ETHNIC	DISABILITY (Max. of 2)	LANGUAGE	BILINGUAL SPECIAL EDUCATION			RELATED SERVICES (Max. of 8)	LRE	RBP	SECTION 14-7.03 ELIGIBILITY			TERM	BEGIN DATE	END DATE	REASON FOR EXIT	ANTICIPATED SERVICES UPON EXIT (Maximum of 6)
					S	A	I				T	P	G					
(4)	(5)	(10)	(11)	(12)	(13)	(14)	(15)	(16)	(17)	(18)	(19)	(20)	(21)	(22)	(23)	(24)	(25)	(26)

ISBE 37-44 (10/00)

Figure 4.1. Individualized Educational Plan from the State of Illinois

DOCUMENTATION OF EVALUATION RESULTS

Complete after an initial evaluation, reevaluation, or review of an independent or outside evaluation

Considering all available evaluation data, record the team's analyses of the student's functioning levels. Evaluation data can include: aptitude and achievement tests, parental input, teacher recommendations, physical condition, social or cultural background, and adaptive behavior. Describe the observed strengths and/or deficits in the student's functioning in the following domains (complete the sections that are applicable to the student, indicate if any section is not applicable):

ACADEMIC PERFORMANCE

COMMUNICATION STATUS

GENERAL INTELLIGENCE

HEALTH

MOTOR ABILITIES

SOCIAL/EMOTIONAL STATUS

HEARING/VISION

ISBE 37-44A (10/00)

Figure 4.1. (continued)

ELIGIBILITY DETERMINATION

Complete after an initial evaluation, reevaluation, or review of an independent or outside evaluation.

The determinant factor for the student's suspected disability is:

☐ Yes ☐ No   lack of instruction in reading
☐ Yes ☐ No   lack of instruction in math
☐ Yes ☐ No   limited English proficiency

If any of the above answers are "yes," the student is not eligible for services under the IDEA. If all of the answers are "no," complete, as appropriate, the following boxes.

SPECIFIC LEARNING DISABILITY

Complete only for students suspected of having a specific learning disability. Observation in a regular classroom setting by a team member other than the student's regular teacher is required, or for a preschool student, an observation in an age-appropriate environment.

RELEVANT BEHAVIOR NOTED DURING THE OBSERVATION

RELATION OF BEHAVIOR TO THE STUDENT'S ACADEMIC FUNCTIONING

EDUCATIONALLY RELEVANT MEDICAL FINDINGS *(If Any)*

☐ Yes ☐ No   A severe discrepancy exists between achievement and ability that is not correctable without special education and related services.
☐ Yes ☐ No   The team has determined that the eligibility determination is not the result of environmental, cultural, or economic disadvantage.
☐ Yes ☐ No   **The student has a specific learning disability.**

Each team member must sign below to certify that the report reflects her/his conclusions. Any participant who disagrees with the team's decision must submit a separate statement presenting her/his conclusions.

☐ Yes ☐ No   _____   ☐ Yes ☐ No   _____

☐ Yes ☐ No   _____   ☐ Yes ☐ No   _____

☐ Yes ☐ No   _____   ☐ Yes ☐ No   _____

COMPLETE FOR ALL STUDENTS SUSPECTED OF HAVING A DISABILITY UNDER THE IDEA.

Step 1 DISABILITY Based on the team's analysis, identify the disability(s).	Step 2 ADVERSE EFFECTS For each disability identified, describe the adverse effect on the student's educational performance.	Step 3 EDUCATIONAL NEEDS State to what extent the disability requires special education and related services to address educational needs.	Step 4 ELIGIBILITY Identify the disability(s) that require special education as determined in steps one through three.

ISBE 37-44 B (10/00)

Figure 4.1. (continued)

PRESENT LEVELS OF EDUCATIONAL PERFORMANCE

Complete for initial IEPs and annual reviews.

When completing this page, include all areas from the following list that are impacted by the student's disability, this may include strengths/adverse effects identified in the most recent evaluation: academic performance, social/emotional status, independent functioning, vocational, motor skills, speech and language/communication

STUDENT STRENGTHS

State how the disability affects the student's involvement and progress in the general curriculum or for preschool children, as appropriate, how the disability affects the child's participation in appropriate activities. **This should reflect the adverse effects identified in the student's most recent evaluation and eligibility determination.**

PARENTAL EDUCATIONAL CONCERNS

ISBE 37-44C (10/00)

Figure 4.1. (continued)

GOALS AND OBJECTIVES/BENCHMARKS

Complete for initial IEPs and annual reviews.
Anyone responsible for implementing the IEP (e.g., goals and objectives/benchmarks, accommodations, modifications and supports) must be notified of her/his specific responsibilities.

The progress on annual goals will be measured by the short-term objectives/benchmarks. Check the methods that will be used to notify parents of the student's progress on annual goals and whether the progress is sufficient to achieve the goals by the end of the IEP year:

☐ report cards ☐ progress reports ☐ parent conference ☐ other *(specify)*_____

The goals and short-term objectives or benchmarks shall: meet the student's educational needs that result from the student's disability, including involvement in and progress in the general curriculum, or for preschool students, participation in appropriate activities, reflect consideration of the State Goals and Illinois Learning Standards.

STATEMENT OF PRESENT LEVEL OF PERFORMANCE

GOAL STATEMENT

TITLE(S) OF GOAL IMPLEMENTER(S)

SHORT-TERM OBJECTIVE/BENCHMARK FOR MEASURING PROGRESS ON THE ANNUAL GOAL

EVALUATION CRITERIA	EVALUATION PROCEDURES	SCHEDULE FOR DETERMINING ACHIEVEMENT	DATES REVIEWED/ EXTENT OF PROGRESS
☐ ____ % Accuracy ☐ ____ of ____ attempts ☐ Other *(specify)*	☐ Log of Observations ☐ Chart ☐ Tests ☐ Other *(specify)*	☐ Daily ☐ Weekly ☐ Quarterly ☐ Semester ☐ Other *(specify)*	

SHORT-TERM OBJECTIVE/BENCHMARK FOR MEASURING PROGRESS ON THE ANNUAL GOAL

EVALUATION CRITERIA	EVALUATION PROCEDURES	SCHEDULE FOR DETERMINING ACHIEVEMENT	DATES REVIEWED/ EXTENT OF PROGRESS
☐ ____ % Accuracy ☐ ____ of ____ attempts ☐ Other *(specify)*	☐ Log of Observations ☐ Chart ☐ Tests ☐ Other *(specify)*	☐ Daily ☐ Weekly ☐ Quarterly ☐ Semester ☐ Other *(specify)*	

SHORT-TERM OBJECTIVE/BENCHMARK FOR MEASURING PROGRESS ON THE ANNUAL GOAL

EVALUATION CRITERIA	EVALUATION PROCEDURES	SCHEDULE FOR DETERMINING ACHIEVEMENT	DATES REVIEWED/ EXTENT OF PROGRESS
☐ ____ % Accuracy ☐ ____ of ____ attempts ☐ Other *(specify)*	☐ Log of Observations ☐ Chart ☐ Tests ☐ Other *(specify)*	☐ Daily ☐ Weekly ☐ Quarterly ☐ Semester ☐ Other *(specify)*	

ISBE 37-44 D (10/00)

Figure 4.1. (continued)

EDUCATIONAL ACCOMMODATIONS

Complete for initial IEPs and annual reviews.
Anyone responsible for implementing the educational accommodations must be notified of her/his specific responsibilities.

CONSIDERATION OF SPECIAL FACTORS

Check the boxes to indicate if the student requires any supplementary aids and/or services due to the following factors. **For any box checked "yes," the IEP must state the supplementary aids and/or services that will be provided.**

☐ Yes ☐ No ☐ NA   **all students - assistive technology devices and services**
☐ Yes ☐ No ☐ NA   **all students - communication needs**
☐ Yes ☐ No ☐ NA   deaf/hard of hearing - language and communication needs
☐ Yes ☐ No ☐ NA   limited English proficiency - language needs
☐ Yes ☐ No ☐ NA   blind/visually impaired - provision of Braille instruction
☐ Yes ☐ No ☐ NA   behavior - strategies, including positive behavioral interventions and supports to address behavior. **This may include a Functional Behavioral Assessment and/or a Behavioral Intervention Plan. If so, attach any completed form(s).**

SUPPLEMENTARY AIDS

Specify what accommodations are needed in regular education classes and other education-related settings to enable the student to be educated with nondisabled peers (e.g., accommodations for daily work, tests, quizzes, environmental accommodations, moving from class to class, etc.). This must include any accommodations or alternate assessments/methods needed for the student to participate in classroom-based assessments.

☐ Yes ☐ No ☐ NA   Student requires accommodations to participate in classroom-based assessments.
☐ Yes ☐ No ☐ NA   Student requires alternate assessment/methods to participate in classroom-based assessments.

STATE AND DISTRICT-WIDE ASSESSMENTS

The State assessments are the Illinois Standards Achievement Test (ISAT) at grades 3, 4, 5, 7 and 8 and the Prairie State Achievement Exam (PSAE) at grade 11.

Students will:

☐ participate in the entire State assessment with no accommodations
☐ participate in the entire State assessment with accommodations
☐ participate in part(s) of State assessment (specified below)
☐ NOT participate in the State assessment

☐ participate in the entire district-wide assessment with no accommodations
☐ participate in the entire district-wide assessment with accommodations
☐ participate in part(s) of the district-wide assessment (specified below)
☐ NOT participate in the district-wide assessment

If the student is completing the assessment(s) with accommodations, specify the needed accommodations (e.g., extended time, alternate setting, auditory testing).

If the student will not participate in part or all of the assessment(s), specify why the assessment is not appropriate and document the alternate assessment to be given, including any needed accommodations.

LINGUISTIC AND CULTURAL ACCOMMODATIONS

☐ Yes ☐ No ☐ NA   The student requires accommodations for the IEP to meet her/his linguistic and cultural needs. **If yes, specify any needed accommodations:**

☐ Yes ☐ No ☐ NA   Special education and related services will be provided in a language or mode of communication other than or in addition to English. **If yes, specify any needed accommodations:**

ISBE 37-44 E (10/00)

Figure 4.1. (continued)

EDUCATIONAL SERVICES AND PLACEMENT

Complete for initial IEPs and annual reviews.
Anyone responsible for implementing special education services must be notified of her/his specific responsibilities.

PARTICIPATION IN REGULAR EDUCATION CLASSES AND OTHER EDUCATION-RELATED SETTINGS

The IEP must specify if the student will participate in regular physical education.

REGULAR EDUCATION - No supplementary aids

REGULAR EDUCATION - with supplementary aids, as specified in the "Supplementary Aids" section of the IEP

SPECIAL EDUCATION	Location	Amount/Frequency of Services	Initiation Date	Duration of Services

RELATED SERVICES	Location	Amount/Frequency of Services	Initiation Date	Duration of Services

Provide an explanation of the extent, if any, to which the student will not participate with nondisabled students in regular education classes and extracurricular and other nonacademic activities. *(Check and complete all that apply)*

☐ Special classes: _____
☐ Separate schooling: _____
☐ Removal from the regular education environment: _____

is/are required because the nature or severity of the student's disability is such that education in regular classes with the use of supplementary aids and services can not be achieved satisfactorily.

☐ None of the above are applicable. All special education services are provided in the regular education class(es) with access to extracurricular and other nonacademic activities.

PLACEMENT DETERMINATION

The placement shall be appropriate to the student's needs and least restrictive of the student's interaction with nondisabled children; based on the student's IEP and located as close as possible to the student's home, unless the IEP requires some other arrangement, in the school he/she would attend if not disabled; and consistent with the findings of the case study evaluation.

PLACEMENT OPTIONS CONSIDERED When determining the placement, consider any potentially harmful effect either on the student or the quality of services that he/she needs. **After determining the student's placement, complete the "Placement" section on page 1.**	TEAM ACCEPTS PLACEMENT
	☐ Yes ☐ No
	☐ Yes ☐ No
	☐ Yes ☐ No

ISBE 37-44 F (10/00)

Figure 4.1. (continued)

TRANSITION

☐ Yes ☐ No   Consideration of service needs, goals, and support/services is required (by age 14, the team must address transition service needs). **If yes, complete the "Transition Services" section of the IEP.**

☐ Yes ☐ No   Consideration of "Home-Based Support Services Program for Mentally Disabled Adults" for eighteen-year-old student is required. **If yes, complete the "Transition Services" section of the IEP.**

TRANSFER OF RIGHTS

☐ Yes ☐ NA   Seventeen-year old student informed of her/his rights under the IDEA that will transfer to the student upon reaching age 18.

TRANSPORTATION

Check all that apply

☐ Yes ☐ No   Special transportation is required to and from schools and/or between schools.

☐ Yes ☐ No   Special transportation is required in and around school buildings.

☐ Yes ☐ No   Specialized equipment (such as special or adapted buses, lifts, and ramps) is required.

SUPPORTS FOR SCHOOL PERSONNEL

☐ Yes ☐ No   Program modifications or supports for school personnel are needed for the student to advance appropriately toward attaining the annual goals, participate in the general curriculum, and be educated and participate with other students in educational activities. **If yes, specify what modifications and/or supports are needed.**

EXTENDED SCHOOL YEAR

☐ Yes ☐ No   Extended school year services are needed. **If yes, the IEP must indicate the type and amount of services to be provided and the duration of the services.**

ADDITIONAL INFORMATION

Figure 4.1. (continued)

MANIFESTATION DETERMINATION

Complete when determining whether a student's behavior was a manifestation of her/his disability.

INCIDENT(S) THAT RESULTED IN DISCIPLINARY ACTION

Consider and document the relevant information in terms of the behavior subject to disciplinary action:

EVALUATION AND DIAGNOSTIC RESULTS (including the results or other relevant information supplied by the parents)

OBSERVATIONS OF THE STUDENT

THE STUDENT'S IEP AND PLACEMENT

Based upon the above information, the team has determined that:

☐ Yes ☐ No   In relationship to the behavior subject to disciplinary action, the student's IEP and placement were appropriate and the special education services, supplementary aids and services, and behavior intervention strategies provided were consistent with the student's IEP and placement. **If no, specify: 1) why the IEP was not implemented and 2) whether the failure to implement the IEP impacted on the student's behavior.**

☐ Yes ☐ No   The student's disability impaired her/his ability to understand the impact and consequences of the behavior subject to disciplinary action. **If yes, the behavior must be considered a manifestation of the student's disability.**

☐ Yes ☐ No   The student's disability impaired her/his ability to control the behavior subject to disciplinary action.
If yes, the behavior must be considered a manifestation of the student's disability.

Check the appropriate box:

☐   The student's behavior **WAS NOT** a manifestation of her/his disability. The relevant disciplinary procedures applicable to students without disabilities may be applied to the student in the same manner in which they are applied to students without disabilities. *If the district initiates disciplinary procedures applicable to all students, the district shall ensure that the special education and disciplinary records of the student with a disability are transmitted for consideration by the person or persons making the final determination regarding the disciplinary action.*

☐   The student's behavior **WAS** a manifestation of her/his disability. The team must review and revise the student's IEP as appropriate and the district must take appropriate action.

ISBE 37-44 G (10/00)

Figure 4.1. (continued)

TRANSITION SERVICES

Complete for students age 14 and older, and when appropriate for students younger than age 14.

TRANSITION SERVICE NEEDS (address by age 14)

Indicate which components of the student's IEP include a statement of *transition service needs* that focus on her/his course of study. (If none, indicate "none.")

TRANSITION GOALS (address by age 14 1/2)

EMPLOYMENT GOAL(S) (If none, indicate "none")

POST-SECONDARY EDUCATION GOAL(S) (If none, indicate "none")

COMMUNITY LIVING ALTERNATIVES GOALS (If none, indicate "none")

TRANSITION SUPPORTS/SERVICES (address by age 14 1/2)

INSTRUCTION (If none, indicate "none")	Provider Position
	Provider Agency
RELATED SERVICES (If none, indicate "none")	Provider Position
	Provider Agency
COMMUNITY EXPERIENCES (If none, indicate "none")	Provider Position
	Provider Agency

Figure 4.1. (continued)

ADDITIONAL SERVICES (when appropriate)	
ACQUISITION OF DAILY LIVING SKILLS	Provider Position
	Provider Agency
FUNCTIONAL VOCATIONAL EVALUATION	Provider Position
	Provider Agency
LINKAGES TO AFTER GRADUATION SUPPORTS/SERVICES	Provider Position
	Provider Agency

HOME-BASED SUPPORT SERVICES PROGRAM FOR MENTALLY DISABLED ADULTS

☐ Yes ☐ No   The student may become eligible for the program after reaching age 18 and when no longer receiving special education services. **If yes, complete the following statements:**

Plans for determining the student's eligibility for home-based services: _____

_____

_____

_____

_____

Plans for enrolling the student in the program of home-based services: _____

_____

_____

_____

_____

Plans for developing a plan for the student's most effective use of home-based services after reaching age 18 and when no longer receiving special education services.

_____

_____

_____

Figure 4.1. (continued)

BEHAVIORAL INTERVENTION PLAN

Complete when the team has determined a Behavioral Intervention Plan is needed.

STUDENT	GRADE	DATE

SUMMARY OF FUNCTIONAL BEHAVIORAL ANALYSIS (may attach completed form)

STUDENT'S STRENGTHS

SUMMARY OF PREVIOUS INTERVENTIONS ATTEMPTED

COMPLETE PAGE 2 PRIOR TO THESE SECTIONS:
DATA COLLECTION PROCEDURES AND METHODS FOR MONITORING INTERVENTIONS

PROVISIONS FOR COORDINATING WITH THE HOME

Figure 4.1. (continued)

TARGETED BEHAVIOR	POSITIVE BEHAVIORAL INTERVENTIONS	SUPPORTS (if needed)	RESTRICTIVE INTERVENTIONS (if needed)

Figure 4.1. (continued)

NOTES

1. Kukic, S., & Schrag, J. (1998). *IEP connections for a dynamic, living, and practical process: IEP team member's manual.* Longmont, CO: Sopris West.

2. U.S. Department of Education. Office of Special Education Programs IDEA Institute Series: Training for trainers 1998. In New York State Education Department, VESID. (1999). *A New Direction for IEPs.* Albany: Vocational and Educational Services for Individuals with Disabilities.

3. New York State Education Department, VESID (1999), pp. 12–13.

Part I Bibliography

Allen, K. E., & Cowdery, G. E. (2005). *The exceptional child: Inclusion in early childhood education*. New York: Thomson/Delmar Learning.

Alper, S., Ryndak, D., & Schloss, C. (2001). *Alternate assessment of students with disabilities*. Boston: Allyn & Bacon.

CASE. (1999). *Section 504 and the ADA: Promoting student access—a resource guide*. (2nd ed.). Arlington, VA: Council of Administrators of Special Education.

Corbett, J. (2001). *Supporting inclusive education: A connective pedagogy*. London: Falmer Press.

Couchenour, D., & Chrisman, K. (2004). *Families, schools, and communities: Together for young children*. New York: Thomson/Delmar Learning.

Council for Exceptional Children (CEC). (1993). CEC policy on inclusive schools and community settings. *Teaching Exceptional Children, 25*(4).

De Bettencourt, L. U. (2002). Understanding the difference between IDEA and Section 504. *Teaching Exceptional Children, 34*(3), 16–23.

Deschenes, C., Ebeling, D., & Sprague, J. (1994). *Adapting curriculum and instruction in inclusive classrooms: A teacher's desk reference*. Bloomington, IN: Center for School and Community Integration.

Developing quality IEPs: A case-based tutorial. Upper Saddle River, NJ: Merrill Prentice Hall.

Feldman, J. (2000, June). How to draft a legally defensible IEP: Legal overview and update. Paper presented at New York State School Boards Association Conference, Melville, New York.

Friend, M., & Bursuck, W. D. (1999). *Including students with special needs: A practice guide for classroom teachers*. Boston: Allyn & Bacon.

Gestwicki, C. (2004). *Home, school, and community relations*. New York: Thomson/Delmar Learning.

Hahn, J. (1989). The politics of special education. In D. K. Lipsky & A. Gartner (Eds.), *Beyond separate education: Quality education for all* (pp. 225–241). Baltimore: Paul H. Brookes Publishing Co.

Heron, T., & Harris, K. (1993). *The educational consultant: Helping professionals, parents and mainstream students.* (3rd ed.). Austin, TX: Pro-ed.

Hickson, L., Blackman, L., & Reis, E. (1995). *Mental retardation: Foundations of educational programming.* Boston: Allyn & Bacon.

Higher Education Task Force on Quality Inclusive Schooling. (2000). *Standards for inclusive teacher preparation programs.* Syracuse: New York State Higher Education Support Center for Systems change.

Kochhar, C. A., West, L. L., & Taymans, J. A. (2000). *Successful inclusion: Practical strategies for a shared responsibility.* Upper Saddle River, NJ: Prentice Hall.

Kukic, S., & Schrag, J. (1998). *IEP connections for a dynamic, living, and practical process: IEP team member's manual.* Longmont, CO: Sopris West.

Lipsky, D. K., & Gartner, A. (1996). Inclusion, school restructuring, and the remaking of American society. *Harvard Educational Review, 66*(4), 762–796.

LRP. (1994). *Full inclusion: Educating students with disabilities in the regular classroom.* Danvers, MA: LRP Publications.

McLoughlin, J., & Lewis, R. (2001). *Assessing students with special needs.* Upper Saddle River, NJ: Prentice Hall.

Murphy, M. (1994, March). Full inclusion case law. Paper presented at LRP conference, Cherry Hill, New Jersey.

New York State Education Department, VESID. (1999). *A new direction for IEPs.* Albany: Vocational and Educational Services for Individuals with Disabilities.

New York State Education Department, VESID. (1999). Practical questions to guide IEP Development.

O'Neil, J. (1995). Can inclusion work? A conversation with Jim Kauffman and Mara Sapon-Shevin. *Educational Leadership,* 7–11.

Overton, T. (2000). *Assessment in special education: An applied approach.* Upper Saddle River, NJ: Prentice Hall.

Sailor, W. (1991). Special education in the restricted school. *Remedial and Special Education, 12*(6), 8–22.

Salvia, J., & Ysseldyke, J. (1998). *Assessment.* (7th ed.). Boston: Houghton Mifflin.

Sheehan, V. (2000, June). Section 504 and the Americans with Disabilities Act—An update. Paper presented at New York State School Boards Association Conference, Melville, New York.

Stainback, S., & Stainback, W. (1992). *Curriculum considerations in inclusive classrooms: Facilitating learning for all students.* Baltimore: Paul H. Brookes Publishing Co.

Strickland, B., & Turnbull, A. (1993). *Developing and implementing Individualized Education Programs.* (3rd ed.). Upper Saddle River, NJ: Merrill.

Taylor, R. (1997). *Assessment of exceptional students: Educational and psychological procedures.* Boston: Allyn & Bacon.

Taylor, S. J., & Searl, S. J., Jr. (1987). The disabled in America: History, policy, and trends. In P. Knoblock (Ed.), *Understanding exceptional children and youth* (pp. 5–64). Boston: Little, Brown.

Thomas, C. C., Correa, V. I., & Morsink, C. V. (2001). *Interactive teaming: Enhancing programs for students with special needs.* Upper Saddle River, NJ: Merrill/Prentice Hall.

Tilton, L. (1996). *Inclusion: A fresh look. Practical strategies to help all students succeed.* (3rd ed.). Shorewood, MN: Coveington Cove Publications.

Turnbull, A., & Turnbull, R. (1997). *Families, professionals and exceptionality: A special partnership.* Upper Saddle River, NJ: Merrill.

Turnbull, A., Turnbull, R., Shank, M., & Leal, D. (1999). *Exceptional lives: Special education in today's schools.* Upper Saddle River, NJ: Merrill/Prentice Hall.

Turnbull, A., Turnbull, R., Shank, M., & Leal, D. (2002). *Exceptional lives: Special education in today's schools.* (3rd ed.). Upper Saddle River, NJ: Merrill/Prentice Hall.

University of the State of New York. (1995). *Test access and modification for individuals with disabilities.* New York: SUNY.

U.S. Department of Education. (2001). *Twenty-second annual report to Congress on the implementation of the Individuals with Disabilities Act.* Washington, DC: U.S. Department of Education.

U.S. Department of Education. Office of Special Education Programs IDEA Institute Series: Training for trainers 1998. In *A new direction for IEPs.*

Villa, R. A., & Thousand, J. S. (Eds.). (1995). *Creating an inclusive school.* Alexandria, VA: Association for Supervision and Curriculum Development.

Waterman, B. (1994). Assessing children for the presence of a disability. *NICHCY News Digest, 4,* 1–27.

Worona, J., & Sokol, P. (1996, June). Educating children with disabilities: Legal overview and update. Paper presented at New York State School Boards Association Conference, Melville, New York.

Worona, J., & Sokol, P. (2000, June). Educating children with disabilities: Legal overview and update. Paper presented at New York State School Boards Association Conference, Melville, New York.

Ysseldyke, J. E., Algozzine, B., & Thurlow, M. L. (2000). *Critical issues in special education.* Boston: Houghton Mifflin.

Zirkel, P. (1999, August). Legal workshop on inclusion. Paper presented at Nassau BOCES Sliver Grant Inclusion Training, Rockville Centre, New York.

PART II

Research, Theory, and Practice for Teachers

CHAPTER 5

Instructional Techniques to Facilitate Inclusive Education

Darra Pace and Melissa Price

Imagine, if you will, that four individuals are required by an employer to attend a meeting in New York City, one week from today, at 2:00 P.M. Attendance at this meeting is a requirement for continued advancement in the company. All travel expenses will be reimbursed. The individual circumstances of each employee's life dictate certain realities about their travel arrangements.

Employee 1 lives in California and has no car, no cash, and no credit. Employee 2 lives in Florida, loves to fly, and uses a wheelchair. Employee 3 lives in Wisconsin now, but grew up in New York City. Employee 4 lives in Maine and is fearful of traveling in New York City.

If you were working to facilitate travel for this group of individuals, would you expect that they would all use the same mode of transportation? Would you expect them all to have the same departure and arrival time? Each traveler has unique needs and abilities. While the goal is the same, the manner of travel is different. Likewise, learners may have a common standard toward which they strive, but the ways they work to achieve that goal may differ. However, customizing instruction is rarely considered a typical instructional procedure. It is interesting to note that in this simple analogy, poverty or a lack of resources presents the greatest challenge in solving this puzzle.

THE PRIMARY THEMES OF THE INCLUSIVE CLASSROOM

Community, curriculum development, and instructional strategies are the overarching themes of the inclusive classroom.

Community Building

The first step for building a truly inclusive classroom is self-reflection on the part of the teacher. One of the most important concerns of the inclusive classroom should focus on creating a community in which all students feel that they belong. This usually starts when adults are more open to others, children and adults alike. Students will look to their teacher to set the tone that makes it possible for community building to occur. Community building is contingent upon the teacher's willingness to view all students as valued participants in the life of the class. If teachers regard others with skepticism, wariness, or defensiveness, students will sense this incongruity and respond to their actions, not their words. Teachers who view students with special needs as an imposition on the class, or their inclusion as a privilege rather than a right, communicate that belief (directly or indirectly) to their students. Teachers who draw attention to the individual differences or disabilities of certain students are often accentuating differences in a negative way. It is more realistic to address issues as they develop over time and to discuss questions openly. When students can speak and advocate for themselves, it accomplishes more than when an adult tries to intervene.

Teachers who mistake adult domination for classroom control miss the opportunity to develop students' social responsibility. In successful classroom communities, student independence as manifested in self-direction and autonomy is complemented by student interdependence. The class members come to view their relationships with one another as the primary impetus for social and academic interaction. Each member of the class needs and is needed by another. The teacher's role is to facilitate the development of the healthy balance of these relationships and not to build dependency upon an adult figure to answer all questions, solve all dilemmas, and direct all activities.

Curriculum Development

Curriculum must be reflective of the need to incorporate unique individuals into a community of learners. As a classroom is physically, emotionally, and socially inclusive, so it must be academically inclusive. To achieve this, teachers need to understand the strengths and needs of each learner and to develop learning opportunities that build on individual strengths and encourage learners to push themselves to new limits.

Traditional teach-to-the-middle approaches do little to address the fact that most learners are not "in the middle." More and more students enter our schools today with diverse cultural, educational, and linguistic requirements. The concept of universal design should be employed in curriculum development so that the needs of all students are built into the curriculum, not added on. Universal design is an adaptation of the architectural concept of total access. Total-access buildings are constructed complete with ramps and enlarged doorways to serve the disabled. Alterations are not made after construction: the accommodations are integral to the design of the structure. Curriculum should reflect the same forethought.

For example, students with receptive processing issues might find guide questions or important facts pre-highlighted in the margins of texts.

Differentiated Instruction

Differentiated instruction to a group of diverse learners provides, among other things, multiple entry points, tiered assignments, varying questions, and flexible grouping. Many of these instructional strategies have been used for years. Now they are being reconceived to address a class of diverse learners.

Upon becoming familiar with the need for community, curriculum development, and instructional strategies, it is important to take those themes and address the pragmatics of implementing them in the classroom.

ARRANGING THE PHYSICAL ENVIRONMENT OF THE INCLUSIVE CLASSROOM TO FACILITATE COMMUNITY BUILDING

In the inclusive class, as in the traditional class, the physical structure of the classroom directly ties into the sense of community, management style, and instructional strategies. How the space is managed significantly impacts student behavior and attitudes and seems to affect achievement.[1] The arrangement of the physical layout of the inclusive classroom provides a starting point for effective instruction and learning.

A classroom of diverse learners compels the teacher to consider certain special needs and supports that will help students succeed. The room arrangement must balance structure, organization, and regimentation with freedom, the chance for exploration, and the opportunity for choice.[2] All of these points become part of the issue of the management of the physical environment.

The layout of the room is more than an assemblage of furniture. Within the confines of the classroom students develop a sense of community during the school year. It is here that children learn about personal and public space.[3] Socialization and, increasingly, collaboration are part of each day. The classroom needs flexibility to meet the demands of different instructional styles, as well as push-in and pull-out services. The management of the space must acknowledge the environmental limitations of the room while making it barrier-free. Also of importance are the aesthetics of the environment. An aesthetically appealing room increases the students' desire to spend time there.

Certain practical guidelines facilitate classroom organization. Maximum attention must be given to the learning goals and the types of tasks students will be involved in. Traditional rows work well when introducing new information or for independent work. There is more direct eye contact with the teacher, and on-task behavior is promoted. Horseshoe or circle arrangements create good student interaction during discussion. Since instructional groups vary in the inclusive class, being able to change the structure quickly with a minimum of disruption is important. To facilitate transitions from group work, or to minimize distractions as students leave or return from services, traffic patterns would be carefully considered as well.[4]

Classrooms are multidimensional. They are crowded and busy places that need to work for all the people in them, including those with disabilities. Classrooms should be wheelchair accessible. Thought must be given to line of vision when the desks are arranged. Can materials and resources be easily reached? Since many things are happening at the same time in the room, the arrangement must allow the teacher to monitor the activities of all the students in the class.

The physical arrangements of a classroom can encourage appropriate behavior.[5] When the room is comfortable, and resources and opportunities for instruction are accessible, student frustration is reduced.

All of the above-mentioned room arrangement factors apply to all classrooms. Another critical consideration is the relationship between the physical layout and instruction. In an inclusive classroom, that means a setting that allows for different types of collaboration, groupings, and cooperative learning.

The physical environment of the room is the starting point for the learning community that will evolve over the year. In an inclusive setting that translates into accommodating differences and responding to the diversity of the learners in the class. Inclusion is about different people working together, whether students or professionals. Collaboration between teachers and other service providers is an integral part of inclusive education. The space must respond to the professional collaboration evident in inclusive settings.

DIFFERENTIATED INSTRUCTION: ADDRESSING INDIVIDUAL NEEDS AND THE STANDARDS

Many state and local governments have developed a uniform set of standards toward which all students are expected to strive. In many places, promotion and/or graduation credentials are dependent upon students performing in adherence to prescribed standards. While this philosophy may seem directly in conflict with the expectation that inclusive classrooms address the individual needs of learners, this need not be the case. To view standards simply as an instructional methodology misses their potential value. Well-meaning individuals in the disability service community have sometimes addressed the individual needs of students with disabilities with an eye toward the student's own personal goals and interests, to the exclusion of the larger community in which these students might hope to function. The result has been an overreliance on separate special education programs. A better balance of expectations seems to be the intent of IDEA'97, which calls for access to general education. By definition, the least restrictive environment (LRE) calls for both access to education with nondisabled peers and the provision of special education services. No student should be called upon to give up student-centered instructional planning in pursuit of the higher expectations posed by the standards movement. This chapter's opening anecdote is helpful in explaining this seeming contradiction. While the goal of the travelers is the same, the manner of travel is different. Likewise, learners may have a common standard toward which they strive, but the manner in which they work to achieve that goal is different.

How does this analogy relate to the inclusive classroom? Simply put, it illustrates the use of differentiated instruction, which incorporates the needs of all learners (travelers) as an integral part of the curriculum (travel plan), instruction, and assessment, not as an add-on. It would be impractical to give all the employees in the analogy the same directions, and then amend them individually. Differentiated instruction in the classroom seeks to avoid that cumbersome approach by creating diversity in instruction through variety in lesson formats, materials, instructional arrangements, teaching strategies, and support.[6] It provides multiple entry points to access curriculum as it is presented. Many teachers are already doing differentiated instruction to some degree. The diversity of learners in the inclusive classroom calls for an extension and expansion of the techniques in use.[7]

Teaching in the inclusive classroom asks teachers to see, accept, and respect students as individuals with distinct abilities and needs. Carol Ann Tomlinson calls on teachers to bring a new set of beliefs into the classroom. "The differences in students are significant enough to make a major impact on what students need to learn, the pace at which they need to learn it, and the support they need from teacher and others to learn it.[8] Differentiating instruction draws on the need to look at different learning styles[9] and multiple intelligences.[10] Tables 5.1 and 5.2 show the different ways in which Gardener and Johnston look at students. Both "Let Me Learn"[11] and multiple intelligence theory expand teacher understanding of the diversity of the learners in their classes.

TEACHING STRATEGIES THAT STUDENTS USE IN THE INCLUSIVE CLASSROOM

To address learning strategies, we need to recognize the array of the differences in the class and the different curriculum areas in question. While each learner would benefit from strategies that specifically address their learning difference or disability, certain general strategies apply across disabilities.

Table 5.1.
Multiple Intelligence Theory

Multiple Intelligence	Description
Linguistic	Skilled manipulators of language—like to read, write, tell stories
Logical-Mathematical	Question the world, explore patterns and relationships, like to work with numbers, excel at math, logic, and problem solving
Spatial	Pictures created in mind's eye and recreates—enjoys demonstrations and hands-on work
Bodily-Kinesthetic	Excellent fine and gross motor skills—needs to move, touch, maneuver
Musical	Enjoys anything related to music, makes meaning out of sound
Interpersonal	Socialers, extroverted, innate understanding of people and feelings—mediate, communicators, need to share
Intrapersonal	Introspective, good understanding of self—works alone and at own pace
Naturalist	Makes consequential distinctions about the natural world—enjoys ordering, classifying, categorizing, environmental issues

Source: Adapted from Gardener, H. (1983). *Frames of mind: The theory of multiple intelligences*. New York: Basic Books.

Lesson Presentation

In a class of diverse learners, not everyone will be able to process the material in the same way. Boyles and Contadino give a number of strategies for supporting learners with receptive language disorders.[12] These suggestions have been generalized to the range of learning differences and disabilities, since everyone in the class must learn the material presented. This multisensory approach to presentation demonstrates sensitivity to differences and disabilities.

- Supplement oral information with written materials and demonstration so students receive information in multiple ways.

Table 5.2.
Let Me Learn

Learning Combination	Description
Sequential	This type learner seeks explicit directions, is a planner and a neat worker.
Precise	This type of learner values details and data.
Technical	This learner prefers hands-on projects that are relevant and real.
Confluent	This learner is creative, intuitive, and a risk taker.

Source: Adapted from Johnston, C. A. (1998). Using the learning combination inventory. *Educational Leadership, 55*(4), 78–82.

- Try to keep directions simple. If more complex directions are needed, write them out so students can refer to them independently.

- Monitor your presentation speed and ask students in the class to re-phrase the information in their own words. This allows for repetition in addition to a different presentation of the content.

- Adjust the pace of your presentation to correspond to the type of material you are presenting. Curriculum presented for the first time needs more time than a review session.

- Stress the target concept. Pause between phrases or sentences to allow all the students to process the material. Chunking information helps students make connections between the fact and ideas being presented. Examples and non-examples illuminate new information in a very concrete way.

- Wait time between concepts is critical. Not everyone can process the material or contribute to the lesson at the same rate. Many students need time to organize their thoughts. Turn and erase the board just to give those extra moments to process and organize. The extra time can serve as encouragement for a reluctant student to participate and feel part of the group discussion. This makes it safe for him or her to take the few minutes needed to become actively involved in the lesson.

Instructional Strategies for Diverse Learners

Much of teacher preparation involves finding ways to ensure that all the students understand the information and ideas presented. This concern grows as the appreciation of the differences in an inclusive setting is realized. Stanovich reported that teachers found the type of instruction used directly affected the success or failure of inclusion.[13] They favored four types of instruction: (1) student-centered activities; (2) cooperative learning; (3) guided discovery; and (4) inquiry-based projects.

The following instruction adaptations and modifications were considered particularly helpful:

1. *Print material available in different reading levels.* It would be ideal to supply multiple forms of print material. More often, one text or handout is used. In that case Salend offers several techniques to assist students who have difficulty with reading and comprehension.[14]

   - Preview the material, including new vocabulary and word pronunciation. This can motivate students and access previous knowledge.

   - Have students respond to teacher questions before, during, and after reading.

   - Have student and teacher take turns summarizing and discussing the reading (reciprocal teaching).

   - Story map the major elements of the reading in a visual format.

2. *Graphic organizers.* Visual displays help students organize information and concepts for comprehension and learning.[15] Organizers like Venn diagrams, semantic webs, genealogical trees, and frames can be used to clarify concepts as well as semantics, and to show relationships. (See Figure 5.1.)

3. *Visual aids.* Most instruction is auditory, delivered by lecture. The efficiency of this method cannot be denied. However, to differentiate instruction, you must utilize more than one dominant delivery method, or at the very least augment it. Visual aids do that by graphically illustrating what is being presented in a lecture. For example, show students a completed, written report or model of a hands-on project.

4. *Adjustments in the length, time, or difficulty of assignments.* Salend's tiered assignments are tailored to the needs of the individual student, from presentation of the material to the final assignments required from the students.[16] Options offered can include written assignment, oral presentation, or physical model.

   - *Break down assignment into manageable units.* Task analysis plays an integral part in special education. In the inclusive classroom this skill can be used by both teacher and student. To Mercer and Mercer, task analysis consists of dividing a learning project into parts to determine the skills need to successfully complete it.[17] Mastro-

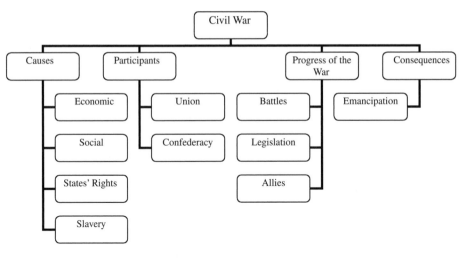

Figure 5.1. Graphic Organizer

prieri and Scruggs extend the process of task analysis to students.[18] Students are taught to look at an assignment, decide what must be done, sequence the steps required, and estimate the amount of time they will need to complete it. An example of task analysis follows.

Terminal behavior: Write letters of the alphabet.

1. Able to hold writing implement (pincer movement).
2. Able to maintain appropriate posture at desk.
3. Position paper correctly on the writing surface.
4. Draw a straight line.
5. Draw a circle.
6. Draw curves.
7. Move writing implement across paper with the proper combination of lines and curves.

5. *Rubrics.* Rubrics are assessment tools that look at a whole or part of a performance or finished product. They describe criteria for the work being assessed on a number of performance levels (e.g., excellent, good, acceptable, unacceptable). Among the many advantages attributed to rubrics by Martin-Kniep is that students have a clearer understanding of teacher expectations.[19] The various de-

scriptions of criteria also serve as scaffolding as students move from one level to another.

6. *Grouping.* It has been documented that students with learning disabilities of all grade levels preferred working in pairs or groups to working alone or as a whole class.[20] The researchers found that all students, both disabled and nondisabled, appreciate the chance to help others and enjoy group assignments. Further, this study revealed that all students, with or without disabilities, have definite preferences for instructional techniques. Students felt that varying the pace of instruction as needed to explain material and assignments, and teaching curriculum in a variety of ways, ensured everyone the opportunity to learn.

Flexible Grouping in the Inclusive Classroom

Student learning groups should be flexible. Problems arise when groups become static and expectations stagnate. Homogeneous grouping or tracking may be done for the convenience of the teacher, and is not in the best interest of all students. There is some evidence to suggest that tracking "works" for the high-ability students[21] in the sense that teachers provide more opportunities for critical thinking and problem solving around high-quality course content. However, lower-ability students are not typically offered these opportunities. The inequity of tracking exacerbates the naturally occurring differences in learning style or speed.

In *Inclusive Schooling Practices: Pedagogical and Research Foundations*,[22] McGregor and Vogelsberg identify a number of small group structures that encourage collaboration in heterogeneous groups:

- Peer tutoring—Students work together to read aloud to each other and edit each other's written work.[23]

- Study teams—Teams are encouraged to ensure that all members learn materials through a reward system based on the performance of the entire group.[24]

- Learning together—Heterogeneous groups share and support group member learning, but mastery is measured by individual test/grades or group products.[25]

- Jigsaw—Students are divided into groups and assigned one portion of an assignment or topic.[26] They become an expert group and are responsible for investigating and reporting back to the main group. (See Figure 5.2.)

- Group investigations—Similar to jigsaw except that the activity starts as a whole group discussion.[27] Students are subsequently divided into small groups based on their interest and skill to investigate one com-

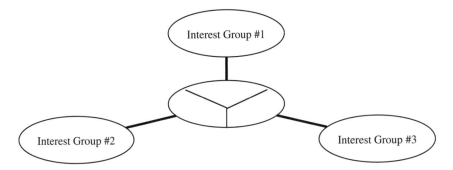

Figure 5.2. Jigsaw Sharing

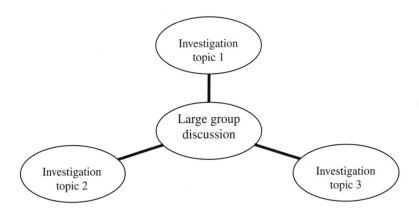

Figure 5.3. Group Investigation

ponent of the problem and report back to the main group. (See Figure 5.3.)

- Numbered heads together—Engages students during adult-led instruction and discussion.[28] Students are organized into four-member learning teams. Each team member is numbered 1, 2, 3, or 4. In response to a question, students are instructed to put their heads together to reach a consensus answer. All members of the group must know the answer. Then, the teacher calls for an answer from one member of each group (e.g., "Which number 4 can answer this question?"). (See Figure 5.4.)
- Literature circles/text sets—Groups of students choose and read the same book or article.[29]
- Think-pair-share—Temporary pairing of students with partners to share ideas and develop responses.[30] All students participate.

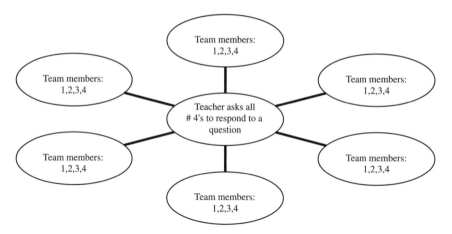

Figure 5.4. Numbered Heads

- Cross-age tutoring—Older students from a different class or grade work with needy students.
- Task groups—Students divided according to parts of a lesson, unit, or theme-based activity (see Figure 5.5). In a second grade classroom, for example, students were divided into groups to work with the general educator, a special educator, and the reading teacher. Students rotated to each station, thereby giving each educator the opportunity to interact with all of the students while consistently delivering content information.

Sometimes students do need one-to-one attention. This is often the case with writing assignments. In a collaborative classroom, "make an appointment" groups can achieve this organization. (See Figure 5.6.)
Other small group configurations include:

- Station teaching—Teachers work with groups of students who progress through different learning centers or stations.
- Parallel teaching—Each teacher instructs half of the class at the same time using the same instructional materials (at a different pace, for example).
- Pre-teaching/extension instruction—One teacher pre-teaches a group of students who may need support to prepare for an upcoming unit of study while another teacher re-teaches a completed unit or provides extension activities for enrichment.

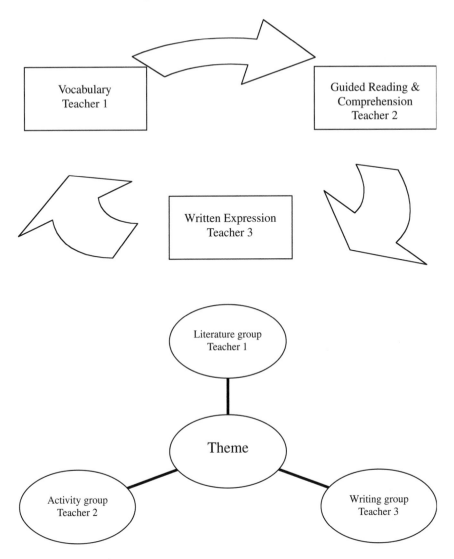

Figure 5.5. Task Groups A

Whole group instruction still exists in inclusive classrooms, but some new opportunities occur as teachers work in collaboration with one another. This configuration is sometimes misused to establish a hierarchy of personnel. In truly collaborative relationships, these roles are interchangeable. Consider the following:

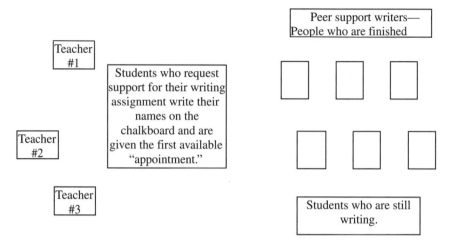

Figure 5.6. Task Groups B

- One teaches, one observes—One teacher delivers direct instruction while another gathers observational data.
- One teaches, one drifts—One teacher delivers direct instruction while another assists students with work, monitors behavior, and corrects assignments.
- Co-teaching partners—One teacher delivers instruction; one reinforces instruction, supplementing the delivery with clarifying questions or examples.

Since no two teachers or their students are the same, it will be necessary to experiment to determine which configurations work best for each situation. The synergy of the collaborative teams offers tremendous opportunities for instructional groupings.

SUMMARY

Creating an inclusive classroom is about rethinking the traditional approach to teaching. Students with disabilities are no longer segregated in self-contained classes apart from more typical learners. The inclusive model asks for the creation of a new learning community, one in which diversity is valued and differences are incorporated into the fabric of school life. This is a challenge that asks teachers to examine what they teach, both consciously and unconsciously, and how they can best teach all the children in their classroom.

This chapter offers teachers some strategies for instruction while keeping in mind that instruction goes hand and hand with curriculum development and creating a community in which all students feel they belong. No strategy or technique can work without an understanding that it is just one component in a new approach to education. Flexible grouping will not be effective if the curriculum does not offer multiple entry points or if a student feels unaccepted by classmates or the teacher.

Many of these strategies are familiar to experienced teachers and have been used successfully. They are the means to address learning differences

Tips for Educators

- Students possess multiple kinds of intelligences and learning styles.
- Student differences must be incorporated into curriculum planning.
- Different learning styles and intelligences must be addressed in instructional strategies.
- Differ print reading level.
- Use graphic organizers.
- Use visual aids.
- Tier assignments.
- Break down assignments into easy-to-do units.
- Use rubrics.
- Use flexible grouping.

and disabilities among the students in an inclusive setting and facilitate the learning of all the children in the class.

NOTES

1. Bellon, J.J., Bellon, E., & Blank, M. (1992). *Teaching from a research knowledge base: A development and renewal process.* New York: Macmillan.

2. Polloway, E.A., Patton, J.R., & Serna, L. (2005). *Strategies for teaching learners with special needs.* Upper Saddle River, NJ: Prentice Hall.

3. Rosenberg, M.S., O'Shea, L., & O'Shea, D.J. (1999). *Student teacher to master teacher.* Upper Saddle River, NJ: Prentice Hall.

4. Rosenberg, O'Shea, & O'Shea (1999).

5. Daniels, V.I. (1998). How to manage disruptive behavior in inclusive classrooms. *Teaching Exceptional Children, 30*(4), 26–31.

6. Kluth, P. (2000). Community-referenced learning and the inclusive class-

room. *Remedial and Special Education, 21*(1), 19–27; and Kluth, P. (2003). *You are going to love this kid! Teaching students with autism in the inclusive classroom.* Baltimore: Paul H. Brookes Publishing Co.

7. Kluth (2000); Kluth (2003).

8. Tomlinson, C. A. (2000). Reconcilable differences? Standards-based teaching and differentiation. *Journal of the Association for Supervision and Curriculum Development, 58*(1), 5–11.

9. Johnston, C. A. (1998). Using the learning combination inventory. *Educational Leadership, 55*(4), 78–82.

10. Gardener, H. (1983). *Frames of the mind: The theory of multiple intelligences.* New York: Basic Books; and Armstrong, T. (1994). *Multiple intelligences in the classroom.* Alexandria, VA: ASCD.

11. Johnston (1998).

12. Boyles, N. S., & Contadino, D. (1998). *The learning differences sourcebook.* Los Angeles: Lowell House.

13. Stanovich, P. J. (1999). Conversations about inclusion. *Teaching Exceptional Children, 31*(6), 54–58.

14. Salend, S. J. (2001). *Creating inclusive classrooms: Effective and reflective practices.* Upper Saddle River, NJ: Prentice Hall.

15. Dye, G. A. (2000). Graphic organizers to the rescue: Helping students link and remember information. *Teaching Exceptional Children, 32*(3), 72–76.

16. Salend (2001).

17. Mercer, C. D., & Mercer, A. R. (2005). *Teaching students with learning problems.* Upper Saddle River, NJ: Prentice Hall.

18. Mastroprieri, M. A., & Scruggs, T. E. (2000). *The inclusive classroom: Strategies for effective instruction.* Upper Saddle River, NJ: Prentice Hall.

19. Martin-Kniep, G. O. (2000). *Becoming a better teacher: Eight innovations that work.* Alexandria, VA: Association for Supervision and Curriculum Development.

20. Klingner, J. K., & Vaugh, S. (1999). Students' perceptions of instruction in inclusion classrooms: Implications for students with learning disabilities. *Exceptional Children, 66*(1), 23–37.

21. Oakes, J. (1985). *Keeping track: How schools structure inequality.* New Haven, CT: Yale University Press.

22. McGregor, G., & Vogelsberg, R. T. (1998). *Inclusive schooling practices: Pedagogical and research foundations. A synthesis of the literature that informs best practices about inclusive schooling.* Baltimore: Paul H. Brookes Publishing Co.

23. Zemelman, S., Daniels, H., & Hyde, A. (1993). *Best practice: New standards for teaching and learning in America's schools.* Portsmouth, NH: Heinemann.

24. DeVries, D. L., Slavin, R. E., Fennessey, K. M., Edwards, K. J., & Lombardo, M. M. (1980). *Teams—games—tournament: The team learning approach.* Englewood Cliffs, NJ: Educational Technology Publications.

25. Johnson, D. W., & Johnson, R. T. (1991). *Learning together and alone: Cooperative, competitive, and individualistic learning.* (3rd ed.). Englewood Cliffs, NJ: Prentice Hall.

26. Aronson, E., Blaney, N., Stephan, C., Sikes, J., & Snapp, M. (1978). *The jigsaw classroom.* Beverly Hills, CA: Sage.

27. Kagan, S. (1985). Dimensions of cooperative classroom structures. In R.

Slavin, S. Sharan, S. Kagan, R. Hertz-Lazarowitz, C.D. Webb, & R. Schmuck (Eds.), *Learning to cooperate, cooperating to learn* (pp. 67–96). New York: Plenum Press; and Sharan, S., & Hertz-Lazarowitz, R. (1980). A group-investigation method of cooperative learning in the classroom. In S. Sharan, P. Hare, C.D. Webb, & R. Hertz-Lazarowitz (Eds.), *Cooperation in education* (pp. 14–46). Provo, UT: Brigham Young University Press.

28. Kagan (1985).

29. Zemelman, Daniels, & Hyde (1993).

30. Lyman, F. (1992). Think-pair-share, thinktrix, thinklinks, and weird facts. In N. Davidson and T. Worsham (Eds.), *Enhancing thinking through cooperative learning*. New York: Teachers College Press.

CHAPTER 6

Including Students Who Are Linguistically and Culturally Diverse

Nancy L. Cloud

Esmeralda Martinez is seven years old and one of four children. Her family is from the Dominican Republic, having moved to the United States before she was born. Until she went to school, she spoke only Spanish at home with her family. Once she started school, she was placed in a transitional bilingual kindergarten program and began to learn English. Currently, she predominantly uses Spanish with her parents, but speaks both English and Spanish about equally with her siblings. All of the school-age children attend the same school.

In the first grade, Esmeralda's teacher noticed that she was having difficulty learning, and so she referred her to the child study team. Almost immediately, they found that Esmeralda had undetected mild sensory impairments (vision and hearing) which could be affecting her learning. She was provided with a hearing aid for her left ear as well as corrective lenses. This year, the school is also providing assistive technology in the classroom designed for her needs, since her teachers note that she is still not at grade level in reading and mathematics.

While she receives related services from an audiologist and a speech pathologist, she is now placed in a team-taught inclusion class where she continues to receive native language and ESL (English as a second language) support from her bilingual teacher, as appropriate. The inclusion teacher works with Esmeralda during reading and writing. As Esmeralda moves through the grades in her elementary school, what should all school personnel know in order to provide her with the most appropriate and effective instruction? What should school personnel advise Esmeralda's parents about language use at home and how best to support her achievement?

UNDERSTANDING THE SPECIAL LEARNING CHARACTERISTICS OF STUDENTS WHO ARE CULTURALLY AND LINGUISTICALLY DIVERSE (CLD)

According to Waggoner,[1] and based on the Office of Civil Rights, U.S. Department of Education, 1998 Sample Survey, American public schools are increasingly diverse places. According to the report, whites constitute around 69 percent of the total school-age population, while 17 percent of school-age children are African American, 14 percent are Hispanics, 4 percent are Asian and Pacific Islanders, and 1 percent are American Indian or Alaska Natives. In several states, students of color comprise the clear majority, among them Hawaii, New Mexico, California, and Texas, and other states will quickly join their number.

In addition to the rich cultural diversity these students bring to American classrooms, they also bring great linguistic diversity to enrich classroom life. In the 2000–2001 school year, 9.6 percent of the total public school population was identified as English language learner (ELL), a 32.1 percent increase over the reported 1997–98 public school ELL enrollment. In descending order, the following states enroll the greatest numbers of ELL students: California, Texas, Florida, New York, Illinois, and Arizona.[2] In these states ELLs comprise from 10 percent to 23 percent of the public school enrollment, a significant percentage of the population.[3] Not only has the number of ELL students in U.S. schools almost doubled over the past decade, it has also increased at nearly eight times the rate of total student enrollment.[4] Because of the significant and rapid increases in this school-age population, some researchers project that by 2030, 40 percent of school-age children will be ELL.[5]

In an address given by former Secretary of Education Richard Riley in 2000, it was confirmed that in the near future, Hispanics would become the largest U.S. minority.[6] He referred to this demographic shift as "a transformation of historic proportions," noting that by 2050, nearly one-quarter of the U.S. population will be Hispanic. U.S. Census figures further confirmed that the Hispanic population is fast-growing and young. The Hispanic population increased by 57.9 percent from 1990 to 2000, compared with an increase of 13.2 percent for the total U.S. population. Three-quarters (76.8 percent) of Hispanics lived in seven states, where their numbers reached 1 million or more: California, Texas, New York, Florida, Illinois, Arizona, and New Jersey. Hispanics in New Mexico made up 42.1 percent of the total population, the highest proportion for any state. Furthermore the median age for Hispanics was 25.9 years, while the median age for the entire U.S. population was 35.3 years. According to Riley, of the 6.5 million Hispanic students enrolled in American classrooms, 2.3 million, or 34.9 percent, are English language learners, while 21 percent of

Asian and Pacific Islanders and 10 percent of American Indian and Alaska Native students are so categorized.[7]

These statistics help to demonstrate that the concept of inclusion must be broadened to encompass not only the notion of accommodating children of varied ability backgrounds, but also children of diverse cultural and linguistic backgrounds (those with and without identified disabilities) if education is to truly be responsive. This chapter is designed to help teachers do just that. While the rest of this volume discusses ways of accommodating learners of diverse ability backgrounds, this chapter focuses on ways to accommodate the added dimensions of learners' cultural and linguistic characteristics.

This is an extremely pressing need since the teaching corps is not as diverse as the student population in terms of racial, ethnic, and linguistic characteristics.[8] This is also true of special educators. According to Wald, whereas in 1995 some 68 percent of special education students where white, an overwhelming 86 percent of special education teachers were so identified.[9] While 16 percent of students were black, only 10 percent of their teachers so identified. Even less representative in composition, Hispanic students made up 12 percent of the special education student population, but only 2 percent of their special education teachers were so identified. While attaining representative proportions of persons of color among the teaching corps is an important goal for this nation, clearly effective teaching relies on more than mere proportional representation. Indeed, to deliver effective special education programs, all teachers must know how to work effectively with culturally and linguistically diverse learners. This chapter is designed to contribute to that effort.

The Impact of Culture on Teaching and Learning

Cultural knowledge and cultural values provide the underpinnings for understanding and interpreting meaning.[10] Teaching and learning environments are profoundly influenced by culture. As noted elsewhere,[11] the curriculum and instruction provided, classroom management techniques employed, counseling and support services offered, and parent outreach efforts conducted are embedded in particular cultural frames of reference which in turn are predicated on certain values, beliefs, knowledge bases, and experiences. To the extent that these match the characteristics of learners, learning is facilitated. To the extent that they do not, learning can be compromised. Jacobs notes that schools are so deeply culturally embedded that they operate largely without conscious awareness.[12] Because of this, teachers must actively reflect on how their curriculum, instruction, and classroom environments are structured in order to modify them as needed to better accommodate the needs of individual learners.

For example, in the all-important areas of academic and literacy instruction, we know that the knowledge and experience (schema) learners bring to the classroom become the starting place for all new learning.[13] According to Hollins:

> Children begin formal schooling with "learning in progress." They have learned the language, behaviors, perceptions, and values appropriate with the home-culture from their families, friends, and other significant people in their lives. Meaningful school learning is directly linked to that already in progress in ways that extend and build on the knowledge that has already been acquired as well as that being processed.[14]

Different cultural groups value and promote different content and life experiences as important and necessary, creating differences in what our learners bring to school. In a culturally diverse society, teachers must survey their learners' background knowledge and be cognizant of their rich and varied life experiences in order to plan instruction around these all-important dimensions. If they fail to consider these variables in relation to their learners, the effectiveness of their instruction will be negatively affected.

At the deepest level, the values level, teachers must understand important differences that exist across different ethnolinguistic groups. Representative of the different values inculcated in children through the cultural transmission process were the findings of an American Association of Retired Persons study of grandparent interaction with grandchildren.[15] It documented that about twice as many white grandparents as black grandparents feel that morals and integrity are the most important values to pass on to children (44 percent compared with 22 percent), whereas more blacks than whites want to transmit ambition and the urge to succeed (35 percent compared with 20 percent). At the same time, more African American grandparents believe that it is important to teach their grandchildren about their own hobbies and interests than do whites. While these examples are restricted to just a few aspects of two groups, they help to show the differences that exist in values and interests upon which teachers can capitalize in their work with children and families. The study also shows that surveying our students' families is one way of gathering the information we need to be successful.

Teacher-pupil and pupil-pupil interactions are also culturally influenced. Because of this, communication patterns and interpersonal interaction styles favored by individuals vary from culture to culture. For example, some students may not feel comfortable participating in class, answering questions in front of a group, or joining in discussions.[16] In cases where teachers understand the importance of these factors, they construct effective environments for learners and establish supportive relationships with and among their students. In cases where they do not know their learners' preferred ways of interacting and communicating, they may unwittingly create distancing and disempowering environments for their learners—conditions that detract from or even prevent learning.

A final example of the interface of cultural background and program development is that of materials selection. When teachers select materials to support high levels of reading comprehension, texts that draw from the life experiences of students and build upon their prior knowledge will be more easily comprehended than those which are distant from them. In culturally diverse classrooms, a broad range of literature, spanning varied topics and themes and written from diverse perspectives, must be available to provide teachers and their learners with needed resources.

How to Facilitate Second Language Learning

Research on acquiring a second language has established that there are two major types of language children must acquire to be successful in their communities and at school: social language and academic language. Acknowledging this, Teachers of English to Speakers of Other Languages (TESOL) has established the following goals for ESL students in grades pre-K–12: (1) students should use English to communicate in social settings, and (2) students should use English to achieve academically in all content areas. Students should not be considered proficient when they can socialize in English; rather, teachers must assure that they acquire the academic English they need to be successful at school. When teachers conceptualize "proficiency" as the merely ability to speak and understand spoken English in everyday interactions, they may erroneously attribute students' lack of success in academic environments (e.g., the inability to read the textbook successfully and respond to questions in writing, or poor performance on tests given in English) as signs of a learning disability rather than as what is more likely the case—the continued need for second language instruction so that academic English can be acquired. Research has shown that while social English is generally acquired by students within two years' time, it takes much longer to develop academic English—between four and seven years for most students, by most estimates.[17] This finding is understandable, since daily social interactions are rather routine and limited, whereas academic English is limitless. Indeed, this is why we send children to school—so that they can understand and communicate effectively about the academic subjects they study. Since the learning is continuous in this area—a moving target, so to speak—it is understandable that it would take ELLs longer to reach this moving target than to reach a more stable target such as the language of daily interactions, which is somewhat finite and fixed in nature.

Language proficiency develops in predictable stages across the areas of listening, speaking, reading, and writing. Children need time to learn a new language and make "errors" along the way; such errors indicate their hypotheses about their new language and show the influence their first language is exerting upon their guesses about their second language. Teachers can facilitate second language development by recognizing and responding to the student's current stage of proficiency. They should choose activities and structure the classroom discourse to support students' continued development to the next higher stage of proficiency (a type of "developmentally appropriate practice").

An important ingredient in language learning is the opportunity to use language or interaction in the target language. Second language learners make good use of peer models, and it is especially important for them to have planned interactions with proficient speakers. This holds true for written as well as spoken English. For this reason, we try to use many models and demonstrations when teaching English to second language learners because we know that they benefit tremendously from hearing or seeing how proficient speakers, readers, and writers of English perform.

Second language learners benefit from face-to-face interaction and the provision of opportunities to "try out" or use their new skills. The more stage-appropriate language learning opportunities provided, the more learning that can take place. When ESL learners are part of whole class activities, they may remain silent and not participate very much, because they may feel overwhelmed. However, if they are placed in smaller groups or pairs, they will have less threatening and more encouraging conditions in which to try out their new skills. In face-to-face interactions, students can get feedback about their performance (e.g., whether they are being understood, whether they are reading/writing something correctly).[18] Grouping structures that maximize student participation and active learning are therefore highly beneficial to ELLs.[19]

Another feature that assists ELLs is the provision of social support, which again can be the result of placing students in supportive group activities. Because working in a second language produces anxiety, tension, and often fatigue, having a partner or partners can help to lessen these detracting forces. The social support provided by working in a small group or with a partner is very beneficial to the learning process because partners can provide encouragement and feedback, and can also share the workload in completing projects and assignments.[20]

A final aspect that assists second language learners is to receive stage-appropriate input and for teachers to use elicitation or questioning strategies that encourage stage-appropriate output from learners.[21] Because second language learning proceeds in recognizable stages, teachers who control their discourse make it possible for students to be full participants in the classroom. "Scaffolded" second language instruction—that is, verbal instruction that is accompanied by visuals, actions, demonstrations, models, and the like—is very helpful to English language learners because the message is coming through several channels at once. Thus, multisensory instruction is very beneficial. Checking on comprehension is another important step when working with second language learners to be sure that the messages are getting through.

Table 6.1 describes the characteristics of learners at different stages and how teachers can modify their interactions with each group of learners (e.g., the ways each group of learners could be asked to respond during instruction) to ensure their participation.[22]

In discussing second language acquisition, it is important to remember the importance of the student's first language as it relates to the acquisition of the second language. This is because a student's native language serves as the base for second language development. When solidly developed, it provides students with capabilities and skills that act as a springboard for the development of the second language. When underdeveloped, it can undermine future language learning.[23]

Rumberger and Larson have documented that greater fluency in English, in and of itself, does not necessarily equate to educational success for Latino students, whereas bilingualism and biculturalism do.[24] These researchers found that students who had a strong foundation in their native culture and a comfortable command of English had the best academic performance. They had higher grades, showed more commitment to education, and were more likely to be on track with their high school credits than were either English only or limited English proficient students. They conclude that "ethnic identity does affect success" and that schools need to ensure that students feel proud of their heritage and culture.[25]

Solid native language development promotes a strong identity as a speaker of a particular language. This, in turn, can positively influence self-esteem and self-confidence, two qualities essential to high levels of achievement and school success. Maintenance of the native language also supports healthy family functioning in cases where parents are predominantly speakers of a language other than English.[26] Therefore, teachers should demonstrate a healthy respect for students' native languages and act in ways that protect the language rights of children and families. At the same time, they also have an obligation to promote the learning of English, but this can be done in an "additive" way rather than one that "takes away" from who students are and what they need to fully function in the wider community.

The value of bilingualism and biliteracy and the concept of language as asset were endorsed by former Secretary of Education Richard Riley when he stated, "It is high time we begin to treat language skills as the asset they are, particularly in this global economy. Anything that encourages a person to know more than one language is positive—and should be treated as such."[27] He urged American educators to encourage bilingualism, biculturalism, and biliteracy among all young people and to challenge young

Table 6.1.
Characteristics of Learners at Different Stages of Language Acquisition

Preproduction	Early Production	Speech Emergence	Intermediate Fluency
minimal comprehension no verbal pro- duction	limited comprehension one/two word responses	increased comprehension; simple sentences	very good comprehension; more complex sentences
listen	name	recall	analyze
point	label	retell	create
move	group	define	defend
mime	respond	explain	debate
match	discriminate	compare	predict
draw	list	summarize	criticize
select	categorize	describe	simplify
choose	tell/say	role-play	evaluate
act out	answer	restate	justify
circle	identify	contrast	support
underline	complete	differentiate	generate
chart	classify	record	hypothesize
find	produce	recite	synthesize
follow		speak	formulate
locate			infer
			develop
			expand
			modify
			propose
			systematize

people with high standards, high expectations, and curriculum in two languages.

The National Association for the Education of Young Children (NAEYC) urges teachers to recognize that children can and will acquire the use of English even when their home language is used and respected.[28] Therefore, it is unnecessary, even counterproductive, to urge students to cease to use their primary language in favor of English. Instead, teachers should counsel parents to support and preserve home language usage as the foundation for future linguistic and cognitive development at school.

Teachers and parents alike need to fully understand that a mother tongue is as important to development as having a mother; it impacts children's emotional, social, cognitive, and linguistic development in similarly profound ways. (Some strategies for promoting the primary languages of all students, irrespective of whether or not school personnel speak these languages, are outlined in the Tips for Educators at the end of this chapter.)

HOW TO COLLABORATE WITH BILINGUAL/ESL TEACHERS AND PARAPROFESSIONALS TO DELIVER INSTRUCTION TO STUDENTS

The Difference Between Bilingual Education and ESL

Bilingual education is a type of school program in which a language other than English is used along with English to provide instruction to students. Bilingual education programs are of several major types: transitional bilingual education (TBE), developmental or maintenance bilingual education (DBE), and two-way bilingual education or dual language immersion programs. According to Cloud, Genesee, and Hamayan, transitional bilingual education (also referred to as early-exit bilingual education) is a program in which language minority students' primary language is used for some instruction for a limited number of years—in most states, three.[29] Such instruction is designed to promote the students' mastery of academic material while they are learning English and to aid students with the transition to an all-English program. TBE programs do not aim to maintain or develop the students' primary language; rather, the emphasis is on exiting as quickly (and hopefully successfully) as possible to participate in mainstream, or all-English, classrooms. Developmental bilingual programs, on the other hand, do intend to develop and maintain full proficiency in the students' home language while promoting full proficiency in English. This program is also known as late-exit bilingual education and, like TBE, is designed for language minority students only. A third major type of bilingual education program, two-way bilingual education (also known as two-way immersion [TWI] and dual language immersion [DLI]) serves both language minority and language majority students in the same classrooms. Two-way programs use both languages for instruction—that of the minority and that of the majority group—and aim for bilingualism and biculturalism for both groups of students.

English as a second language (ESL) instruction is a part of all of these programs and provides students with the opportunity to learn English as a second or additional language. Thus, ESL can be offered in conjunction with a bilingual education program or as a stand-alone program. In ESL classes or stand-alone programs, in addition to helping students to learn social English (the type needed to communicate in social situations) and academic English (the type needed to be successful in school settings and to master academically challenging material in English), teachers also assist students with the cultural adaptation process. Thus, ESL instruction has three goals: cultural adaptation, acquisition of social English, and the development of academic English to succeed on grade level. Currently, many districts are offering students "sheltered English" content area classes in addition to traditional ESL classes, where they learn subject-specific academic English while they learn the grade-level content associated with particular subject area classes required for their grade level. Thus, for example, students might have a designated ESL class, plus several sheltered English content area classes (social studies, mathematics, science, health, etc.) that make up their instructional day.

As can be seen by this discussion, bilingual education and English as a second language have many important features in common in their attempts to assist English language learners in achieving success at school. The main difference between the two is that bilingual education actively uses a student's native language as well as English to promote academic achievement, whereas ESL programs do not make use of the student's native language in any substantive way to support learning. The relative merits of each approach depend on the needs of students and the educational goals set by the district.[30] Educational outcomes vary predictably by the model selected, the resources available to support the model, the educational needs of students, and the wishes of families and communities for particular educational outcomes for their youngsters. Yet, research shows that students enrolled in strong bilingual programs—those with rich cognitive and academic instruction in students' primary languages—benefit from these programs and that the benefits are cumulative. The more years first-language–based plus English-language–based instruction is present, the greater the students' eventual English-based achievement.[31]

How Best to Plan for Language Use at School and at Home

Whether or not a bilingual approach is used to educate students at school, families should always use their most proficient language to interact with their children at home. This is because when parents use their most proficient language with their children, (1) they serve as better (more competent) linguistic models for their children; (2) they typically interact more frequently with their children because they have greater comfort communicating in that language; (3) the cognitive load (cognitive complexity and cognitive content) of their messages is higher because they are capable of fully expressing their exact meaning and sharing their thinking process more completely with their child; and (4) they have more enriching and more frequent mediated learning interactions with their children. The truth is that the quantity and quality of child-parent interactions in the home are far more important than in what language these interactions take place. Indeed, children with strong foundations in their primary language, especially those who develop literacy in their native language, make the transition to English more smoothly than those without such foundations.[32]

To help your children develop cognitively, linguistically, and academically to their fullest potential, you should:

- Speak your strongest language to your child, and interact often with your child so that he/she hears and uses lots of language.
- Give your child access to English spoken by proficient speakers outside of school if possible (for example, through after-school or community-based activities).
- Read to and with your child, and have your child read as much as possible.
- Actively support and maintain the native language at home so your child can have the advantages of proficient bilingualism.

To answer many of the questions you might have about raising your child bilingually, including your child with special learning needs, see *The Bilingual Family: A Handbook for Parents* (second edition, 2003), by Edith Harding-Esch and Philip Riley. This book has practical advice for parents who want their child to grow up to be a proficient bilingual.

This advice is particularly crucial for parents of students with special learning needs, since their cognitive and/or linguistic abilities may be compromised. Language use and development policies at school must consider students' current and future communicative needs at home and in the community. It is not adaptive to blindly teach children in English only when we know that to be adaptive in their homes and communities they must be able to communicate in a language other than English. We know that the family support they will need to be successful must be strengthened, not weakened, and therefore we will want to make sure that communication at home is strengthened by the policies promoted by school personnel with respect to language use and development. Sometimes this will mean that the language recommended for use at home will differ from the one being used at school, especially where the family speaks a low incidence language which is impossible to offer to students at school.

One way of unifying what goes on at school with what goes on at home is to work on the same goal or objective across languages. For example, if the school is working with a student on an expressive language objective such as naming and requesting items, the home could be instructed to work on the same objective in the home language. Researchers have documented that, even in cases where cognitive functioning is compromised (say in the case of students with moderate mental retardation), spontaneous transfer from one language to another and separation of the two languages can be accomplished.[33] Indeed, Greenlee concludes that

> bilingual proficiency is not beyond the grasp of children experiencing developmental disabilities. Rather, the extent to which individual children have in fact, progressed toward this goal has probably not been fully appreciated . . . one need not assume that a single-language policy is most beneficial; in fact, it may ignore linguistic skills which are important to the child and his community.

Gutierrez-Clellen agrees, stating that "children who are learning two languages may benefit from a bilingual approach in intervention. . . . [M]ediation in the native language does not slow development or learning of a second language."[34]

Therefore, if it is true that children develop language to the extent of their cognitive capacity, they are capable of acquiring the same range of skills in all of their primary learning environments (and in the language required by the environment). This learning can be actively facilitated by all parties by working together on the same learning goals across the child's learning and linguistic environments. If the home and school are able to work in the same language, of course this is desirable, but the development of students' skills and abilities can occur within the same language or across languages as necessary.

Ways to Collaborate with Bilingual/ESL Teachers and Paraprofessionals to Deliver Instruction to Students

There are so many ways special educators and general educators can collaborate with bilingual and ESL teachers and paraprofessionals to deliver instruction to students. These run the same gamut of options as with any other type of instruction delivered through a collaborative service delivery arrangement.

Kang outlines three types of collaboration that may prove useful: (1) coordination of curriculum and instruction; (2) collaborative creation of resources; and (3) training and consultation among teachers and specialists.[35] While Kang's recommendations were formulated to assist second language readers in mainstream content area classes, they will be applied more broadly to all collaborative efforts of teachers in the discussion that follows.

Coordination of curriculum and instruction can be accomplished through collaborative planning, a mechanism that helps teachers overcome the all-too-frequent fragmentation that can exist for students across their instructional day. This type of planning not only strengthens instruction for students by linking what they are learning in one environment with what they are learning in another, but also improves the collegial atmosphere of schools and teaching satisfaction.

The collaborative creation of resources is a second way of strengthening instruction. When working together, the ESL or bilingual teacher can adapt materials for the language and cultural needs of learners, while the special educator can assist in adapting materials for the special learning needs of students. In this manner, materials are fully adapted to ensure success, rather than partially modified for one learner characteristic while leaving the others completely unaddressed.

By sharing their knowledge and expertise, teachers can get needed advice on specific students and their needs, on teaching approaches and curriculum materials, and on how to successfully interact with culturally diverse families. Over time, through the process of collegial collaboration, the ability of all teachers to function independently and successfully with culturally and linguistically diverse exceptional learners will be attained. Voltz describes various ways for professionals to share their knowledge and expertise, including (1) information-sharing sessions where experts can share their knowledge with teachers; (2) peer exchange sessions, where teachers can brainstorm ways to assist students who are experiencing difficulty; and (3) peer coaching, where teachers who are implementing new strategies are given support and feedback from their more experienced peers.[36] She suggests that collaborative consultation can take place among professionals and/or among professionals and families to better support the educational process.

HOW TO PLAN CULTURALLY RESPONSIVE CURRICULUM AND INSTRUCTION

Dimensions That Make Curriculum and Instruction Culturally Relevant

Curriculum/Materials. As previously noted, use of materials that represent the values and norms, life experiences, and culturally determined background knowledge of students can greatly facilitate learning. Materials should also be free from stereotypes and positively represent the great diversity that exists within American classrooms. Santos, Fowler, Corso, and Bruns outline tips for selecting culturally appropriate materials for early childhood special education programs. They suggest, for example, that teachers get to know the children and families they serve in order to check for congruence between the curriculum materials and practices they are implementing.[37] At a minimum, teachers should survey the materials in use to ascertain if the materials represent well the families and communities they serve. One curriculum diversification strategy is use of multicultural children's literature[38] to honor the students in the classroom, develop an appreciation for diversity, and prompt critical inquiry about self and others.

Teaching Strategies/Approaches. Methods and strategies must be culturally responsive. This means that teachers must carefully consider whether cooperative versus competitive, adult-directed versus learner-centered, or discovery learning versus direct teaching approaches are best suited to the needs and characteristics of particular learners. Initially, culturally familiar strategies and routines could be used; however, over time, students' repertoires should be expanded to create comfort with teaching strategies and approaches commonplace in American classrooms.

Interpersonal Interactions. Children acquire preferred communication patterns and interpersonal interaction styles through culturally specific childrearing processes. From their interactions in their families and communities children learn (1) the amount of verbalization expected in interactions; (2) the distance maintained between speakers; (3) the amount of physical contact expected; (4) the amount and type of interaction expected across gender and age lines; and (5) the dominant roles they should assume in communicative interactions (listener/speaker).[39] All of these expectations come to school with children and affect classroom life. Teachers must fully understand the sociocultural dimensions of teaching/learning environments so that they can interact with learners in ways that create comfort in the classroom.[40] They also must interpret behavior in culturally appropriate ways—for example, not mislabeling a child who is behaving according to his/her cultural standards as "shy," "reluctant," "nonparticipatory," etc.

Management of Space and Time. Two dimensions are worth note in this category: wait time and personal space. Each cultural group has norms as to how a person is to be questioned, how many times a question can be asked before it is assumed the speaker cannot provide a response, how long one waits for a response to be given, and what the listener might do during the wait time to encourage a response (e.g., ask the question again, gently urge the speaker to respond, wait quietly, etc.). These norms can vary tremendously. The Anglo-American wait time norm is relatively brief, as indicated by the times generally indicated on norm-referenced, standardized tests—as short as fifteen to thirty seconds. However, for other cultural groups, the wait time can be extensive and feel excruciatingly painful to someone socialized to wait only thirty seconds. If teachers wait their "normal" amount of time and students fail to answer, they may assume erroneously that students cannot answer, whereas the students may be working within their own expected time frame to construct and provide a response, or may be waiting to be asked a second time before answering in order to be perceived as sufficiently well mannered or polite.

Likewise, the concept of "personal space" varies tremendously among cultural groups. The traditional Anglo-American norm is to have desks in rows with sufficient space between them (i.e., personal space). Even in co-operatively arranged classrooms, space is engineered in certain ways to give each student "enough" space. Where the distance provided is greater or less than that required by some students, this can trigger negative perceptions among the participants (e.g., "s/he's all over me") or overall discomfort in the learning environment (e.g., students feeling they cannot work well in the space provided).

A simple solution is to ask students their preferences—"Did I give you enough time to think about your answer?" "How shall we arrange the desks so we can work well with each other?" Differences among students can be discussed in class meetings and flexible arrangements made wherever possible to accommodate everyone who has a strong preference. Personalizing the learning environment is very important, especially in culturally diverse classrooms.

How to Design Linguistically Responsive Instruction

How to Make Classroom Instruction Comprehensible for Second Language Learners. According to Zehler, an accepting and predictable environment is very important for second language learners because when students understand classroom expectations and routine tasks, they are free to concentrate on learning.[41] Zehler notes that teachers have two major teaching objectives: to maximize opportunities for language use and to provide support for students' communicative interactions.[42]

This means that teachers must (1) monitor and adapt their speech for the particular stages of proficiency present in their ELL student population; (2) guide and facilitate students' efforts to communicate; (3) provide additional supports so that students can understand instruction provided in English (realia, visuals, graphic organizers, etc.); (4) interact frequently with ELLs; and (5) provide peer support and assistance through use of paired activities or small group learning.[43]

The following suggestions are frequently given for making instruction comprehensible for second language learners:

- Simplify your language as needed.
- Use demonstrations and modeling.
- Make use of all senses.

- Check frequently for understanding.
- Actively involve students.
- Allow more time for reaction.
- Adapt materials (language level; amount of text).
- Pair with students who speak the same language.
- Offer tutoring support outside of class.
- Write down important information (if literate).
- Use books in the primary language (if literate).
- Provide audiotapes for re-listening.
- Have varied ways of assessing students.
- Set reasonable expectations (in-class; grading policy).
- Offer tutoring inside/outside of class (peer; adult).

Critical Differences to Be Aware of When Teaching Reading to Second Language Learners

This section highlights five important aspects of teaching reading in a second language. First, it is important to remember that reading depends on sufficient oral language development[44] of young children; this will mean that, if initial reading is to be taught in a second language, the teacher should allow sufficient time to develop an adequate oral language base upon which literacy skills will be developed. With older children, especially in cases where literacy has already been developed in the primary language, a whole language approach should be used so that literacy and oral language in a second language are developed in tandem and deliberately.[45]

Second, students' background knowledge must be considered in the selection of texts (especially initial readers), as background knowledge and experience are important in assuring reading comprehension—even more important than surface vocabulary knowledge.[46] Likewise, culturally familiar topics should be used to promote writing development, since use of unfamiliar topics will inhibit students' ability to express themselves in writing.[47]

Third, bilingual/biliterate students have skills to transfer to English. Teachers should value literacy development in the primary language and support it, since it is well documented that knowing how to read and write in the first language supports the development of reading and writing in the second language.[48] Specific transfer effects should be expected and facilitated.[49]

Fourth, second language readers need multiple cueing systems to ensure comprehension. This means that use of texts with known vocabulary and predictable or patterned language is a great aid to students. Having pictures that correspond to the text is also very helpful in supporting second language learners' reading comprehension, because if the linguistic cues are not understood, the picture is there for backup. Indeed, the selection of supportive, stage-appropriate text is probably the single most important thing teachers can do to support second language learners in learning to read in a second language.[50] Fifth, it is typically not very easy for second language learners to use phonics-based decoding approaches, especially in the early stages, as the phonemes of the second language are not very well established, if at all, and may compete with phonetic knowledge the learners bring from their primary languages. This would be identical to asking an English speaker who is new to Japanese to "sound it out," an improbable task when the speaker is completely new to the sounds of Japanese. Since learners are still acquiring these sounds, they will most likely rely instead on the phonics they do know (in this case not Japanese sounds, but English ones) to try to comply with the request. For this reason, whole word/sight word approaches (meaning-centered approaches) are much more appropriate for the early stages of second language literacy development than "synthetic" approaches where sounds are put together to build words. While it is true that phonics is very important, especially to writing, the timing of the introduction of this skill is important when working with second language learners, making certain that you are drawing on sounds that have been established. It is also important to note that in terms of use of "inventive" spelling in writing, teachers will notice "cross-lingual inventive" spelling—where letters are selected to represent sounds drawing from what learners know about phonics from all of their languages (for example, students who write "escul" for "school" are using what they know about both Spanish and English sound-symbol correspondence and drawing on their pronunciation of the word and letter/sound correspondence in Spanish to represent that word in writing).

How to Adapt Textbooks for Second Language Learners

Materials must be appropriate to the age level, grade level, and proficiency characteristics of learners. Often, this means that materials must be adapted, since, while materials might be appropriate to the age or grade level, they might exceed the proficiency characteristics of learners of English. In order to modify materials, Short recommends that teachers (1) create a graphic depiction of the text (photographs, drawings, graphic organizers); (2) highlight main points in the text or provide an outline of the text; (3) write a summary of the text simplifying the language (controlling the vocabulary used, simplifying the grammar, and structuring paragraphs carefully); (4) shorten the amount of reading required; (5) create audiotapes to accompany the text or to stand alone in place of the text; (6) provide live demonstrations (e.g., role plays) or use film to bring the text material to life; and/or (7) use alternate materials (low readability, high interest materials; native language materials).[51] Teachers can also use marginal glosses (notes in the margin calling students' attention to specific details of importance), vocabulary guides (explanations written at the student's language level), and structured overviews or advanced organizers (which orient students to key concepts and vocabulary in a unit) to assist students in comprehending textbooks written in English.[52]

How to Group Students to Maximize the Language and Cross-Cultural Learning Opportunities in the Classroom

How to Use Peer Support to Aid Second Language Learners. There is substantial evidence that peer interaction is very beneficial to language learning.[53] This is because, through peer interaction, learners gain opportunities to use language and to get feedback on their language use—two crucial prerequisites for language development. Because students are not directly focused on language learning but rather use language to interact with others as they socialize or study meaningful and challenging content, language acquisition takes place as a by-product of these interactions with others. Some believe that the critical social interaction that promotes language development can best be accomplished by having students work with others on projects, through the use of cooperative learning activities[54] or through other active learning methodologies, such as using manipulatives, constructing visual organizers, use of one-on-one conferencing, dialogue journals, etc.[55]

Some Basic Ways to Use Grouping to Facilitate Learning. According to Fern, Anstrom, and Silcox, "small group, one-on-one instruction with the teacher, peer dyads, and individual student-directed activities should be used."[56] Student groupings can be homogeneous or heterogeneous in nature, accounting for both language proficiency characteristics of the students and their content level knowledge or skills levels. Most experts agree that use of a range of groupings, or flexible grouping, is the best approach. By using homogeneous and heterogeneous group composition and varied group structures (dyads, triads, small groups, large groups), teachers can maximize their teaching effectiveness. The teaching objective, phase of the lesson, and nature of the learning activity should determine the grouping structure to be used. For example, whole class instruction is common when introducing a new topic to students, when clarifying a concept, or when reviewing at the end of a unit. Small groups are useful when providing direct instruction to ability groups, for projects, or to encourage discussion. Pairs are very useful when practicing skills and for providing individual support and feedback. Individual practice (independent work) is also necessary to advance skill development.

One way in which grouping has proved beneficial in special education and second language settings is through the use of peer tutoring. Cross-age and peer tutoring have a range of positive outcomes for students. These student-centered learning arrangements have been shown to positively contribute to social, language, and cognitive development of both the tutors and the tutees. Learning, friendship, and social growth are frequent outcomes of such learning arrangements because they provide opportunities for skill learning through peer modeling, assistance, and emotional support.[57] However, it is important to note that such grouping arrangements must be carefully planned and structured, with adequate training provided to the tutors, in order for these grouping structures to achieve their beneficial results.[58]

Grouping also permits teachers to give students more plentiful feedback or to encourage peer or self-evaluation to take place. The provision of feedback is critical to language acquisition. Explicit correction, especially self-correction, seems to be more useful to learners than implicit correction (recasting a student's utterance to make it correct); however, such feedback needs to be done sensitively (with encouragement) and with a focus on the meaning conveyed.[59] Peer and self-assessment provides students with a greater sense of responsibility for and involvement in their own learning. With such assessment, students come to understand the criteria that define expert performance and the objectives of instruction. They can also learn to identify their own strengths and weaknesses and begin to understand where they need to place more attention in order to attain greater success.[60]

Community building is enhanced through cooperative learning and small group approaches. This is important because it is well accepted that language learning takes place best where the "affective filter" is low,[61] meaning where anxiety is low and students feel comfortable and capable. Likewise, in special education environments, we know that the provision of peer and adult support is very important to maintaining motivation and to overall student achievement and success. Working on projects in groups, establishing well-functioning learning teams, having students give each other encouragement and feedback, and providing opportunities for students to share what they know are all concrete ways of helping students to establish the social connections that support learning. In turn, these improved relationships among students lead to better attitudes toward school, increased learning, and higher self-esteem—all goals of quality programs.[62]

HOW TO WORK EFFECTIVELY WITH CLD FAMILIES

The importance of family involvement to student achievement is undisputed. Family involvement is also guaranteed in all special education legislation, particularly in the development and monitoring of the student's Individualized Education Plan (IEP). Yet, differential patterns of parental participation with schools have been noted across socioeconomic, ethnic, and linguistic lines.[63] Since this is the case, the economic, cultural, linguistic, and psychological factors that contribute to these patterns need to be understood by school personnel in order to establish strong working relationships with families.[64]

This section is organized to provide some insights into why certain patterns may exist and how school personnel might address the factors that prevent parents from becoming full participants. In some cases, the mechanisms traditionally used to foster parental participation may need to be reshaped to reach particular parent groups. Even more fundamental to the whole notion of parental participation, the very definition of what it means to participate may need to be reconsidered in order to honor and acknowledge the culturally determined notions of "participation" that are so deeply rooted in the consciousness of the parents of our students as well as in us.

First and foremost, the definition of "family" needs to correspond to that of the particular group in question. School personnel need to determine if "the family" is restricted to members of the nuclear family or involves members of the larger extended family. For example, in some attenuated families, "the family" may be comprised of a mother and her children along with live-in grandmothers, aunts, and cousins, rather than the more traditional father, mother, and children.

The roles played by the members of the extended family may be significant. For example, the aforementioned study by the American Association of Retired Persons documented that 11 percent of all grandparents are either raising a grandchild or providing daycare on a regular basis.[65] Among African Americans, about 20 percent, or one in five grandparents, are doing so; in contrast, one in ten white grandparents are this closely involved in their grandchildren's lives.[66] Therefore, in addition to determining the members of the family, providers must also understand the roles of each member, how responsibility for childrearing is distributed, and who will participate in making school-related decisions if we are to collaborate successfully in planning for the child.[67]

How Culture Influences Parental Expectations of Schools

The literature on parent involvement suggests that the following types of parental involvement are helpful to students enrolled in U.S. schools:

(1) provision of a stimulating literacy and material environment; (2) high expectations and moderate levels of parental support and supervision; (3) appropriate monitoring of television viewing and homework completion; (4) participating in joint learning activities at home; (5) emphasis on effort over ability; and (6) autonomy-promoting parenting practices.[68]

Expectations of "parental involvement" need to be framed in culturally sensitive ways.[69] Whereas in the United States parental involvement is usually defined as engagement in school activities (parent meetings, participation in school events) and support provided at home around school-related tasks (supervision of homework completion, asking students what is going on at school, reading to students at home), in some cultures parents consider that they are fully performing their role if they fulfill their parental obligations—for example, meeting the basic needs of their child and providing a loving home environment. They view school professionals as having the training necessary to educate their child and as best equipped to make school-related decisions.[70] Therefore, in cases where parents view each party as having dramatically different and completely independent roles to play in the life of the child, they truly do not understand why they are being asked to make educational decisions or why school personnel are involving themselves in matters of the home.

Education in many Latin American countries is fashioned after the European model, which is highly centralized at the national level. Major policy decisions are made by a ministry of education with limited or virtually no control by parents.[71] There are no such organizations as PTAs, and democratic decision making does not exist; rather, the system is hierarchical. When parents come from countries in which all decision making was done above and without them, they have no reason to expect, or skills to engage in, active participation with schools.

According to DeGaetano, Williams, and Volk, whether or not parents participate in the ways American school personnel have come to expect, several assumptions should always underlie partnerships established with parents by school personnel.[72] Among them are the following:

- All parents want the best for their children, despite the fact that some parents know how to enable their children to obtain these things, while others do not.

- A lot of learning goes on in the home that can have a positive effect on children's overall growth and development, and much of it is not school-related but complementary to it.

- Parents support their children's school learning in a variety of ways irrespective of socioeconomic levels. For example, some may verbally encourage their children, but they may not actively help them do their homework. Others may sit with their children while they do their homework, while still others may not encourage their children's schoolwork in any way. This wide variability in parents' abilities, skills, and motivation to help, as well as in the time they have available to do so, must be assessed realistically and respectfully understood by school personnel.

At the same time, families of children with disabilities may have additional stresses that make it difficult for them to play the roles that schools may want them to play in the education of their children. It is important to understand the "big picture" and not to detract from the parents' ability to perform their most essential functions—that of providing for the emotional well-being and physical needs of their child—by overwhelming them with additional demands that they may not feel competent or able to fulfill.

For all of these reasons, an individualized parent involvement approach is recommended, since "we recognize that parents will participate at different levels and in different ways depending on their own educational experiences, their interests, comfort levels, and understandings."[73] Gaetano, Williams, and Volk recommend that we offer parents ways of being involved at home and at school, as well as at the district level. Since the school and district level roles are better known by teachers, the paragraph that follows describes parents who feel most comfortable restricting their efforts to the home. To date, this essential role of parents has been undervalued, but recent research[74] shows that parental engagement at home is even more important than parental involvement at school.

Those parents that are involved solely at home make sure their children are healthy, safe, and cared for. They can also provide schedules for children to do homework, listen to them read, and listen and respond to them as they talk about what happened at school, as time and comfort level with these tasks permits. Such tasks are consistently associated with school success.[75] To facilitate teacher-parent communication, teachers can communicate with parents when they drop off or pick up their children at school, or through phone calls, notes, periodic newsletters, personal letters, or home-school communication journals or notebooks. When possible, teachers might also make home visits or hold meetings in sites that are familiar to the parents. Social events can lead to more formal school-based information-sharing events once trust is established, yet all meetings must respond to some need or concern of parents, rather than just the needs of school personnel.[76] Whatever the best mechanism for each individual family, teachers will want to ask for parents' input and ideas, invite parents to share their concerns, and maintain warmth and respect in all their communication.

It is essential to remember that if parents do not come into the school, this should not automatically be construed to mean that they do not care about their child's education. It may only mean that they may feel more comfortable in caring for and nurturing the child's development at home or that they believe that this is the "proper" role for parents—not "meddling" at school. In addition, many of these families view the concept of a "well-educated" person broadly, within which academic development at school is only a part. Therefore, they see the role they play at home in "educating" their child to be as important as what goes on at school in terms of the child's overall well-being and healthy functioning as a member of a family and of society.[77]

Overcoming Known Barriers to Working Effectively with CLD Families

As outlined by Winzer and Mazurek, some barriers to effective parent-school partnerships include (1) giving parents late notices of meetings or being inflexible when scheduling conferences; (2) limited time for conferences; (3) emphasis on documents rather than participation; (4) use of distancing jargon; (5) a structure of power in which parents feel at a disadvantage, or parental perception that educators are authority figures to be avoided; (6) lack of information about rights and duties under federal special education policy; (7) minimal parental participation at conferences and meetings; and (8) the intimidating formality of the structure of the IEP itself.[78] In addition, Greene and Nefsky point out that the parents' dominant language and level of acculturation, their cultural group's attitudes toward persons with disabilities, the family's knowledge of and comfort with the school infrastructure, as well as special educators' level of knowledge about and sensitivity to linguistically and culturally diverse peoples, can also serve to limit meaningful collaboration.[79] Because meetings often take place in a language in which the parents do not yet have full proficiency or through a translator, the failure to establish a true and meaningful collaboration with families is likely. Add to this the limited time some parents have available due to their need to support themselves and to adjust to a new life in a new language and culture, and it is even easier to understand why parent-school collaboration is difficult to establish. However, what is important in interpreting parents' limited participation, especially their ability to come to school, is not to presume that this speaks to their interest in their child's education. Parents may be very interested in their child's education, but long working hours, economic needs, and educational, psychological, cultural, and linguistic barriers may make it difficult for them to participate in the traditional ways.[80]

Some solutions proposed for overcoming these barriers are personalizing communication and helping parents understand the importance of their role; engaging in more open-ended communication with parents (e.g., sending questions to parents to consider prior to the meeting so that they can be better prepared to make substantive contributions); making home visits or making schools more welcoming to parents when they arrive at the school; having parent advocates on staff (e.g., school counselors); giving parents extra time at meetings and the opportunity to ask questions; avoiding educational jargon and explaining terms fully; fully and clearly informing parents as to the special education policies and procedures as well as the meaning of the decisions being made as they pertain to their child's education; and conducting the meeting in the language of the parent.[81]

Effective communication practices are central to this process—use of bilingual professionals, reduction of technical jargon, decreased reliance on written communication in cases where such communication is not very effective, increased face-to-face communication, active listening to both verbal and nonverbal messages communicated by parents, providing liaison personnel to parents through whom they can establish communication with the school and its personnel, and, most important, giving parents real options and choices and allowing them to choose what is best for their child.[82]

Making Proper Use of Translators and Interpreters

According to Winzer & Mazurek, when an interpreter is used, "that person should be trained in cross-cultural interpretation, have knowledge of the special education system, and be proficient in the language of the family and English."[83] Langdon[84] and Langdon and Cheng[85] specify that while having translators can facilitate parental involvement, translators should be well selected (e.g., demonstrate proficiency and cross-cultural competence) and explicitly trained for the roles they will perform. They must learn how to schedule parent-teacher conferences, administer tests, and interpret results during conferences when IEPs are formulated; they must understand and be able to explain special education terminology to parents; they must be culturally sensitive and responsive; they must know the special education administrative procedures and placement alternatives required under the law and be able to explain the full range of options to parents; they must be able to read and write both languages; and they must be trustworthy and maintain all rules of confidentiality.

SUMMARY

All teachers must have the ability to work with students with diverse learning needs. This includes children of varied ability backgrounds from culturally and linguistically diverse homes.

In this chapter, we have reviewed the practical things teachers can do to support students who are learning through a second language and to make their instruction more culturally responsive. We have also reviewed pertinent information about working with culturally and linguistically diverse families.

The ability to include students who are culturally and linguistically diverse is an essential skill for today's special educator. In addition to consulting the additional resources and references mentioned in this chapter, teachers may wish to contact professional associations and organizations (for example, the Division of Culturally and Linguistically Diverse Exceptional Learners [DDEL] at http://www.cec.sped.org) to connect with other interested educators or for additional information.

Tips for Educators

✎ Understand the value of and demonstrate respect for students' languages and cultures. Encourage parents to interact with their children in the language in which they are most proficient and to strengthen their children's cultural identities.

✎ Recognize and respond to students' current stage of English language proficiency in all instructional interactions. Tailor instructional language demands to make sure that students receive "comprehensible input." Complement verbal instruction with nonverbal support (visuals; hands-on, multisensory experiences).

✎ Learn as much as possible about the cultural values, norms, and preferred modes of interaction of the students you teach. Make curriculum, teaching strategies, interpersonal interactions, and use of time and space as culturally responsive as possible.

✎ Use familiar themes when teaching reading and writing to support comprehension and expression. Build oral language to support literacy activity. Emphasize getting and expressing meaning over isolated skill development.

✎ Enhance collaboration among all professionals working with the student to ensure that instruction makes sense. Reach out to families to coordinate efforts at school and at home.

✎ Use environmental print in the home languages of students in classrooms.

✎ Provide the school and classroom libraries with books, magazines, and other resources in languages other than English.

✎ Encourage students to publish books in their native languages and to share their stories in languages other than English.

✎ Have students read and write with others (aides, parents, or other students) who speak their native languages.

✎ Use professionally and student-produced multimedia (video, audio, CD-ROM, software) resources to support academic learning and raise self-esteem.[86]

Tips for Parents

✎ Let teachers know how you support your child at home (for example, providing encouragement; making sure your child gets enough sleep and completes assignments; talking with and reading to your child; taking your child on weekend excursions or other family trips; talking with your child about the importance of school).

✎ Let teachers know of any constraints that make it difficult for you to participate as much as you would like in school-related activities (for example, meetings about your child's progress). For example, let teachers know if your work schedule, lack of transportation, or childcare responsibilities make it difficult for you to make meetings during the day. Let teachers know if other family priorities make it difficult for your child to complete all assigned schoolwork.

✎ Let teachers know of any concerns you have about your child and ask how they might assist you to investigate and respond to these concerns.

✎ Let teachers know of your child's strengths, special gifts, and talents.

✎ Let teachers know of family wishes for your child regarding the maintenance and development of the primary language. If you intend for your child to be bilingual, enlist the support of teachers in promoting this goal.

TO LEARN MORE

- *Developing Cross-Cultural Competence: A Guide for Working with Children and Their Families,* by Eleanor W. Lynch and Marci J. Hanson. 2nd ed. Baltimore: Paul H. Brookes Publishing Co., 1998. In addition to defining cross-cultural competence, provides information regarding Anglo-European families, Native American families, African American families, Latino families, Filipino families, Native Hawaiian and Samoan families, and Middle Eastern families.

- *Hispanic Children and Youth in the United States: A Resource Guide,* by Angela L. Carrasquillo. New York: Garland Publishing, 1991. Describes the diversity present within the Hispanic population (Mexican American, Puerto Rican, Cuban, Dominican, Central and South American) and refugee students. Also covers the greater Hispanic culture and its family structure and organization.

- *Kaleidoscope: A Multicultural Approach for the Primary School Classroom*, by Yvonne DeGaetano, Leslie R. Williams, and Dinah Volk. Upper Saddle River, NJ: Merrill, 1998. The chapter entitled "Culture: The Way to Begin" discusses ways of discovering the cultures of students and ways of understanding culture in the community.
- *Multicultural Students with Special Language Needs: Practical Strategies for Assessment and Intervention,* by Celeste Roseberry-McKibbin. 2nd ed. Oceanside, CA: Academic Communication Associates, 2002. Discusses cultural and linguistic variables affecting service delivery for immigrant and refugee families; religiously diverse learners; and Anglo European, African American, Hispanic, Asian, Native American, Pacific Islander, and Middle Eastern students.
- *Teaching Language Minority Students in the Multicultural Classroom*, by Robin Scarcella. Englewood Cliffs, NJ: Prentice Hall Regents, 1990. Has chapters titled "Interacting with Parents" and "Appreciating Cultural Diversity in the United States" providing information on specific Asian, Southeast Asian, and Latino groups.

NOTES

1. Waggoner, D. (2000, March). Public school districts report LEP enrollment. *Numbers and Needs* (Ethnic and Linguistic Minorities in the United States), *10*(2), 1–2.

2. Padolsky, D. (2002a). *How has the limited English proficient student population changed in recent years?* Ask NCELA No. 8. Washington, DC: National Clearinghouse for English Language Acquisition and Language Instruction Educational Programs.

3. Waggoner (2000, March), pp. 1–2.

4. Padolsky (2002a).

5. Thomas, W. P., & Collier, V. P. (2002). *A national study of school effectiveness for language minority students' long-term academic achievement. Final Report: Project 1.1.* Santa Cruz, CA: Center for Research on Education, Diversity and Excellence.

6. Riley, R. W. (2000, March 15). Excelencia para todos—Excellence for all: The progress of Hispanic education and the challenges of a new century. Speech delivered at Bell Multicultural High School, Washington, DC.

7. Riley (2000, March 15).

8. Archer, J. (2000, March). Minority teachers. *Number and Needs, 10*(2), 4.

9. Wald, J. L. (1996). *Culturally and linguistically diverse professionals in special education: A demographic analysis.* Reston, VA: National Clearinghouse for Professions in Special Education, the Council for Exceptional Children, p. 11.

10. Trueba, H. T. (1989). Cultural embeddedness: The role of culture on [*sic*] minority students' acquisition of English literacy. In *Competing visions of teacher knowledge: Proceedings from an NCRTE seminar for education policymakers, Vol. 2: Student diversity* (pp. 77–90). East Lansing: Michigan State University, National Center for Research on Teacher Education.

11. Cloud, N. (2002). Culturally and linguistically responsive instructional planning. In A.J. Artiles and A.A. Ortiz (Eds.), *English language learners with special education needs: Identification, assessment, and instruction* (pp. 107–132). Washington, DC: Center for Applied Linguistics; and Cloud, N. (1993). Language, culture and disability: Implications for instruction and teacher preparation. *Teacher Education and Special Education, 16*(1), 60–72.

12. Jacobs, L. (1991). Assessment concerns: A study of cultural differences, teacher concepts, and inappropriate labeling. *Teacher Education and Special Education, 14*(1), 43–48.

13. Hollins, E.R. (1996). *Culture in school learning: Revealing the deep meaning.* Mahwah, NJ: Lawrence Erlbaum Associates; and McDiarmid, G.W. (1989). What do teachers need to know about cultural diversity? Restoring subject matter to the picture. In *Competing visions of teacher knowledge,* pp. 91–106.

14. Hollins (1996).

15. AARP. (1999, November). The AARP grandparenting survey. Media, PA: IRC Survey Research.

16. Zehler, A.M. (1994, Fall). *Working with English language learners: Strategies for elementary and middle school teachers.* NCBE Program Information Guide Series, 19. Washington, DC: National Clearinghouse for Bilingual Education.

17. Collier, V.P. (1995, Fall). Acquiring a second language for school. *Directions in Language and Education, 1*(4); and Cummins, J. (1981). The role of primary language development in promoting educational success for language minority students. In *Schooling and language minority students: A theoretical framework* (pp. 3–49). Los Angeles: Evaluation, Dissemination, and Assessment Center, California State University.

18. Kagan, S. (1995, May). We can talk: Cooperative learning in the elementary ESL classroom. *ERIC Digest* (EDO-FL-95-08). Washington, DC: ERIC Clearinghouse on Languages and Linguistics, Center for Applied Linguistics.

19. Herrell, A., & Jordan, M. (2004). *Fifty strategies for teaching English language learners.* (2nd ed.). Upper Saddle River, NJ: Pearson/Merrill, Prentice Hall.

20. Kagan (1995, May); and Kagan, S. (1986). Cooperative learning and sociocultural factors in schooling. In California Department of Education (Ed.), *Beyond language: Social and cultural factors in schooling language minority students* (pp. 231–298). Los Angeles: California State University.

21. Collier (1995, Fall); and Herrell & Jordan (2004).

22. Wiessbrot, S. (1995). "Ensuring Quality Bilingual/ESL Instruction in New York City Schools. Paper presented at NYC Second Language Workshop.

23. Baker, C. (2001). *Foundations of bilingual education and bilingualism.* Clevedon, UK: Multilingual Matters; Cummins (1981); Gutierrez-Clellen, V. (1999). Language choice in intervention with bilingual children. *American Journal of Speech-Language Pathology, 8,* 291–302; TESOL. (1996). Promising futures: ESL standards for pre-K–12 students. TESOL Professional Paper #1. Alexandria, VA: Teachers of English to Speakers of Other Languages; and TESOL. (1997). *ESL standards for pre-K–12 students.* Alexandria, VA: Teachers of English to Speakers of Other Languages.

24. Rumberger, R.W., & Larson, K. (1998, May/June). *LMRI [Linguistic Minority Research Institute] Newsletter.*

25. Rumberger & Larson (1998, May/June), p. 1.

26. NAEYC. (1996). NAEYC position statement: Responding to linguistic and cultural diversity—Recommendations for effective early childhood education. *Young Children, 51*(2), 4–12.

27. Riley (2000, March 15).

28. NAEYC (1996).

29. Cloud, N., Genesee, F., & Hamayan, E. (2000). *Dual language instruction: A handbook for enriched education.* Boston: Heinle & Heinle.

30. Genesee, F. (Ed.) (1999). *Program alternatives for linguistically diverse students.* Santa Cruz, CA: Center for Research on Education, Diversity and Excellence (CREDE); and Rennie, J. (1993, September). ESL and bilingual program models. *ERIC Digest* (EDO-FL-94-01). Washington, DC: ERIC Clearinghouse on Languages and Linguistics, Center for Applied Linguistics.

31. Center for Research on Education, Diversity and Excellence. (1998, April 8). Findings on the effectiveness of bilingual education [press release]. Santa Cruz, CA: CREDE.

32. TESOL (1996); and TESOL (1997).

33. Greenlee, M. (1981). Specifying the needs of a "bilingual" developmentally disabled population: Issues and case studies. *NABE Journal, 6*(1), 55–76.

34. Gutierrez-Clellen (1999), p. 299.

35. Kang, H. W. (1994). Helping second language readers learn from content area text through collaboration and support. *Journal of Reading, 37*(8), 646–652.

36. Voltz, D. L. (1995). Learning and cultural diversities in general and special education classes: Frameworks for success. In B. A. Ford (Ed.), *Multiple voices for ethnically diverse exceptional learners* (pp. 1–11). Reston, VA: Division for Culturally and Linguistically Diverse Exceptional Learners, Council for Exceptional Children.

37. Santos, R. M., Fowler, S. A., Corso, R. M., & Bruns, D. A. (2000, January/February). Acceptance, acknowledgment, and adaptability: Selecting culturally and linguistically appropriate early childhood materials. *Teaching Exceptional Children, 32*(3), 14–22.

38. Taylor, S. V. (2000, January/February). Multicultural is who we are: Literature as a reflection of ourselves. *Teaching Exceptional Children, 32*(3), 24–29.

39. Cloud (2002); and Cloud (1993).

40. Zehler (1994, Fall).

41. Zehler (1994, Fall).

42. Zehler (1994, Fall).

43. Echevarria, J., Vogt, M. E., & Short, D. J. (2004). *Making content comprehensible for English language learners: The SIOP Model.* (2nd ed.). Boston: Allyn & Bacon; and Herrell & Jordan (2004).

44. Cloud, Genesee, & Hamayan (2000); Lynn, L. (1997). Language-rich home and school environments are key to reading success. Harvard Education Letter Research Online, http://www.edletter.org/past/issues/1997-ja/languages.html; and Pinnell, G. S., & Jaggar, A. M. (1991). Oral language: Speaking and listening in the classroom. In J. Flood, J. M. Jensen, D. Lapp, & J. R. Squire (Eds.), *Handbook of research on teaching the English language arts* (pp. 691–729). New York: Macmillan.

45. Cloud, Genesee, & Hamayan (2000); and Freeman, D. E., & Freeman, Y. S. (1992). *Whole language for second language learners.* Portsmouth, NH: Heinemann.

46. Cloud (2002); and Cloud (1993).

47. Cloud (2002); and Cloud, Genesee, & Hamayan (2000).

48. Thonis, E. (1983). *The English-Spanish connection.* Northvale, NJ: Santillana Publishing Co.

49. August, D., Calderon, M., & Carlo, M. (2001). The transfer of skills from Spanish to English: A study of young learners. *NABE News, 13.* Available at http://www.ncbe.gwu.edu/miscpubs/jeilms/vol13/transf13.htm; Cloud, Genesee, & Hamayan (2000); and Thonis (1983).

50. Cloud, Genesee, & Hamayan (2000).

51. Short, D. J. (1989, September). Adapting materials for content-based language instruction. *ERIC/CLL News Bulletin, 13*(1), 1, 4–8.

52. Leverett, R. G., & Diefendorf, A. O. (1992, Summer). Students with language deficiencies. *Teaching Exceptional Children, 24*(4), 30–34.

53. TESOL (1996); Herrell & Jordan (2004); and Gaies, S. J. (1985). *Peer involvement in language learning.* Orlando, FL: Harcourt Brace Jovanovich and the Center for Applied Linguistics.

54. Gallagher, J. (1998, October). The language of learning: Attacks on bilingual education ignore the varied needs of non-native speakers. *Middle Ground, 2*(2), 6–10, 24.

55. Fern, V., Anstrom, K., & Silcox, B. (1994). Active learning and the limited english proficient student. *Directions in Language and Education, 1*(2). Washington, DC: National Clearinghouse for Bilingual Education.

56. Fern, Anstrom, & Silcox (1994), p. 3.

57. Thomas, R. L. (1993). Cross-age and peer tutoring. *ERIC Digest* (EDO CS-93-01). Bloomington, IN: ERIC Clearinghouse on Reading and Communication Skills.

58. Thomas (1993).

59. Cloud, Genesee, & Hamayan (2000), pp. 77–78.

60. Cloud, Genesee, & Hamayan (2000), p. 159.

61. Krashen, S. (1982). *Principles and practice in second language acquisition.* Oxford, UK: Pergamon.

62. Collaborative for Academic, Social, and Emotional Learning (CASEL). (2003). *Safe and sound: An educational leader's guide to evidence-based social and emotional learning programs.* Chicago: CASEL.

63. Berliner, D. (1985). Is parent involvement worth the effort? *Instructor, 95,* 20–21; Garcia, D. (1990). Factors that determine and influence Hispanic parental involvement: Creating Parental Involvement. In D. Garcia, *A manual for school children and parents interacting program* (pp. 51–55). ERIC Reproduction Service Number ED 323 273. Miami: Florida International; University; Lynch, E. W., & Stein, R. (1987). Parent participation by ethnicity: A comparison of Hispanic, black and Anglo families. *Exceptional Children, 87,* 105–111; and Sontag, J. C., & Schacht, R. (1993). Family diversity and patterns of service utilization in early intervention. *Journal of Early Intervention, 17,* 431–444.

64. Garcia, S. B. (2002). Parent-professional collaboration in culturally sensitive assessment. In A. J. Artiles and A. A. Ortiz, pp. 87–103; Garcia (1990); Greene, G., & Nefsky, P. (1999). Transition for culturally and linguistically diverse youth with disabilities: Closing the gaps. In B. A. Ford (Ed.), *Multiple voices for ethnically diverse exceptional learners 1999* (pp. 15–24). Reston, VA: Council for Exceptional

Children; and Marion, R. L. (1982). Communicating with parents of culturally diverse exceptional children. In C. H. Thomas and J. L. Thomas (Eds.), *Bilingual special education resource guide* (pp. 52–65). Phoenix, AZ: Oryx Press.

65. AARP (1999, November).

66. Waggoner (2000, March), pp. 1–2, 4.

67. Garcia, S. B. (2002); and Garcia, S. B. (1995, June 12–13). Cultural influences on teaching and learning. Presentation at the Multicultural Special Education Summer Institute, Omaha, Nebraska.

68. Baker, A.J.L., & Soden, L. M. (1998). The challenges of parent involvement research. *ERIC/CUE Digest No. 134.* New York: ERIC Clearinghouse on Urban Education, Institute for Urban and Minority Education, Teachers College, Columbia University.

69. DeGaetano, Y., Williams, L., & Volk, D. (1998). *Kaleidoscope: A multicultural approach for the primary school classroom.* Columbus, OH: Merrill.

70. Greene & Nefsky (1999).

71. D. Garcia (1990); and DeGaetano, Williams, & Volk (1998), pp. 184–185.

72. DeGaetano, Williams, & Volk (1998), pp. 187–188.

73. DeGaetano, Williams, & Volk (1998), pp. 187–188.

74. Finn, J. D. (1998). Parental engagement that makes a difference. *Educational Leadership, 55*(8), 20–24.

75. Finn (1998).

76. Inger, M. (1992, August). Increasing the school involvement of Hispanic parents. *ERIC Digest No. 80.* New York: ERIC Clearinghouse on Urban Education, Institute for Urban and Minority Education, Teachers College, Columbia University.

77. Greene & Nefsky (1999).

78. Winzer, M. A., & Mazurek, K. (1998). *Special education in multicultural contexts.* Upper Saddle River, NJ: Merrill, p. 231.

79. Greene & Nefsky (1999), pp. 16–19.

80. S. B. Garcia (2002); and Winzer & Mazurek (1998), pp. 245–256.

81. S. B. Garcia (2002), pp. 87–103; and Winzer & Mazurek (1998), pp. 245–256.

82. S. B. Garcia (2002); and Greene & Nefsky (1999).

83. Winzer & Mazurek (1998), p. 263.

84. Langdon, H. W. (2002). *Interpreters and translators in communication disorders: A practitioner's handbook.* Eau Claire, WI: Thinking Publications.

85. Langdon, H. W., & Cheng, L. L. (2002). *Collaborating with interpreters and translators: A guide for communication disorders professionals.* Eau Claire, WI: Thinking Publications, p. 234.

86. Freeman, D. E., & Freeman, Y. S. (1993). Strategies for promoting the primary languages of all students. *The Reading Teacher, 46*(7), 552–558.

CHAPTER 7

Including Students with Emotional/Behavioral Problems

Melissa Price

Jeanette starts an argument with the teacher every time an independent writing assignment is given during class time. The argument typically escalates until Jeanette is sent to the principal's office. The end result is that the student waits in the main office for an overly taxed administrator who lectures about compliance and returns the student to her next scheduled class.

REASONS TO INCLUDE STUDENTS WITH EMOTIONAL/BEHAVIORAL DIFFICULTIES IN GENERAL EDUCATION CLASSROOMS

The question is not whether we should include students with emotional/behavioral difficulties; it is how we can best include them. Participation in the general education environment is not a question of privilege; it is a question of rights.[1] Students with emotional disabilities have the same rights as other students to gain access to the general education environment, given that the supports and services they need are provided to them. So the legal question is not whether we should include these students, but what it would take to successfully include them.

By definition, students with emotional/behavioral difficulties are not cognitively impaired (as a primary disability) and therefore have a good potential to succeed academically if their social/emotional needs are satisfactorily addressed. To succeed academically, students need access to the general education curriculum, which is most efficiently and effectively delivered in the general education setting by content area specialists who know the material. McGregor and Vogelsberg's review of research on inclusive practices cites forty-eight studies that seem to indicate that inclusion offers benefits to the social and academic life of students with disabilities.[2] Traditional self-contained special education classes tend to put similarly classified students together in small groups with well-intentioned special education teachers trained in behavior management techniques, but not typically well prepared to deal with a wide range of curriculum content.

Since the majority of research on the efficacy of inclusive programs has indicated positive social and emotional outcomes for all students, inclusion has the potential to be particularly advantageous to students with emotional/behavioral difficulties. Opportunities for positive relationships with nondisabled students are more likely to occur in inclusive classrooms that have structured supports.[3] Models of socially acceptable behaviors are less likely to exist in a self-contained, homogeneously grouped classroom.

IDENTIFYING STUDENTS WITH EMOTIONAL/ BEHAVIORAL DIFFICULTIES

Before we identify students, we must first consider what constitutes a behavior problem. The definition of a behavior "problem" is relative to the person defining the event. Calling an event "a problem" conveys the reality that someone perceives the event through a particular negative lens. Another question that might be asked is, "Whose problem is it?" If the person initiating an event, the peers viewing the event, and the parents of the initiator do not perceive the event as a problem, is it a problem simply because a teacher perceives it that way? This question leads us to issues of cultural and personal values. Often the difference between typical programs, alternative programs, and special education programs is how narrowly these lines are drawn. Interpersonal differences and tolerance levels of individual teachers may be the difference between a referral to special education and a casual annoyance with a student.

Respect and Compliance

Consider the following scenario and questions. If a student wears a baseball cap to class, his peers wear baseball caps to class, and parents consider this acceptable behavior, should the teacher discipline a student for this behavior or should school rules be adjusted to allow the event? Looking more deeply at the question of hats in school, what is the reason behind this rule? Is the underlying value statement best conveyed through this rule? Educators and administrators generally perceive removing one's hat in school as a measure of respect as demonstrated through compliance. Is an argument with a student over removing a hat the best way to build respect? If a culture of respect already exists, this is a request that most students will comply with quickly. However, where mutual respect is lacking, this argument is often a symptom of the problem and not the cause. Further, is unquestioning compliance always a desired outcome? A student who has experienced hair loss as a result of chemotherapy, for example, may value personal dignity above compliance with rules.

In situations like this, the values of the system (school, classroom, teacher) seem to differ from those of individual students. Starratt discusses this dilemma in educational administration as the conflict between the ethic of justice (consistent expectations applied to all) and the ethic of critique (the need to address the special circumstances of individuals and marginalized groups).[4] While it is important to consider special needs, erring on the side of the individual justice can be problematic as well. If illicit drug use is the cultural norm for a group of young people, should a student be excused from responsibility for illegal activities because he/she is responding to a different value system?

Certainly this debate continues in our larger society, but it is a particular burden to schools and teachers to feel the need to resolve issues that have immediate implications for students. These are the decisions plaguing schools and communities as they struggle to define the limits of individual rights versus universal justice. Schools routinely struggle with issues of dress code. Students have been suspended for carrying Midol, Tylenol, or other readily available over-the-counter medications under tougher "no drug rules." Recognition of and respect for cultural and personal value differences do not constitute a disregard for the "rules." An examination of the criteria for the selection and enforcement of the rules is the responsibility of each educator. This is where a school-wide discipline code that has been developed through consensus with the community, students, and school personnel is essential. The real questions are, whose "rules" are they, and are these rules valid? These fundamental questions are not merely academic philosophic ramblings. The first question heard from a confronted rule violator is often, "Yeah, who says??!!" Those in authority must have a satisfactory justification to meet this challenging response.

So, who are students with emotional/behavioral difficulties? If we are using a functional definition, not all students identified as having a behavioral problem will also have a disability. Most behavioral problems are defined in terms of frequency, duration, and intensity relative to the established expectations of the setting. Upon review, case studies of students identified as having behavior problems typically share three phenomena:

- students who have a pattern of acting out or violent behavior;
- behavior plans that stress consequences for inappropriate behaviors; and
- students whose values or needs are different from those of the authority figure reporting the problems.

SEVERE BEHAVIOR

Typically, acting out or violent behaviors illustrate an advanced degree of intensity. It only takes one violent episode to draw a "severe" label. However, some behaviors that persist despite interventions or whose duration outlasts the patience of an authority figure may fit this category as well. Students who are persistently verbally aggressive, belligerent, or simply disobedient may be identified as having severe behavior problems as well. Subtle, self-abusive, or self-deprecating behaviors may fit this category if they are persistent or become threatening to the well-being of the individual.[5] Consider the student who has an eating disorder. While this behavior is not necessarily intrusive to the classroom environment, it is no less destructive for the individual. Students with "behavior problems" are not synonymous with students with disabilities. "Emotional disability" is a label applied to students who are judged to meet the criteria for this definition.[6] The application of labels is inconsistent and often context reliant.[7] Similarly behaving students may be classified quite differently. One might be diagnosed as having emotional disabilities while others may be considered "socially maladjusted," "juvenile delinquents," or "at risk." First-time violent offenders may never have been previously identified, and students judged to have psychiatric disorders introduce yet another system of classifications.

Unless a label can serve as a doorway to remediation or alleviation, it is often useless at best, and stigmatizing at worst. Even labeling the behavior itself as "severe" provides little enlightenment with regard to solutions. No single definition of a "severe" behavior problem is available, and therefore no single intervention can easily be applied. Human nature is too complex for cookbook solutions, and, much to the dismay of many frustrated teachers, no simple remedies are available. Yet, this may be viewed as an exciting opportunity for professionals to engage in the art of teaching!

Concerns About Physical Safety in the Classroom

This question belies the stereotype that all students with emotional and/or behavioral difficulties are violent. As discussed earlier, acting-out behaviors are only one type of behavioral problem. Having said that, we must acknowledge that some students have the potential for violence and/or disruption, and no one wants to see anyone hurt. IDEA '97 acknowledges the right of the system to overrule the least restrictive environment (LRE) provision in certain situations. However, the *Oberti v. Clementon, New Jersey* case made it clear that it is the school's responsibility to develop an IEP, which seeks to preclude behavioral incidents through the provision of supplementary aids and services.[8] In the case of a student with emotional/behavioral difficulties, the recommended supplementary aids and services might include the services of a teacher with special education certification, professional development activities for individuals working with the student, modification of the curriculum, integrated or coordinated counseling or mental health services, and most important, a thoughtful behavior support plan. IDEA gives students the right to a functional behavioral assessment and a behavior support plan. Any district that has failed to implement this process for a student with emotional or behavioral difficulties runs the risk of violating a student's least restrictive environment rights and doing a disservice to that student, his/her peers, and school personnel.

IDEA 2004

For the past decade there has been great controversy surrounding the provisions in IDEA regarding discipline and emotional/behavioral disabilities. In particular, the provisions related to determining whether a student's behavior is a manifestation of his disability have been problematic. In the new bill, IDEA 2004, language has been added giving schools the authority to view individual cases and unique circumstances in the placement of a student who violates school conduct criteria.

Violent Events in the Classroom

While preventing a violent episode is always the goal, only on very rare occasions does violence occur in classrooms. It is important to know what provisions your school already has in place to address these events. Is there an evacuation plan? Are there clear channels for communication between classrooms, school leadership, and emergency services? Have backup systems been identified? When mental health services are incorporated into a school program, it has been helpful to assign a silent pager for individuals with emotional disabilities that will notify school personnel in the event of a crisis and permit them to respond quickly. In all cases, it is essential that school personnel plan, train, and rehearse for these episodes so that they may act in concert should the need arise. This type of planning should not be left to a single individual, but must be the result of consensus planning by community leaders, emergency services, mental health providers, school personnel, and other individuals who can constructively contribute to planning for crisis intervention.

Professional Responsibilities for Working with Students with Emotional and Behavioral Disabilities

Since students with emotional and behavioral disabilities participate in community activities, ride the school bus, and walk our streets daily, it is important that anyone who is responsible for the supervision of young people in the community take a role in understanding their needs. When the attempt is made to shove those responsibilities off onto bewildered parents, "special" teachers, the mental health communities, or the criminal justice system, we deny the reality that we are a co-dependent network of individuals and that the acts of some influence all of us.

In the school setting, students with emotional/behavioral difficulties traditionally have been relegated to special education programs and school counselors. While such programs may be of some help, all educators need to be prepared to meet the needs of students. Any student with or without a disability may have an emotional/behavioral problem.

It is difficult to imagine a situation in which any school employee would fail to understand constructive options for addressing situations involving the health and well-being of students. Unfortunately, schools often fail to provide every employee with opportunities to consider or learn anything more than emergency responses to these situations.

Anderson describes the Team Training Inservice Project, which has established interagency state-level training teams in twenty-one states.[9] This training includes collaboration, team building, conflict resolution, and communication skills for service providers as well as content about functional behavioral assessment and positive behavioral support plans. If responsibility for prevention and instruction is relegated to one specialist, we miss the opportunity to build and capitalize on existing supports and expertise, which may benefit both the school and the community.

TYPES OF SERVICES

What services are most appropriate for individuals with emotional disabilities? There is no one-size-fits-all answer to this question. To determine which services will best meet the needs of any given student, it is necessary to conduct a functional behavioral assessment. When functional behavioral assessment is viewed as a holistic problem-solving technique, it fits well into the dynamics of person-centered planning[10] and the collaborative teaching model.[11] Functional behavioral assessment should do the following:

- Identify and define the problem behavior.
- Describe strengths, interests, and skill deficits.
- Describe general health and well-being.
- Describe the student's quality of life.
- Identify specific settings, activities, and situations.
- Identify the function(s) of the problem behavior.
- Identify contributing variables.
- Identify tentative hypotheses to guide the creation of a behavior support plan.

The information considered during a functional behavioral assessment should encompass a broad array of sources and perspectives, and may include formal psychological evaluation, academic testing, parental input, social history, medical history, student and peer interviews, interviews with school personnel, and school records. While it is important to examine the situations in which problem behaviors occur, it may be even more useful to identify situations in which no problems occur.[12] If one is able to identify the critical components that contribute to "nonoccurrences," conditions might be replicated to generalize successful participation in other settings. The functional behavioral assessment results in a hypothesis that may explain the purpose of the behavior. The behavior may be an attempt to communicate frustration, boredom, anger, or numerous other messages. The context in which the behavior occurs and patterns of its repetition are often clues to the purpose of the behavior. Once this purpose is identified, it may be possible to intervene and provide another alternative behavior for its expression. Remember Jeanette, the student in the opening anecdote who started an argument with the teacher every time an independent writing assignment was given? In this very common scenario, Jeanette might be avoiding an independent writing assignment. A functional behavioral assessment would help to identify whether or not this is a fairly consistent pattern, whether Jeanette has difficulty with written expression, and if she has been successful with writing assignments in other scenarios. Rather than viewing the problem as a simple matter of noncompliance, we may come to understand that Jeanette perceives herself as a poor writer. The behavior support plan then might address the problem by providing prewriting structure, a spell-checker, a peer coach, or possibly even supplemental instruction for written expression. The hypothesis generated from the information gathered during the functional behavioral assessment will guide the brainstorming session that begins the behavioral support planning process.

PLACEMENTS

Small Group Setting

Some students do benefit from small group settings, but the purpose, composition, and management of the group are critical to success. The ultimate purpose of any program is to return the student to typical settings with their peers as soon as possible. Unfortunately, traditional special education has had a tendency to lock students into small group, special education settings with few prospects for returning to the general education setting. It may be better to ask what elements of the small group setting have proven beneficial to the student. If a smaller student-teacher ratio has been beneficial, then additional support personnel might serve in the general education classroom to the benefit of all students. If a greater degree of organization or structure is the component of the small group setting which has proven most beneficial, it would be important to identify a general education setting which is also highly structured and organized. If social skill instruction is a beneficial component, it may be useful and helpful to weave this instruction into the general education program to the benefit of all students. Additional services may continue to be necessary outside of the general education setting. However, the goal of the LRE requirement is to provide the necessary special education supports while meeting the student's educational needs to the maximum extent appropriate as compared with other students who do not have disabilities.

Delivering Services in the General Education Setting

There is no one set of "specialized techniques" that best meets the needs of all students with emotional/behavioral difficulties. Each student's behavior intervention plan or positive behavioral support plan is unique and is based on the findings of the functional behavioral assessment.

INTERVENTION PLANS

Prevent, Treat, Respond

Of particular note is the use of a positive behavior support plan model first developed by Syracuse University's Child-Centered Inservice Training and Technical Assistance Network (1989) and refined by Janney and Snell.[13] In this model, the plan would identify strategies to prevent behavior difficulties, teach alternative responses, and respond in crisis situations. What makes this model so appealing is that its proactive components seek to support and develop the student. Typical behavioral plans often consist solely of consequences, rewards, or emergency intervention strategies.[14] While these elements may be necessary for some students, all of these strategies are reactive, only to be used after an event. Potentially, these responses are engaged after the damage is done (to one's self, environment, or others). Schools need to consider prevention and teaching as the most salient and individualized components of the behavioral support plan and to devote the bulk of the plan to these elements. A schoolwide discipline plan should provide elements that support both the prevention and crisis intervention elements of this plan. While the philosophical orientation of providers may vary from behaviorism to an ecological approach, what must result is a plan that clearly identifies the intended outcome for the student, uses effective strategies that are culturally and personally respectful, and employs a means for evaluating the effectiveness of implementation.

Selecting the Appropriate Intervention

No single individual should be responsible for the functional behavioral assessment or the development of the behavioral support plan. Group consensus in planning is essential to ensure that strategy selection will be amenable to all of the parties involved. For this reason, student participation in the planning process is important. Ultimately, self-management, which moves the locus of control out of the hands of teachers and parents, is a desired outcome. If students can achieve self-management, there is an increased likelihood of continued successful interactions across multiple settings. It is helpful to consider several criteria when selecting strategies and interventions. Building on the work of Meyer and Evans,[15] I propose the following criteria:

Physical safety

Psychological safety

- Builds upon strengths
- Culturally responsive
- Maintains and enhances dignity

Context appropriateness

- Socially acceptable
- Age appropriate
- Minimally intrusive to the learning and social environment
- Congruence or closeness of approximation to typical expectations

Capacity building

- Generalizability
- Increases opportunities for self-management
- Enhances opportunities for positive interaction with others

Sustainability

- Resources (time, personnel, materials, etc.)
- Consensus support

Effectiveness

- Research supported
- Personal efficacy

Clearly, aversive procedures such as electric shock, restraint, and corporal punishment do not meet these criteria, and are not endorsed. Likewise, it is important to note that the imposition of this plan by any party without the buy-in of the stakeholders has a diminished likelihood for success. For this reason, educators are strongly encouraged to use outside consultants only as group facilitators. A positive behavioral support plan, on the other hand, is a collaborative effort at addressing a student's behavior. Let's consider Jeanette's response to a writing assignment. Table 7.1 is an example of a behavior plan developed for a specific student and a particular behavior.

SUMMARY

Students with serious emotional problems have traditionally been viewed through a negative lens. These students present a variety of behaviors, some that may include extreme acting out to the point of violence. The challenge is obvious: How do we meet the needs of these students within the school environment? The answer is as complex as the question. A few things are clear. The responsibility for educating students with severe emotional problems is a collaborative one. All members of the educational community involved with these students need training to assist in determining the most beneficial placement and strategies. There is no one set of "specialized techniques." Understanding the needs of these students begins with a functional behavioral analysis. Educators working together can then develop preventive strategies to facilitate positive changes in student behavior across educational and social settings.

Tips for Educators:

✎ Use your lesson plan book as a chart to record behavioral or emotional incidents. Detailed lesson plans may provide clues to patterns that influence behavior.

✎ Inventory your resources. These resources include personnel and volunteers, agency support systems and communication systems, as well as time, space, and funds.

✎ Use a team approach to functional behavioral assessment and positive behavioral support planning. This team will become a natural support group.

✎ Involve peers, parents, and the student in problem solving whenever possible. These individuals are closest to the situation.

✎ Know yourself. Understand your personal reactions and tendencies to help you plan careful responses to behavioral problems. Seek support for yourself. Remember, if teaching students with emotional/behavioral problems were easy, you wouldn't be reading this.

Table 7.1.
Sample Behavioral Plan for Jeanette

Problem Statement: After being assigned an in-class, individual writing assignment, the student starts an argument with the teacher or a peer.
Hypothesis: The student is insecure about her writing abilities and therefore avoids the task.

Prevent	Teach	Respond
• Student has accurate self-knowledge of her writing abilities based on conferences with teacher and assessment data.	• All students will learn that each of us has individual strengths and weaknesses.	• Ignore student's attempt to start an argument.
• Create a classroom environment that encourages risk taking by:	• All students will learn how to use the spell-checker, dictionary, and word processor.	• Redirect student to alternative ways to communicate needs.
• Sharing autobiographies of famous writers to illustrate that writing is a process that challenges many of us.	• All students will learn how to access resources during or after class time to facilitate writing.	• If the argument becomes physical, follow schoolwide discipline plan for intervention.
• Demonstrating teacher's need to revise writing samples and correcting own mistakes.	• All students will learn how to self-assess using a writing rubric.	
• Using pre-writing strategies like graphic organizers to help students gain momentum for the task.	• All students will learn peer editing process for revisions.	
	• All students will role play strategies for dealing with writer's block and other writing frustrations.	

Table 7.1.
(continued)

Prevent	Teach	Respond

• Assigning journal writing assignments that will remain unread and uncritiqued by anyone except the author.
• Vary the tasks involved in writing assignments:
  — group writing
  — jigsaw writing
  — individual writing assignments done at home
  — individual writing assignments dictated to a tape recorder at home
  — in-class individual writing
• Provide writing rubrics for self-evaluation.
• Don't use red pen for editing.
• Don't write on student products—use Post-it notes or write a separate critique or word process edits one-on-one with students.
	• Teach all students to ignore attempts to start an argument when the purpose of that behavior is avoidance.
	• Teach all students to redirect another to other problem resolution strategies (e.g., tell the teacher that you don't know where to start with this assignment).	

NOTES

1. Individuals with Disabilities Education Act, 20 U.S.C. 1400 (1997).

2. McGregor, G., & Vogelsberg, R. T. (1998). *Inclusive schooling practices: Pedagogical and research foundations. A synthesis of the literature that informs best practices about inclusive schooling.* Baltimore: Paul H. Brookes Publishing Company.

3. Janney, R., & Snell, M. (2000). Teachers' guides to inclusive practices: Behavioral support. Baltimore: Paul H. Brookes Publishing Co.

4. Starratt, R. (1991). *Building an ethical school: A practical response to the moral crisis in schools.* Boston: Falmer Press.

5. Pipher, M. B. (1994). *Reviving Ophelia: Saving the selves of adolescent girls.* New York: Putnam.

6. Individuals with Disabilities Education Act (1997).

7. Biklen, D. P. (1992). *Schooling without labels: Parents, educators, and inclusive education.* Philadelphia: Temple University Press.

8. *Oberti v. Board of Education of the Borough of Clementon School District* (1993).

9. Anderson, J. (1999). Reflections about positive behavioral supports. *TASH Newsletter, 25*(11), 4–6.

10. Giangreco, M., Cloninger, C. J., & Salce Iverson, V. (1998). *COACH: Choosing outcomes and accommodations for children* (2nd ed.). Baltimore: Paul H. Brookes Publishing Co.

11. Friend, M., & Cook, L. (2000). *Interactions: Collaboration skills for school professionals.* (3rd ed.). White Plains, NY: Longman.

12. Dunlap, G., Kern, L., dePerczel, M., Clarke, S., Wilson, D., Childs, K. E., White, R., & Falk, G. D. (1993). Functional analysis of classroom variables for students with emotional and behavioral disorders. *Behavioral Disorders, 18*(4), 275–291.

13. Janney & Snell (2000).

14. Amos, P. (1999). What restraints teach. *TASH Newsletter, 25*(11), 28–29.

15. Meyer, L. H., & Evans, I. M. (1989). *Nonaversive intervention for behavior problems.* Baltimore: Paul H. Brookes Publishing Co.

CHAPTER 8

Related Services

Beverly Rainforth

Kayla has a significant learning disability. She leaves her classroom promptly at 9:30 A.M. every Monday, Wednesday, and Friday for speech therapy. The classroom teacher is not sure what Kayla does there or how it will improve her communication, especially when she misses portions of the language arts lesson three times a week. And there seems to be no opportunity to discuss any of this.

James is struggling with a variety of family issues and presents challenging behavior. A school counselor is available to meet with James when he first arrives at school and at lunchtime, if needed, to help him deal with concerns before they interrupt his classes.

DEFINING RELATED SERVICES

Many children who receive special education also receive one or more related services such as speech therapy or counseling. Teachers may have a general understanding of what these services are, but all too often related service providers have little communication with classroom teachers beyond the schedule of services (i.e., what time a student will be absent from the classroom).

When students receive related services in isolation from the educational program, as Kayla does, it works against the goal of inclusive education. Certainly, "isolated related services" is an oxymoron, and providing services in this way also appears to contradict the intent of the related service provision under IDEA. In contrast, consider James. Each quarter, James's counselor also co-teaches a unit on conflict resolution with a different group of teachers, achieving both direct services to students and collaboration with staff. Although these services require planning and flexibility, there have been clear benefits for individual students as well as the school climate overall.

Related services can be important supports that enable students like James and Kayla to participate and succeed in inclusive education. In fact, related services can be important "supplementary aids and services" that ensure access to general education as the least restrictive environment (LRE), as required by IDEA. Achieving this goal requires a clear understanding of what related services are and how they can support inclusion of students with disabilities.

IDEA DEFINITIONS OF "RELATED SERVICES"

The term "related services" means transportation and developmental, corrective, and other supportive services, including speech-language pathology and audiology services; psychological services; physical and occupational therapy; recreation, including therapeutic recreation; social work services; counseling services; including rehabilitation counseling; orientation and mobility services, and medical services, except that such medical services shall be for diagnostic and evaluation purposes only, as may be required to assist a child with a disability to benefit from special education, and include the early identification and assessment of disabling conditions in children.[1]

This definition lists examples of several types of related services and explains the purpose of related services. Teachers can increase the likelihood that they and their students will receive the support needed for inclusive education when they know what each service is and who provides it; how to determine if a service is warranted; and how related services should be provided.

Related Service Providers

Related services run the gamut of assistance from how to assess a student's needs to how to facilitate help. These various providers are special education teachers, counselors, and therapists. Table 8.1 provides definitions of the various related services listed in IDEA and gives Internet addresses for professional organizations where additional information can be found.

Table 8.2 lists some of the services commonly provided by related service professionals and other members of special education teams. It is important to note that professionals from several different disciplines might provide the same or similar services. For example, Table 8.2 lists several different professions that could provide students and their families with counseling related to emotional difficulties. In other instances, several professions appear to offer the same service, but each has a distinct focus. For example, a variety of specialists might develop or guide selection of adapted equipment and materials, but each would be oriented toward a particular area of need (e.g., academics, communication, mobility, seating, self-care).

Table 8.1.
Related Services Definitions and Professional Organizations

Service	Definition (unless otherwise noted, definitions come from the IDEA Rules and Regulation, 34 CFR 300.24 (b))	Professional Organization
Audiology	Identification of children with hearing loss; determination of the range, nature, and degree of hearing loss, including referral for medical or other professional attention for the habilitation or hearing; provision of habilitative activities, such as language habilitation, auditory training, speech reading (lipreading), hearing evaluation, and speech conservation; creation and administration of programs for prevention of hearing loss; counseling and guidance of children, parents, and teachers regarding hearing loss and determination of children's needs for group and individual amplification, selecting and fitting and appropriate aid, and evaluating the effectiveness of amplification.	American Speech, Language, and Hearing Association www.asha.org
Counseling	Services provided by qualified social workers, psychologists, guidance counselors, or other qualified professionals.	American School Counselor Association www.schoolcounselor.org
Early Identification and Assessment	Implementation of a formal plan for identifying a disability as early as possible in a child's life.	Conducted by any appropriate members of educational team
Medical	Services provided by a licensed physician to determine a child's medically related disability that results in the child's need for special education and related services.	American Academy of Pediatrics www.aap.org

Occupational Therapy	Services provided by a qualified occupational therapist, including improving, developing, or restoring functions impaired or lost through illness, injury, or deprivation; improving ability to perform tasks for independent functioning if functions are impaired or lost; and preventing, through early intervention, initial or further impairment of loss of function.	American Occupational Therapy Association www.aota.org
Orientation and Mobility	Services provided to blind and visually impaired students by qualified personnel to enable those students to attain systematic orientation to and safe movement within their environments in school, home, and community; these services include teaching students the following, as appropriate: (a) spatial and environmental concepts and use of information received by the senses (such as sound, temperature, and vibrations), to establish, maintain, or regain orientation and line of travel (e.g., using sound at a traffic light to cross the street); (b) use of the long cane to supplement visual travel skills or as a tool for safely negotiating the environment for students with no available travel vision; (c) understanding and using remaining vision and distance low vision aids; and (d) other concepts, techniques, and tools.	Association for Education and Rehabilitation of the Blind and Visually Impaired www.aerbvi.org
Parent Counseling and Training	Assisting parents in understanding the special needs of their child; providing parents with information about child development; and helping parents to acquire the skills necessary to support the implementation of their child's IEP or Individualized Family Service Plan (IFSP).	Conducted by any appropriate members of educational team; See also Exceptional Parent Magazine www.eparent.com

Table 8.1.
(continued)

Service	Definition (unless otherwise noted, definitions come from the IDEA Rules and Regulation, 34 CFR 300.24 (b))	Professional Organization
Physical Therapy	Care and services provided by or under the direction and supervision of a physical therapist; these includes examining and evaluating patients with health-related conditions, impairments, functional limitations, and disability in order to determine a diagnosis, prognosis, and intervention; alleviating impairments and functional limitations by designing, implementing, and modifying therapeutic interventions; preventing injury, impairments, functional limitations, and disability, including promoting and maintaining fitness, health, and quality of life in all age populations; and engaging in consultation, education, and research. (Definition from American Physical Therapy Association, 1985.)	American Physical Therapy Association www.apta.org
Psychology	Administering psychological and educational tests and other assessment procedures; interpreting assessment results; obtaining, integrating, and interpreting information about child behavior and conditions relating to learning; consulting with other staff members in planning school programs to meet the special needs of children as indicated by psychological tests, interviews, and behavioral evaluations; planning and managing a program of psychological services, including psychological counseling for children and parents; and assisting in developing positive behavioral intervention strategies.	National Association of School Psychologists www.nasponline.org/

Recreation	Assessment of leisure function; therapeutic recreation services; recreation programs in schools and community agencies; and leisure education.	National Therapeutic Recreation Society www.nrpa.org
Rehabilitation Counseling	Services provided by qualified personnel in individual or group sessions that focus specifically on career development, employment preparation, achieving independence, and integration in the workplace and community of a student with a disability. The term also includes vocational rehabilitation services provided to a student with disabilities by vocational rehabilitation programs funded under the Rehabilitation Act of 1973, as amended.	American Rehabilitation Counseling Association www.nchrtm.okstate.edu/ARCA
School Health	Services provided by a qualified school nurse or other qualified person. Prevention of illness and disability; early detection and correction of health problems; management of children with special health care needs in the school setting and support of their families. (Definition excerpted from National Association of School Nurses Home Page, www.nasn.org.)	National Association of School Nurses www.nasn.org American School Health Association www.ashaweb.org
Social Work	Preparing a social or developmental history on a child with a disability; group and individual counseling with the child and family; working in partnership with parents and others on those problems in a child's living situation (home, school, and community) that affect the child's adjustment in school; mobilizing school and community resources to enable the child to learn as effectively as possible in his or her educational program; and assisting in developing positive behavioral intervention strategies.	National Association of Social Workers, Section on School Social Work www.naswdc.org/

Table 8.1.
(continued)

Service	Definition (unless otherwise noted, definitions come from the IDEA Rules and Regulation, 34 CFR 300.24 (b))	Professional Organization
Speech-Language Pathology	Identification of children with speech or language impairments; diagnosis and appraisal of specific speech or language impairments; referral for medical or other professional attention necessary for the habilitation of speech or language impairments; provision of speech and language services for the habilitation or prevention of communicative impairments; and counseling and guidance of parents, children, and teachers regarding speech and language impairments.	American Speech, Language, and Hearing Association www.asha.org
Transportation	Travel to and from school and between schools; travel in and around school buildings; and specialized equipment (such as special or adapted buses, lifts, and ramps) if required to provide special transportation for a child with a disability.	Architectural and Transportation Barriers Compliance Board www.access-board.gov

Table 8.2.
Services Provided by Various Members of the Special Education Team

Specific Service	Related Service Provider	Other Educational Team Member
Accessibility (for transportation)	Occupational therapist Physical therapist	
Adapted equipment and materials	Occupational therapist Orientation-mobility specialist Physical therapist Speech-language pathologist	Special education teacher
Assessment (for early identification, IEP planning, diagnostics)	All	Special education teacher Other educators
Augmentative communication	Speech-language pathologist	Special education teacher
Counseling	Guidance counselor Psychologist Rehabilitation counselor Social worker	Special education teacher
Health and health education	School nurse	Physical education teacher
Hearing	Audiologist	Deaf education teacher
Independent living	Occupational therapist School nurse	Special education teacher Home and careers teacher
Motor development	Occupational therapist Physical therapist	Physical education teacher Adapted physical education teacher
Oral motor control (eating)	Speech-language pathologist Occupational therapist	
Play, leisure, and recreation	Occupational therapist Recreation therapist	Special education teacher
Positive behavior assessment	Psychologist	Special education teacher

Table 8.2.
(continued)

Specific Service	Related Service Provider	Other Educational Team Member
Sensory awareness and processing	Audiologist Occupational therapist Orientation-mobility specialist	Deaf-education teacher Special education teacher
Speech and language	Speech-language pathologist	Deaf-education teacher Special education teacher Teacher of English as second language
Vocational testing and preparation	Occupational therapist Vocational counselor	Special education teacher

Unfortunately, the demarcations among all the special education and related service professions are very fuzzy. State laws often define who can provide certain services (usually medical services—for example, dispensing medication), whether there are specific procedures a discipline cannot provide, or whether a physician referral is needed to provide services (e.g., often required for physical therapy). For most of these professions, however, a license or certification does not clearly define the scope of practice. Instead, expertise evolves from the combination of formal preparation at a college or university, advanced education (degree programs or nondegree seminars/workshops), personal and professional experience, and personal preference. For example, Table 8.2 lists several services that might be provided by an occupational therapist, but few occupational therapists are expert in all these areas. Special education teachers also bring expertise in a variety of areas, and in some situations they are able to meet student needs without related services. Given these ambiguities, teachers are most likely to receive the kind of support they need for their students when they clearly define the concern to be addressed and ask who on the team has the expertise needed to address that concern.[2]

Determination of Related Services

IDEA states that the multidisciplinary team (MDT) will make decisions about a student's goals and objectives, and whether related services are required to achieve those goals and objectives. A variety of strategies have been used to make these decisions, however, and some contradict the spirit of the law.

Disability Labeling. Frequently, a service is proposed simply because the student has a particular disability, rather than to meet specific educational goals. For example, the MDT for a young child with a physical disability may automatically recommend occupational therapy, physical therapy, or both. These therapists then conduct assessments, identify deficits, and present the MDT with their therapy objectives for the student. Unfortunately, services designed around a disability label are likely to be disconnected from the rest of the student's educational program. On the other hand, when MDT base service recommendations on a disability label for an older student, they are less likely to propose occupational or physical therapy, because motor development has reached a plateau. For both the younger student and the older one, however, the MDT should focus instead on whether the related services would "assist a child with a disability to benefit from special education," that is, to achieve IEP goals and objectives.

Eligibility Criteria. Focusing on a student's disability, rather than on educational goals, has also resulted in establishment of "eligibility criteria" for related services. These criteria typically require a discrepancy between a student's overall performance and her/his performance in the area of development to be addressed by the related service. The underlying rationale is that a student could not benefit from speech therapy, for example, unless his language development fell below his overall intellectual development. Although the intent of eligibility criteria is to use limited resources carefully, the criteria are based on questionable assumptions about "intelligence" as a construct separate from other areas of ability or disability. Furthermore, the U.S. Department of Education has deemed such eligibility criteria unacceptable because their use interferes with the MDT's responsibility to make individualized decisions about whether a student would benefit from related services.[3]

Availability/Advocacy of Services. Other variables that often influence whether a multidisciplinary team will recommend related services are availability of services and advocacy. Teachers report that they are often told not to request a particular service at an MDT meeting, because the service is not available. Clearly this interferes with consideration of whether related services would help a student achieve educational goals and objectives. In contrast, a strong advocate may succeed in securing extensive services for a child. Giangreco noted that "more is better" is the value that often guides decision making about related services, based on the belief that disabilities will be corrected by intensive services.[4] Although early intervention is important, and may reduce the impact of disabilities, be aware that excessive services may take away from opportunities for children to learn through more normative experiences, such as interacting with peers and participating in the regular education curriculum.

Setting Goals and Objectives. In contrast with the approaches described above, the MDT should start by identifying one set of goals and objectives for a student. While related service providers contribute to this discussion as part of the team, they do not have separate goals or objectives. Remember, decisions to recommend related services are based on whether one or more services are required to achieve a student's IEP goals and objectives in the context of the student's overall educational priorities. In a process called VISTA (Vermont Interdependent Services Team Approach), Giangreco recommends using the value of "only as special as necessary" to guide these decisions.[5] Team members can put this value into practice by asking themselves questions about how they will address each objective on a student's IEP.

VISTA Guidelines

For each objective on a student's IEP, the team should ask the following questions:

1. Does this objective contribute to the student's overall educational participation and achievement? If yes, how? If no, is it a priority for the IEP?
2. Does the regular education teacher have the expertise required to address this need? Does the special education teacher?
3. If neither one, who does have the expertise?
4. If more than one person has the expertise, do they bring the same or different perspectives? Are there gaps, overlaps, or contradictions?
5. Looking at all the objectives on this student's IEP, who is essential to support the classroom teacher in addressing the IEP?[6]

Carefully considering each of these questions will help determine which, if any, related services are "required to assist a child with a disability to benefit from special education." The last question also reminds the IEP team that communication and coordination to meet student needs are more effective when the smallest group with the required competence assumes responsibility for the entire IEP.

Providing Related Services

IDEA addresses this question in three ways. First, IDEA defines special education as "specially designed instruction" and states a clear preference for that instruction to be provided in regular education settings. As an integral part of the special education program, related services should meet these same standards. Second, IDEA specifies that related services be "required to assist a child with a disability to benefit from special education." This suggests that related services should be provided in ways that allow the student to receive greater benefit from the educational program than if such services were not provided. Finally, related services may be recommended as "supplementary aids and services" needed to support the student in regular education as the least restrictive environment.

These principles can be illustrated by looking at the services provided for Kayla and James, described at the beginning of this chapter. When Kayla leaves her classroom for speech therapy, it is not clear if she is receiving instruction that is specially designed to meet her unique needs, or if the services have any relationship to her participation and achievement in regular education. The services are not provided in ways that allow her to remain in the regular education setting or to achieve greater benefit from her educational program than if the services were not provided. Thus, these services do not meet IDEA's intent for related services. Unfortunately, many related service professionals have been educated in a "medical model" in which service providers work alone in clinical settings. Learning to collaborate with others and to provide services in educational settings is very challenging for some related service providers, but it is necessary.

In contrast to Kayla's situation, James's counselor has responded to the needs of James and his teachers in ways that allow James to participate in regular education more consistently and more successfully. James is learning to recognize issues that are troubling him and to go to a safe place to "vent" rather than explode at times and in places that cause more trouble for him and others. James, along with his classmates and teachers, is learning a variety of strategies to deal with conflicts constructively. There are still times when James must leave his classroom, but his team monitors these incidents carefully to make sure his emotional and educational needs are being met using the least restrictive alternative. The team also recognizes that related services may not be enough to meet all the needs of James and his family, so they have started developing "wraparound" services that address James's needs outside of school in collaboration with a community mental health provider.[7]

Tekra has physical disabilities and serious health impairments. Once a day, she goes to the nurse's office for treatments to clear her lungs. Although this service does not relate directly to performance objectives on Tekra's IEP, it is an important related service because it maintains her health and allows her to benefit from her educational program.[8] As she travels to and from the nurse's office, Tekra is also learning to operate her power wheelchair. A physical therapist worked closely with Tekra to develop her driving skills. The therapist also met with Tekra's teacher to identify transitions when Tekra should work on driving, taught a paraprofessional to provide driving instruction, monitors Tekra's (and the paraprofessional's) performance by talking with the paraprofessional and observing instruction, and makes changes in the program when needed. Although this service does not improve academic performance, the IEP team determined that independent mobility is an important educational objective for Tekra because it improves her overall ability to participate. By planning the related service with the classroom teacher, instruction occurs during natural transitions and the physical therapist has ensured that instruction will support and not detract from Tekra's participation in regular education.

Recent research confirms that related services have an impact on students' school performance when teachers are involved in making referrals, setting objectives, and consulting with related service providers.[9] Teachers also report greater satisfaction when they collaborate with service providers. Despite these benefits, classroom teachers often find it challenging to collaborate with the range of service providers who work with students with disabilities.

Working with Related Service Providers to Support Inclusion of Students with Disabilities. Teachers are most likely to find effective ways to collaborate with related service providers when (1) the service addresses a classroom need; (2) specific objectives are understood; and (3) related service methods can be incorporated into classroom routines.

Definition of the Need for Related Services. Although there may be times when a specialist sees a need that the classroom teacher does not, experienced teachers are usually well aware of their students' exceptional needs. As with any other special education need, the classroom teacher would carefully describe and document the need, and share this information with the principal or a child study team. A special education teacher or related service professional might be asked to observe the student, to corroborate or help define the need, and to help determine which, if any, related service might be appropriate to help address the need.

Quan, for example, receives special education to address a variety of learning needs. Since the start of the school year, Quan's teacher has become more concerned about his general disorganization, distractibility and impulsivity, and clumsiness affecting gross and fine motor abilities (e.g., writing, cutting). She and the special education teacher had been using a combination of developmentally appropriate practice and behavioral strategies to address these needs, which correspond with objectives on Quan's IEP. Now the classroom teacher sees growing differences between Quan and his classmates, but with so many needs, she is not sure who else might help. After discussing her concerns with the special education teacher, the school principal, and Quan's mother, they all agree to ask an occupational therapist (OT) to observe Quan. The OT's schedule does not permit her to observe during the activities Quan finds most challenging, so the two teachers videotape Quan and provide a written description of their concerns. The OT sees evidence that Quan may have sensory processing problems, and has several ideas for instructional strategies to help Quan become better focused on his work (reducing disorganization, distractibility, and impulsivity) and improve coordination for classroom tasks. The school principal agrees to refer Quan back to the IEP team to recommend occupational therapy as a related service. Because the classroom teacher defined the needs to be addressed, the outcomes of the OT service are clearly related to the educational program.

The Goals of Related Services. The building principal, special education director, or special education teacher should provide classroom teachers with IEPs for each of their students. The IEPs should list the students' goals and objectives and required services, but may not clearly state which services are to help address which objectives. Upon reviewing this background, it is appropriate for teachers to contact each related service provider to request clarifications or additional information. In some schools, a related service professional will provide services for the same students for two or more years, and may already know the students better than the classroom teacher. In other situations, teachers and related service providers will be getting to know students at the same time. Either way, both the classroom teacher and related service providers benefit from meeting to discuss their expectations for students and support services. It is particularly important to share perspectives about (1) how the services relate to student performance in regular education settings; (2) how much service will be provided in the regular class or school routines; (3) what methods can be incorporated into routine activities; and (4) how the teacher and related service provider will communicate and coordinate their efforts.

Parents may not know the specific expectations or opportunities in their child's class, but they do know their child better than any other member of the team. It is not unusual for a child to demonstrate abilities and needs at home or in the community that differ from those seen at school. For example, a speech-language pathologist was surprised to see that a child who was quiet, withdrawn, and often tearful at school was very active, interactive, and vocal at home. An occupational therapist discovered that a child was nearly independent while dressing and undressing at home and at swimming lessons in the community, but at school he complied passively while staff assisted him with all his clothing. A psychologist agreed to assist a family with challenging behavior at home and quickly understood that their child with autism was under considerable pressure to "hold it together" during the school day, only to "fall apart" when she got home. Teams can draw parents in as active members, and develop more complete and accurate pictures of their students, by asking parents to describe their child's abilities and needs. To convey the importance of parents' knowledge of their child, this invitation needs to come at the start of conversations, not after all the professionals already have drawn their conclusions. There is no substitute for a home visit to open the eyes of the professionals, but when logistics make this difficult, parents often welcome the invitation to share videotapes of their child. Knowing that a child performs differently in different settings shifts the emphasis from teaching new skills to understanding the conditions under which the child is able to demonstrate abilities and perform more consistently.

The same inconsistencies are seen between student performance in isolated related service settings and regular education settings. When related service providers work in isolated settings, they cannot understand the opportunities or demands of classroom settings, and classroom teachers cannot expand their repertoire of strategies to help all their students succeed. In schools where related services have not been well connected with regular education, related service providers are likely to be either pleasantly surprised by the invitation to collaborate with classroom teachers or resistant to any change from their traditional role. Although some related service providers have responsibilities for so many students, schools, or administrative tasks that collaboration is difficult, they are still more likely to meet student needs if they collaborate with classroom teachers than if they devote the same time to providing isolated services.

Pull-out Services. When students leave their classroom for related services, they often leave in the middle of one lesson or activity and return in the middle of another one. The result is that students who most need consistency, continuity, intensity, and intent of instruction are subjected to disruptions and disconnections. Often, the teacher is given several schedules to follow, with students leaving class for a variety of services. This can be disconcerting for the teacher and disruptive for the entire class. For these reasons alone, it is important to reduce pull-out services as much as possible. When students leave their classroom, they also miss important instruction, and may actually receive less instruction than if they received no additional services. Finally, as discussed previously, pull-out services are less likely to be designed to relate to and support student performance needs in regular education.

Pull-in Options. Many people refer to classroom-based related services as "push-in" services. This terminology suggests that related services personnel must force their way into someplace they are not wanted. It is easy to understand why related service providers would not want to engage in this kind of professional assault, when their hope is to collaborate for the benefit of shared students. Unfortunately, however, many related service providers do feel as though they are unwanted and must force their way into classrooms. A better option, both practically and sematically, is for classroom teachers to invite others to work with them. The language and practice of "pull-in" services are preferable to "push-in" services. When therapists provide their services within inclusive classrooms and address skills that are immediately useful to students, teachers judge the therapists' contributions positively and want therapists to spend more time in the classroom.[10]

There are a variety of ways that teachers can make their classrooms inviting to related service providers, even those who reject the idea at first. Teachers can ask for suggestions to address student needs during routine class activities, demonstrating their interest in collaboration. For example, Kayla's teacher might ask the speech-language pathologist about strategies to help Kayla improve her articulation and speak in longer sentences. As the teacher starts to understand the kinds of strategies and activities the speech-language pathologist favors, the teacher might ask for Kayla to stay in the classroom for a special activity and invite the speech-language pathologist to join them. (With speech therapy services often provided to small groups of students, the teacher may need to be prepared to invite the whole group.) The teacher could ask for suggestions to adjust or expand the activity to provide better opportunities to address communication needs. Each of these overtures signifies the teacher's ongoing interest in collaboration, as well as willingness to adjust her own curriculum and methods to support the speech-language pathologist's priorities.

These overtures can be important to entice related service providers out of their isolation. Over the long term, however, these "teacher deals" are tiring, and need to be replaced with systemic support for services to be provided in ways that are relevant and supportive to inclusive education, consistent with collaboration models developed with special education teachers. Systemic change must begin with IEP teams reexamining their bases for recommending related services and adopting the value of "only as special as necessary"[11] Scheduling can be a barrier to related service providers being able to work within classrooms;[12] therefore, schools may also consider ways of clustering students who need a particular service, so that the related service provider can work with children in fewer classrooms and collaborate more extensively with those teachers.[13]

COLLABORATION

Teams Promote Continuity

Collaboration is also enhanced when teams have opportunities to work together for successive years. For example, a multigrade team agreed to become the "home" for certain students with emotional disabilities as they proceeded through grades three, four, and five. The students all received counseling as a related service, and the structure of the team allowed the counselor to develop long-term relationships with the students and their teachers. Having a major responsibility to this team also allowed the counselor to provide classroom-based services on a regular basis. When arranging to cluster students in these ways, however, great care must be taken not to overload a class, making it a de facto special class.

Related Services Without Disruption

Some related service providers have the talent and flexibility to arrive in a class during almost any lesson and find ways to provide the specialized services needed by individual students. Although every educator finds the need to make some adaptations on the spot, it is unacceptable as a long-term strategy because it is draining for service providers and not intentional enough to meet the needs of students with disabilities. Furthermore, on-the-spot adaptations often result in the teacher and the related service provider inadvertently competing for student attention. Time in the class-room will be most productive for related services and least disruptive for the rest of the class when activities are planned to address both the regular education curriculum and the related service needs. This can occur in several ways.

First, teachers can carefully examine their class routines and the ways students participate. A teacher can provide related service professionals with the class schedule, noting which activities would be most conducive to communication, gross motor activity, fine motor activity, problem solving, individualized variations, and so on, as relevant to the particular service. At the secondary level, different classes often provide opportunities for different types of services, so it is helpful if teachers discuss their instructional methods with related service providers or the special education teacher who coordinates a student's services, to determine where matches are possible.

Teachers at Dansville (New York) Primary School expanded on this approach to improve inclusive education for their students with severe or multiple disabilities. The teachers delineated the class routine and how most students participated in the routine, then listed the ways a student with severe/multiple disabilities participated. Table 8.3 outlines a portion of the routine for a kindergarten class that included Sara, a student with developmental disabilities affecting her speech, language, academic, and motor development. The kindergarten teacher sent this chart to Sara's mother as well as her special education teacher, speech-language pathologist, occupational therapist, and physical therapist. Each member of the team completed the third column, suggesting ways Sara might participate and skills she might work on during each activity. The teacher pasted all the "third columns" together, copied the page onto legal-size paper, and distributed copies to all team members. Then the team met and set priorities to be addressed during each activity so that Sara's greatest needs would be met in the course of the daily classroom routine. As a result, related service providers also understood optimal times to work with Sara in the course of the day. This strategy is time-consuming, and the teams used it primarily for students with severe or multiple disabilities, who received more services and whose needs were less familiar to classroom teachers. As a result of planning this way for students

Table 8.3.
Class Routine for Opening Circle in Kindergarten

Class Participation	What Sara Does Now	What Sara Could Do
Opening Activity (song, finger play, record): Children sit on floor and move hands, use voices, etc., as required by activity, or do large motor movements if required by activity.	Sits in chair or lies on floor. Occasionally sits on floor supported by aide. Watches and smiles during song and movement activities. Participates as she is able.	
Helpers: Choral reading of jobs and names.	Watches and listens. Raises hand if name is on Helpers chart.	
Chart Story: Sit and listen, focusing on chart and print. May chime in and read with teacher.	Same as other children. Does not usually chime in.	
Calendar: One child finds correct number and hangs it on proper space on calendar. Others watch and give reinforcement and assistance as needed.	If calendar person, needs adult help to walk to calendar. Needs help to find correct number. Otherwise, she watches.	
Weather: "Weather person" looks out window and chooses two weather conditions to record on chart by turning arrow. Rest of class says weather poem that requires weather person's response.	Same as above. If weather person, aide helps choose weather conditions (identifies cloudy, etc.). Otherwise, says part of poem as she is able.	
Number Line: Count with teacher to determine next number to write.	Counts lower numbers to 10 with aide holding up her fingers.	

Source: Example provided by Christine Spoor, kindergarten teacher at Dansville (New York) Primary School.

with severe/multiple disabilities, the teams found that they had a more holistic perspective on planning for all their students.

It is unlikely, however, that a related service provider's schedule will match well with every teacher's schedule. Therefore, the second way to make this time productive is for teachers to adjust their schedules so, for example, silent reading is switched with an activity having opportunities for gross motor work when the physical therapist can be with the class. Another strategy is for teachers and related service providers to plan activities together and then teach them together.

Small Gestures Yield Powerful Results

Teachers have found that even small adjustments in their lessons can be powerful, and often the changes made for one student benefit others as well. For example, a teacher found that the manipulatives used for math lessons were quite challenging for a student with visual-spatial and fine motor difficulties. The occupational therapist devised a cardboard template to help this student keep the manipulatives grouped properly as ones, tens, and hundreds (see Figure 8.1). Soon the teacher realized that this adaptation would be useful for several other students, and additional templates were made for the class. Another teacher was planning to introduce a unit on money with the poem "Smart" by Shel Silverstein.[14] The counselor working with students in the class suggested using the book *Alexander, Who Used to Be Rich Last Sunday* by Judith Viorst,[15] which would also offer opportunities to discuss emotions such as envy and disappointment, and how to deal with them. This discussion could be expanded into an assignment for the students' "buddy journals,"[16] which the counselor would read.

Plan Often and Plan Ahead

Classroom teachers may not even see related service providers, so it can be hard to imagine finding time to meet with them all. When related service providers work primarily in one school, an expectation can be set that they will meet with each classroom teacher at least once a month, preferably in a team meeting that involves the special education teacher. When related service providers serve more than one school, it is advisable that they meet with special education teachers at least once a month. In some schools, special education teachers and related service providers meet more frequently (at least once a week), and the special education teachers assume responsibility for coordinating services and integrating them into class routines and activities. Because planning a coordinated effort is important, it is appropriate for each student's IEP to list planning time under "supplementary aids and services" and for related services to include time for team

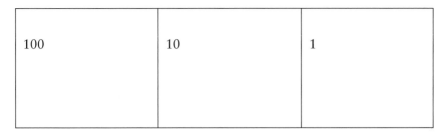

100	10	1

Figure 8.1. Cardboard Template to Organize Math Manipulatives

planning (e.g., one hour per month for each service), in addition to direct services and classroom consultation. If, as discussed earlier in this chapter, there were a compact core team, the classroom teacher would have a limited number of people to meet with each month. The specific time for team planning can be determined by a schoolwide schedule or through arrangements among the individuals involved.

Teams have found that they can optimize their planning time when classroom teachers can provide the team with lesson plans for at least the next week and, ideally, the next month. Even when related service providers do not have time to meet with every teacher, they will usually review lesson plans left in a mailbox. When related service providers work in more than one building, teachers can fax or e-mail ideas for lessons. Related service providers will usually appreciate the opportunity to review lesson plans and make suggestions about how the lesson can support their participation.

Incidental Skill Sharing

When members of special education teams were asked during a series of workshops what they wanted to learn from other service providers, a common response was, "We want to know what you do." As long as related services are provided in isolation from the educational program, teachers are likely to imagine that they involve highly specialized intervention techniques. In fact, related service providers do have specialized knowledge and skills, as do all members of an educational team. Each team member draws on specific knowledge and skills during student assessment and intervention planning. All members of the team, however, can readily learn certain aspects of these skills. Once appropriate methods are identified to address a student's needs, however, related services will have the greatest impact if teachers and paraprofessionals incorporate these methods into their own instructional repertoire. Sometimes new methods are adopted through incidental learning, as teachers and paraprofessionals see others model these practices.

Role Release

When incidental learning is not adequate, teachers, paraprofessionals, and related service providers can engage in an intentional process of "role release."[17] To release portions of their roles in a responsible and effective manner, team members who are instructing others must complete three steps. During role release, each instructor (1) models a strategy and points out critical features; (2) exchanges roles with the learner; and (3) provides corrective feedback to the learner.

This process is repeated until the learner has adequate competence to use the new method safely, but not perfectly. To increase competence, the instructor provides monitoring and feedback during subsequent visits to the classroom. When the student's needs change, the method is revised and the process of role release is repeated. Although it is expected that related service providers will release some of their roles to teachers and paraprofessionals, it is also important for related service providers to learn from other team members. Classroom teachers, for example, have important knowledge and skills related to the regular education curriculum and large group management that others would benefit from learning.

Some professionals argue that it took many years of education and experience to learn their methods, and that role release is neither appropriate nor possible. This is a misconception.[18] Role release does not require all knowledge and skills to be taught to others. It requires teaching specific skills to be used with specific students in specific situations. Related service providers may know techniques that are too complicated or too dangerous to be taught to others through role release, but it is unlikely that these techniques would be appropriate for use in educational settings, or that they could be used frequently enough to have a real impact on a student. One exception to this guideline would be health procedures that, by state law, may only be performed by a school nurse. For methods that must be performed in a precise way (e.g., positioning of a child with brittle bones, intermittent catheterization), instructors can only achieve the necessary level of competence through systematic instruction, written or pictorial reminders of critical steps and details, sign-offs on training, and ongoing supervision.[19] Having two or more people competent in specialized procedures reduces the risk of injury or forced absence when a single service provider is not available.

This chapter has provided many examples of how related service strategies have been incorporated into class routines. It is appropriate for teachers to ask related service providers for specific recommendations to deal with specific needs during routine activities. For example, a speech-language pathologist provided a teacher with lists of words for a student to practice articulation of initial consonant sounds, and taught the teacher to cue the sounds with which the student had the most difficulty. The teacher referred to the word list when planning lessons, making sure there were ample opportunities for the student to work on articulation. Because a paraprofessional often worked with individual students or small groups in the class, the teacher also asked the speech-language pathologist to teach the paraprofessional to cue the student to correct his articulation. With permission from the student, two peers were also taught these cues so that they could provide gentle reminders during paired reading activities.

Paraprofessional and Peer Involvement

The previous examples serve as reminders of the value of involving peers and paraprofessionals. Far too often, paraprofessionals are assigned major responsibilities in inclusive classrooms, with minimal training or supervision and less than satisfactory results.[20] Teachers can begin by clearly stating their own expectations of paraprofessionals and providing guidance and feedback about their performance. It is also appropriate to ask related service providers to work with paraprofessionals to develop effective methods of teaching and to support students with disabilities. To ensure that the paraprofessional does not assume the teacher's leadership role, the teacher can routinely exchange classroom roles with the related service providers as well as the paraprofessionals. For example, the paraprofessional could lead the class through the opening routine, and the teacher could assist a student who is learning to use an augmentative communication device. When the speech-language pathologist works in the class later that day, both the teacher and the paraprofessional could spend a few minutes with him, to learn more about how to use the device and teach this student.

The Importance of Collaboration

Classrooms that are truly inclusive are learning communities where everyone helps each other. This culture makes it comfortable to involve students in using some of the methods introduced by related service providers. For example, Seth is a fifth grade student with multiple disabilities who receives occupational therapy, services for the blind, and several other services. During a social studies lesson, students worked in small groups to list characteristics of certain cultural events. As a matter of routine, Seth's group talked about how Seth would participate in the task, and decided to write their list on a red transparency clipped to a "light box" because that would encourage Seth to hold his head up and use his residual vision. When Seth's head drooped, another fifth grader squeezed his hand gently to bring his attention back to the group. None of this seemed to distract anyone from the task at hand. When the class moved from tables to the floor for a large group discussion, a member of Seth's group found the device Seth would need to sit on the floor, and put it in place for the paraprofessional to position Seth. Although Seth's abilities are limited, he was a valued member of his group because other students had learned ways to include him from teachers, paraprofessionals, and related service providers working in the classroom.

SUMMARY

IDEA has made provisions for students with disabilities to receive related services, not as isolated health and mental health services, but as integral parts of the special education program. Some thirty years ago, special education teams found that "transdisciplinary teamwork," characterized by role release[21] and integrated therapy,[22] were effective strategies for professionals from many disciplines to share their expertise with each other, and to provide specialized interventions in the context of students' routine educational activities. As students have moved from isolated special education classes and schools to more inclusive schools, great attention has been given to the need for collaboration, but has focused almost exclusively on teachers. Collaboration with related service providers has generally been viewed as something to address "later," after teachers become comfortable and competent in their new roles and relationships. Unfortunately, getting around to "later" can be elusive. Beware too, that the cohesive teams and coordinated classroom-based supports that students with disabilities need and deserve must also be pursued with determination. To be sure, adding related services to the mix makes collaboration more complicated, but also offers great benefits, for both students and the professionals who educate them. This chapter has applied the concepts of transdisciplinary teamwork, role release, and integrated therapy to the special education programs of today. Making related service providers integral members of each child's educational team will help the team move closer to achieving its goal of inclusive education.

Tips for Educators

✎ Invite related service providers to be part of your classroom team. They may not accept your invitation at first, but they are more likely to remove other barriers if invited to join you, rather than having to "push in" to a class where they do not feel welcome.

✎ Share your daily schedule with related service providers. Together you may discover times that it "makes sense" to provide some related services within your scheduled activities.

✎ Find times to meet with the related service providers. Meeting just once a month with one person will allow you to share important information.

✎ Invite related service providers to tell you what they are doing with your students and why. Many of their methods are probably easy to incorporate into your own instruction.

✎ Invite related service providers to co-teach with you. Try planning and teaching one lesson or one unit together, and build on your successes.

Tips for Parents

✎ Be an active member of your child's team. When your child has new team members, provide a concise written summary of essential things to know about your child.

✎ Inform the team about your experiences with your child; often a child shows different abilities at school than at home and in the community, so you may see very different strengths and difficulties. A videotape can help illustrate.

✎ Be clear about the outcomes you want your child to achieve. Stay focused on the function (e.g., to tell how he feels when upset) but be flexible about the form (e.g., speech vs. sign language vs. drawing) and the related services methods (e.g., vocabulary lessons in class vs. one-on-one counseling) as long as your child is happy and making satisfactory progress.

✎ Learn about the specialties and methods of the related service providers at your child's school, so you don't mistakenly assume that, for example, all (or only) occupational therapists are experts at teaching handwriting, or that the new physical therapist will use the same methods as the last one.

✎ Share methods with your child's team. Let them know what has and has not worked for you; ask what has and has not worked for them. Discuss when it is important to use the same methods and when variety is acceptable or even helpful.

✎ Check to see if your child is getting plenty of opportunities to learn and practice (with support) important skills in the situations where those skills are needed.

✎ Tell your child's team members about priorities and possibilities for communication with you; find out when and how you can best communicate with them.

NOTES

1. Regulations for IDEA also identify school health services as a related service (20 U.S.C. § 602 (22)).

2. Giangreco, M. F. (1996). *Vermont Interdependent Services Team Approach (VISTA): A guide to developing educational support services.* Baltimore: Paul H. Brookes Publishing Co.

3. Letter to Rainforth, 17 *Education of the Handicapped Law Report* 222 (OSEP 1990).

4. Giangreco (1996).

5. Giangreco (1996).

6. Giangreco (1996).

7. Duckworth, S., Smith-Rex, S., Okey, S., Brookshire, M. A., Rawlinson, D., Rawlinson, R., Castillo, S., & Little, J. (2001). Wraparound services for young schoolchildren with emotional and behavioral disorders. *Teaching Exceptional Children, 33*(4), 54–60; Eber, L., Nelson, C. M., & Miles, P. (1997). School-based wraparound for students with emotional and behavioral challenges. *Exceptional Children, 63*(4), 539–555; and Stevenson, R. A. (2003). Wraparound services: A community approach to keep even severely disabled children in local schools. *School Administrator, 60*(3), 24–25, 27.

8. Katsiyannis, A., & Yell, M. L. (2000). The Supreme Court and school health services: *Cedar Rapids v. Garret F. Exceptional Children, 66*(3), 317–326.

9. King, G. A., McDougall, J., Tucker, M. A., Gritzan, J., Malloy-Miller, T., Alambets, P., Cunning, D., Thomas, K., & Gregory, K. (1999). An evaluation of functional, school-based therapy services for children with special needs. *Physical and Occupational Therapy in Pediatrics, 19*(2), 5–29.

10. Barnes, K. J. (2003). Service delivery practices and educational outcomes of the related service of occupational therapy. *Physical Disabilities: Education and Related Services, 21*(2), 31–47.

11. Giangreco (1996).

12. Barnes (2003).

13. Rainforth, B., & England, J. (1997). Collaborations for inclusion. *Education and Treatment of Children, 20*(1), 85–104.

14. Silverstein, S. (1974). *Where the sidewalk ends.* New York: Harper & Row.

15. Viorst, J. (1980). *Alexander, who used to be rich last Sunday.* New York: Athenaeum.

16. Bromley, K. D. (1989). Buddy journals make the reading-writing connection. *Reading Teacher, 43*(2), 122–129.

17. Rainforth, B., & York-Barr, J. (1997). *Collaborative teams for students with severe disabilities: Integrating therapy and educational services.* Baltimore: Paul H. Brookes Publishing Co.; and Snell, M. E., & Janney, R. (2000). *Teachers' guides to inclusive practices: Collaborative teaming.* Baltimore: Paul H. Brookes Publishing Co.

18. York, J., Rainforth, B., & Giangreco, M. F. (1990). Transdisciplinary teamwork and integrated therapy: Clarifying some misconceptions. *Pediatric Physical Therapy, 2*(2), 73–79.

19. Heller, K. W., Frederick, L. D., Best, S., Dykes, M. K., & Cohen, E. T. (2000). Specialized health care procedures in the schools: Training and service delivery. *Exceptional Children, 66*(2), 173–186.

20. Giangreco, M. F., Edelman, S. W., Luiselli, T. E., & MacFarland, S.Z.C. (1997). Helping or hovering? Effects of instructional assistant proximity on students with disabilities. *Exceptional Children, 64*(1), 7–18; Marks, S. U., Schrader, C., & Levine, M. (1999). Paraeducator experiences in inclusive settings: Helping, hovering, or holding their own? *Exceptional Children, 65*(3), 315–328; and Pickett, A. L., & Gerlach, K. (2003). *Supervising paraeducators in educational settings: A team approach.* (2nd ed.). Austin, TX: Pro-Ed.

21. Hutchison, D. J. (1978). The transdisciplinary approach. In J. B. Curry & K. K. Peppe (Eds.), *Mental retardation: Nursing approaches to care* (pp. 65–74). St. Louis: C. V. Mosby.

22. Sternat, J., Messina, R., Nietupski, J., Lyon, S., & Brown, L. (1977). Occupational and physical therapy services for severely handicapped students: Toward a naturalized public school service delivery model. In E. Sontag, J. Smith, & N. Certo (Eds.), *Educational programming for the severely and profoundly handicapped* (pp. 263–287). Reston, VA: Council for Exceptional Children.

CHAPTER 9

The Changing Roles of Teachers and Teaching in Inclusive Settings

Nancy Dubetz, Neil Garofano, and Joan M. Black

Sal is a special education teacher who has volunteered to co-teach with Jean, a fourth grade general educator. Sal has experience working in a resource room as well as in self-contained programs. Although he has had some opportunity to collaborate with other teachers to plan for the instruction he provides to their students attending his resource room, he has not had any experience co-teaching in an inclusive classroom setting. Jean, a certified elementary education teacher, has taught for three years in a fourth grade general education classroom and has received tenure for her work at the Bay Elementary School, located within a suburban school district. Jean sees herself as a sensitive and caring teacher, and up to this year believed that her students with special needs would benefit more from the instruction offered in the resource room from the special educator in language arts and math.

Creating an inclusive school culture involves a change process that can be both controversial and time-consuming. Inclusive education is controversial because it challenges the traditional structure of schools in ways that can make administrators, teachers, and parents feel uncomfortable, even fearful or hostile. Traditionally, schools address student differences through compensatory programs like remedial reading, resource room, or English as a second language (ESL) classes. In most schools, teachers are socialized to view themselves as effective educators in one area, for example, special education, reading, or secondary math. In addition, schools are structured so as to encourage teachers to work independently rather than collectively. Teachers view their work as a private endeavor and work in relative isolation from each other. Inclusion challenges these views of schools and teaching because it demands collaboration and ongoing sharing of practice and expertise.

Research focusing on how school reform initiatives such as inclusion affect the members of a school community offers several insights into the change process. First, it suggests that change occurs in stages or phases that involve conflict and reassessment of the change initiative during the process.[1] Second, individuals within a school community react to change differently depending on where they are professionally when a reform initiative is undertaken and what attitudes they hold about the initiative. When it comes to inclusion, some teachers will immediately embrace the opportunity to work with colleagues, while others will be filled with doubts and fears.[2] Finally, successful initiatives are systemic, that is, they affect all layers of an institution.[3] As a school reform initiative, including students with disabilities in general education classrooms will affect assessment and curriculum practices and teacher roles throughout the school.

In this chapter we will look at three central challenges to changing a school culture to one that values and practices inclusion. We will illustrate how co-teaching can serve as a way to transform these challenges into opportunities for professional growth and effective inclusive practice. Three challenges to creating an inclusive school culture are (1) ensuring that all students in an inclusive school meet high standards; (2) dealing with changing professional roles brought about by inclusive schooling; and (3) providing effective, ongoing staff development for those new to inclusive education.

THE CHALLENGE OF ENSURING THAT ALL STUDENTS MEET HIGH STANDARDS

Most teachers are well aware of the increasing accountability placed on educators to ensure that all students reach high standards. The standards movement is a result of efforts to assess the status of public education in the United States beginning in the early 1980s. Reports published during this period (e.g., *A Nation at Risk*) suggested that U.S. schools were not remaining competitive with those in other industrialized countries. It was argued that U.S. schools needed to raise expectations for learners. During the 1990s, national standards were developed to describe the content and skills students must acquire in a variety of disciplines (e.g., mathematics, the natural and social sciences, language arts) in order to fully participate in a democratic society and compete in the new global marketplace. At the state level, the national standards have been used to develop curriculum frameworks and assessments that hold schools, districts, and/or individual students accountable for meeting the standards. In some states, a school's funding or accreditation is tied to the percentage of students meeting state standards, and in others students must individually meet state standards to receive a high school diploma.[4] In 2001, the No Child Left Behind (NCLB) Act was passed by Congress, proposing sweeping changes in the way schools are held accountable for meeting the needs of disadvantaged children. The legislation mandates that schools report annual progress toward raising the academic achievement of students of color, English language learners, and children with disabilities. It demands a rigorous accountability system involving standardized assessment of all children, including the subgroups of children mentioned above.

The changes in public policy described above have led to a revisiting of the status of children with disabilities in meeting standards and participating in large-scale assessments. Historically, local and state policy makers have encouraged special educators to resist having children with disabilities participate in large-scale curriculum-based assessments. Advocates of the new standards and policies like NCLB, however, have not only been interested in raising expectations for the best and brightest students; they have argued that a successful democracy depends on all of its citizens reaching their fullest potential, and thus all students must meet higher standards. The reauthorization of the Individuals with Disabilities Education Act in 1997 included changes that supported higher standards for students with disabilities. According to IDEA, students with disabilities must be included in state and district assessments, either with appropriate accommodations or an alternate assessment when they are not able to participate in the general assessment. NCLB requires that 95 percent of various subgroups of children in every school, including children with disabilities, be assessed and that the states must provide reasonable accommodations in the process.

States are responding to these mandates in varying ways. While most states have developed the same standards for all students, a few have developed separate standards for students with disabilities. Most states are working on alternative assessments for the few students with disabilities who cannot succeed with testing accommodations alone. In inclusive settings, it is extremely important that teachers, administrators, and parents are aware of their state's policies regarding standards and assessment for students with disabilities and are preparing these students to meet the standards.

The Challenge of Meeting New Standards in Inclusive Settings

At the core of the push to have all children meet high standards is the belief that all students can learn. However, advocates for learners with disabilities argue that the scope of the new standards is limited to a narrow set of academic content and skills, and current approaches to assessment too narrowly define the ways in which students demonstrate their learning. Although there has been much discussion about the existence of multiple intelligences,[5] standards and standardized exams, for the most part, continue to value a narrow set of these intelligences. Efforts are under way to explore forms of assessment that allow learners to demonstrate their knowledge in multiple ways; however, most state assessments continue to be limited to pencil/paper tests that primarily measure verbal/linguistic and logical/mathematical intelligences.

Darlene's Case. The implications of such state assessment limitations are illustrated in Brogdon's description of Darlene, a special education student who is frustrated by her inability to graduate from high school.[6] Her successful work in an early childhood setting, combined with her ability to read above a fourth grade level, has convinced her teachers that she can be successful, but her interpersonal intelligence is not measured by the high school exams. Helping students with disabilities succeed under such conditions is extremely challenging. In an inclusive school, administrators and teachers must be sure that classrooms are designed to help students with disabilities reach the standards and be able to demonstrate what they know in multiple ways.

A second challenge to ensuring that students with disabilities are successful in meeting new standards is determining how the new standards are affecting the learning of students with disabilities. In inclusive settings, this means that teachers must understand what modifications and adaptations support learning in the general education classroom. Despite changes in federal policy, the percentage of students with disabilities who participate in state assessments varies dramatically from state to state.[7] One of the leading barriers to the participation of students with disabilities in state assessment is the lack of exposure of these students to test content.[8] In most states, the multidisciplinary team (MDT) is responsible for linking individual student goals with state content standards and determining how to assess student performance.[9] Teachers who work with students with disabilities need to be able to align individual student goals with state standards and define appropriate performance standards to measure learning.

The success or failure of a school community to meet standards has become an increasingly public affair as a result of federal and state pressure to disseminate student performance results and link funding to student outcomes. The popularity of school report cards is an indicator of this growing emphasis on results-oriented accountability. As a result, school administrators and teachers feel pressured to demonstrate high student achievement regardless of the nature of the student population. Teachers and administrators resist the inclusion of students with disabilities in the general education classroom because they fear that they will be unable to help students with academic or behavioral needs meet the same standards as other students. Parents resist inclusion because they fear that teachers will lower their expectations for more able students to meet the needs of students with disabilities. As students with disabilities are included in more substantial ways in general education classrooms, the existing system will change, and teachers and administrators who advocate for inclusion will have to address resistance in productive ways.

THE CHALLENGE OF DEALING WITH CHANGING
ROLES AND RESPONSIBILITIES

For inclusion to be successful, those involved need to work together in collaborative ways to promote the learning of diverse pupils in classrooms. Teachers, administrators, and parents need to join together and assume new roles that may be unfamiliar and overlapping; most share the responsibility of providing effective learning opportunities for students with disabilities.

In creating inclusive classrooms, the job description of the regular and special educator needs to be revisited with a collaborative lens. A well-planned collaborative model needs to be implemented in order to best address the diverse needs of students with and without disabilities within the inclusion classroom.[10]

For inclusion to work, a collaborative and trustworthy relationship between the regular education and special education teachers needs to be developed, so that teachers no longer feel that they must do everything themselves and can share in goal setting, decision making, and accountability for the learning of students. Collaboration is necessary for increasing differentiated instruction to address diverse pupil needs in and outside of the classroom setting.

A successful collaborative model challenges teachers to change from a teaching style that is isolationist to one that includes a team approach of sharing resources and responsibilities and planning the instructional program together.[11] A situation of interdependence rather than independence needs to be created, with the regular and special educators supporting one another to help students in inclusive programs benefit and grow. For collaboration to work, teams of teachers need to recognize and value one another's strengths and expertise. They need to build an instructional program together that reflects their common beliefs and philosophy of teaching, focusing on the improvement of learning by all students.

The Changing Roles of Administrators

If a collaborative model is to work in the schools, administrators need to view their role in different ways as well. The administrator of an inclusive school needs to promote collaboration and cooperation rather than competition within the school culture, and help to create and reward teacher partnerships at different stages of implementation. Setting a tone for open sharing and risk taking will support teachers in creating inclusive classrooms that are truly collaborative and innovative. Faculty meetings and staff development that realistically reflect the needs of teachers who are striving to succeed with more inclusive practices is an important administrative function as well. The sharing of successful inclusive practices by colleagues and having the opportunity to observe model collaborative classrooms firsthand have been reported as effective ways that teachers feel supported and best prepared for inclusion.[12]

Administrators need to show their support by arranging collaborative planning time on a regular basis for teachers, and by providing effective and relevant professional development opportunities. In addition, teachers need to be given more decision-making responsibilities in creating collaborative models like co-teaching that will work to fit their personalities and teaching styles, and that will best address pupil needs. Teachers need to know that they are regarded as major players in making decisions rather than merely serving as an advisory group and sounding board for the principal's ideas and mandates. Administrators also should provide necessary technological support and resources to help further inclusive practices within the classroom program.

Administrators can help to convey a sense of confidence in the inclusive model by helping to educate parents about the benefits their students will receive and encouraging them to volunteer in the classrooms to see inclusion at work. Helping to organize classrooms with a reasonable balance of students with disabilities in an equitable and productive way is another way administrators can support inclusion.[13]

Possible Reactions to the Changing Roles Created by Inclusion

Inclusion requires a change in roles and openness to collaboration that may prove to be challenging and difficult for those involved. Teachers trained for general education may not feel prepared as inclusive teachers who need to provide accommodations and adaptations for learners with disabilities within their classrooms. In addition, they may be anxious about getting all students within their classrooms to meet state standards and grade level expectations and being expected to instruct students with disabilities with strategies with which they are not familiar.

Special education teachers involved in inclusive models may worry about their students feeling overwhelmed within the regular classroom. They may also be concerned that the general educator will treat them as teaching assistants rather than as respected co-teachers. These issues as well as others need to be addressed before successful inclusion can take place.[14]

Administrators need to be increasingly willing to share more decision-making responsibilities, be flexible in arranging schedules to fit teacher needs to collaborate, and provide professional development that addresses teacher needs and requests related to inclusive practices. They also need to be strong advocates of the collaborative model to gain the support of parents and the school community at large.

Parents of students with and without disabilities may also have negative reactions to or strong reservations about having their children educated in inclusive classrooms due to their unfamiliarity with the model. Parents of children with disabilities may worry that their son or daughter will not receive sufficient services within the regular classroom setting. A parent of a student without a disability may feel that the special needs learners may slow down the class and prevent others from achieving as much as they should. Parent education on inclusive practices needs to take place so that parents will support inclusion and co-teaching efforts once they come to understand and appreciate the benefits for all those involved.

THE CHALLENGE OF PROVIDING EFFECTIVE, ONGOING PROFESSIONAL DEVELOPMENT

Researchers at the National Center on Educational Restructuring and Inclusion (NCERI) have determined that support in the way of time and staff development is among the essential factors necessary for inclusion to succeed.[15] Support through staff development becomes especially crucial since collaboration, co-planning, and co-teaching are new ways of working for many teachers who will require a set of specialized skills for student learning and refined interactive strategies when embarking on inclusion.[16]

Support Systems Necessary for Inclusion to Succeed

It is clear that a main ingredient in a successful environment of collaboration and co-teaching is time for planning. Repeatedly, research on teaching, collaboration, co-planning, and teaming points to time as the key issue. When a system that supports planning time is not actively maintained, collaborative activities are restricted, often informal, and less a part of the culture of the school.[17] It is essential to recognize that time for collaborative planning needs to be over and beyond the traditional preparation period.

While allocation of time for collaborative planning is a necessary part of the support system, it is clearly not sufficient to promote an effective inclusive teaching culture. Since most teachers are socialized and trained to plan in a solitary and isolated environment, a professional development program focusing on collaborative planning techniques and strategies is needed. Experienced co-teachers, while emphasizing the importance of co-planning, readily report on the awkwardness of the process as it is getting established. Staff development programs are needed to help teachers learn about good co-planning, which includes efficient use of limited time, effective communication techniques, the development of co-planning routines, and the use of technology to enrich collaboration.

A major thrust of support needed for inclusion must be opportunities for teachers to learn about modifying curriculum, learning instructional behaviors, implementing learning strategies, adapting materials, and designing alternative assessment tools. When general and special educators learn about and practice techniques such as these, studies have demonstrated a concomitant improvement in student achievement.

A well-funded and well-organized staff development program that educates teachers in the management of time and energy will likely decrease stress and increase productivity for those in a co-teaching and co-planning arrangement. When describing schools that have been successful at cultivating a climate of collaboration, researchers point to the important contributions of teacher teams in the design, delivery, and evaluation of staff development.[18] Further, when these teams work together as a follow-up to the staff development, they attain a better implementation rate as compared to the implementation rate for teachers with no collegial support.

A significant portion of the success of inclusion hinges on educators' collaborative and co-teaching skills along with their ability to adapt curriculum and accommodate to students' learning needs. If we are to be more successful with inclusion than we were during the "open school" and "open plan" movement of the 1960s and 1970s, then we must learn from the mistakes of that era. Most team teachers in the "open classrooms" lacked professional preparation and planning time needed to establish and enrich their programs.[19] Now, some thirty to forty years later, support in the way of professional development must be a significant part of the inclusion movement.

In conclusion, the real challenge of providing effective staff development is to deliver a program that is different from the top-to-bottom design of traditional efforts. General and special educators need to learn of collaborative methods together in a systemic, ongoing staff development program that consistently responds to the needs and questions that arise from inclusive practices in planning and teaching.

CO-TEACHING AS A MODEL FOR TRANSFORMING CHALLENGES INTO OPPORTUNITIES

In order to face the challenges that come with creating an inclusive school culture, change must occur where learning takes place: in the classroom. It has long been recognized that teachers' first allegiance in schools is to their students and that their greatest reward is feeling that they have made an impact on them.[20] Teachers overwhelmingly prefer to spend additional work time on activities related to their classrooms rather than on schoolwide matters.[21] Co-teaching presents general and special educators with the opportunity to fundamentally change the way children with and without disabilities are educated in the classroom. Research on inclusion has yielded data suggesting that both students and teachers benefit from the experience.[22] Despite the professional and personal challenges, inclusion teachers in a co-teaching arrangement find that their existing pedagogical and planning skills are refined and that they develop new skills when involved in an effective co-teaching arrangement.[23] Teachers report that their careers are enhanced when the classic isolation of the profession fades into a collegial and trusting peer collaboration.[24] Co-teaching in an inclusive school offers teachers ways to help all children meet higher standards, deal with the changing roles and responsibilities that result from collaboration, and grow professionally by acquiring new knowledge and skills through ongoing professional development.

Defining Co-teaching

As the inclusion movement has grown, a sizable number of inclusive trends have grown with it. One of these trends has been to deliver services in the general education classroom by co-teaching. Friend and Cook define co-teaching as two or more professionals delivering instruction jointly to a diverse and blended group of students who are in a single classroom space.[25] Dettmer et al. add that an essential element for true inclusive co-teaching is a shared responsibility for both planning and delivering intense and individualized instruction within the framework of the curriculum used in the general education setting.[26]

One of the inherent advantages of co-teaching is the flexibility it affords teachers who are faced with designing and delivering instruction to a highly diverse group of students with unique learning needs. Co-teaching arrangements have been described by Bauwens and Hourcade,[27] Friend and Cook,[28] Dettmer, Dyck, and Thurston,[29] and Walther-Thomas, Korinek, McLaughlin, and Williams.[30] The models that will now be summarized offer teachers opportunities to use a variety of pedagogical styles in large or small group teaching situations in inclusive classrooms.

Interactive Teaching

The interactive model is the most commonly used style of co-teaching since its variations offer wide flexibility when preparing and delivering instruction. The interactive model has been referred to by several other names, among them "team teaching," "teach and monitor," "speak and chart," "speak and add," "duet,"[31] and "one teach-one observe" or "one teach-one drift."[32] Whatever the name, however, each of the interactive models emphasizes the importance of both partners' active engagement in the teaching and learning process. In general, the interactive model calls for a lead and a support partner who alternate roles periodically so as to help students recognize the co-equal status of the teachers and give each teacher an opportunity to view the teaching/learning process and students' behaviors from both perspectives.

Clearly, when comparing all of the co-teaching models, interactive teaching offers the greatest flexibility. As one teacher leads the discussion, teaches a new concept, or presents a lesson, the other teacher is free to assume several roles during the same lesson. Should the "support" teacher recognize confusion on the students' faces, clarifying comments or questions can be introduced into the lesson in order to both improve learning and encourage student question skills. Sometimes the support teacher may purposefully roam and drift in order to assist students who require focusing reminders or who are confused by the content or instructions. The beauty of the interactive model is that there is less delay in student support, since the "floating" teacher can address students' needs almost immediately and in private, which can minimize any potential student embarrassment and promote better learning.

Alternative Teaching

Friend and Cook describe alternative teaching as a highly advantageous strategy when considering the diverse needs of students within the inclusive classroom.[33] Co-teachers who utilize the alternative teaching models divide instruction into two groups of students, one large and one small.

As in interactive teaching, one partner assumes responsibility for teaching a large group of students. The co-teacher, however, instead of providing spontaneous support, and so on, convenes a smaller group of students who require extension activity, additional instruction, guided practice, pre-teaching, adaptations, repetition, or assessment.

Obviously, the alternative teaching model can be very useful when considering the learning style needs of students with disabilities as well as students who would benefit from advanced learning opportunities. For example, students with behavioral, attentional, or learning problems may need an occasional opportunity to work in a small group with a teacher and, perhaps, a student collaborator/tutor. Likewise, students who may have already met the learning objectives for the large groups could use the alternative small groups to extend their learning through inquiry training, problem solving, or experimentation.

When planning for alternative teaching, caution is in order. Should the same students or teacher be repeatedly assigned to the smaller group format, they may be labeled and/or stigmatized by the arrangement. It is essential, therefore, that roles and memberships between and among the teachers and the small and the large groups be carefully encrypted, rotated, and fluid. The alternative teaching strategy is not designed to promote a "self-contained" atmosphere for students with disability. Therefore, if general education and special education teachers are co-teaching, both should take responsibility for the small group when it is designed for students with disabilities.

Station Teaching

Station or rotation teaching is a co-teaching strategy that calls for the designing of at least three workstations or learning centers where students rotate in and out in small groups. The pedagogical possibilities of station teaching are valuable, but the planning and potential pitfalls deserve very careful consideration.

Typically, after careful planning, the co-teachers divide responsibilities for the lesson and then take a station at one of the learning centers in the environment. In addition to two stations attended by a co-teacher, at least one other station must serve as a location for independent work related to the lesson or a place for peer tutoring or paraprofessional supervised activities. While the station teaching format has all the advantages of small group instruction, it gives the partners an opportunity to immediately complement each other's teaching and encourage a better understanding and deep learning via lesson-related discussions and/or activities.

As with the alternative co-teaching model, teachers are cautioned to plan carefully when selecting students for station learning. It is important to recognize once again how social and learning stigmas can result if the same group of students is too often rotated together. As Walther-Thomas et al. point out, rotation teaching carries with it the potential problems of high voice levels and monitoring difficulties.[34] Furthermore, should a rotation for independent work be utilized, the teachers must carefully consider those students whose independent learning strategies are suspect.

Parallel Teaching

As in station teaching, parallel teaching utilizes small versus whole group instruction. However, unlike station teaching, where complementary activities are designed, parallel teaching is used to present the same material or content but in differing ways. Typically, when preparing for parallel teaching, co-teachers split the class so that group diversity is maintained, and carefully prepare their responsibilities so that eventually the same instruction is delivered. These guidelines for implementation make parallel teaching inappropriate for introductory materials or content but very useful for activities such as drill and practice, concept reviews, or ongoing projects.

THE CO-TEACHING RELATIONSHIP

Learning to co-teach can be compared to the adjustment process encountered in cross-cultural learning.[35] As teachers move from the relative comfort of their "own" classroom to the shared space and time occupied by their co-teachers, they should be aware of the stages of psychological integration that often occur. New co-teachers will face stages of behavior and emotional reactions that we shall call the "E's of co-teaching": enthusiasm, establishment, and enrichment.

Stage 1: Enthusiasm

Since co-teaching should be most importantly a voluntary professional activity,[36] willing participants are usually intrigued and energized by the prospect of entering a partnership. Co-teaching often brings together self-motivated, enthusiastic professionals ready to engage in mutual work to enrich their classrooms, their students, and their professional lives.

Prior to the actual co-teaching experience, most teaching partnerships are characterized by a perception of exciting challenges that lie ahead. Anticipating a co-teaching opportunity provokes a sense of curiosity and novelty that seems to energize the participants and generate a healthy sense of optimism.

Prior to actual engagement, the members of the new co-teaching team often assume a professional psychological profile that serves them and the new partnerships well despite some preconceptions or preconceived ideas. These new team members, while anticipating hard work and unconventional challenges, usually enter the collaborative arrangement willingly, energetically, and optimistically. In fact, should any of the collaborators lack this sort of psychological profile, the emerging co-teaching team will likely enter the establishment phase encumbered.

Stage 2: Establishment

During the establishment phase of co-teaching, the members engage in active collaboration. The teachers now establish their routines, review their early plans, and begin arranging their preferred and/or assigned roles and responsibilities. At this point, a very powerful set of psychological and personality forces may emerge which must be coped with healthfully and professionally if the co-teaching arrangement is to flourish and enrich the learning of all its constituents. A sense of disequilibrium often emerges among co-teachers during the establishment phase. As some of the preconceived notions are dispelled and partners begin to work with new and differing pedagogical styles, preferences, and values, it is not unusual for members of the co-teaching arrangement to experience some frustration and discouragement.

While the enthusiasm stage is characterized by a general air of optimism and anticipation, the establishment phase may bring a sense of doubt and a tinge of regret. ("What have I gotten myself into?") These disturbing early reactions emerge as increased time pressures and the discomforts of change are assimilated into the teachers' professional lives. Practitioners discover that planning and performing one's professional duties are no longer an isolated self-reflective process and confront a new set of circumstances born of the partnership. Members are forced to examine their personality style regarding criticizing, setting boundaries, objecting, disagreeing, maintaining an open mind, and remaining flexible, among many others!

It is essential to recognize that the stress of co-teaching may be at its peak during the establishment phase. The constant demand to adjust and function well often becomes difficult to accept. Many co-teachers struggle with the need to voice their opinions, objections, and preferences while remaining respectful and polite. For most teachers used to conducting a classroom "my" way, the demands of assertive negotiations can be temporarily perceived as burdensome.

It is useful at this time to review the co-teaching research, which suggests that the challenging establishment phase characterizes the first year of a new co-teaching arrangement. However, most co-teachers reported that their efforts at laying the foundation for the team paid off soon thereafter.[37]

In successful co-teaching arrangements the establishment phase serves a very useful purpose. The struggles encountered by patient team members promote a healthy sense of acceptance without complacency and a reflective working relationship bonded in a spirit of collaboration. As the establishment phase passes, the co-teachers begin to understand how the differences that once caused exasperation and angst are among the ingredients that allow for enrichment.

Stage 3: Enrichment

As the team passes through the establishment phase, successful co-teachers come to the realization put forth by Dettmer, Dyck, and Thurston: "In order to serve students best, educators do not need to think alike—they need to think together."[38]

Upon transition into the final phase of collaboration, many co-teachers experience a "quality burst" in their ongoing partnership. Successful practitioners in a prolonged collaboration report increases in trust, efficiency, and a sense of value, creativity, and humor as hallmarks of the enrichment phase of co-teaching.[39]

Once the familiar isolation of what Hunter referred to as the "armed camp"[40] diminishes, a climate of respect and collegiality begins to permeate the partners and the process. As the process moves along in the enrichment phase, a comfortable co-teaching rhythm sets up. The teachers develop a sense of harmony as the enriching interchange helps to orchestrate the invention of new pedagogies built on one another's work. And now, instead of discounting the collaboration as unfamiliar, awkward, and time-consuming, veteran co-teachers use each other's differences to identify problems, generate solutions, evaluate performance, improve learning, and enrich their professional lives. As the rhythm builds, successful co-teachers no longer focus on the problems and obstacles of co-teaching. Instead, they recognize and value a certain "ease of co-teaching."

Opportunities During the Establishment Phase: Planning for Successful Co-teaching

Since the co-teaching model may very likely be different from the one most teachers have been trained for and are comfortable following, there may be a good deal of anxiety and resistance to pursuing a classroom co-teaching partnership. Teacher concerns regarding ownership of the classroom and one's students, the large amount of time needed for planning lessons collaboratively, the difficulty in establishing a process for jointly evaluating students, and one's discomfort level at having other adults in the classroom are possible reactions from teachers when asked to work together in inclusive classrooms. Not knowing exactly what each partner's job responsibilities are supposed to be may discourage and inhibit people from participating in a co-teaching model unless handled appropriately.

In a successful inclusive classroom, the general educator's role is providing instruction for all students as s/he collaborates with the special educator for the strategies and the accommodations they will both be providing to different groups of learners. Consequently, in this arrangement the special educator's role is expanded to a respected co-teacher working with many pupils, not only those with disabilities. The special education teacher is not perceived as the one who is solely responsible for the behavior of the learners with IEPs or the only one to monitor the learning of only a small group of students within the general education classroom. Successful co-teaching team members have a sense of equity in terms of the ownership of the classroom and its learners. Once the expertise of each of the co-teachers is recognized, an instructional program of varying teaching formats with strategies for accommodations and adaptations can be jointly organized and implemented.

With planning ahead for the appropriate administrative support, parent involvement, and teacher collaboration, many of the problems related to a change in roles in inclusive classrooms can be prevented. Co-teaching offers teachers endless opportunities to learn from one another, share responsibilities, and help each other reflect on the learning process and needs of their students.

Factors to Consider for a Successful Co-teaching Process

To make co-teaching work and continue successfully beyond the enthu-siasm and establishment stages, a good deal of advance planning needs to take place before its actual implementation in inclusive classrooms. Areas for planning involve the following six aspects that schools need to consider with thoughtfulness and sensitivity:

1. Identify a shared philosophy, common goals, and basic rules.
2. Schedule meetings and plan subsequent Instruction.
3. Define roles and responsibilities.
4. Identify and select a variety of instructional formats.
5. Set up a process to deal with student problems.
6. Plan an assessment process.

After each of these aspects is described, they will be further illustrated through a case study discussion.

Identify a Shared Philosophy, Common Goals, and Basic Rules

Co-teachers need to formulate a common philosophy and goals that will drive the instructional program they will be implementing. A shared set of philosophical beliefs and values has been cited as an important factor in successful collaboration.[41] For co-teaching to work, it is essential that both team members have communicated and have agreed upon a set of desired outcomes for their collaborative program. In addition, co-teachers need to identify their ideas and expectations about daily routines and procedures that involve classroom management, grouping practices, and discipline.

We'd like to reintroduce Sal and Jean, the two teachers described in the anecdote at the beginning of this chapter, to illustrate the planning process that needs to take place for collaboration to be successful. If you'll remem-ber, Sal is a special education teacher who has volunteered to co-teach with Jean, a fourth grade general educator. Sal has not had any experience co-teaching with another teacher within an inclusive classroom setting. Jean sees herself as a sensitive and caring teacher and up until this year believed that her students with special needs would benefit more from language arts and math instruction offered in the resource room rather than in her classroom.

When the principal of the Bay Elementary School asked for volunteers to co-teach in a classroom to further promote the school's effort for inclu-sion, Sal and Jean agreed to work as partners. The district provided funds for Sal and Jean to plan their program together during the summer prior to the start of the inclusion model. They designated a week in July and a week in August to meet to design their program and to plan ahead for the success of the co-teaching experience. Their classroom was to have a paraprofessional and twenty-five students, seven of whom have IEPs.

Schedule Regular Meetings and Plan Subsequent Instruction

Meeting collaboratively on a regular basis to examine the instructional program and its effects on classroom learners is a crucial component for successful co-teaching. The team needs to adhere to the planned agenda in a timely manner. Important resolutions and actions to be taken, the identification of the person(s) responsible for their implementation, and designated target dates should be recorded and distributed to team members for implementation.[42]

First off, Jean and Sal agreed to set aside designated meeting times each week to assess the impact of the classroom instructional program on student learning as well as to reflect on how the co-teaching model was working. They also created a process to record highlights of their meetings. They would take turns writing minutes of the meetings and completing a helpful form that identified the action to be taken, the lesson(s) to be planned, and the designated person to assume responsibility for the task's implementation.

Define Roles and Responsibilities of Co-Teachers

Although roles may change through the establishment and enrichment stages, the more the responsibilities and tasks of each team member are discussed at the beginning of the establishment stage, the better the chances are that the co-teaching partnership will be one of parity and satisfaction.

In September, Jean and Sal decided to try different models of co-teaching based on the subject matter and the needs of their students in the particular area of the curriculum. Since Jean's favorite subject to teach was science, the team decided that Jean would lead science instruction. Sal drifted and assisted students, following the interactive teaching model. For language arts, both teachers believed in the importance of small group instruction and chose to follow a form of the alternative teaching format. To start, Jean would work with the advanced readers, while Sal would offer structured phonics instruction and strategic reading lessons to two small groups of learners struggling in language arts, some of whom had disabilities. In math, the teachers chose to follow a parallel teaching model, with Sal teaching the advanced math students at a more rapid pace. This served to offer Sal newer insights into the learning of successful learners, and to present him as a teacher of all students in the class, not only of those with disabilities.

Identify and Select a Variety of Instructional Formats Incorporating Accommodations and Adaptation

Co-teachers should review together the different strategies and models of teaching that they will be using in their collaborative classroom. Inductive learning, direct instruction, and cooperative learning experiences may be considered for individualized, small group, and large group instruction to address the diverse learning styles and needs of classroom pupils and the objectives of the curriculum. In addition, it is important for the team to share successful strategies with one another for providing accommodations and adaptations as soon as the needs and learning styles of students are assessed.

Set Up a Process to Deal with Student Problems

Identifying problem-solving procedures will also be helpful before the program is in full gear. One needs to expect that once teachers begin to co-teach, problems will emerge that can become wonderful opportunities for teacher learning and collaboration. Even the best planners cannot predict all the potential problems that may arise once they are sharing a classroom and a group of pupils. It is important, therefore, to have a process in place for solving problems collaboratively.

According to Friend and Cook, a problem is a discrepancy between what exists and what is desired.[43] Although problem identification may sound easy, it is often the most difficult part of the problem-solving process. A problem needs to be defined in specific, concrete language. For example, describing a student as unmotivated offers little specific information. On the other hand, describing the current behaviors that lead one to believe that a student is unmotivated, as well as the behaviors that would be desirable, offers important information that can help the teachers in both selecting an intervention and evaluating its potential. Without clearly defining the problem, it is impossible to determine whether the problem can be solved relatively quickly, or whether the co-teaching team will need to gather extensive data over time. In addition, when describing a problem, it is important to use multiple sources of information. The advantage of co-teaching is that there are two observers to offer insights into the problem. Problems can have many solutions. It is important to dedicate adequate time to brainstorming for all possible solutions without evaluating them. During brainstorming all ideas are accepted. Once a list of possible solutions is developed, teachers can evaluate them by exploring the positive and negative consequences of each. This process will narrow the list of possible solutions. It is then appropriate to outline what task would need to be performed for each possible solution to determine which would be the most feasible given the circumstances.

In order to implement the plan, Friend and Cook suggest that a chart be developed to record descriptions of each activity/intervention that will be implemented, the individual(s) who will be responsible for the actions, the expected outcomes of each activity/intervention, and a target date for evaluating the success of each activity/intervention.[44] This process or any other should be examined and planned for before the establishment stage is under way.

Plan for an Assessment Process to Monitor Success of the Co-teaching Experience

It is crucial for the co-teachers to establish a strong working relationship of trust and respect for one another for inclusion to work. Striving for an environment of open dialogue to share one's fears and concerns is important for the co-teaching model to work. Creating opportunities to reflect on classroom practices and regular discussion of how the co-teaching model is going are other important areas to consider. Planning for a process of open dialogue ahead of time may reduce the stress and discomfort when an incident or concern arises once the co-teaching model is implemented. Team members must recognize the need to adhere to confidentiality, to respect the diversity of opinions, and to recognize the importance of hearing each other out before arriving at a decision.

During the establishment phase of collaboration, co-teachers need to plan for how they will monitor their success as a team. It is difficult to measure how students are experiencing co-teaching if the co-teachers themselves are not aware of their own process. Teachers need to reflect on their collaborative experiences on an ongoing basis. In a sense, they must step out of their roles as co-teachers and look at what they are experiencing as co-observers or co-investigators. With the many decisions that need to be made on a daily basis, it is not easy to find time for either individual or collaborative reflection; however, it is critical to the ultimate success of the team. An easy way to do this is to dedicate some time to debriefing after a particularly positive or negative co-teaching experience. A second, more powerful way to engage in reflection is to videotape a co-taught activity or a planning meeting. A video provides an excellent stimulus for discussing and evaluating an experience in the role of co-investigators.

Let's return to our case study and see how Jean and Sal engage in analyzing their co-teaching experiences. First, they begin each planning session with a discussion of their co-teaching process. To do this, they use a set of questions for reflection:

What specific evidence was there that we were sending the message to our students that we are equal partners in instruction?

Did our roles change since the last time we taught together, and if so, how?

Who made what decisions during a co-taught lesson?

How did we address differences of opinion?

What did we do when a problem arose that we had not anticipated?

This is a "starter" set of questions. The teachers might focus on only one at a meeting, or they might add a new one. What is important is that this guided reflection occurs before they begin planning for the next set of activities. This helps them focus on the importance of their relationship in developing a community of inclusion in the classroom.

Co-teachers commit to a long-term relationship. As in any long-term relationship, they will not always agree, and conflicts will emerge. Conflicts are a natural outgrowth of even the most constructive collaborative relationships. If co-teachers have planned effectively, they have already explored potential similarities and differences in their approaches to planning and delivering instruction, managing behavior, assessing students' work, and completing paperwork. However, it is not uncommon for co-teachers to deal with negative feelings toward each other during the establishment phase. Common sources of conflict are when one teacher perceives that the other is doing more of the decision making or less of the work, or when one perceives that the other is grading students using a different set of criteria or values.

Addressing conflicts collaboratively is not easy. Teachers, like all human beings, have been socialized to deal with conflict in diverse ways depending on their cultural backgrounds and personal experiences with conflict as members of families and communities. Some have been socialized to avoid conflict, while others have been socialized to see conflicts as win-lose battles. Fortunately, effective strategies for resolving conflicts exist that help teachers address concerns while also maintaining their working relationship. Strategies such as forcing or persuading the other person to yield to one's decision or withdrawing from the person may resolve the problem but do not create opportunities to further strengthen the partnership.[45] One strategy that serves as a way to both resolve the conflict and maintain a productive relationship between co-teachers is a conflict negotiation process described by Raider.[46]

According to Raider, effective negotiation occurs in four stages: ritual sharing, defining the issues, reframing the issues, and finding common ground. In the remainder of this section, we will use our case study teachers to illustrate the stages.

Conflicts commonly arise around classroom management because, traditionally, general education teachers tend to depend on a common set of strategies for managing the class as a whole, whereas special educators are accustomed to individualizing their strategies because they work with such a diverse range of disabilities.

By late September, Sal has observed that Jean is disciplining Millie, a child with ADHD, in a way that he believes is not effective. Jean expects children to be in their seats unless they have been given permission to move, and she has been telling Millie to sit down every few minutes. Yesterday, Jean demanded that Millie stay in the class seated at a desk during recess because she was out of her seat multiple times during the morning. Sal is getting aggravated because he doesn't think Jean is being sensitive to Millie's disability, but Jean feels that in a class of twenty-five children, kids have to be expected to remain seated. She also thinks that ten-year-olds are mature enough to be held accountable for following classroom rules. Tension begins to grow in the relationship and affects how Sal works with Jean during co-teaching. Sal decides that they need to sit down and talk about the situation.

SHARING RITUAL

The purpose of ritual sharing, the first stage of the negotiation process, is to get the negotiation off to a good start. Social rituals such as cordially greeting each other or sharing something humorous help build rapport. Co-teachers may have already developed such rituals, whether consciously or unconsciously. Sal and Jean choose to discuss the situation during their regular planning time, and they often start off these meetings with a visit to the coffeepot and a comment about how they are feeling that day.

Identification of Issues

The next stage is to identify the issues. In this stage each person shares his/her position and needs with the other. A position is often framed as a point of view that one person is taking. Thus, Sal's position is that Jean's approach to disciplining Millie isn't working. Jean's position is that Millie is not following the class rules and must be disciplined. A need is framed as a statement of what one desires. Thus, Sal's need is to see that Millie be disciplined in a way that effectively modifies her inappropriate behavior. Jean's need is that Millie be seated when the rest of the students are seated. The focus of effective conflict negotiation is on needs and not positions, though teachers should share background explanations or justifications for their points of view as well during this stage. Attacking the other person is not useful in resolving the conflict. If both people have not been truthful about what they need at this stage, then they will not be able to come to agreement on a solution later in the process.

Reframe Issues

The third stage is to reframe the issues. This stage can only occur once the two people have made clear their issues and needs. Once each is well informed about the other's needs, they can collaborate and combine two points of view into a single problem in need of a solution. One way of doing this is by having teachers list the issues on a sheet of paper, ask themselves how they can work together, and address both sets of needs. Sal and Jean reframe their issue in the following way: We need to develop an effective disciplinary strategy for Millie that works for her and works for both of us.

Brainstorm

At this point the brainstorming stage is undertaken, following the same structure described earlier as a problem-solving activity. It is important that both teachers contribute ideas, that all ideas are included for consideration, and that no one's ideas are criticized. Once both participants have agreed that they have no more ideas, they review the list and select ideas they both agree with. Jean and Sal came up with a set of three discipline plans for Millie and implemented one that they believe will best change Millie's behavior using both rewards and punishment. This agreement helps them monitor each other's reactions to Millie when she is seated and when she gets out of her seat without permission. They agree to discuss Millie's progress and their own progress in following the plan during their reflection time. Now their co-teaching relationship is back on track, the tension is gone, and the next conflict will be easier to address because of their newly developed skills.

As with learning any new skill, negotiation may seem awkward at first, especially if one does not have much experience with it. Only an overview of conflict negotiation is provided here, and it will be important for teaching teams to have access to experts in conflict resolution to help them develop the skills needed to address conflict constructively. Once teachers are able to resolve their conflicts, they are able to more effectively help their students resolve conflicts.

Opportunities During the Enrichment Phase: Studying the Impact of Co-teaching on Children

Once teachers reach the enrichment phase, they are ready to begin undertaking serious analysis of the impact of their efforts on students and the school culture. The "quality burst" that co-teachers experience at this phase can be used to transform the challenges described in the early part of the chapter into opportunities for effectively addressing a diverse range of student needs and promoting an inclusive school culture. Teacher research is an opportunity to solve problems in ways that will serve teachers in and outside the classroom in the present and the future. Cochran-Smith and Lytle define teacher research as "systematic, intentional inquiry by teachers about their own school and classroom work."[47] Teacher research presents an opportunity for teachers to investigate the relationship between their practice and its impact on students. In teacher research, teachers define the questions they wish to investigate. For co-teachers in inclusive settings, teacher research is a vehicle for the study of the impact of inclusive strategies on the academic, behavioral, and social development of students.

The teacher research cycle generally involves four phases: planning; action; observation and data collection; and reflection and revision.

The first step in launching an investigation of a new problem or existing practice is to identify a question to investigate. New problems that emerge as co-teachers proceed offer a rich pool of ideas for research. The research question may emerge from informal conversations or from a more formal problem-solving process like the one described earlier. Teacher research is labor intensive, so it is important to choose a question that is answerable and will be useful to the team in future practice.

Teacher research offers co-teachers a way to study specific questions related to their classroom. Sal and Jean could choose from the following: How is our approach to reading affecting our included students? How are three of our learning disabled children responding to a modification that enables them to work with primary documents during social studies? Are disabled and nondisabled students learning from each other in our inclusion classroom? Such research into inclusive practices will not only provide insights for the teachers, but will also offer important findings to be shared with administrators, parents, and colleagues who may be skeptical about inclusive schooling. At present there is relatively little data on the impact of inclusive education on students because the reform is so new in most schools. Earlier in the chapter, we described some of the concerns that have emerged with the increasing pressure on schools to demonstrate achievement on state assessments. Evidence gathered in the classroom is a powerful tool for establishing local policy and addressing attitudes of resistance.

Once the research question is formed, the teachers need to see what knowledge base is already available about the new or existing practice under study. It is here that teacher research transforms an opportunity to resolve a classroom problem into an opportunity to develop professionally and learn more about inclusive education. Next, teacher researchers need to plan for how they are going to record changes between what is currently occurring and what they wish to see occur. Teachers need to decide what kind of information they want to gather to document changes. Descriptive information can be collected through observations, interviews, journals, and samples of student work. There are a variety of commercial materials available for helping teachers make decisions about appropriate methods for gathering information. Once the planning is completed, the teachers are ready to begin their research.

Whether the teachers are implementing an intervention or evaluating a current practice, they need to document what they are doing. The observation and data collection may be occurring while the intervention is implemented, or it may happen before and after the intervention. Without this documentation, it will be difficult later to determine how the intervention affected the outcomes. It is easy to become involved in resolving new issues and neglect to collect adequate information to examine the practice under investigation. Once the data has been collected, the final step is to reflect, and if necessary, revise the original plan. It is important for co-teachers to set aside time for discussing their research. Co-teaching offers wonderful opportunities for collaborative reflection, and the most exciting results of teacher research are having the power to modify practice based on what has been learned and to share what has been learned with others in the immediate school community or at professional conferences.

SUMMARY

All signs point to an accelerated trend toward educating all students in inclusive settings. In the process, schools are often radically altering traditional classroom ecologies and the roles and responsibilities of most of the professionals working in these new environments. This process of change is usually slow, painstaking, and replete with challenges. While the concept of inclusion has become a valued fundamental principle embraced by many in our educational system, there is no precise formula for the development of an "inclusive classroom." Unfortunately, some districts have begun developing and implementing their own brand of "inclusion" without careful consideration of and planning for the many complex challenges that must be faced by students, professionals, and parents. As a result, poorly implemented versions of "inclusion" have sprung up around the country.

In this chapter, we have attempted to present some of the challenges all schools and their constituents should anticipate as they move from the traditional special education models to a culture of inclusion. We recognize especially the critical challenges of the standards movement, professional development programs, and collaboration. Embedded in these challenges, however, we have found professional opportunities to improve teaching and student learning.

It is our belief that co-teaching is an essential opportunity and tool for teachers intending to embark upon the challenges of inclusion. While co-teaching is a significant change for most teachers, it is also a very powerful dynamic process when planned and implemented patiently and properly. Through co-teaching, teachers can better fortify themselves and their students for the challenges of inclusion. Through co-teaching, powerful problem-solving strategies and pedagogical techniques can improve learning for all. And through co-teaching, inclusion can be more than an educational fad and instead become an opportunity for all students to be meaningfully involved in the mainstream of education.

Tips for Educators

🖎 Familiarize yourself with policies that explain how children with disabilities are to be evaluated in relation to learning standards in your district and/or state.

🖎 Insist on adequate administrative support and resources for pre-planning and ongoing planning once you implement your program.

🖎 Set up a scheduled time for co-teacher meetings.

🖎 Decide which model(s) of co-teaching you will use and for what purposes.

🖎 Define what each teacher's role will be in the model(s) you choose to implement.

🖎 Share each teacher's strengths, areas of expertise, and concerns.

🖎 Discuss and plan for instructional formats that incorporate accommodations and adaptations.

🖎 Determine how you will address problems when they arise.

🖎 Decide how you will build in opportunities for reflection on your co-teaching process.

🖎 Expect conflicts to arise and plan for how you will deal with them.

🖎 Develop a plan for how you will study the effects of your work on your students.

Tips for Parents

🖎 Familiarize yourself with policies that explain how children with disabilities are to be evaluated in relation to learning standards in your district and/or state. Much of this information is available through district offices and state and federal Web sites.

🖎 Answers to frequently asked questions for parents and educators about No Child Left Behind can be found at www.NoChild LeftBehind.gov.

🖎 Most state departments of education have a Web site that can be located on the Internet by using a search engine such as Google.com or by requesting the information from your school.

✎ Your school should have a plan for preparing parents for placing their children in inclusion programs. There should be an orientation and information about how the program is designed and the benefits and challenges it offers. If not, insist that such an orientation be provided before placing your child in an inclusive program.

✎ If teachers are effectively co-teaching, you should be able to meet with both or either of them to get information on how you child is doing.

NOTES

1. Fullan, M. (1982). *The meaning of educational change.* New York: Teachers College Press.

2. Bradley, D. F., King-Sears, M. E., & Tessier-Switlick, D. M. (1997). *Teaching students in inclusive settings: From theory to practice.* Needham Heights, MA: Allyn & Bacon.

3. Bradley King-Sears, & Tessier-Switlick (1997); and Fullan (1982).

4. Erickson, R. (1998). *Special education in an era of school reform: Accountability, standards, and assessment.* Washington DC: Federal Resource Center for Special Education.

5. Gardner, H. (1983). *Frames of mind: The theory of multiple intelligences.* New York: Basic Books.

6. Brogdon, R. E. (1993). Darlene's story: When standards can hurt. *Educational Leadership, 50*(5), 76–77.

7. Thompson, S., & Thurlow, M. (2000). State alternative assessments: Status as IDEA alternate assessment requirements take effect. Synthesis Report 35. Minneapolis: University of Minnesota, National Center on Educational Outcomes.

8. Thompson & Thurlow (2000).

9. Erickson (1998).

10. Friend, M., & Cook, L. (2000). *Interactions: Collaboration skills for school professionals* (3rd ed.). White Plains, NY: Longman; and Snell, M. E., & Janney, R. (2000). *Social relationships and peer support.* Baltimore: Paul H. Brookes Publishing Co.

11. Snell & Janney (2000).

12. Snell & Janney (2000).

13. Friend & Cook (2000).

14. Friend & Cook (2000); and Snell & Janney (2000).

15. Dettmer, P., Dyck, N., & Thurston, L. P. (1999). *Consultation, collaboration and teamwork for students with special needs.* Boston: Allyn & Bacon.

16. Friend & Cook (2000).

17. Friend, M., & Bursuck, W. D. (1999). *Including students with special needs: A practical guide for classroom teachers.* Boston: Allyn & Bacon, pp. 75–77.

18. Darling-Hammond, L. (1997). Principals and teachers must devise new struc-

tures to meet the challenges of education in the 21st century. *Principal, 77*(1), 5–11.

19. Dickenson, T.S., & Erb, T.O. (Eds.). (1996). *We gain more than we give: Teaming in middle schools.* Columbus: OH: National Middle School Association.

20. Lortie, D. (1975). *Schoolteacher: A sociological study.* Chicago: University of Chicago Press.

21. Lortie (1975).

22. Walther-Thomas, C., Bryant, M., & Land, S. (1996). Planning for effective co-teaching: The key to successful inclusion. *Remedial and Special Education, 17*(4), 255–266.

23. Walther-Thomas, C. (1997). Co-teaching experiences: The benefits and problems that teachers and principals report over time. *Journal of Learning Disabilities, 30*(4), 395–399.

24. Walther-Thomas (1997).

25. Friend & Cook (2000).

26. Dettmer, Dyck, & Thurston (1999).

27. Bauwens, J., & Hourcade, J.J. (1995). *Cooperative teaching: Rebuilding the schoolhouse for all students.* Austin, TX: Pro-Ed.

28. Friend & Cook (2000).

29. Dettmer, Dyck, & Thurston (1999).

30. Walther-Thomas, C., Korinek, L., McLaughlin, V.L., & Williams, B. (1999). Collaboration to support students' success. *Focus on Exceptional Children, 32*(3), 1–19.

31. Walther-Thomas (1997).

32. Friend & Bursuck (1999).

33. Friend & Cook (2000).

34. Walther-Thomas, Korinek, McLaughlin, & Williams (1999).

35. Cushner, K., McClelland, A., & Safford, P. (1992). *Human diversity in education: An integrative approach.* New York: McGraw-Hill, pp. 28–30.

36. Mostert, M.P. (1998). *Interprofessional collaboration in schools.* Boston: Allyn & Bacon.

37. Mostert (1998).

38. Dettmer, Dyck, & Thurston (1999).

39. Walther-Thomas (1997), 397–407.

40. Hunter, M. (1984). Knowing, teaching, and supervising. In P.L. Hosford (Ed.), *Using what we know about teaching.* Alexandria, VA: ASCD.

41. Fishbaugh, M.S. (1997). *Models of collaboration.* Boston: Allyn & Bacon; and Kochhar, C.A., West, L.L., & Taymans, J.M. (2000). *Successful inclusion: Practical strategies for a shared responsibility.* Upper Saddle River, NJ: Prentice Hall.

42. Snell & Janney (2000).

43. Friend & Cook (2000).

44. Friend & Cook (2000).

45. Johnson, D.W., & Johnson, R.T. (1995). Teaching students to be peace makers: Results of five years of research. *Peace & Conflict, 1*(4), 417–429.

46. Raider, E. (1992). Solving conflicts—not just for children. *Educational Leadership, 50*(1), 14–18.

47. Cochran-Smith, M., & Lytle, S. (1993). *Inside-outside: Teacher research and knowledge.* New York: Teachers College Press, p. 450.

Part II Bibliography

Amos, P. (1999). What restraints teach. *TASH Newsletter, 25*(11), 28–29.

Anderson, J. (1999). Reflections about positive behavioral supports. *TASH Newsletter, 25*(11), 4–6.

Archer, J. (2000, March). Minority teachers. *Number and Needs, 10*(2), 4.

Armstrong, T. (1994). *Multiple intelligences in the classroom*. Alexandria, VA: ASCD.

Aronson, E., Blaney, N., Stephan, C., Sikes, J., & Snapp, M. (1978). *The jigsaw classroom*. Beverly Hills, CA: Sage.

Artiles, A. J., & Ortiz, A. A. (Eds.) (2002). *English language learners with special education needs: Identification, assessment, and instruction*. Washington, DC: Center for Applied Linguistics.

August, D., Calderon, M., & Carlo, M. (2001). The transfer of skills from Spanish to English: A study of young learners. *NABE News, 13*. Available at http://www.ncbe.gwu.edu/miscpubs/jeilms/vol13/transf13.htm.

Baker, A.J.L., & Soden, L. M. (1998). The challenges of parent involvement research. *ERIC/CUE Digest* No. 134. New York: ERIC Clearinghouse on Urban Education, Institute for Urban and Minority Education, Teachers College, Columbia University.

Baker, C. (2001). *Foundations of bilingual education and bilingualism*. Clevedon, UK: Multilingual Matters.

Barnes, K. J. (2003). Service delivery practices and educational outcomes of the related service of occupational therapy. *Physical Disabilities: Education and Related Services, 21*(2), 31–47.

Bauwens, J., & Hourcade, J. J. (1995). *Cooperative teaching: Rebuilding the schoolhouse for all students*. Austin, TX: Pro-Ed.

Bellon J. J., Bellon, E., & Blank, M. (1992). *Teaching from a research knowledge base: A development and renewal process*. New York: Macmillan.

Berliner, D. (1985). Is parent involvement worth the effort? *Instructor, 95*, 20–21.

Biklen, D. P. (1992). *Schooling Without labels: Parents, educators, and inclusive education*. Philadelphia: Temple University Press.

Boyles, N. S., & Contadino, D. (1998). *The learning differences sourcebook.* Los Angeles: Lowell House.

Bradley, D. F., King-Sears, M. E., & Tessier-Switlick, D. M. (1997). *Teaching students in inclusive settings: From theory to practice.* Needham Heights, MA: Allyn & Bacon.

Brinkley, J., & Armstrong, J. (1997). What are you trying to tell me?—The Role of Communication in Behavior: Instructional Support System of Pennsylvania. Tri-State Consortium on Positive Behavior Support. Paper presented at TASH Conference, December, 1997.

Brogdon, R. E. (1993). Darlene's story: When standards can hurt. *Educational Leadership, 50*(5), 76–77.

Bromley, K. D. (1989). Buddy journals make the reading-writing connection. *Reading Teacher, 43*(2), 122–129.

Cassella, R. A., Kluth, P., Taney, S., & Brunken, K. (2000). *Tools for schools: Differentiated instruction, a tool for all students.* Albany: University of the State of New York and the New York State Education Department.

Center for Research on Education, Diversity and Excellence. (1998, April 8). Findings on the effectiveness of bilingual education [press release]. Santa Cruz, CA: CREDE.

Cloud, N. (1993). Language, culture and disability: Implications for instruction and teacher preparation. *Teacher Education and Special Education, 16*(1), 60–72.

Cloud, N. (2002). Culturally and linguistically responsive instructional planning. In A. J. Artiles and A. A. Ortiz (Eds.), *English language learners with special education needs: Identification, assessment, and instruction* (pp. 107–132). Washington, DC: Center for Applied Linguistics.

Cloud, N., Genesee, F., & Hamayan, E. (2000). *Dual language instruction: A handbook for enriched education.* Boston: Heinle & Heinle.

Cochran-Smith, M., & Lytle, S. (1993). *Inside-outside: Teacher research and knowledge.* New York: Teachers College Press.

Cohen, L., & Spenciner, L. J. (2005). *Teaching students with mild and moderate disabilities: Research-based practices.* Upper Saddle River, NJ: Prentice Hall.

Collaborative for Academic, Social, and Emotional Learning (CASEL). (2003). *Safe and sound: An educational leader's guide to evidence-based social and emotional learning programs.* Chicago: CASEL.

Collier, V. P. (1995, Fall). Acquiring a second language for school. *Directions in Language and Education, 1*(4).

Cook, L., & Friend, M. (1995). Co-teaching guidelines for creative effective practices. *Focus on Exceptional Children, 28*(2), 1–12.

Cummins, J. (1981). The role of primary language development in promoting educational success for language minority students. In *Schooling and language minority students: A theoretical framework* (pp. 3–49). Los Angeles: Evaluation, Dissemination, and Assessment Center, California State University.

Cummins, J. (1986). Empowering minority students: A framework for interaction. *Harvard Review, 56,* 18–36.

Cushner, K., McClelland, A., & Safford, P. (1992). *Human diversity in education: An integrative approach.* New York: McGraw-Hill.

Daniels, V. I. (1998). How to manage disruptive behavior in inclusive classrooms. *Teaching Exceptional Children, 30*(4), 26–31.

Darling-Hammond, L. (1997). Principals and teachers must devise new structures to meet the challenges of education in the 21st century. *Principal, 77*(1), 5–11.

DeGaetano, Y., Williams, L., & Volk, D. (1998). *Kaleidoscope: A multicultural approach for the primary classroom.* Columbus, OH: Merrill.

Demchak, M. (1993). Functional assessment of problem behaviors in applied settings. *Intervention in School and Clinic, 29*(2), 89–93.

Dettmer, P., Dyck, N., & Thurston, L. P. (1999). *Consultation, collaboration and teamwork for students with special needs.* Boston: Allyn & Bacon.

DeVries, D. L., Slavin, R. E., Fennessey, K. M., Edwards, K. J., & Lombardo, M. M. (1980). *Teams—games—tournament: The team learning approach.* Englewood Cliffs, NJ: Educational Technology Publications.

Dickenson, T. S., & Erb, T. O. (Eds.). (1996). *We gain more than we give: Teaming in middle schools.* Columbus, OH: National Middle School Association.

Duckworth, S., Smith-Rex, S., Okey, S., Brookshire, M. A., Rawlinson, D., Rawlinson, R., Castillo, S., & Little, J. (2001). Wraparound services for young schoolchildren with emotional and behavioral disorders. *Teaching Exceptional Children, 33*(4), 54–60.

Dunlap, G., & Foster-Johnson, L. (1993). Using functional assessment to develop effective, individualized interventions for challenging behaviors. *Teaching Exceptional Children, 25*(3), 44–50.

Dunlap, G., Kern, L., dePerczel, M., Clarke, S., Wilson, D., Childs, K. E., White, R., & Falk, G. D. (1993). Functional analysis of classroom variables for students with emotional and behavioral disorders. *Behavioral Disorders, 18*(4), 275–291.

Dye, G. A. (2000). Graphic organizers to the rescue: Helping students link and remember information. *Teaching Exceptional Children, 32*(3), 72–76.

Eber, L., Nelson, C. M., & Miles, P. (1997). School-based wraparound for students with emotional and behavioral challenges. *Exceptional Children, 63*(4), 539–555.

Echevarria, J., Vogt, M. E., & Short, D. J. (2004). *Making content comprehensible for English language learners: The SIOP Model.* (2nd ed.). Boston: Allyn & Bacon.

Erickson, R. (1998). *Special education in an era of school reform: Accountability, standards, and assessment.* Washington, DC: Federal Resource Center for Special Education.

Fern, V., Anstrom, K., & Silcox, B. (1994). Active learning and the limited English proficient student. *Directions in Language and Education, 1*(2). Washington, DC: National Clearinghouse for Bilingual Education.

Finn, J. D. (1998). Parental engagement that makes a difference. *Educational Leadership, 55*(8), 20–24.

Fishbaugh, M. S. (1997). *Models of collaboration.* Boston: Allyn & Bacon.

Fradd, S. H. (1992, December). Collaboration in schools serving students with limited English proficiency and other special needs. *ERIC Digest* (EDO-FL-91-10). Washington, DC: ERIC Clearinghouse on Languages and Linguistics, Center for Applied Linguistics.

Freeman, D. E., & Freeman, Y. S. (1992). *Whole language for second language learners.* Portsmouth, NH: Heinemann.

Freeman, D. E., & Freeman, Y. S. (1993). Strategies for promoting the primary languages of all students. *The Reading Teacher, 46*(7), 552–558.

Freund, R., & Rich, R. (2005). *Teaching students with learning problems in the inclusive classroom.* Upper Saddle River, NJ: Prentice Hall.

Friend, M., & Bursuck, W. D. (1999). *Including students with special needs: A practical guide for classroom teachers.* Boston: Allyn & Bacon.

Friend, M., & Cook, L. (2000). *Interactions: Collaboration skills for school professionals.* (3rd ed.). White Plains, NY: Longman.

Fullan, M. (1982). *The meaning of educational change.* New York: Teachers College Press.

Gaies, S. J. (1985). *Peer involvement in language learning.* Orlando, FL: Harcourt Brace Jovanovich and the Center for Applied Linguistics.

Gallagher, J. (1998, October). The language of learning: Attacks on bilingual education ignore the varied needs of non-native speakers. *Middle Ground, 2*(2), 6–10, 24.

Garcia, D. (1990). Factors that determine and influence Hispanic parental involvement: Creating parental involvement. In D. Garcia, *A manual for school children and parents interacting program* (pp. 51–55). ERIC Reproduction Service Number ED 323 273. Miami: Florida International University.

Garcia, S. B. (1995, June 12–13). Cultural influences on teaching and learning. Presentation at the Multicultural Special Education Summer Institute, Omaha, Nebraska.

Garcia, S. B. (2002). Parent-professional collaboration in culturally sensitive assessment. In A. J. Artiles and A. A. Ortiz (Eds.), *English language learners with special education needs: Identification, assessment, and instruction* (pp. 87–103). Washington, DC: Center for Applied Linguistics.

Gardener, H. (1983). *Frames of the mind: The theory of multiple intelligences in the classroom.* New York: Basic Books.

Genesee, F. (Ed.). (1999). *Program alternatives for linguistically diverse students.* Santa Cruz, CA: Center for Research on Education, Diversity and Excellence (CREDE).

Giangreco, M. F. (1996). *Vermont Interdependent Services Team Approach (VISTA): A guide to developing educational support services.* Baltimore: Paul H. Brookes Publishing Co.

Giangreco, M. F., Cloninger, C. J., & Salce Iverson, V. (1998). *COACH: Choosing outcomes and accommodations for children.* (2nd ed.). Baltimore: Paul H. Brookes Publishing Co.

Giangreco, M. F., Edelman, S. W., Luiselli, T. E., & MacFarland, S. Z. C. (1997). Helping or hovering? Effects of instructional assistant proximity on students with disabilities. *Exceptional Children, 64*(1), 7–18.

Greene, G., & Nefsky, P. (1999). Transition for culturally and linguistically diverse youth with disabilities: Closing the gaps. In B. A. Ford (Ed.), *Multiple voices for ethnically diverse exceptional learners 1999* (pp. 15–24). Reston, VA: Council for Exceptional Children.

Greenlee, M. (1981). Specifying the needs of a "bilingual" developmentally disabled population: Issues and case studies. *NABE Journal, 6*(1), 55–76.

Gutierrez-Clellen, V. (1999). Language choice in intervention with bilingual children. *American Journal of Speech-Language Pathology, 8,* 291–302.

Harry, B. (1992). *Cultural diversity, families, and the special education system: Communication and empowerment.* New York: Teachers College Press.

Heller, K. W., Frederick, L. D., Best, S., Dykes, M. K., & Cohen, E. T. (2000). Specialized health care procedures in the schools: Training and service delivery. *Exceptional Children, 66*(2), 173–186.

Herrell, A., & Jordan, M. (2004). *Fifty strategies for teaching English language learners.* (2nd ed.). Upper Saddle River, NJ: Pearson/Merrill, Prentice Hall.

Hollins, E. R. (1996). *Culture in school learning: Revealing the deep meaning.* Mahwah, NJ: Lawrence Erlbaum Associates.

Hudson, P. J. (1989). Instructional collaboration: Creating the learning environment. In S. H. Fradd & M. J. Weismantel (Eds.), *Meeting the needs of culturally and linguistically different students: A handbook for educators* (pp. 106–129). Boston: College-Hill.

Hunter, M. (1984). Knowing, teaching, and supervising. In P. L. Hosford (Ed.), *Using what we know about teaching.* Alexandria, VA: ASCD.

Hutchison, D. J. (1978). The transdisciplinary approach. In J. B. Curry & K. K. Peppe (Eds.), *Mental retardation: Nursing approaches to care* (pp. 65–74). St. Louis: C. V. Mosby.

Inger, M. (1992, August). Increasing the school involvement of Hispanic parents. *ERIC Digest* No. 80. New York: ERIC Clearinghouse on Urban Education, Institute for Urban and Minority Education, Teachers College, Columbia University.

Jacobs, L. (1991). Assessment concerns: A study of cultural differences, teacher concepts, and inappropriate labeling. *Teacher Education and Special Education, 14*(1), 43–48.

Janney, R., Black, J., & Ferlo, M. (1989). *A problem-solving approach to challenging behaviors: Strategies for parents and educators of people with developmental disabilities and challenging behaviors.* Syracuse, NY: Syracuse City Schools.

Janney, R., & Snell, M. (2000). *Teachers' guides to inclusive practices: Behavioral support.* Baltimore: Paul H. Brookes Publishing Co.

Johnson, D. W., & Johnson, R. T. (1991). *Learning together and alone: Cooperative, competitive, and individualistic learning.* (3rd ed.). Englewood Cliffs, NJ: Prentice Hall.

Johnson, D. W., & Johnson, R. T. (1995). Teaching students to be peacemakers: Results of five years of research. *Peace & Conflict, 1*(4), 417–429.

Johnston, C. A. (1998). Using the learning combination inventory. *Educational Leadership, 55*(4), 78–82.

Kagan, S. (1985). Dimensions of cooperative classroom structures. In R. Slavin, S. Sharan, S. Kagan, R. Hertz-Lazarowitz, C. D. Webb, & R. Schmuck (Eds.), *Learning to cooperate, cooperating to learn* (pp. 67–96). New York: Plenum Press.

Kagan, S. (1986). Cooperative learning and sociocultural factors in schooling. In California Department of Education (Ed.), *Beyond language: Social and cultural factors in schooling language minority students* (pp. 231–298). Los Angeles: California State University.

Kagan, S. (1995, May). We can talk: Cooperative learning in the elementary ESL classroom. *ERIC Digest* (EDO-FL-95-08). Washington, DC: ERIC Clearinghouse on Languages and Linguistics, Center for Applied Linguistics.

Kang, H. W. (1994). Helping second language readers learn from content area text through collaboration and support. *Journal of Reading, 37*(8), 646–652.

Katsiyannis, A., & Yell, M. L. (2000). The Supreme Court and school health services: *Cedar Rapids v. Garret F. Exceptional Children, 66*(3), 317–326.

Kincaid, D., & Knoster, T. (1999). Effective school practice in educating students with challenging behavior. *TASH Newsletter, 25*(11), 8–11.

King, G. A., McDougall, J., Tucker, M. A., Gritzan, J., Malloy-Miller, T., Alambets, P., Cunning, D., Thomas, K., & Gregory, K. (1999). An evaluation of functional, school-based therapy services for children with special needs. *Physical and Occupational Therapy in Pediatrics, 19*(2), 5–29.

Klingner, J. K., & Vaugh, S. (1999). Students' perceptions of instruction in inclusion classrooms: Implications for students with learning disabilities. *Exceptional Children, 66*(1), 23–37.

Kluth, P. (2000). Community-referenced learning and the inclusive classroom. *Remedial and Special Education, 21*(1), 19–27.

Kluth, P. (2003). *You are going to love this kid! Teaching students with autism in the inclusive classroom.* Baltimore: Paul H. Brookes Publishing Co.

Kochhar, C. A., West, L. L., & Taymans, J. M. (2000). *Successful inclusion: Practical strategies for a shared responsibility.* Upper Saddle River, NJ: Prentice Hall.

Krashen, S. (1982). *Principles and practice in second language acquisition.* Oxford, UK: Pergamon.

Langdon, H. W. (2002). *Interpreters and translators in communication disorders: A practitioner's handbook.* Eau Claire, WI: Thinking Publications.

Langdon, H. W., & Cheng, L. L. (2002). *Collaborating with interpreters and translators: A guide for communication disorders professionals.* Eau Claire, WI: Thinking Publications.

Leverett, R. G., & Diefendorf, A. O. (1992). Students with language deficiencies. *Teaching Exceptional Children, 24*(4), 30–34.

Lortie, D. (1975). *Schoolteacher: A sociological study.* Chicago: University of Chicago Press.

Lyman, F. (1992). Think-pair-share, thinktrix, thinklinks, and weird facts. In N. Davidson & T. Worsham (Eds.), *Enhancing thinking through cooperative learning.* New York: Teachers College Press.

Lynch, E. W., & Stein, R. (1987). Parent participation by ethnicity: A comparison of Hispanic, black and Anglo families. *Exceptional Children, 87*, 105–111.

Lynn, L. (1997). Language-rich home and school environments are key to reading success. Harvard Education Letter Research Online, http://www.edletter.org/past/issues/1997-ja/language.shtml.

Marion, R. L. (1982). Communicating with parents of culturally diverse exceptional children. In C. H. Thomas and J. L. Thomas (Eds.), *Bilingual special education resource guide* (pp. 52–65). Phoenix, AZ: Oryx Press.

Marks, S. U., Schrader, C., & Levine, M. (1999). Paraeducator experiences in inclusive settings: Helping, hovering, or holding their own? *Exceptional Children, 65*(3), 315–328.

Martin-Kniep, G. O. (1999). *Capturing the wisdom of practice: Professional portfolios for educators.* Alexandria, VA: ASCD.

Mastroprieri, M. A., & Scruggs, T. E. (2000). *The inclusive classroom: Strategies for effective instruction.* Upper Saddle River, NJ: Prentice Hall.

McDiarmid, G. W. (1989). What do teachers need to know about cultural diversity? Restoring subject matter to the picture. In *Competing visions of teacher knowledge: Proceedings from an NCRTE seminar for education policymakers. Vol. 2: Student diversity* (pp. 91–106). East Lansing: Michigan State University, National Center for Research on Teacher Education.

McGregor, G., & Vogelsberg, R. T. (1998). *Inclusive schooling practices: Pedagogical and research foundations. A synthesis of the literature that informs best practices about inclusive schooling.* Baltimore: Paul H. Brookes Publishing Co.

Mercer, C. D., & Mercer, A. R. (2005). *Teaching students with learning problems.* Upper Saddle River, NJ: Prentice Hall.

Meyer, L. H., & Evans, I. M. (1989). *Nonaversive intervention for behavior problems.* Baltimore: Paul H. Brookes Publishing Co.

Mostert, M. P. (1998). *Interprofessional collaboration in schools.* Boston: Allyn & Bacon.

NAEYC. (1996). NAEYC position statement: Responding to linguistic and cultural diversity—Recommendations for effective early childhood education. *Young Children, 51*(2), 4–12.

Natheson-Mejia, S. (1989). Writing in a second language. *Language Arts, 66*(5), 516–526.

Oakes, J. (1985). *Keeping track: How schools structure inequality.* New Haven, CT: Yale University Press.

Padolsky, D. (2002a). *How has the limited English proficient student population changed in recent years?* Ask NCELA No. 8. Washington, DC: National Clearinghouse for English Language Acquisition and Language Instruction Educational Programs.

Padolsky, D. (2002b). *How many school-aged English language learners (ELLs) are there in the U.S.?* Ask NCELA No. 1. Washington, DC: National Clearinghouse for English Language Acquisition and Language Instruction Educational Programs.

Pennsylvania Department of Education, Bureau of Special Education. (1995). Guidelines: Effective Behavioral Support. Harrisburg: Pennsylvania Department of Education.

Pickett, A. L., & Gerlach, K. (2003). *Supervising paraeducators in educational settings: A team approach.* (2nd ed.). Austin, TX: Pro-Ed.

Pinnell, G. S., & Jaggar, A. M. (1991). Oral language: Speaking and listening in the classroom. In J. Flood, J. M. Jensen, D. Lapp, & J. R. Squire (Eds.), *Handbook of research on teaching the English language arts* (pp. 691–729). New York: Macmillan.

Pipher, M. B. (1994). *Reviving Ophelia: Saving the selves of adolescent girls.* New York: Putnam.

Polloway, E. A., Patton, J. R., & Serna, L. (2005). *Strategies for teaching learners with special needs.* Upper Saddle River, NJ: Prentice Hall.

Raider, E. (1992). Solving conflicts—not just for children. *Educational Leadership, 50*(1), 14–18.

Rainforth, B. (2003). Using activity routines to design inclusive education for students with severe disabilities. In B. Rainforth & J. Kugelmass (Eds.),

Curriculum and instruction for all learners: Blending systematic and constructivist approaches in inclusive elementary schools (pp. 241–267). Baltimore: Paul H. Brookes Publishing Co.

Rainforth, B., & England, J. (1997). Collaborations for inclusion. *Education and Treatment of Children, 20*(1), 85–104.

Rainforth, B., & England, J. (2000). Educational teams for students with diverse needs: Structures to promote collaboration and impact. In V. Risko & K. Bromley (Eds.), *Collaboration for diverse learners: Viewpoints and practices.* Newark, DE: International Reading Association.

Rainforth, B., & York-Barr, J. (1997). *Collaborative teams for students with severe disabilities: Integrating therapy and educational services.* Baltimore: Paul H. Brookes Publishing Co.

Rennie, J. (1993, September). ESL and bilingual program models. *ERIC Digest* (EDO-FL-94-01). Washington, DC: ERIC Clearinghouse on Languages and Linguistics, Center for Applied Linguistics.

Riley, R. W. (2000, March 15). Excelencia para todos—Excellence for all: The progress of Hispanic education and the challenges of a new century. Speech delivered at Bell Multicultural High School, Washington, DC.

Rosenberg, M. S., O'Shea, L., & O'Shea, D. J. (1999). *Student teacher to master teacher.* Upper Saddle River, NJ: Prentice Hall.

Salend, S. J. (1999). So what's with our inclusion program? *Teaching Exceptional Children, 32*(2), 46–54.

Salend, S. J. (2001). *Creating inclusive classrooms: Effective and reflective practices.* Upper Saddle River, NJ: Prentice Hall.

Santos, R. M., Fowler, S. A., Corso, R. M., & Bruns, D. A. (2000, January/February). Acceptance, acknowledgment, and adaptability: Selecting culturally and linguistically appropriate early childhood materials. *Teaching Exceptional Children, 32*(3), 14–22.

Sharan, S., & Hertz-Lazarowitz, R. (1980). A group-investigation method of cooperative learning in the classroom. In S. Sharan, P. Hare, C. D. Webb, & R. Hertz-Lazarowitz, (Eds.), *Cooperation in education* (pp. 14–46). Provo, UT: Brigham Young University Press.

Short, D. J. (1989, September). Adapting materials for content-based language instruction. *ERIC/CLL News Bulletin, 13*(1), 1, 4–8.

Silverstein, S. (1974). *Where the sidewalk ends.* New York: Harper & Row.

Snell, M. E., & Janney, R. (2000a). *Social relationships and peer support.* Baltimore: Paul H. Brookes Publishing Co.

Snell, M. E., & Janney, R. (2000b). *Teachers' guides to inclusive practices: Collaborative teaming.* Baltimore: Paul H. Brookes Publishing Co.

Sontag, J. C., & Schacht, R. (1993). Family diversity and patterns of service utilization in early intervention. *Journal of Early Intervention, 17,* 431–444.

Stanovich, P. J. (1999). Conversations about inclusion. *Teaching Exceptional Children, 31*(6), 54–58.

Sternat, J., Messina, R., Nietupski, J., Lyon, S., & Brown, L. (1977). Occupational and physical therapy services for severely handicapped students: Toward a naturalized public school service delivery model. In E. Sontag, J. Smith, & N. Certo (Eds.) *Educational programming for the severely and profoundly handicapped* (pp. 263–287). Reston, VA: Council for Exceptional Children.

Stevenson, R. A. (2003). Wraparound services: A community approach to keep even severely disabled children in local schools. *School Administrator, 60*(3), 24–5, 27.

Taylor, S. V. (2000, January/February). Multicultural is who we are: Literature as a reflection of ourselves. *Teaching Exceptional Children, 32*(3), 24–29.

TESOL. (1996). Promising futures: ESL standards for pre-K–12 students. TESOL Professional Paper #1. Alexandria, VA: Teachers of English to Speakers of Other Languages.

TESOL. (1997). *ESL standards for pre-K–12 students.* Alexandria, VA: Teachers of English to Speakers of Other Languages.

Thomas, R. L. (1993). Cross-age and peer tutoring. *ERIC Digest* (EDO CS-93-01). Bloomington, IN: ERIC Clearinghouse on Reading and Communication Skills.

Thomas, W. P., & Collier, V. P. (2002). A national study of school effectiveness for language minority students' long-term academic achievement. Final Report: Project 1.1. Santa Cruz, CA: Center for Research on Education, Diversity and Excellence.

Thompson, S., & Thurlow, M. (2000). State alternative assessments: Status as IDEA alternate assessment requirements take effect. Synthesis Report 35. Minneapolis: University of Minnesota, National Center on Educational Outcomes.

Thonis, E. (1983). *The English-Spanish connection.* Northvale, NJ: Santillana Publishing Co.

Tomlinson, C. A. (2000). Reconcilable differences? Standards-based teaching and differentiation. *Journal of the Association for Supervision and Curriculum Development, 58*(1), 5–11.

Trueba, H. T. (1989). Cultural embeddedness: The role of culture on [*sic*] minority students' acquisition of English literacy. In *Competing visions of teacher knowledge: Proceedings from an NCRTE seminar for education policymakers.* Vol. 2: *Student diversity* (pp. 77–90). East Lansing: Michigan State University, National Center for Research on Teacher Education.

Turnbull, A., & Turnbull, H. R. III. (1999). Group action strategy as a plan for providing comprehensive family support. In L. K. Koegel, R. L. Koegel, & G. Dunlap (Eds.), *Positive behavioral support: Including people with difficult behavior in the community* (pp. 99–114). Baltimore: Paul H. Brookes Publishing Co.

U.S. Census Bureau. (2001). *The Hispanic population. Census 2000 brief.* C2KBR/01-3. Washington, DC: U.S. Department of Commerce, Economics and Statistics Administration, U.S. Census Bureau.

Viorst, J. (1980). *Alexander, who used to be rich last Sunday.* New York: Athenaeum.

Voltz, D. L. (1995). Learning and cultural diversities in general and special education classes: Frameworks for success. In B. A. Ford (Ed.), *Multiple voices for ethnically diverse exceptional learners* (pp. 1–11). Reston, VA: Division for Culturally and Linguistically Diverse Exceptional Learners, Council for Exceptional Children.

Waggoner, D. (2000, March). Public school districts report LEP enrollment. *Numbers and Needs* (Ethnic and Linguistic Minorities in the United States), *10*(2), 1–2, 4.

Wald, J. L. (1996). *Culturally and linguistically diverse professionals in special education: A demographic analysis.* Reston, VA: National Clearinghouse for Professions in Special Education, the Council for Exceptional Children.

Walther-Thomas, C. (1997). Co-teaching experiences: The benefits and problems that teachers and principals report over time. *Journal of Learning Disabilities, 30*(4), 395–399.

Walther-Thomas, C., Bryant, M., & Land, S. (1996). Planning for effective co-teaching: The key to successful inclusion. *Remedial and Special Education, 17*(4), 255–266.

Walther-Thomas, C., Korinek, L., & McLaughlin, V. L. (1999). Collaboration to support students' success. *Focus on Exceptional Children, 32*(3), 1–19.

Winzer, M. A., & Mazurek, K. (1998). *Special education in multicultural contexts.* Upper Saddle River, NJ: Merrill.

York, J., Rainforth, B., & Giangreco, M. F. (1990). Transdisciplinary teamwork and integrated therapy: Clarifying some misconceptions. *Pediatric Physical Therapy, 2*(2), 73–79.

Zehler, A. M. (1994, Fall). *Working with English language learners: Strategies for elementary and middle school teachers.* NCBE Program Information Guide Series, 19. Washington, DC: National Clearinghouse for Bilingual Education.

Zemelman, S., Daniels, H., & Hyde, A. (1993). *Best practice: New standards for teaching and learning in America's schools.* Portsmouth, NH: Heinemann.

PART III

For Parents and Families

CHAPTER 10

Parent Participation in Inclusive Schooling

Darra Pace, Linda Milch, and Lillian Sanabria-Hernández

Will and Alice are the parents of two school-age children. Paul is a typical fourth grader with no health or school problems. Brianne, age six, was born with multiple health issues and has had numerous hospitalizations. Neither parent had a positive experience in school, nor have they completed high school. Will works a factory job for minimum wage, while Alice is a health aide in a nursing home. Despite some financial assistance from their parents and their church, Will and Alice feel overwhelmed with the expense of caring for Brianne. Learning to deal with the health care system and early intervention recommendations has been difficult, and not completely mastered by either parent. Now Brianne's school is asking for meetings to discuss concerns about her. Both Will and Alice have great trepidation about getting involved with yet another group of professionals and the school system itself. How can they get the help they need?

NAVIGATING SCHOOL CULTURE

Welcome to your neighborhood school! The images that might pop into a visitor's mind are directly related to his or her own personal history and experience from books, movies, and television shows. Reality might well prove to be different, in both positive and negative ways, from memories or media interpretation.

For parents new to the American school system, or to those harboring negative memories of their own educational experiences, the school and the educational system can be very intimidating and inhospitable. In addition, the professional culture of schools, with unfamiliar educational jargon and business dress, can increase feelings of trepidation. To deal with this system, parents have to learn just what rights they have to ensure the best education for their children. Parents like Will and Alice, who have already been involved with bureaucracies such as the medical system and the department of health, may understandably not be eager to take on the public schools.

Schools are complex places with their own set of routines, rules, and regulations designed to provide a safe and productive place in which students can learn. For educator and parent alike, knowing how schools work, and the culture of education, increases the chances of facilitating the kind of education that benefits all students.

Getting in the Door

Today, schools are very conscious of the need for security. These precautions are responses to troubling issues in the real world, such as terrorism, weapons, and gangs. The aim of security is to make school safe and to avoid potential trouble while still allowing children to be comfortable and grow and prosper.[1] Although these precautionary measures can be off-putting for parents, it is important for them to understand that locked doors, sign-in procedures, closed-circuit televisions and cameras, hall patrols, digital surveillance, and even metal detectors are meant to deter crime, or at least make someone feel uncomfortable about committing a crime.[2] Security is not meant to make parents unwelcome. In fact, these procedures are in place to reassure parents that their children are being well taken care of. Parents, along with students, teachers, administrators, and school personnel, are considered wanted and welcomed members of the school community.

What Is School Culture?

Much as any home or workplace has its own atmosphere, or "culture," so does a school. Every school is unique, with its own culture. According to Kent Peterson, "School culture is the set of norms, values and beliefs, rituals and ceremonies, symbols and stories that make up the 'persona' of the school."[3] Both educators and parents need to understand their roles and how they contribute to creating the very culture that they are involved in. Peterson writes about "unwritten expectations" that evolve over time as the administrators and teachers work with students and parents. How these expectations develop is very much a result of the interactions of all the stakeholders in the school. Parents are not tangential to the school culture; they are very much a part of it. Consequently it is important that parents understand the norms of the school their child attends. They also need to understand that as their child advances through the school system and changes schools, each experience will require both students and parents to learn and adjust to a new school culture.

To understand a school culture, we must look at the values and beliefs of the educational system as well as the ceremonies, rituals, and traditions that are part of each school community.[4] Parents new to the system may be unfamiliar with yearly traditions such as holiday concerts, field day, or school fairs. Not only are families and school personnel welcome at these events, their participation is needed for the traditions to continue. Ceremonies such as graduation or award nights are opportunities to be part of the school program, and must be presented as such. The limitations of parental involvement during certain events, on the other hand, must be clearly stated. On Open School Night, for example, teachers present curriculum and expectations for the year, and do not discuss individual students. Parents need to know ahead of time that this is not the forum to discuss individual children and that other arrangements can be made to meet with the teacher.

The school calendar is an important planning resource that lists events and important dates throughout the year. It is very helpful in planning availability for special school occasions. In addition, calendars usually list important telephone numbers, including those for individual schools, administrators within the district, the attendance and health office, and so on.

Written communication is the primary manner in which schools and teachers maintain contact with parents.[5] Generally a written notice is prepared to publicize school functions and other important information. Particularly important announcements are mailed home; others are sent home with the students. It is necessary that parents ask their children not only what happened at school that day but also what they have brought home from school.

Written correspondence can be problematic if it is not in the native language of the family. Schools should be sensitive to this issue, and make sure that all families receive information they can read.

STANDARDS OF STUDENT ACHIEVEMENT

Individual student achievement is a major focus of the American educational system. Students take tests that are expected to measure achievement and raise academic standards, while holding educators and students accountable for reaching high educational goals.[6] These tests are used not only to track student progress but also for promotion and graduation. Each year parents receive a report of their child's score in comparison to other students in their school district as well as to students across the country.

When student performance falls below a certain standard, parents are invited to meet with school personnel to discuss and address the student's needs. The outcome of this meeting may involve a variety of options, from extra help to repeating a grade. Or the child's needs may suggest placement in the special education system. Special education offers students a wide range of services and supports in the general education classroom as well as in separate placements.

BRIDGING THE CULTURE GAP

Despite the best intentions and a determined need, the core values of special education—individualism, equity, and choice—can conflict with those of parents.[7] Parents may be more accepting of their child and might not believe that their child needs to be "fixed."

Parents' acceptance of a child's disability can conflict with a system that stresses choice and equity as means to ensure that students receive an individually tailored education. Schools might view lack of active parental involvement in pursuing the educational values of the system as indifference when in actuality it is a response to a different set of values.

Cultural dissonance can also play a significant role between a school and a family. The school must be willing to recognize, for example, that the culture of the family may not value individual independence, but instead how the child fits into a group, thereby assuring his or her future.[8] The parents, by the same measure, need to appreciate that schools *do* focus on the individual student and may not be aware of the parents' value of collectiveness.

Meetings or conferences are intended to be a true dialogue between educators and parents.[9] A conference, however, can cause real concern for everyone involved. Parents are anxious about what teachers will say, and teachers worry about parental response. Both sides want and need to be clearly understood. The meeting venue is meant to afford parents and teachers the opportunity to partner in the education of the child they both care about. So what are some things that can help in making these exchanges positive?

- Write down topics you want to share in advance. It is easy to forget something you want to discuss when you are actively involved in a dialogue.
- Listen carefully. Take notes, and don't be afraid to ask questions to clarify anything you don't understand or feel is vague.
- Remember that time is limited. Both parent and teacher have other obligations, so keep in mind that a follow-up conference might need to be scheduled. If meeting in person is difficult, perhaps a phone conference can be arranged.
- Summarize the meeting. Review the major points and the conclusions of the conference. Again, make sure everything is clear. Don't be afraid to ask questions.

Educators understand that many parents are not familiar with the intricacies of the school process. No question is foolish, especially those that ask for further explanation of unfamiliar topics such as special services, evaluation, and placement.

PARENTS' RIGHTS IN THE SPECIAL EDUCATION PROCESS

One of the core principles stated in the Code of Federal Regulations to implement IDEA demands parental involvement in the individual educational decision-making process. Children with disabilities are entitled to a free and appropriate public education (FAPE). Parents of children with disabilities are empowered to ensure that their children receive the services they require in order to fulfill the FAPE mandate. While this is an important entitlement for parents, many parents such as Will and Alice are intimidated about getting involved.

IDEA emphasizes and mandates parental involvement in the special education process through meetings between parents and educators to discuss any concerns they have based on a child's disability or even the suspicion of a disability that might impact a child's education. Specifically, IDEA "requires that parents have an opportunity to participate in meetings with respect to the identification, evaluation, and educational placement of the child, and the provision of FAPE to the child."[10]

Each local education agency (LEA), or school district, is required to have meetings to determine initial and continued eligibility for special education services. Since there is so much at stake for families, it is important that they understand the special education process for their state and their school. Each state may have its own name for the formal meeting whose purpose is to discuss eligibility for special education services. It may be called an IEP (Individualized Education Program) meeting or a CSE (Committee on Special Education) meeting or possibly the eligibility meeting. This meeting can be requested by a parent or staff member. Once a meeting is requested in writing:

- Parents have a right to be involved at every step of the process. Prior to any evaluation the school district must obtain written consent. Educators should explain to parents what evaluations are being done, and why.

- The school must conduct a comprehensive evaluation in a timely fashion so that a meeting can be held and services put in place by the sixtieth school day.

- Any evaluations necessary to determine whether or not a youngster has a disability under IDEA or Section 504 must be conducted at no cost to parents.

- If parents choose to have evaluations done at their own expense, those evaluations must be considered along with any evaluations the school has conducted.
- Evaluations should be conducted in the child's native language or mode of communication.
- A variety of assessment tools should be used.
- For a child with limited English proficiency, assessment tools must be selected that measure disability, not the child's English language skills.

Any information the parent provides, including information related to the child's ability to be involved in the general curriculum, should be considered in determining whether a child has a disability and in the development of the child's IEP.

THE IEP MEETING

Once all the necessary evaluations are completed, the IEP meeting can be held. It is of crucial importance for parents to attend this meeting, as they are important members of the IEP team. In recognition of this, IDEA mandates that the meeting take place at a time and place mutually agreed upon by the parent and the school district. If the parents cannot make a scheduled meeting they want to attend, they should notify the school district as soon as possible.

Parents can and should play a major role in determining the child's involvement in the general curriculum and his or her participation in state and district-wide assessments. They can also have input into what services the school district will provide and in what setting those services will be provided. Together, the IEP team must determine if the student meets one of the thirteen disability categories listed in IDEA. That having been decided, an IEP can be developed that includes the goals and objectives the child is expected to achieve.

Parents may invite individuals of their choosing to the IEP meeting. While it is not a requirement, parents are encouraged to inform school personnel of their intention to bring others to the meeting. This will facilitate a productive, child-centered meeting. The goal of IDEA, and specifically the Amendments of 1997, is for parents to work in partnership with their child's school. If a parent attends an IEP meeting and finds that the IEP has been developed without parental input, there has been a violation of IDEA. It is important to note that according to Appendix A of IDEA, it is not permissible for an agency to have the IEP completed before the IEP meeting begins. Agency staff may come to an IEP meeting prepared with evaluation findings and proposed recommendations regarding IEP content, but the agency must make it clear to the parents at the outset of the meeting that the services proposed by the agency are only recommendations up for review and discussion with the parents. Parents have the right to bring questions, concerns, and a recommendation to an IEP meeting as part of a full discussion of the child's needs and the services to be provided to meet those needs before the IEP is finalized.

Once the initial IEP is developed, the team comes to a consensus regarding the appropriate services by which the IEP goals can be met. Appendix A of IDEA makes it very clear that it is not appropriate to make decisions based on a majority vote. Furthermore, Appendix A states, "If the team cannot reach consensus, the public agency must provide the parents with prior written notice of the agency's proposals or refusals, or both, regarding the child's education program, and the parents have the right to seek resolution of any disagreements by initiating an impartial due process hearing."[11]

In addition to asserting their due process rights, the parents can seek mediation or an independent educational evaluation at school district expense. When a parent requests an independent evaluation, the school district must make arrangements to have the evaluation done or convene a hearing to demonstrate that an evaluation is not necessary. While any of these measures are being implemented, the agreed upon services remain in place. An IEP must exist in order for a child to begin receiving special education and related services. However, if the parents agree, an interim IEP can be developed to determine an appropriate placement for a child.

Sometimes it takes more that one meeting to determine initial eligibility for services, develop an IEP, and make recommendations. However, once it is determined that a child needs special education and related services, the IEP must be in place within thirty days.

Parental rights and involvement do not end with the development of the first IEP. Once a child has been classified as having a disability, the IEP team must meet at least once every twelve months to review the IEP and determine whether the annual goals are being achieved, and revise the IEP if necessary. When appropriate, the results of any reevaluations will be presented. If the parents or school team have any new information, it should be discussed at this time, as well as any anticipated needs. The parents, and when appropriate, the student, will be invited to attend and participate in every IEP meeting. The parents, sometimes in conjunction with the school staff, determine if the attendance of the child will be helpful in developing the IEP or if it would be of some benefit to the child to be present. Student participation at IEP meetings, particularly during the discussion of transition services in the adolescent years, will be discussed later in this chapter.

If the parents believe the placement and/or services are no longer appropriate during the course of the year the IEP is in effect, they can request a meeting. How can parents know whether or not their child's IEP or the services are appropriate? When IDEA was reauthorized in 1997, a mechanism was specifically added so that parents could be meaningfully involved in their child's special education program throughout the year and not be surprised at the end of the year about their child's progress. A number of provisions in Part B of IDEA keep parents informed of their child's progress.

IDEA requires that parents be informed of the child's present levels of educational performance. This statement can be used by parents as a way of measuring progress from year to year.[12] Additionally, the law requires that the IEP indicate how the disability affects the child's involvement and progress in the general curriculum.

IDEA also requires that parents be regularly informed of their child's educational progress.[13] The IEP must state how the child's progress toward goals will be measured. The IEP report to parents must indicate the progress toward annual goals and whether the progress is sufficient to enable the child to achieve the goals by year's end. This gives parents the information they need to either set up informal meetings with school personnel or request a CSE meeting if the child's lack of progress continues.

A major objective of the IEP is that it will remain appropriate for the full year it is in effect and that the student will demonstrate ongoing progress. However, children do not follow a guidebook and can sometimes change unexpectedly. If a child is not progressing at the rate anticipated by the IEP, parents and professionals can first meet informally to review the IEP and examine the child's progression. The team will want to rule out any possible physical cause for the lack of progress, such as ear infections or poor vision. The parent and teacher may want to review the evaluations with or without the assistance of a psychologist to determine if a different method of instruction might benefit the student. If the child is still not progressing after review and modification of instruction, the parent or the teacher can request an IEP meeting. All requests made regarding eligibility and the IEP should be made in writing.

When IDEA was reauthorized in November 2004, multiyear IEPs created at the child's natural transition points were introduced. The effectiveness of this type of IEP is subject to review. Multiyear IEPs must clearly state how a student's progress toward the annual goal is being ascertained and when reports will be issued on that progress.

As we know, IDEA requires that all students with disabilities be provided with a free and appropriate public education. In addition to ensuring that students meet high educational standards while they are in school, FAPE also requires that a student's IEP prepares him or her for employment and independent living. An essential purpose defined in the IDEA

Amendments of 1997 is to prepare students for "later educational challenges and employment."[14] There are specific requirements on how the IEP must reflect transition services, which are defined as

> a coordinated set of activities for a student with a disability that—
> (1) is designed within an outcome-oriented process, that promotes movement from school to post-school activities, including postsecondary education, vocational training, integrated employment (including supportive employment), continuing and adult education, adult services, independent living, or community participation; (2) is based on the individual student's needs, taking into account the student's preferences and interests; and (3) includes (i) instruction; (ii) related services; (iii) community experiences; (iv) the development of employment and other post-school adult living objectives; and (v) if appropriate, the acquisition of daily living skill and functional vocational evaluation.[15]

The Committee Report on the IDEA Amendments of 1997 clarifies: "The purpose . . . is to focus attention on how the child's educational program can be planned to help the child make a successful transition to his or her goals for life after secondary school."[16] The report elaborates: "If for example, for a child whose transition goal is a job, a transition service could be teaching the child how to get to the job site on public transportation."[17] This is clearly a student-driven process. In fact, when the purpose of an IEP meeting is to discuss transition services, the student must be invited to participate. If the student does not attend, the school must make sure that the student's preferences and interests are considered.[18] Parents can assist their children in identifying and asserting their interests, including assuring that appropriate vocational assessments help their youngster identify personal strengths and interests. The IEP's transition services for students must begin no later than age sixteen (sooner if appropriate). Once transition goals are in place, they must be evaluated yearly in the same way that all IEP goals are evaluated.

While this process has many steps, it is usually achieved to the satisfaction of all the parties involved. Sometimes, however, parents do not agree with the recommendations made by the IEP team, and need to request mediation. Mediation is a voluntary process whereby parents and professionals discuss their disagreements with a trained mediator. Any agreed upon decision facilitated by the mediator is binding for the school district. The mediation is conducted at no cost to either the parents or the local education agency.

When parents are not in agreement with the evaluations used by the IEP team, they are entitled to request an independent education evaluation (IEE) at school district expense.[19] Once the evaluation is completed, the IEP team reconvenes and once again attempts to reach a consensus decision.

DUE PROCESS

The right of due process allows parents to review and inspect educational records, including the special education placement of their child. Parents should request a review of their child's records in writing. Each local school agency will have a written process by which they make records available to parents. Parents may be charged a reasonable fee to obtain copies of records unless the cost prevents them from making copies. If parents believe that the records contain inaccurate information, they can request that the school remove that information. If the school refuses, parents are allowed to place a written statement in the records explaining their disagreement with the stated record. Parents may also appeal to the federal government if a school refuses to let them see or seek revision in their child's school record. Complaints should be sent to the Family Policy Compliance Office, U.S. Department of Education, Washington, DC 20202-4605. The laws on parents' rights regarding school records are explained fully in both federal and state laws and in the Family Educational Rights and Privacy Act (FERPA).

Additional due process rights include prior notice, procedural safeguards notice, and parental consent.

Prior Notice

Prior notice must be provided when the school proposes or refuses to initiate or change the identification, evaluation, or educational placement of the child or the provision of FAPE.[20]

In 1999 further amendments required that prior written notice must include

- an explanation of why an action was proposed or refused;
- a description of any other options the agency considered;
- the reasons those options were rejected;
- a description of each evaluation procedure, test, record, or report the agency used as a basis for the proposed or refused action;
- a description of any other factors that are relevant to the agency's proposal or refusal;
- a statement that the parents have protection under the procedural safeguards; and, if this is not an initial referral for evaluation,

- the means by which a copy of a description of the procedural safe-guards can be obtained and sources for parents to contact to obtain assistance in understanding these provisions.

The notice must be in understandable language.

Procedural Safeguards

Procedural safeguards notice[21] must be given to parents upon initial referral for evaluation; upon each notification of an IEP meeting; upon reevaluation of the child; and upon receipt of a request for due process under CFR 300.50. The content of the notice must include a full explanation of the procedural safeguards available and the state's complaint procedures. A mechanism for parents to file a written complaint to their own state is required as part of IDEA.

Parental Consent

The parental consent requirement means that informed consent must be obtained before conducting an initial evaluation or reevaluation and the initial services to a child with a disability.[22]

Although the special education process may seem intimidating to parents, it is clear that the laws designed to protect students count on parental participation. For this reason parent information centers designed to assist parents are located throughout the country. (A partial listing is included at the end of the chapter.) In addition, Figure 10.1 illustrates the special education process, providing a visual summary of the various steps parents and educators go through to ensure the appropriate services for a child with disabilities.

SUMMARY

Parents are often faced with difficulties identifying needs and seeking help for their children and families. Obstacles may seem to multiply if a member of the family has disabilities, particularly if the family has limited resources. The stress of dealing with a disability may result in feelings of isolation, frustration, and inadequacy. It is important to remember that you are not alone. There is plenty of help available, regardless of your ability to pay. Your local school district can be an invaluable resource to help you identify and meet the needs of your child to best prepare him or her for a successful and rewarding adult life. Outside of the schools, additional resources are readily available: books, Internet sites, and support groups, to name a few. Internet access is available free of charge in most public libraries. Remember, you are an expert member of your child's support team—and your child's best advocate. Your input is necessary and invaluable. You know your child better than anyone else.

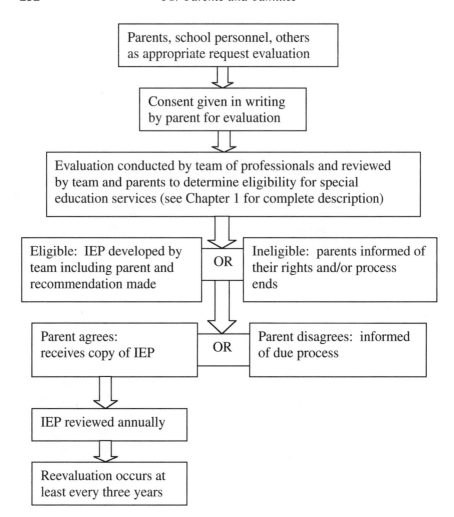

Figure 10.1. The Special Education Process

Tips for Educators and Parents

- The key to any successful partnership is to establish a relationship of mutual respect and appreciation.
- Cultural sensitivity helps to build trust.
- Open communication and active listening promote understanding.

- Teachers can help parents become active partners in supporting learning by sharing information about class routines and activities.

- Parents can help educators by sharing important and relevant information about their child.

- Advocating for a child with disabilities is the first step in building a partnership.

RESOURCES

The following list of Internet sites may be very useful to parents. Many of these sites have information available in different languages, and many have links to other international sites. Some sites were established by parents who have "been there, done that," and have decided to reach out and help facilitate learning.

General Sites

ABLEDATA. http://www.abledata.com
An electronic database of information on assistive technology and rehabilitation equipment available from domestic and international sources to consumers, organizations, professionals, and caregivers in the United States.

Advocacy Center. http://www.advocacycenter.com
A Rochester-based organization serving fifteen Finger Lakes and western New York counties. Provides education, advocacy, and support for individuals with developmental disabilities or traumatic brain injuries and their families. Site contains information about resources and training opportunities, as well as database of local recreational facilities.

Caregivers Web site. http://www.stls.org/caregiver
Information and resources to assist caregivers of people with developmental disabilities; developed by the Southern Tier Library System.

Disability Information and Resources. http://www.makoa.org/
Jim Lubin, creator of this Web site, is a C2 quadriplegic, completely paralyzed from the neck down and dependent on a ventilator to breathe. He uses a keyboard/mouse emulator with a sip and puff switch to type. The site contains hundreds of links to other disability resources. He constantly adds new sites, although it sometimes takes awhile to get them organized.

The DRM Guide to Disability Resources on the Internet. http://www.disability resources.org
An organization that monitors, reviews, and reports on the best disability resources on the Internet. Over 160 separate disabilities and disorders are listed in the index to specific disabilities.

National Library Service for the Blind and Physically Handicapped. http://www.loc.gov/nls/

The NLS, a service of the Library of Congress in cooperation with a network of regional and subregional libraries, provides free library service to persons who are unable to read or use standard printed materials because of a visual or physical impairment. Books and magazines in recorded form or in Braille are delivered to eligible readers by postage-free mail and are returned in the same manner. Regional libraries provide a full range of library service to readers with print disabilities.

Legal Issues, Statistics, ADA, and Other Topics

Access to Disability Data. http://www.infouse.com/disabilitydata
The National Institute on Disability and Rehabilitation Research (http://www.ed. gov/offices/OSERS/NIDRR) conducts comprehensive and coordinated programs of research and related activities to maximize the full inclusion, social integration, employment, and independent living of disabled individuals of all ages. The InfoUse project provides access to disability data through an extensive collection of statistical charts, tables, and surveys.

ADA Home Page. http://www.usdoj.gov/crt/ada/adahom1.htm
Provides current information about the Americans with Disabilities Act and its enforcement, including new or proposed regulations, technical assistance program, settlement information, and ADA mediation.

Disability Tables. http://www.icdi.wvu.edu/disability/tables.html
State, national, and international disability tables from the International Center for Disability Information (ICDI) at West Virginia University.

U.S. Census Bureau. http://www.census.gov/hhes/www/disability.html
The Census Bureau maintains a disability site that includes data from the 1990 Census. It also includes statistics released in March 2001. Americans with Disabilities: 1997 (http://www.census.gov/hhes/www/disable/sipp/disable97.html) provides an excellent overview of the demographics and characteristics of America's disability population.

U.S. Department of Justice. http://www.usdoj.gov/crt/ada/cguide.htm
This "Guide to Disability Rights Laws" describes ten federal laws that prohibit discrimination and establish the rights of people with disabilities to have a life of independence and dignity in the mainstream of America. It lists 800 numbers and Web sites that tell where to turn for help.

Wrightslaw: The Special Ed Advocate. http://wrightslaw.com
A well-organized site that provides accurate, up-to-date information about effective advocacy for children with disabilities. Includes the text of federal statutes and regulations, advocacy articles, correspondence, case reports, and the archives of its free *Special Ed Advocate Newsletter*.

Learning Disabilities

Attention Deficit Disorder Association. http://www.add.org
ADDA is especially focused on the needs of adults and young adults with ADD. Articles, personal stories, interviews with ADD professionals, book reviews, and links to other ADD-related sites are included.

Children and Adults with Attention Deficit Disorders. http://www.chadd.org

A nonprofit organization representing children and adults with attention deficit /hyperactivity disorder, founded in 1987. Includes information about legislative action, articles about AD/HD, research studies, links, and a chat room.

International Dyslexia Association. http://www.interdys.org
This international nonprofit organization has forty-two branches in the United States offering informational meetings and support groups. IDA provides referrals for testers, tutors, and schools specializing in dyslexia as well as information on technology, Individualized Education Programs (IEPs), Individuals with Disabilities Education Act (IDEA) legislation, and the ADA.

LD Online. http://www.idonline.org
This service of PBS station WETA's "The Learning Project," LD Online, is a comprehensive Web site that includes basic and in-depth information about learning disabilities, recommended resources, links, a newsletter, research findings, articles, and political news.

Learning Disabilities Association. http://www.ldanatl.org
The Web site of this national organization includes fact sheets, publications, listings of state LDA pages, a resource center of over 500 publications, alerts, and bulletins. LDA does not endorse any method, curriculum, treatment, program, etc., for individuals with learning disabilities.

National Center for Learning Disabilities. http://www.ncld.org
Basic information about learning disabilities and an extensive resource section. NCLD also offers referral services, develops and supports innovative educational programs, and advocates for more effective policies and legislation to help individuals with learning disabilities.

National Information Center for Children and Youth with Disabilities. http://www.nichcy.org
NICHCY is one of four clearinghouses established by Congress to provide specialized information on disabilities and disability-related issues for families, educators, and other professionals. Their special focus is children and youth (birth to age twenty-two).

Additional Sites of Interest

Ability OnLine Support Network. http://www.ablelink.org
An electronic mail system that connects young people with disabilities or chronic illnesses to disabled and nondisabled peers and mentors.

Adoption: A Family Choice. http://www.geocities.com/Heartland/Hills/2940/disabilities.html
Links to sites of interest to parents of children with disabilities. Topics include medical information, parent support, blindness, children affected by drugs, Down syndrome, attachment disorder, and school inclusion. Maintained by a parent who has several children with disabilities.

The DRM WebWatcher. http://www.disabilityresources.org/PARENTS-OF.html
Contains links to sites for, by, and about kids with disabilities and chronic illnesses in *Disability Resources Monthly*'s "Just for Parents (and Service Providers)" section.

Family Village. http://www.familyvillage.wisc.edu/

A Web site that attempts to bring together valuable information for parents of individuals who have disabilities.

Family Voices. http://www.familyvoices.org

National grassroots clearinghouse for information and education concerning the health care of children with special health needs.

The Parenting Factor. http://www.theparentingfactor.com

Founded in the belief that "it takes a village to raise a child," this organization and Web site were created by parents, for parents in an effort to bridge gaps between organizations, professions, genders, cultures, etc., in order to better serve our children.

NOTES

1. Kennedy, M. (2002). Balancing security and learning. *American School and University,* 74(6), 8–11.

2. Lupinacci, J. (2002). A safe haven. *American School and University,* 74(6), 8–11.

3. Peterson, K. D. (2002). Positive or negative. *Journal of Staff Development,* 23(3), 21–30.

4. Stolp, S., & Smith, S. (1994). School culture and climate: The role of the leader. *OSSSC Bulletin* (Eugene: Oregon School Study Council).

5. Mercer, C., & Mercer, A. R. (2004). *Teaching students with learning problems.* Upper Saddle River, NJ: Prentice Hall.

6. Heubert, J. P., & Hauser, R. M. (Eds.) (1999). *High stakes: Testing for tracking, promotion and graduation.* National Research Council. Washington, DC: National Academy Press.

7. Harry, B., & Kalyanpur, M. (1999). *Culture in special education: Building reciprocal family provider relationships.* Baltimore: Paul H. Brookes Publishing Co.

8. Harry & Kalyanpur (1999).

9. Bauer, A. M., & Shea, T. M. (2003). *Parents and schools.* Upper Saddle River, NJ: Prentice Hall.

10. Section 300.501 (a)(2).

11. Individuals with Disabilities Education Act. Pub. L. 104–17, 111 Stat. 37, Appendix A.

12. Section 300.347 (a)(1).

13. Section 300.347 (a)(7).

14. H. Rep. No. 105–95, p. 82 (1997); S. Rep. No 105–17, p. 4 (1997).

15. H. Rep. No. 105–95, p. 82 (1997); S. Rep. No 105–17, p. 4 (1997).

16. H. Rep. No. 105–95, pp. 101–102 (1997); S. Rep. No. 105–107, p. 22 (1997).

17. H. Rep. No. 105–95, p. 102 (1997); S. Rep. No. 105–107, p. 22 (1997).

18. Section 300.344 (b).

19. Section 300.502.

20. Section 615 (c); Section 300.503.

21. Section 615 (d); Section 300.504.

22. Sections 614 (a)(1)(c) and (c)(3); Section 300.503.

CHAPTER 11

Promoting Competency, Independence, and Self-Advocacy

Gloria Lodato Wilson

Ivan is a teenage boy with learning disabilities who is facing the new demands of adolescence. His story illustrates the relationship between academic disabilities and the development of competence and independence.

Ivan's Story

If we lived in a society where reading and math were not important, I would never have had any problems. I couldn't read, write, or do math until I was twelve. Some people think that that is a real problem, and it was, but my father read history books and newspapers to me, and we would sit and discuss ideas every day, so I've always known a lot of information. Besides reading and talking to me, my father also used to coach my soccer team. That worked out well, because sometimes when I would forget the rules or be on the opposite side of the field, he was there to remind me. My idea of the spacing was different than everybody else's and I could only anticipate one player at a time rather than the whole team. My dad made me the goalie so that I could see the whole field and I knew to keep my back to the goal.

My mother said that when I was a baby I was a crawler for a long time and my specialty was crawling backwards! I spoke later than my peers and had difficulty with some sounds. Some of the mothers of my friends in the neighborhood said that I couldn't play with their children because my speech sounded garbled and they thought their children would start sounding like me but their kids always wanted to play with me. I made up great games and everyone thought that the games that I made up were more interesting than the ones they played. Best of all I could remember the rules to the games I made up. That inventiveness made me the leader of my groups.

Growing up was very difficult for me because of my learning problems. When we were young, my sister was the one who always got things right. She read all the time; I didn't know the alphabet. She walked to our neighborhood schools; I got bussed to a private one. She was in the orchestra; I was in speech therapy. My sister was in advanced classes and everyone in her class won awards; everyone in my class had something wrong with them. My sister had a boyfriend who lived across the street, but the only girl from my school who lived nearby took pills every day at lunch and always had to go to her psychiatrist.

RATIONALE FOR PROMOTING COMPETENCE

"Our kids will always disappoint us." That's how the father of two sons with attention deficit disorder opened his keynote to a group of parents and teachers of children with disabilities. Why? His children were not fitting into what families and schools expected. As teachers, students with disabilities will disappoint us. Why? Because, as teachers and parents, we want to be successful, but we find that we can't go along and teach or parent in the ways that we thought worked before. And ultimately we will disappoint our children and our students, who look to us for relief and might not find it.

Take a moment to reflect. If asked to describe a person with learning disabilities, or mental retardation or autism or vision impairment, what adjectives would you use? The usual responses include:

- poor reader
- poor writer
- difficulties with following directions
- poor thinking skills
- poor memory
- difficulty moving about
- moving about too much
- poor speaking skills

The list goes on. How different is a conception based on competence? What attributes could we list if we switched our thinking from one of deficits to one of competence; if we acknowledged the disability but didn't define the person by the disability? We might describe the same individuals in drastically different ways:

- artistic
- humorous

- athletic
- good friend
- strong
- fast runner
- kindhearted
- creative
- determined

In fact, the life stories of adults with disabilities reveal compensatory skills that revolved around areas of competence.[1] Indeed, Anne and Rud Turnbull, pioneers in the field of special education, propose a value system that is the antithesis of disappointment and deficits. They have delineated six values that can guide our thinking and our actions toward all children, but particularly children with special needs:

Envisioning Great Expectations. Students have many capabilities that have not been tapped. We can develop new visions of what is possible. These visions can become realities. We need new perspectives of what life can be as well as support for fulfilling these dreams.

Enhancing Positive Contributions. Students contribute positively to their families, schools, friends, and communities. We need to develop greater opportunities for these contributions.

Building on Strengths. Students and families have many natural capacities. They need opportunities for educational programs to identify, highlight, and build upon their strengths.

Acting on Choices. Students and families can direct their own lives. Enabling them to act on their own preferences promotes their self-determination.

Expanding Relationships. Connections are crucial to quality of life. Students and families need to connect with each other, educators, and friends in the community.

Ensuring Full Citizenship. Less able does not mean less worthy. All students, including those with exceptionalities, and their families are entitled to full participation in American life.[2]

A competence model differs tremendously from a deficit model and can make all the difference in a person's life. The world is beginning to change because we are changing how we think, which, in turn, changes how we act. If we reflect upon these values each day in our dealings with children with special needs, we will begin to discover that we are actually looking for solutions instead of being paralyzed by problems. We will begin to see possibilities where none existed before. We will no longer be disappointed, and our children will thrive. A disability can influence a person's image. It can also affect motivation. How does a disability influence a person's motivation? What does learned helplessness mean, and how does a student show signs of learned helplessness?

When deficits are highlighted and what people cannot do is valued more than what they can do, some devastating things begin to happen. Many children become caught in a vicious circle of what is called "learned helplessness." The term, coined by Seligman, is descriptive of a sequence based on failure.[3] It begins when a child attempts to learn something; s/he tries very hard but fails, and this happens time and again. Eventually, the child learns not to equate effort with success and tends to think that no matter how much effort is exerted there is no payoff. This leads to not trying at all.

Now this isn't quite the "American way." Part of the fabric of our culture is the premise that if you work hard you will achieve success, and anything is possible for anyone. We think that there is a direct correlation between effort and success. But this does not occur in the experience of many children with disabilities. What happens then is that the child, if successful at all, tends to think that the success was due to external circumstances—it was an easy test or someone else helped. Some children will try to protect themselves from internalizing failure and will begin to blame others. They might complain that the teachers are stupid or don't know how to teach, or that the test was ridiculously hard. Figure 11.1 is a useful survey to give students to ascertain to what they attribute their success or failure.

What happens when a child stops trying? Nothing good, that's for sure. Parents get frustrated, teachers feel the student doesn't care, and the child receives more negative feedback and becomes more certain of failure. So the signs of learned helplessness are quite clear. The child stops trying and starts depending on others to get work done, if at all.

How is the cycle of learned helplessness broken? Partially it comes from not defining the child solely in terms of the disability; by following the six values prescribed by the Turnbull et al.;[4] by being interested enough to find a child's interests and skills and making strengths more important than the disability; by participating in Person Centered Planning (PCP) activities; by using effective praise; and by understanding the role of helping.

Finding a Child's Strengths and Interests

The notion of attending to a person's disability while trying to find strengths is tricky. After all, a student is in school to learn a set of skills and a core of knowledge. A teacher's competence is judged by how well students learn. So how can a teacher cope with what seem on the surface to be mutually exclusive terms: disability and competence?

When you do well in school, is it usually because: (rate the importance of each explanation)					
	Not a reason at all				An important reason
You studied hard?	1	2	3	4	5
You studied the right things?	1	2	3	4	5
You are smart?	1	2	3	4	5
The teacher explained things well?	1	2	3	4	5
Someone helped you?	1	2	3	4	5
The work was easy?	1	2	3	4	5
When you do poorly in school, is it usually because:					
You didn't study enough?	1	2	3	4	5
You studied the wrong things?	1	2	3	4	5
You are not smart?	1	2	3	4	5
The teacher didn't explain things well?	1	2	3	4	5
No one was there to help you?	1	2	3	4	5
The work was hard?	1	2	3	4	5

Figure 11.1. Measure of Attributions for Performance on Academic Tasks

Source: Adapted from Stipek, D. (1993). *Motivation to learn: From theory to practice*. (2nd ed.). Boston: Allyn and Bacon. Copyright © 1993 by Pearson Education. Reprinted by permission of the publisher.

The answer again rests partially on a teacher's ability to orchestrate the learning environment to promote competence in academic, social, and emotional areas. A teacher in an inclusive classroom becomes concerned with the difficulty level of tasks; how tasks are introduced, formatted, and presented; and the appropriateness of curriculum and evaluation procedures. A teacher in an inclusive classroom also is keenly tuned in to how the student with special needs is perceived by and interacts with others, and the impact of each student on the dynamics of the class as a whole.

However, a teacher who is supported by a group of other caring individuals interested in a particular student can be even more effective. Person Centered Planning is a vehicle for understanding student strengths.[5]

Person Centered Planning and How This Process Can Support Teachers' Efforts

In Person Centered Planning, students, assisted by school professionals, family members, and friends, uncover and reveal their strengths, hopes, dreams, and nightmares. Together, through group routines, participants think creatively to plan for the resources and supports needed for fulfillment of dreams. Group tools used include Personal Futures Planning or Making Action Plans, I Have a Dream, Dream Cards, Good Experience, The Other Way,[6] and others. All of these activities focus on student strengths and interests. The process is proactive, and the activities result in a plan for some specific action. The planning can involve a class of students and usually takes several class periods over a span of time to implement, or parents can organize the meetings at home. Through the Person Centered Planning activities, personal capacities and opportunities for growth are found at school and at home. Because Person Centered Planning is just beginning to become incorporated into public school systems, a professional trained in Person Centered Planning usually facilitates the activities. However, the role of the teacher is essential to success. Classroom teachers can create the positive climate for class participation that is necessary for productive sessions, and their knowledge of the student can lead to group insight. For online information, go to www.pacer.org/tatra/personal.htm.

Components of Effective Praise

Praise is different from the ordinary feedback a teacher gives to indicate whether an answer is right or wrong. Praising entails congratulating a student for a job well done. Praise usually encourages a student to go on and gives some satisfaction that efforts were recognized. Yet, praising a child can sometimes backfire. Teachers and parents may feel that they need to use praise even if the work is not satisfactory in order to keep the child motivated. Parents and teachers need to reflect on how they praise children and use effective praise and realistic encouragement techniques.[7] According to Stipek, "if praise is not contingent on high effort or good performance, it will not increase the likelihood of either one. If poor performance is just as likely to be praised as good performance, or if students are praised regardless of their efforts, students learn that praise is not based on anything they do and they discount it."[8] So, if a teacher or a parent tells a child that s/he did a good job, when, in fact, the work is not good, or tells a child that s/he is putting in great effort when s/he is not, the cycle of learned helplessness is supported once again. This is particularly true if praise supports success of very easy tasks. Students can interpret this as indicating that adults have very low expectations and perceptions of their abilities.

Effective praise specifies particular aspects of the performance that are noteworthy, recognizes genuine effort in completing difficult assignments, and values the accomplishment. For example, a teacher can praise a student for a particular answer on a test even if the total test performance was less than stellar. Likewise, a parent can praise the attempt, the effort, or the improvement of a skill that the child has not yet mastered.

Supporting Independence When a Child Depends on Adults and Peers Throughout the Day

We want children to succeed and we want to support that success, but we must be extremely careful of overhelping. Overhelping occurs when adults come to a child's rescue without being asked for help or before the child has tried. It is often an attempt to alleviate the person's struggle, or to get a better, more polished version of the assignment. Think back to a time when a child gave you a handmade gift. Usually, the gift is crudely made, with irregular shapes or poorly painted. Yet the gift is almost always treasured and remembered because of the pride of the child with which it is associated. If a teacher, a parent, or a caring adult had improved on that gift, evened out the edges, or smoothed out the color lines, the gift would have been more presentable, but not likely to be as cherished, nor the creator as proud. So too, in our efforts to help students achieve a more polished report or project or assignment, we are actually preventing them from struggling a bit and from feeling the pride of a job done on their own.

This is a very complex issue because we do not want to set kids up for failure or to create stressful situations. Most overhelping is a response to tasks that are too difficult for children to accomplish on their own. Many parents fall into the trap of overhelping with homework assignments. Fearful that their child will be continually penalized for incomplete or incorrect homework, they spend hours each night prodding the child, and often, in frustration, complete the homework themselves. This also happens with well-meaning paraprofessionals and special education teachers placed in the role of supporting and aiding students with special needs. Many general education teachers are dumbfounded when they try to figure out how a student with special needs produces assignments that are better than those turned in by the most talented students in the class!

Overhelping, then, needs to be avoided, while supporting success needs to be promoted. Assignments or projects should be well thought out, adapted, and modified appropriately and gauged so that children can meet with a reasonable amount of success by completing them, themselves. A supportive structure, such as scaffolding, should exist in the classroom so that a student experiencing difficulty is able to ask for and receive appropriate assistance. Scaffolding instruction, described by Bos and Vaughn, "relates to the role of the teacher or the expert, who encourages learners by providing temporary and adjustable support as they develop new skills, strategies, and knowledge."[9] The important concept in scaffolding instruction is the relinquishing of support. Oftentimes, children are given appropriate supports for inappropriate lengths of time, thus making them dependent on others and uncertain of their own abilities.

COMPETENCE AND CURRICULUM ISSUES

Addressing Academic Areas of Need and Promoting Feelings of Competence

It is possible to address academic areas of need and promote competence. Take some time to look at the classroom demands and change them so that effort can pay off and strengths can be found. For instance, Ivan, the student in the opening vignette, had tremendous difficulty reading, yet his dad nourished his curiosity by reading to him so that they could discuss world affairs.

As a teacher, you might show students *how* to study, not just tell them *to* study. Teach the process of getting to the final answer; don't just expect students to get there. You might give a few open notebook quizzes where students who have done their homework can find the answers but those who haven't would be lost. You can praise the effort, not just reward the product, by saying things like "I see that you really have been keeping up with the assignments and your participation in class is really bringing some insight into this topic" or "I can see that you have been really trying and it's beginning to show. Keep it up." You might give students choices for assignments and have the assignments cover an array of approaches to addressing the topic.

Modifications to materials and use of technology are essential to addressing areas of academic need in a manner that will support effort and learning. In addition, reconceptualizing curriculum and implementing the principles of universal design can enrich the learning of all students in your classroom while addressing learning diversities.

PLANNING PYRAMIDS AND UNIVERSAL DESIGN

Planning a Curriculum That Can Meet the Needs of All the Students in My Class

Vaughn, Bos, and Schumm provide teachers with a conceptual and practical framework to address curriculum issues in a diverse classroom.[10] The Planning Pyramid is based on the diversity of interests, skills, and motivation in a class and guides the teacher to conceptualize the curriculum within three parameters the authors call the Degrees of Learning.[11] The Pyramid (Figure 11.2) is divided into three horizontal levels, each of which addresses a different curriculum question. Starting at the base level, the question answered is, "What do I want *all* students to learn?" The middle level answers the question, "What do I want *most* students to learn?" The top level is guided by the question, "What information will some students learn?"[12] The authors caution against the misinterpretation of the Planning Pyramid and the Degrees of Learning into thinking that students are partitioned and only taught or exposed to limited curriculum:

- All students must have the opportunity to be presented with or exposed to the same information, although presentation of the information may vary somewhat according to a student's needs.
- All students must have equal access to information that represents all levels of the Pyramid.
- Students should not be assigned to a particular level of the Pyramid based on their ability—students who learn at the middle and top levels do so based on their interests, prior knowledge, or personal experience.
- Activities at the base of the Pyramid should no be less stimulating (e.g., dittos, worksheets) than those at the other levels, nor should the upper levels be viewed as the place for creative, fun activities.[13]

Figure 11.3 presents the format for the Unit Planning Form.

Elements of Universal Design

The term "universal design" was first popularized in the field of architecture during the 1980s to describe efforts to create accessible housing and barrier-free living for all people. Universal design elements help teachers develop curriculum, address areas of need, and promote competence. Introduced into education in the late 1990s to address diversity in the classroom,

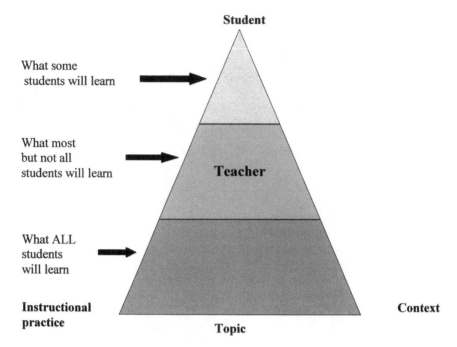

Figure 11.2. The Planning Pyramid

Source: Figure from Schumm, J. S., Vaughn, S., & Leavell A. G. (1994, May). "Planning pyramid: A framework for planning for diverse students' needs during content area instruction." *The Reading Teacher, 47*(8) 608–615. Reprinted with permission of Jeanne Shay Schumm and the International Reading Association. All rights reserved.

the concepts of universal design are beginning to be incorporated in inclusive settings throughout the country. Integral to universal design in learning is the idea that modifications, adaptations, and materials used are built into the curriculum from its inception. Materials and procedures are pre-adapted and technologically supported, freeing teachers from time-consuming modifications and providing more time for teaching.[14]

In "Universal Design in Education," Bowe outlines the seven essential principles of universal design developed by the Center for Universal Design at North Carolina State University.[15] The essential principles are presented in Table 11.1.

A framework for guidance in curriculum development that can also assist the general education teacher when utilizing universal design elements is presented in Table 11.2.

However, it would be an oversimplification to equate universal design with assistive technology. For more on assistive technology, see Chapter 12.

UNIT PLANNING FORM   Date:_____   Class Period:_____

Unit Title:_____

What some students will learn

Materials/Resources:
_____
_____
_____
_____

What most but not all students will learn

Instructional Strategies/Adaptations:
_____
_____
_____
_____

What ALL students will learn

Evaluation/Products:
_____
_____
_____
_____
_____

Figure 11.3. The Unit Planning Form

Source: From Schumm, J. S., Vaughn, S., & Harris, J. (1997). Pyramid power for collaborative planning for content area instruction. *Teaching Exceptional Children, 29*(6), 62–66. Copyright 1997 by The Council for Exceptional Children. Reprinted by permission.

While technology is often integral to the design, Bowe highlights the differences in Table 11.3.

Grading a Child with Deficient Skills

One great way to evaluate students is through the use of rubrics. Rubrics (see Table 11.4) provide a framework for the student to complete an assignment and self-evaluate the product, and they provide the teacher with an objective tool to assign grades. Students learn how their assignments compare with those of others who achieve at different levels, can see what needs to be added for work to improve, and can, in fact, determine what was good about their work no matter what level was attained.

The Degrees of Learning and the Planning Pyramid described earlier offer another way to approach grading. Using the Pyramid when making up an assessment, a teacher can decide to devote 80 percent of the test questions to the material designated as important for *all* students to learn

Table 11.1.
The Seven Principles of Universal Design

Principle of Universal Design	Definition	Classroom Application
Equitable use	The design is useful and marketable to people with diverse abilities	Classroom lectures or notes available to all students on computer disks
Flexibility of use	The design accommodates a wide range of individual preferences	Variety of assignments on a given topic will allow for choice and individual strengths, e.g., group activity, paper, or a test
Simple and intuitive use	Use of the design is easy to understand, regardless of the user's experience, knowledge, language skills, or current concentration level	Assign readings that are understandable and contain the important information for the concept; focus on the big ideas
Perceptible information	The design communicates necessary information effectively to the user, regardless of ambient conditions or the user's sensory abilities	Arrange formats of written material such as tests and assignments in a clean, uncluttered, and clear manner; directions are unambiguous
Tolerance for error	The design minimizes hazard and the adverse consequences of accidental or unintended actions	Use of Slow Keys and Bounce Keys help prevent unintentional key strokes on the computer; key guards for resting hands without touching keys
Low physical effort	The design can be used efficiently and comfortably and with a minimum of fatigue	Adjustable desks and chairs; word expansion word processing programs which predict word use; intermittent reprieves from sitting through group activities
Size and space for approach and use	Appropriate size and space are provided for approach, reach, manipulation, and use regardless of user's body size, posture, or mobility	Moveable desks, tables and chairs; door levers rather than knobs

Source: From Bowe, F. (© 2000). *Universal design in education*. Westport, CT: Bergin & Garvey. Reproduced with permission of Greenwood Publishing Group, Inc., Westport, CT.

Table 11.2.
A Framework for Universal Design in Curriculum Development

Provide Flexible Means of Representation

Alternatives that reduce perceptual barriers	• Digital text (on a computer) can easily be transformed in size, shape, or color and can be automatically transformed into spoken speech for students with learning disabilities, low vision, or blindness.
	• Audio with captions provides flexible alternatives for students who are deaf, who are nonnative speakers of the language, or who have auditory processing problems.
	• Digital images and graphics with verbal description provide access and flexibility for instructional emphasis, clarity, and direction.
Alternatives that reduce cognitive barriers	• Big idea summaries simplify linguistic and conceptual complexity surrounding content.
	• Background knowledge pretests alert a teacher to the need for more preparation.

Provide Flexible Means of Expression

Alternatives that reduce motor barriers to expression	• Pencil and paper exercises present barriers to many students who have difficulty physically forming letters, writing legibly, or spelling words. The same exercises provided in digital form on the computer can provide supports and alternatives enabling more students to succeed. Examples include on-screen scanning keyboards, enlarged keyboard, word prediction, and spell-checkers.
	• Speeches and oral presentations provide a welcome alternative to writing for many students, but present barriers for others. The option to create multimedia presentations provides access to those for whom speech is not a viable presentation method.
	• Graphic design and illustration as means of expression are difficult or impossible for some students. Digital graphic programs and libraries provide needed support for many who cannot draw by hand and helpful scaffolds for all.

Table 11.2.
(continued)

Alternatives that reduce cognitive barriers to expression	• Any formal means of expression requires a series of steps to prepare and execute. In order to succeed, some children need those steps explicitly stated and taught (conspicuous strategies), not leaving any part of the process to intuition. • Scaffolding is a temporary support for learning that is gradually reduced as the student develops confidence with the new content or skills.

Provide Flexible Means of Engagement

Alternatives that support motivation	• For all children, an appropriate balance of support and challenge results in optimal engagement, but for each child the point of balance is different. Providing flexible options for setting the level of challenge and building in supportive scaffolds allows more children, and their teachers, to find the right balance. • Providing flexible options for the amount of repetition, familiarity, randomness, and surprise allows more children to stay engaged. • Providing key concepts in multiple formats and contents provides alternatives that are likely to engage a broader set of children. • The opportunity to contribute to the curriculum by adding one's own images, sounds, words, and texts to what has already been developed often leads to a deeper engagement than in a curriculum that is delivered completely fixed. This type of curriculum is sometimes referred to as being "half full." The term is not meant to imply that the curriculum is unfinished or unplanned, just that it is flexibly structured to allow for direct input from students with differing abilities and able to reach them in more effective ways.

Source: Adapted from ERIC/OSEP Topical Brief. (1998). A curriculum every student can use: Design principles for student access. Appendix: A framework for universal design in curriculum development. http://www.cec.sped.org/osep/appendix.htm.

Table 11.3.
Universal Design versus Assistive Technology

Universal Design	Assistive Technology
Responsibility of designers/developers	Responsibility of user or user's agent
Done while service or product is being developed	Done after product is finished, or while service is being delivered
Serves many people at once	Serves one individual user at a time
Renewable accessibility	Consumable accessibility
Allows for serendipity	Seldom is used in innovative ways

Source: From Bowe, F. (© 2000). *Universal design in Education*. Westport, CT: Bergin & Garvey. Reproduced with permission of Greenwood Publishing Group, Inc., Westport, CT.

and know, with the remaining 20 percent of the questions allocated to the *most* and *some* content. A testing model based on this premise would accommodate and eventually differentiate the attainment levels of all the students in the class and would provide an analysis of what the students actually know that the teacher had determined was important. Misunderstandings that often arise when students are graded on effort and not on knowledge, which can result in inflated grades and miscommunication of skill level, could also be prevented.

In addition, Christiansen and Vogel advocate a decision model and problem-solving framework to "minimize misunderstandings and potential conflict that can arise from differences in grading practices."[16] They review a series of evaluative procedures, including criterion-referenced, where a grade is reflective of attainment of a particular skill; self-referenced, where a grade reflects the growth of a student to him or herself; norm-referenced, where a grade reflects a comparative ranking to the group. Above all, the grading procedures need to be discussed with parents, administrators, and fellow teachers to avoid confusion about the meaning of assigned grades and to maintain consistency with the student's IEP.

COMPETENCE AND SOCIAL ISSUES

Enhancing Social Acceptance

Disability Simulations. Dealing with both the academic and social lives of children is imperative. In a meta-analysis of the social competence of

Table 11.4.
Sample Writing

Name:
Narrative/Descriptive Writing Scoring Guide
Course Outcome: Students will be able to internalize a writing process which includes planning, composing, revising, and self-evaluating.

Assignment:
Date:

Criteria Quality	Focus on and Organization of Task	Narrative	Descriptive	Style and Diction	Grammar, Usage, and Mechanics
Excellent 90+ (A)	• Topic is approached in a unique and imaginative way. • Attitude and point of view remain the same for entire paper. • Paragraphs and sentences are organized and make sense.	• Opening situation is clearly established. • Characters are effectively introduced and developed. • Description is original and vivid. • Conflict is clearly developed. • Conflict is logically and completely solved.	• Very descriptive words or phrases are used. • Details are chosen to create a very clear picture or image for the reader throughout the writing.	• Uses well-chosen and appropriate words all of the time. • Expresses ideas in an imaginative and creative way. • Effective paragraphing. • Varies sentence structure.	• Can correctly use certain parts of speech, ending punctuation, and indentation at all times. • Correctly uses comma and quotations at all times. • Uses proper tense throughout. • Few or no spelling errors. • Capitalization correct throughout.

Quality 80+ (B)	• Topic is understood. • Attitude and point of view are clear, but not used throughout the paper. • Paragraphs are not always organized, but sentences are organized in a pattern.	• Opening situation is established. • Characters are adequately introduced and developed. • Includes some description. • A conflict is developed. • Conflict is solved.	• Descriptive words or phrases are used. • Details are chosen to create a good picture or image for the reader throughout the writing.	• Generally chooses appropriate words. • Expresses ideas clearly. • Some sentence structures are repetitious. • Some errors in sentences. • Correct paragraphing.	• Can correctly use certain parts of speech, ending punctuation, and indentation in most cases. • Correctly uses commas and quotations most of the time. • Uses proper tense throughout. • Minor spelling errors. • Capitalization appropriate.
Acceptable 70+ (C)	• Topic is understood, but ideas are not developed enough. • Attitude and point of view change throughout the writing. • Paragraphs are not always organized, and sentence order does not make sense.	• Opening situation is not appropriate or established. • Characters are not well developed. • Conflict is not established or does not make sense. • Conflict is not completely solved.	• Few descriptive words or phrases are used. • There are not enough details to keep the picture or image in the reader's mind.	• Sometimes chooses inappropriate words. • Meaning is clear, but word choice is not varied. • Some sentences are choppy. • Fragments/runons. • Errors in paragraphing.	• Word usage is limited. • Errors or omissions in the use of commas or quotations. • Errors in verb tense, but meaning is clear. • Several spelling errors, but meaning is clear.

Table 11.4.
(continued)

Name:
Narrative/Descriptive Writing Scoring Guide
Course Outcome: Students will be able to internalize a writing process which includes planning, composing, revising, and self-evaluating.

Assignment:
Date:

Criteria Quality	Focus on and Organization of Task	Narrative	Descriptive	Style and Diction	Grammar, Usage, and Mechanics
Below Expectations	• Topic is not understood. • Attitude, point of view are unclear. • Paragraphs are not organized, nor do the sentences make sense.	• Lacking major elements of narrative structure.	• Almost no descriptive words or phrases are used. • Details, if any, do not create a picture for the reader.	• Chooses incorrect or inappropriate words. • Meaning is unclear or confusing, point is not made. • Many fragments and/or run-ons. • Incorrect or no paragraphing.	• Little or no knowledge of use of parts of speech of ending punctuation. • Commas, quotes, capitalization, punctuation errors throughout the paper. • Spelling errors interfere with understanding. • Constant shifting of verb tenses.

Source: From Salend, S. J. (1998). *Effective mainstreaming: Creating inclusive classrooms.* Upper Saddle River, NJ: Prentice Hall. P. 440. © 1990. Reprinted by permission of Pearson Education, Upper Saddle River, NJ.

students with learning difficulties, Nowicki found these students to be at "greater social risk" compared to students without disabilities.[17] Parents also report that their children with disabilities have lower levels of social competence and higher rates of behavioral problems when compared to normally achieving siblings.[18] But how can social issues be addressed?

Disability simulations are an outstanding way to develop positive attitudes toward students with disabilities. An excellent source is *Kids with Special Needs: Information and Activities to Promote Awareness and Understanding*.[19] This book includes a series of activities, games, and bulletin boards to enhance understanding of what it is like to be a person with a disability. For example, "The Disability Myth Game" is a card game that debunks some commonly held beliefs concerning disabilities. "It's Kind of Blurry" provides directions for making various glasses that can increase awareness of visual impairments.

Discussion of Disabilities. Ongoing discussions and problem-solving conferencing throughout the year are essential. Some teachers provide this support in their classes. They might invite a psychologist, social worker, or counselor to come into the class and run sessions. Parents may want to have brief conversations regarding disabilities and abilities. Ultimately, what is important is an ongoing, open dialogue where children can ask questions, express concerns, and find solutions.

Group Exercises. "Ignoring sessions" can also help classmates respond neutrally to negative behaviors. Often advice is given to ignore inappropriate behavior, only to find that when the negative behavior emerges, most will focus on it rather than ignore it. During "ignoring sessions" students are directly taught how to ignore such distractions. The procedure is as follows:

1. Have all the students in the class focus on a spot on their desk, or on the floor, or on the wall.

2. Instruct them to look at the spot and concentrate; they are not to look away from that spot.

3. Pick a student to play the part of the "distracter." Have this student move about the class and try to draw the other students' attention away from their spot (make jokes, make odd sounds, do funny faces, etc.).

4. Remind the students to ignore the behavior of the distracter and focus on their spots.

5. Suspend this activity after one or two minutes but repeat daily for about two weeks and then intermittently throughout the school year.

What happens as the result of these sessions is that when a student truly is becoming a distraction in the classroom, the teacher can remind the other students to focus on their spots and ignore the deviant behavior. The students do not get distracted, the level of negative activity does not elevate, and the deviant behavior diminishes. This procedure has worked time and time again and has prevented troublesome situations from escalating.

Reading Materials. Books addressing disability issues can also be a vehicle for understanding student diversity and increasing social acceptance. Read and discussed in class, books offer tremendous opportunities for discussion and insight. The books should have characters that are believable and who are not stereotypes, be clearly written, and provide accurate information about the disability; characters with disabilities and without disabilities should share common experiences, feelings, and dreams.[20]

Lists of appropriate books are available from various sources. *A Guide to Children's Literature and Disability, 1989–1994*, published by the National Information Center for Children and Youth with Disabilities (NICHCY), can be viewed online at www.nichcy.org. Choose "Publications" from the menu and then choose "Bibliographies (list of books)."

Encouraging Children of Different Abilities to Work Together

Cooperative Learning. Perhaps the best way to have students with differing abilities work together is through cooperative learning. However, true cooperative learning entails a substantial amount of teacher planning and orchestration, and many teachers confuse group work with cooperative learning. Simply giving students a task to complete within a group will not necessarily be a positive experience for students of differing abilities. In fact, poorly planned groupings could lead to increased emphasis on weaknesses and poor acceptance. Teachers are therefore cautioned when using groupings to make sure that they adhere to the principles of cooperative learning outlined by proponents such Slavin.[21] For online information on cooperative learning, go to www.edletter.org/past/issues/2000-mj/coop erative.shtml.

Cooperative Thinking. Another model teachers can use for effective groupings is "The Cooperative Thinking Strategies," a group of strategies developed to help students think and work cooperatively.[22] The series is divided into five areas, each focused on an integral component for cooperative work. The series develops ways for students to share ideas, organize complex projects, analyze and absorb information, and resolve controversial issues. The "Teamwork Strategy" is a way for students to organize and finish multipart assignments and projects. By working in small groups, students learn how to break a project into smaller parts, assign tasks, give and receive help and feedback from group members, and ultimately complete and evaluate the project. For more information on this model go to www.ku -crl.org.

Fostering Acceptance of Difference. Fairness has to do with giving students what they need. The question of fairness is an important one to consider, and teachers must continually reevaluate what it is that individual students actually need to support success. An open classroom environment where each student feels valuable and valued decreases the likelihood that "fairness" will enter into the discussion. In reality, an inclusive classroom addresses each student's diverse needs by integrating choices and multiple avenues for demonstrating skills and learning. Students come to understand their classmates' differences and begin to recognize strengths and abilities.

A very busy New York City teacher took the time each week to hold what she called "evaluating sessions." At the end of each week students told her how she did or did not fulfill their expectations and how she could improve the following week. In turn, she evaluated her students in the same manner, and students evaluated themselves and each other. This teacher obviously had great skills to be able to conduct these evaluating sessions in a respectful and productive manner. She felt that the sessions gave the students a voice in their education and helped them understand a teacher's role in adjusting to students' needs.

PROMOTING SELF-ADVOCACY

The Importance of Self-Advocacy Skills

Historically, professionals and parents have been the advocates for children with disabilities. This is understandable considering the legal and social challenges that needed to be overcome. However, allowing the voices of students with disabilities to be heard is integral to a model of competence. Children with a voice can feel power and control over their own destinies. This is particularly important for those with special needs whose lives tend to be controlled by others.

Committees make decisions of eligibility, classification, programming, and goal making. A student with special needs once described his anxiety every time the Committee on Special Education met. He said that he was always waiting for a gigantic crane to scoop him up and place him in another class or, worst yet, a different school. He felt powerless. Well-meaning parents and teachers feel that they know what is best for students with special needs. However, input from the students expressing their desires, wishes, dreams, nightmares, and interests can substantially alter decisions.

Self-advocacy skills need to be nurtured as students progress through elementary and secondary school because these skills become vital to young adults with special needs. Once students leave the protective school environment they are expected to make their needs known to employers or professors. Young adults need to know what their disabilities are and be able to explain others how the disability will affect their performance and what accommodations need to be made on their behalf. Poor self-advocacy skills put their future in jeopardy.

The Self-Advocacy Plan

The researcher P. Phillips designed an interesting program to promote self-advocacy.[23] Designed for adolescents with learning disabilities, the Self-Advocacy Plan involves the participation of teachers, parents, and students. In ninth grade the student, together with a special education teacher and a counselor, studies the impact of learning disabilities. The student also becomes more aware of his/her particular learning disability through discussions and learning logs. In tenth grade the student takes part in meetings that inform the general education teachers of his/her learning needs. The student also investigates career interests and opportunities. In eleventh grade the student contacts the general education teachers and discusses learning needs and develops necessary accommodations. This model gives the student support and skills needed for becoming a self-advocate and highlights the need for a planned progression toward independence.

The I Plan

Another option is the Education Planning Strategy: I Plan.[24] Developed through the University of Kansas, this plan aims to help students understand their learning difficulties and abilities and enables them to actively participate in decision making, such as IEP meetings, that affect their lives. Once again, this plan highlights the need for active involvement by teachers to assure students have the skills to become self-advocates. The five steps in the plan include:

Inventory—students become familiar with their strengths and weaknesses.

Provide Your Inventory Information—students learn how to communicate to others their needs and skills.

Listen and Respond—students learn how to listen to others and how to respond to others' ideas.

Ask—students learn how to ask questions during planning meetings.

Name Your Goals—students learn how to make sure their goals are incorporated into the conference.

SUMMARY

Emphasizing disabilities rather than abilities can seriously undermine the education and development of students. Children with disabilities can become entwined in a cycle of learned helplessness and fail to attribute their success to the effort they put forth. Teachers and parents, by understanding both the strengths and weaknesses of their children, can address learned helplessness and increase motivation and learning. Person Centered Planning activities can help parents and teachers to understand student needs, dreams, and strengths. This chapter also reviews elements of effective praise and issues of helping and overhelping in order to identify methods that support competence. The relationship between competence and curriculum issues is addressed, and teachers are introduced to elements of Pyramid Planning and Universal Design. The use of rubrics to deal with the sensitive issue of grading students with special needs is discussed. How academic difficulties affect social interactions and competence is also addressed. Finally, ways to promote independence through self-advocacy are outlined.

Tips for Educators

On a daily basis, teachers can create many opportunities for students' voices to be heard and for students to make decisions.

- ✎ Integrate choices within assignments so students have options for demonstrating knowledge.

- ✎ Teach an array of strategies and routines so students have tools to choose from to support their own learning.

- ✎ Initiate an assignment calendar for the week or the month so students can begin to manage their time more effectively through the choices they make.

Tips for Parents

Take time each day to:

- ✎ Develop your child's talents.

- ✎ Use effective praise and offer realistic encouragement.

- ✎ Create opportunities to open your child to a world that involves learning in nonacademic ways.

- ✎ Encourage and honor self-advocacy.

NOTES

1. McNulty, M. A. (2003). Dyslexia and the life course. *Journal of Learning Disabilities, 26*(4), 363–381.

2. Adapted from Turnbull, R., Turnbull, A., Shank, M., Smith, S., & Leal, D. (2002). *Exceptional lives: Special education in today's schools.* (3rd ed.). Upper Saddle River, NJ: Merrill Prentice Hall. © 2002. Reprinted by permission of Pearson Education, Inc., Upper Saddle River, NJ.

3. Seligman, M.E.P. (1975). *Helplessness: On development, depression and death.* New York: W. H. Freeman.

4. Turnbull, Turnbull, Shank, Smith, & Leal (2002).

5. Mount, B. (1997). *Person centered planning: Finding directions for change using personal futures planning.* New York: Graphic Futures.

6. Mount, B. (1997).

7. Brooks, R.B. (2004). To touch the hearts and minds of students with learning disabilities: The power of mindsets and expectations. *Learning Disabilities: A Contemporary Journal, 2*(1), 1–8; and Marchant, M., Young, Y. K., & West, R. P. (2004). The effects of parental teaching on compliance behavior of children. *Psychology in the Schools, 41*(3), 337–350.

8. Stipek, D.J. (1993), p. 52.

9. Bos, C., & Vaughn, S. (1998). *Strategies for teaching students with learning and behavior problems.* (4th ed.). Boston: Allyn & Bacon, p. 52.

10. Vaughn, S., Bos, C.S., & Schumm, J.S. (2003). *Teaching exceptional, diverse, and at-risk students in the general education classroom.* Needham Heights, MA: Allyn & Bacon.

11. Vaughn, Bos, & Schumm (2003).

12. Vaughn, Bos, & Schumm (2003).

13. From Vaughn, S., Bos, C. S., & Schumm, J. S. (1997). *Teaching mainstreamed, diverse, and at-risk students in the general education classroom.* (2nd ed.). Boston: Allyn and Bacon, pp. 45, 48. Copyright © 1997 by Pearson Education. Reprinted by permission of the publisher.

14. Kame'enui, E. J., & Simmons, D. C. (1999). *Toward successful inclusion of students with disabilities: The architecture of instruction. Vol. 1: An overview of materials adaptations.* Reston, VA: Council for Exceptional Children.

15. Bowe, F. (2000). *Universal design in education: Teaching nontraditional students.* Westport, CT: Bergen & Garvey.

16. Christiansen, J., & Vogel, J. R. (1998, November–December). A decision model for grading students with disabilities. *Teaching Exceptional Children, 31*(2), p. 30.

17. Norwicki, E. A. (2003). A meta-analysis of the social competence of children with learning disabilities compared to classmates of low and average to high achievement. *Learning Disability Quarterly, 26*(3), p. 185.

18. Dyson, L. L. (2003). Children with learning disabilities within the family context: A comparison with siblings in global self-concept, academic self-perception, and social competence. *Learning Disabilities Research, 18*(1), 1–9.

19. Getskow, V., & Konczal, D. (1996). *Kids with special needs: Information and activities to promote awareness and understanding.* Santa Barbara, CA: Learning Works.

20. Forgan, J. W. (2002). Using bibliotherapy to teach problem solving. *Intervention in School and Clinic, 38*(2), 75–82.

21. Slavin, R. E. (1987). *Cooperative learning: Student teams.* Washington, DC: NEA Professional Library; and Slavin, R. E., & Cooper, R. (1999). Improving intergroup relations: Lessons learned from cooperative learning programs. *Journal of Social Issues, 55*(4), 647–663.

22. Vernon, D. S., Schumaker, J. B., & Deshler, D. D. (1993). *The SCORE skills: Social skills for cooperative groups.* Lawrence, KS: Edge Enterprises.

23. Phillips, P. (1990). A self-advocacy plan for high school students with learning disabilities: A comparative case study analysis of students', teachers', and parents' perceptions of program effects. *Journal of Learning Disabilities, 23,* 466–471.

24. Van Reusen, A. K., Bos, C. S., Schumaker, J., & Deshler, D. (1987). *The education planning strategy.* Lawrence, KS: Excell Enterprises.

CHAPTER 12

Technology and Assistive Technology

Vance Austin

Witold Rybczynski asserts that "not being able to run very fast or for very long [man] has grafted onto himself additional feet, until he can travel farther and faster than any other animal, and not only on land but also on and under water and in the air. He can reinforce his eyes with glasses, telescopes, and microscopes."[1] If Rybczynski is correct that humans are prosthetic gods, then it seems reasonable to infer that assistive technology is an extension of our ingenious nature—an attempt to provide access to the same quality of life for persons who are otherwise disabled.

THE STORY OF JOSH

Josh is a fifteen year-old boy placed in a self-contained classroom for students with learning disabilities. Reading has always been a challenge for Josh, who depends primarily on his auditory modality for processing information. The fact that he is succeeding in school in all subjects except English is a testament to his ability to use his auditory processor effectively. However, Josh is currently reading at a grade three level, and this is the cause of much embarrassment. Josh is failing English again, and he is feeling very discouraged.

English class is not the only place his reading disability is causing him to feel like a failure. He also has difficulty reading the inventory lists at his part-time job in a local deli. Fortunately, the owner has a son who has dyslexia and is very sympathetic. Josh is also troubled when he takes a girlfriend out to eat in a nice restaurant and has to order a steak: he is unsure if they will serve steak and too embarrassed to admit he can't read everything on the menu. Josh worries more than most fifteen-year-olds about getting into college or getting a real job because he is smart enough to know one must be literate to obtain a college degree and a job that provides a livable wage.

Josh knows that he is running out of time, and is frustrated that ten years of remedial reading have only helped him improve three reading levels. However, Josh's dream of being able to process text as quickly as he processes sound may be only a few months away, thanks to innovations in optical character recognition (OCR) software, the laptop computer, and a portable scanner. For many students like Josh, assistive technology may be the great equalizer.

In 1993, according to the National Council on Disability's report to Congress, an estimated 75 percent of children with disabilities could remain in general education classes if provided with the appropriate assistive technology (AT). This same report noted that effective assistive devices could reduce the amount of school-related services required by approximately 45 percent of these students.[2]

In reference to Part E of the IDEA, a child who is eligible for special education services must be evaluated to determine his or her technology needs; this includes a functional evaluation in the child's natural environment. Further prescribed in the legislation is the acquisition of assistive devices, involving the selection, designing, fitting, customizing, adapting, maintaining, and replacement of assistive technology devices. In addition, schools are responsible for providing training and technical services to qualified students, their parents, and teachers.

Consistent with the mandates of IDEA '97 legislation,[3] teaching professionals are responsible for helping students and their parents choose and acquire assistive technology devices as well as instructing them in their application.[4] However, while the results of a national survey of teacher preparation programs in special education substantiated the need for technology training,[5] little data currently available shows that teachers and other professionals are being adequately prepared to assist students and their parents in the selection and use of appropriate assistive devices.[6]

ASSISTIVE TECHNOLOGY IN THE CLASSROOM

"Assistive technology" is a generic term that describes everything from an ergonomically designed pencil grip to an optic imaging communicator. More formally, assistive technology refers to a wide assortment of devices that include any item, piece of equipment, or product system, whether acquired commercially, off the shelf, modified, or customized, that is used to increase, maintain, or improve the functional capabilities of children with disabilities.[7]

Whereas many of these assistive devices are prescribed for persons with physical disabilities, a significant percentage have been shown to be effective in the remediation of learning disabilities, coincidentally the highest incidence disability found in most inclusive classrooms.[8] An in-depth examination of assistive devices currently available revealed a profusion of types and models; however, the number appropriate for use in the inclusive classroom is limited. Because most inclusive classroom teachers see the same children 60–80 percent of the week for periods lasting from forty to fifty minutes,[9] whichever assistive devices are used must be easily administered and monitored. Other important criteria to be considered when selecting assistive devices for students with disabilities in inclusive classrooms include the following: (1) the device must be easy to use; (2) the device must be viable and make learning accessible for the student with a disability; (3) the product must be economically feasible; (4) the product should be portable and should be easily packed and unpacked; and (5) the function and operation of the device should be easily understood by the teacher-instructor and not require an inordinate amount of time. Ideally, the assistive devices for use in an inclusive classroom should provide access to one or more of the following academic skills areas: literacy skills (expressive and/or receptive); math skills (word problem and/or reasoning); organizational skills; or metacognitive skills.[10]

Types of Assistive Technologies That Are Effective in Helping Students with Disabilities

There are essentially three contexts in which assistive technology devices and services provide support: the school, the community, and the home. We will focus on those devices and services that facilitate learning within the classroom.

The goal of the classroom teacher in selecting appropriate assistive devices for a particular student is predicated on the belief that such technology is intended to complement effective instruction. (A complete list of assistive technology devices [ATDs] and contact information is found at the end of this chapter.) In this vein, ATDs should support one or more of the following learning goals:

- Help students develop study skills necessary for accessing instruction.
- Include students with disabilities in challenging, standards-based math curricula.
- Provide opportunities for students to learn basic literacy skills.
- Encourage students to communicate effectively through writing.

Essentially, ATDs used in the classroom can be broadly categorized as either low-technology or high-technology. Low-technology devices are devices that are passive or simple, with few moving parts.[11] Examples include ergonomic pencil grips, book holders, Velcro used to secure textbooks and materials, key guards, enlarged print texts, reachers, weighted spoons, magnifying lenses, graphic organizers, and mnemonic devices such as multiplication cards and acrostics. In contrast, high-technology devices are ones that have greater complexity and may operate electronically; examples include computers, power wheelchairs, computer-based augmentative communication devices, robotics, and electronic spell-checkers.

Reading Assistance. To determine what types of ATDs are effective, it is useful to examine generic low-technology and high-technology options. For reading mechanics and comprehension, for example, some low-technology solutions might include nonslip mats and book holders to help students hold the book; rubber fingers; a universal cuff with a pencil and eraser; and a head/mouth stick to facilitate page turning. To assist with the reading of words, a student might use a magnifying glass, a cardboard "jig" to isolate words, and a straight edge to read line by line. Similar high-technology solutions might include electronic page turners, books on tape, the use of scanners and text-to-speech conversion software, an enlarged computer monitor, and spell-check and vocabulary software.

One example of a visual aid that might provide access to print for a student with a visual-processing deficit is the Kurzweil Scanner. This device scans the text document placed into its reader and interprets the image using phonics rules; this information is then sent to the speech synthesizer, which reads the text aloud. Once loaded, the document may be saved as a text file. There is also a version of this program that does not require a computer. Another auditory text processor, the Reading Edge, is an optical character recognition device. This readily transportable reader can interpret and translate written text into synthesized speech at a rate of 550 words per minute. The Navigator is a device that modifies an existing computer system to convert the printed information on the screen to Braille. This is accomplished through sets of pins, which are raised or lowered electromechanically to create a Braille translation of the text. In a different application, Zoomtext is a screen magnification program that enlarges print and allows the user to view the entire monitor screen or specific areas. Zoomtext is compatible with IBM formatted computer systems.

Expressive Language Deficits and Visual Impairments. Expressive language deficits that specifically impact a student's ability to form letters may be alleviated by some low-technology solutions. These include an ergonomically designed pencil grip, a large marker, a splint made from low-temperature plastics, a keyboard mitt with an isolated finger, a universal cuff made with a pencil or dowel, a weighted pen or pencil, or a typing stick. Low-technology devices that facilitate the student's use of paper might include color-coded or textured-line paper, taping the paper to the writing surface, or using a clipboard. A simple low-tech solution to taking written notes might include a fellow student duplicating his or her notes with carbon paper.

High-technology applications include electric typewriters; word processors; orthotics; prosthetics; robotics; software with word prediction, grammar, and spell-check; the use of a tape recorder; and, most recently, voice recognition software.[12] Voice or speech recognition programming has demonstrated great application for students who have difficulty with the mechanics of writing. This technology permits the user to "write" grammatically and syntactically intelligible text by simply speaking into an external microphone. Some computer manufacturers predict that voice recognition technology will replace the keyboard and mouse as the principal means of input for computer commands. Voice or speech recognition programs "learn" to recognize the nuances of the speech patterns of the user by listening to the phonemes and committing them to memory. It does, however, take some time and patience on the part of the user to input sufficient and varied text to make the voice recognition program viable.[13]

Three major voice recognition systems, Dragon Naturally Speaking Preferred, IBM ViaVoice, and Kurzweil VoicePlus, are currently popular. Dragon Naturally Speaking Preferred, marketed by Dragon Systems, works with Windows and Windows NT and can comfortably input 100 words per minute. The IBM ViaVoice program was originally designed to be used in providing Internet access for persons unable to type in keywords or use a mouse; however, it has shown great accuracy and utility as a word processing system and is compatible with Windows NT. The IBM ViaVoice does require that the user spend some time reading in-text passages in order to teach the program the user's vernacular and voice modulations. Finally, the most economical of these programs is the Kurzweil VoicePlus. It is relatively efficient in differentiating phonemic sounds and does not require the operational memory of the other two programs, but compels the user to pause between words, which may represent a problem for students who have difficulty concentrating or remaining focused.[14]

Mathematics. In mathematics instruction, specifically relative to solving word problems and functional math skills, several viable low-tech options are available. These low-tech devices include the use of an abacus, a counter, a ruler to read problems line by line, and graphic templates and manipulatives. High-tech solutions include the use of handheld computers, calculators, and math skills computer software.

Texas Instruments manufactures a wide array of calculators to serve the needs of students with math deficits in computation; one of the most effective is its "talking calculator." A talking calculator has a speech synthesizer, which provides the user with another modality with which to check the accuracy of calculations. The drawback in using any calculator is that while the calculator may improve accuracy and speed in computation, it cannot provide the student with the rationale for the use of a particular operation.[15] Another high-tech device that is effective for math students with learning disabilities is the computer-based spreadsheet program. The benefit of using spreadsheets is that they provide a model or visual representation of the problem, perform the operations required, and allow the student with disabilities to focus attention on understanding the mathematical operations in a real-life context. Finally, a growing number of computer assisted instruction (CAI) math courses on the market reinforce math skills at various levels and have a voice output feature.[16]

Organization and Memory Tasks. Students with learning disabilities often have great difficulty organizing, managing, and remembering information. Low-tech and high-tech assistive devices offer solutions to these challenges. Low-tech options to consider are the use of mnemonic strategies such as acrostics and acronyms, which facilitate the retrieval of stored data, and graphic organizers such as semantic webs, which have demonstrated positive effects in the organization of notes and written work. Daily planners and calendars also help the student remember important dates and appointments.

High-tech solutions include personal data managers, which allow the user to easily store and retrieve large amounts of personal information by simply encoding the important information on a keyboard/keypad for later retrieval; the information is then displayed on a computer monitor or LCD display. Personal data managers are available as software programs and as self-contained handheld units. Two devices on the market, Voice Organizer and Voice It, allow the user to retrieve data by simply speaking into a microphone on the device. The requested stored data is played back in the speaker's own voice.

Another high-tech organization/memory assistive device is the free-form database, a computer version of the Post-it note. These software databases are memory resident and can be activated while in a word processor or other program by simply pressing a hot key. Free-form databases enable the user to store bits of information in the computer's memory that can be easily recalled by typing in any fragment of the information stored. An example of the free-form database is the function of the phonebook storage feature in most cell phones. In order to retrieve a desired number, one need only key in the first few letters of the individual's name and the entire name and telephone number are recalled instantly.

Determining the Best Option

As teachers and educational professionals determine the device or devices that are most appropriate for a particular student, several issues need to be addressed, namely, (1) the individual's unique profile; (2) the function to be performed; and (3) the specific context in which the technology will be employed.[17]

Occasionally, more than one technology is warranted, and the most effective approach may involve the use of several devices. For example, in the case of a student with a physical impairment and a learning disability, a device that facilitates access to a computer keyboard may be necessary to enable the student to use the organizational software installed in the computer.[18]

Remember the IEP

The most important source of information about the unique needs of the individual student with disabilities is the IEP. As far back as August 1990, the

Office of Special Education Programs (OSEP) published a policy statement indicating that assistive technology must be included in the development of the IEP. This document stated that assistive technology needs must be specified in one of the following three areas of a student's IEP: within the annual goals and short-term objectives; in the section detailing supplementary aids or services; or in the list of related services. Furthermore, the OSEP policy letter emphasized that school systems are responsible for providing ATs in accordance with the mandated provision of a free and appropriate public education.[19] The needs of the student to be assessed for the provision of ATs should be studied by a multidisciplinary team (MDT) that may include teachers, therapists, computer design analysts, rehabilitation professionals, social workers, family members, and, of course, most important, the student.[20] Inge and Shepherd[21] suggest nine steps in a systematic process for selecting AT devices:

1. Gather background data, which involves asking students what they want to be able to do and where they want to do it, and determining the kinds of devices that would best facilitate these perceived needs.

2. Observe students in the classroom environment to determine their abilities and needs and how AT can help them achieve their learning objectives.

3. Determine the students' abilities and assistive technology needs involving a more in-depth assessment.

4. Investigate the ideal access system employing interagency collaboration, the state lending library, or vendors or agencies that loan equipment for assessment purposes.

5. Propose an access system.

6. Personalize and maximize the access system.

7. Set goals for instruction and training.

8. Implement the system.

9. Monitor programs and provide follow-up.

Accessibility of Assistive Technology

Unfortunately, there is no central clearinghouse for the collection and distribution of assistive technology, although the Internet offers a wealth of information. Typically, assistive devices are available from companies and their distributors that specialize in the manufacture of technologies for persons with disabilities, and companies and their retail affiliates that provide generic technologies to the general public. There has been an increase over the last several years in the number of companies that have added technologies designed principally for persons with learning disabilities to their product lines (e.g., Intellitools, Mayer-Johnson Inc., Don Johnston Inc., Assistive Technology Inc., Kurzweil Applied Intelligence Inc., Dragon Systems Inc., Prentke Romich Inc., Word+ Inc., and Ablenet). Some of the devices manufactured by these companies were designed primarily for other disabilities such as speech-language, deafness, and blindness and low vision, but, because of their compensatory potential for students with learning disabilities, were adapted and marketed for this population.

Many "standard technologies" marketed to the general population may be appropriately considered assistive technologies for use as compensatory devices in the classroom. Some popular examples of these technologies include personal data managers (such as those distributed by Sharp Electronics Inc.), spell-checkers available from Texas Instruments, and the talking calculators also available from Texas Instruments.

Costs of Assistive Technologies

There are some very effective ways to finance and purchase assistive technologies, but always consider low-tech solutions first. An example of a low-tech solution would be to consider purchasing or borrowing books on tape (no charge if borrowed) rather than buying a costly OCR system for a student with a visual processing disorder. Nevertheless, there may be high-tech assistive devices that are determined to be the most effective option for a student. If this is the case, and the device is required as a part of the student's special education program, then it is clearly the responsibility of the school to obtain it.

Sources of funding include state departments of rehabilitation, private foundations, and service clubs like the Rotary and Kiwanis Clubs. In addition, it may be possible to apply for donations or discounts toward the purchase of new or used equipment. Medicare, Medicaid, and private insurance companies are other possible sources of funding; however, these sources require that the assistive technology support a bona fide medical condition rather than a learning problem, and as such must be prescribed by a physician or other licensed practitioner.[22] Credit financing of assistive technology provided through various state loan programs, such as the New York State Equipment Loan Fund, represents an affordable means by which many students and their families can purchase costly high-tech devices. Created in 1986, the New York State Equipment Loan Fund is a revolving fund administered by the New York State Department of Social Services, which allocates loans of from $400 to $4,000 that can be repaid over a two- to eight-year period. Other states offer similar loans at even lower interest rates. The variable repayment schedule as well as the fixed-rate low interest may make this type of loan more feasible than bank loans for students with disabilities and their families. School administrators and teachers may apply for a grant to purchase assistive technology for their students who need them. In preparing the grant application, it is important to develop a sound rationale that supports the needs of students with disabilities in the school as well as the perceived benefits of the technology to student academic and social development. Mates suggests that including a picture of one of the students using an assistive technology that the grant money will obtain makes a compelling statement.[23]

Next, experts recommend that the funding request reflect the mission statement and criteria for funding published by the funding agency. For example, if the agency states that the grant is intended to fund in-service training for teachers to become proficient in the use of assistive technologies to help students with learning disabilities, then your rationale should underscore your intention to train selected staff to become proficient in its use and to train other staff members and students with disabilities to use these technologies. Finally, once the needs and plan of use have been clearly defied, the applicants should identify an appropriate funding agency. Three good sources of information about possible funding agencies are the Alliance for Technology Access Resource Centers, the Technology Assistance Program, and the *Disability Funding News*, which also alerts the reader to relevant grants available from the federal government as well as private agencies.[24]

However, before making a purchase, it is always advisable to evaluate the advantages and disadvantages of any technology being considered for use through sources such university and college curriculum materials libraries, computer shows, assistive technology and learning disability conferences, as well as technology retail outlets. In addition, many manufacturers of assistive technology permit a trial period before the prospective client is committed to purchasing the device. This policy protects the student and his or her family from making an expensive mistake purchasing assistive technology that is not beneficial.[25]

TRAINING FOR USING ASSISTIVE TECHNOLOGY

Low-technology assistive devices probably do not require training; however, more involved high-technology devices most certainly do. In 1989, the Center for Special Education Technology at the Council for Exceptional Children (CEC) held a state forum that determined that teachers, related service personnel, students with disabilities, and parents needed training that included awareness of technologies as well as a commitment to preservice and continuing education in the implementation of these technologies.

According to Bryant, Wolfu, Candela, and Johnson, and Weikle and Hadadian, effective training is crucial for students with disabilities and their families on how to locate, obtain and use assistive technologies.[26] Furthermore, it is recommended that service providers such as rehabilitation counselors, special and general education teachers, and administrators in schools and agencies be provided with different levels of training in conjunction with their roles as they relate to students with disabilities in schools. Because the student (consumer) and teacher (service provider) have different needs with respect to assistive technology, it follows that they should receive different kinds of training. Students with disabilities need to be apprised of the options available in both low- and high-tech devices that will provide them with optimal compensatory or remedial assistance. Typically, awareness of assistive technologies is facilitated through radio and television ads. Other effective ways in which this information is disseminated include human interest stories presented in television documentaries; information and referral systems provided on the Internet; and demonstrations by vendors at conferences (e.g., the LDA Conference) and technology fairs. What is currently lacking for students with disabilities and their parents, however, is access to high-quality, affordable technical assistance and consultation.[27]

The 1989 Switzer Memorial Seminar on technology and empowerment recommended that service providers such as special and general education teachers be adequately trained in the use of assistive technology. The seminar made the following suggestions to schools to facilitate this training:

- Develop formal (e.g., certifying) and informal (e.g., in-service workshops and conferences) training programs.
- Provide programs for the novice and veteran professional.
- Provide training that is relevant for the technologies used in the school.
- Expand the training to include environments other than the school for which the technology may prove beneficial.

In making the case for effective in-service training, Young noted that service providers of the future must be competent enough in the application of assistive technologies to be able to make appropriate modifications to benefit the student.[28] Sometimes simple adaptations can improve access and utility for a student with a disability and obviate the need to purchase costly new technology. An example of the flexibility required by teacher-trainers is provided by recent modifications made to Israeli fighter jets. The pilots, needing better peripheral vision, simply mounted rearview mirrors from old cars inside the cockpits of their jets, resulting in improved visual perception.

Unfortunately, studies regarding the preparation of teachers to use technology such as computers in their classrooms reveal that the majority have not received sufficient training in technology.[29] Whereas national surveys have indicated that the majority of faculty in teacher preparation programs in special education agree that training in technology should be an integral part of their programs, relatively few require that education majors take a computer technology course or demonstrate competency in using computers to enhance instruction.[30]

In responding to the discrepancy between needed skills and those actually taught in teacher preparation programs, the Council for Exceptional Children developed a set of standards relative to new teachers that includes assistive technology competencies. Furthermore, in a survey of Virginia schools conducted by the Center for Human disAbilities at George Mason University, respondents identified the following skills and responsibilities as preeminent for assistive technology personnel: (a) assessing technology services and devices; (b) determining student eligibility for such devices and services; (c) conducting in-service training on assistive technologies; (d) delivering assistive technology to students; and (e) writing assistive technology goals and objectives on students' individualized education plans.[31]

To provide assistive technology instruction and training to students with disabilities in the classroom, the trainer must first assess the student's learning needs. Next, the teacher-trainer should select the most functional and beneficial device that is maximally accessible to the student, considering low-tech options first. In the case of a low-tech solution such as a "talking" calculator, the teacher may simply read over the instructional booklet, developing from it a simple systematic procedure for the student. In contrast, if a high-tech solution is deemed more beneficial, the teacher-trainer may need to learn the operational and maintenance procedures from an authorized manufacturer representative or technical assistant. This additional training may or may not be included in the purchase price—another point to consider before investment.

Instructional support for standard technologies such as a word processing program like WordPerfect® may be provided by competent peers or family members who are proficient users. Whereas some assistive technologies may be mastered from videotapes provided with the technology (e.g., Voice Pilot and certain OCR devices), for others that are more involved, a tutor may be needed to provide further guided practice after school. Lastly, some of the more popular assistive technologies provide online tutorials and support services. The issue here is not how training is provided, but whether it is beneficial to the student.[32] The following effective training strategies are recommended when implementing new assistive technologies for students with disabilities.

- Employ a multisensory approach to training, incorporating visual, oral, and written instruction; however, break the instructional process into steps for more involved (high-tech) ATs.
- Reinforce training through ample practice.
- Model the use of the technology and allow the student to perform the same procedures modeled.

- Provide constant comprehension checks to ensure that the student understands the concept and procedures.

- Provide meaningful instruction for the student using his or her words to describe the functions taught. Remember the advantages of metacognitive aids such as mnemonics, acronyms, graphic representations or schema, and rhymes to assist the student with the storage and retrieval of the procedures required to use the AT.

- Use concise, clear language in describing functions and operational procedures.

- Provide motivation for the student to want to use the device, particularly when its use is compensatory.

Finally, classmates are an overlooked resource relative to student training and support. They can make the difference in the feasibility of an AT and the inclination of a peer with a disability to use the device. Some of the newer technologies available, such as optical character recognition and speech recognition systems, may be interesting to many students in the classroom. Their natural fascination and curiosity with technology can provide the incentive to teach them the function and operation of the assistive device. Once they have learned the operational procedures of the AT, these classmates can become effective facilitators for the student with a disability.

Consider Josh, the student described at the beginning of the chapter. According to recent literature, Josh might benefit from both the appropriate assistive devices and the support of classmates who can help him work with the technology as well as provide much-needed acceptance and understanding.[33] For example, Josh's teacher may be unable to provide the level of support he may need to negotiate new assistive devices, whereas classmates trained to use the technology could fill this role effectively until Josh gains the necessary expertise. Further, after years of struggling to read and trying to cope with the embarrassment of poor literacy skills, Josh would conceivably benefit from the acceptance of peers who can appreciate his disability.

In their seminal investigation of the effects of training classmates without disabilities to be peer facilitators for students with disabilities who use assistive technology, Church and Glennen developed a list of goals for a peer preparation activity designed to facilitate awareness of the special needs of students with disabilities in the classroom as well as the technologies that help them learn.[34] These purposes are instructive:

- Establish the purpose of the assistive device.
- Establish the procedures for the use of the AT by classmates without disabilities.

- Establish the competencies of the student with disabilities who will use the equipment.
- Encourage the student with a disability using an AT device to plan the instructional presentation of the use of the device.
- Teach classmates the best way to help the student with a disability who uses an AT device.

Following these procedures may optimize the constructive involvement of classmates in facilitating the use of assistive technology by a student with a disability.

SUMMARY

The term "assistive technology" refers to a range of devices designed to increase, maintain, or improve the functional capabilities of children and adults. This technology can provide support in several different venues, but primarily the school, home, and workplace. Further, assistive technology devices should support study skills, standards-based math curricula, and basic literacy skill development, and help improve written and oral communication. In accomplishing these purposes, assistive technology devices may be categorized as either low-technology devices, those that are passive or simple and relatively inexpensive, or high-technology devices, those that are more complex and costly.

To reduce costs to the consumer or institution, low-technology devices should be considered first. When this is not a viable alternative, more expensive assistive devices may be funded by grants provided by private foundations and service clubs or through loans obtained from various state agencies. In addition, quality training in the use of assistive devices is recommended for the students who require them as well as for the service providers and families of these students.

In discussing the issue of assistive technology and equity, Brett and Provenzo noted that such technology, correctly applied, can give students with disabilities "the opportunity to compete on an equal footing in our culture."[35] However, there are two sides to the access issue: if we empower some students through assistive technology, then we surely disenfranchise those who do not have access. In a way, we subordinate those students without access to both students without disabilities and students with disabilities who are empowered through access.[36]

Providing assistive technology to students whose IEP prescribes it is neither an excessive nor an unreasonable accommodation, but is clearly required in accordance with IDEA. In compliance with this mandate, all teachers should be conversant with the more effective of these technologies as they pertain to the classroom. As schools seek to provide access to knowledge for all their students and, where appropriate, to provide instruction for these students in the general education classroom, every teacher needs to be competent in the selection and use of the most effective assistive technologies. Asking questions about the types and uses of assistive devices, the cost of such technology, and the availability of training for both staff and student is critical in the quest to obtain valuable information about current state-of-the-art resources.

Tips for Educators

✎ Explore the feasibility of using low-technology devices before investing in more costly high-tech alternatives.

✎ Consider various sources of funding available to assist in the purchase of expensive assistive technology; examples include service clubs like the Rotary and Kiwanis as well as credit financing through state loan programs. In addition, remember to check with funding agencies like the federal governments Technology Assistance Program, one of the Alliance for Technology Access Resource Centers, as well as the *Disability Funding News*, for valuable information about government and corporate grants for the purchase of assistive technology.

✎ Ensure that the student with disabilities who requires an assistive device and those individuals who will provide support receive the appropriate training. Teachers of these students need to be able to assess their specific AT needs, identify and procure the most effective and affordable devices, and modify the equipment when necessary. Teacher training that adequately addresses these needs should be provided to every teacher, especially those who work with students with disabilities. School administrators need to be made aware of the importance of providing training for their teachers in order to ensure the successful application of this costly technology.

✎ Become conversant with several of the organizations that provide information about various assistive technologies as well as some of the vendors that distribute them. Select a few of the Web sites recommended in this chapter that seem relevant to your student population, and find out about the services and/or products they provide.

✎ Visit a regional assistive technology center near you and ask the staff to give you a tour of the various devices that they have catalogued. You can locate such centers by contacting the office of developmental disabilities in your area, or your state education department.

Tips for Parents

✎ Familiarize yourself with your student's IEP learning goals and objectives and ensure that the use of assistive technologies is included in the document as a required service. Also, make certain that these goals truly reflect your student's needs.

✎ Refer to and study good sources of information about assistive technology, especially those most relevant and beneficial to your student. Many of these are listed in this chapter for your convenience.

✎ Educate yourself about the assistive technologies most recommended by experts in journals and trade publications. If feasible, visit an assistive technology distributor such as Kurzweil Educational Systems or a training center such as the Kornreich Center in Albertson, New York. This chapter provides a list of many of the most popular and reputable manufacturers and distributors to assist you in this endeavor.

✎ Learn how the assistive technology required by your student functions. Many manufacturers and distributors of assistive technologies provide assistance and instruction either by arrangement on-site or via e-mail or telephone.

✎ Ensure that the teachers and aides working with your student are using the most effective and appropriate assistive technology—be proactive and insist on the best!

✎ Make sure that teachers and aides are proficient in the use of the assistive device or technology your student needs to be successful in school.

✎ Learn about potential funding sources, especially if your student requires costly assistive software or equipment. Investigate the more promising of these and share this information with your student's teachers and school administrators.

✎ Keep up to date—educate yourself about promising innovations in assistive technology that are relevant to your student.

✎ Work with your student's teachers, aides, other educational professionals, and the family members of other students who are using assistive technologies to learn. Be supportive of their efforts to provide the best education possible for their students.

✎ Help your school select assistive technologies that will provide optimal access to learning for your student and others who need them.

✎ Consider forming a family advocacy group to provide information about various assistive technologies as well as support to other families with students who require them.

RESOURCES

The following organizations and Internet sites provide teachers, parents, and students with important information about current assistive technology services and equipment relevant to learning in the classroom.

ABLEDATA. www.abledata.com
  Abledata is a federally funded program whose purpose is to provide information on assistive technology and rehabilitative equipment.

Adaptive Technology Resource Centre (ATRC). www.utoronto.ca/atrc
  Clearinghouse for information about access to data, providers, and reviews of assistive technology.

Apple Disability Site. www.apple.com/disability/welcome.html
  This site provides information about available Macintosh assistive technology.

The Archimedes Project. http://archimedes.stanford.edu/
  Provides information about the development of innovative computer-based technology.

AskERIC Virtual Library. http://ericir.syr.edu
  Clearinghouse for information relevant to the field of education.

Center for Computer Assistance to the Disabled, Inc. (C-CAD). www.c-cad.org
  Incorporates links to disability sites, a computer training catalogue, and adaptive software that can be downloaded.

Closing the Gap, Inc. www.closingthegap.com
  Source publishes a monthly newspaper and annual resource guide to assistive technology.

Council for Exceptional Children. www.cec.sped.org
  A source of information for teachers of children with disabilities.

IBM Special Needs Solutions. www.austin.ibm.com/sns/snsvision
  Information clearinghouse for assistive technologies that make computers more accessible to persons with disabilities.

Indie (The Integrated Network of Disability Information and Education). www.indi.ca
  An extensive source of information and products relevant to persons with disabilities.

Jim Lubin's disAbility Resources. www.eskimo.com/~jlubin/disabled
  Disability resource featuring links to a profusion of hardware, software, funding, and training Web sites.

LD Online. www.ldonline.org
  Provides a wealth of information on all aspects of learning disabilities, including resources and links to pertinent sites.

National Center for Disability Dissemination Research (NCDDR). www.ncddr.org
  Disseminates information from NCDDR-funded research projects and increases the accessibility of research results for consumers.

National Center for Learning Disabilities (NCLD). www.ncld.org
  Clearinghouse for information on learning disabilities, including resources.

National Center to Improve Practice (NCIP). www.edc.org
  Advocates the effective use of technology to improve academic outcomes for students with sensory, cognitive, physical, and emotional disabilities.

National Information Center for Children and Youth with Disabilities (NICHCY). www.nichcy.org
Information on all aspects of disability. Site also offers links to regulations, training, and resources that benefit children and youth with disabilities.

National Institute on Disability and Rehabilitation Research (NIDRR). www.ncddr.org
Funds hundreds of projects and programs relative to persons with disabilities. Provides links to online foundations as well as corporate grant programs.

The Productivity Works. www.prodworks.com
Manufactures pwWebSpeak, an Internet browser that provides an auditory as well as a simplified visual presentation, including large character display.

Project DO-IT (Disabilities, Opportunities, Internetworking, and Technology). www.washington.edu/doit
Provides access links and information on assistive technology.

Rehabilitation Engineering and Assistive Technology Society of North America (RESNA). www.resna.org
Professional organization whose mission is to develop products and devices that improve access to technology for persons with disabilities.

Schwab Learning. www.schwablearning.org
This organization provides information on all types of assistive and adaptive technology as well as contact information for the manufacturers.

WebABLE! www.webable.com
The World Wide Web information clearinghouse for persons with disabilities and organizations that provide accessibility solutions.

The following are selected manufacturers who market assistive and adaptive technology devices and equipment to persons with disabilities:

ACCESSABILITY
320 Clement Street
San Francisco, CA 94118
Phone: (888) 322-7200
Fax: (415) 751-5262
Vendor offers a complete line of adaptive computer equipment and assistive devices.

AICOM CORPORATION
5847 Glen Eagles Drive
San Jose, CA 95131
Markets Accent speech synthesizers and Messenger-IC, speech synthesizers for notebook and palmtop computers.

ANN MORRIS ENTERPRISES, INC.
890 Fams Court
East Meadow, NY 11554
Phone: (516) 292-9232; (800) 454-3175
Fax: (516) 292-2522
Mail order catalogue of both high- and low-end assistive devices.

ARKENSTONE
555 Oakmead Parkway
Sunnyvale, CA 94086
Phone: (408) 245-5900; (800) 444-4443
Fax: (408) 328-8484
www.arkenstone.org
  Provides reading machines and talking maps for persons with learning disabilities.

BIOLINK COMPUTER RESEARCH & DEVELOPMENT LTD.
140 West 15th Street
North Vancouver, British Columbia V7M 1R6, Canada
Phone: (604) 984-4099
  Purveyor of screen-reading software for Windows 3.1, Windows 95, and Windows NT. Also provides Protalk for Windows.

CAROLYN'S
1415 57th Avenue West
Bradenton, FL 34207
Phone: (800) 648-2266
Fax: (941) 739-5503
  Providers of various screen-reading and magnification software as well as speech-synthesizer hardware and software.

DON JOHNSTON
1000 North Rand Road, Building 115, P.O. Box 639
Wauconda, IL 60084
Phone: (800) 999-4600
Fax: (708) 526-4177
www.donjohnston.com
  A producer of computer access, augmentative communication, and learning disabilities hardware and software.

DRAGON SYSTEMS INC.
320 Nevada Street
Newton, MA 02160
Phone: (800) 825-5897
Fax: (617) 527-0372
www.dragonsys.com
  Manufactures and markets DragonDictate-30K, a speech recognition system that responds to the voice commands of the user.

FREEDOM OF SPEECH
1524 Fairfield Road, South
Minnetonka, MN 55305
Phone: (612) 544-3333
Fax: (612) 544-7799
  Markets voice recognition technology produced by various reputable manufacturers.

IBM SPECIAL NEEDS
11400 Burnet Road, Building 904/6
Austin, TX 78758
Phone: (800) 426-4832
Fax: (512) 838-8199
www.ibm.com

> Designs and sells assistive devices and software tools that make the computer more accessible for persons with vision, mobility, speech, and attention/memory disabilities.

INTELLITOOLS
55 Leveroni Court, # 9
Novato, CA 94949
Phone: (800) 899-6687
Fax: (415) 382-5950
www.intellitools.com

> Manufacturers of IntelliKeys keyboard, this company designs computer assistive technology for persons with disabilities.

KURZWEIL EDUCATIONAL SYSTEMS
411 Waverly Oaks Road
Waltham, MA 02154
Phone: (800) 894-5374
Fax: (617) 899-3167
www.kurzweiledu.com

> Producers and distributors of software products for persons with reading disabilities as well as persons who are blind or have low vision.

LAUREATE LEARNING SYSTEMS
110 East Spring Street
Winooski, VT 05404
Phone: (800) 562-6801
Fax: (802) 655-4757
www.llsys.com

> Distributors of talking software designed to provide access for persons with various language-based learning difficulties.

MAXI-AIDS
42 Executive Boulevard
P.O. Box 3209
Farmingdale, NY 11735
Phone: (800) 522-6294
Fax: (516) 752-0689
www.maxiaids.com

> A provider of a wide array of low- and high-tech assistive devices.

MICROSYSTEMS SOFTWARE
600 Worcester Road
Framingham, MA 01701
Phone: (800) 828-2600

Fax: (508) 879-1069
www.handiware.com
Manufacturers of various types of software for persons who need screen magnification, adapted access, augmentative communication, or environmental control.

VOILA TECHNOLOGY
54 Castle Road
Rochester, NY 14623
Phone: (716) 321-1451
Fax: (716) 321-1451
Provider of voice input/output systems for persons with various learning disabilities.

XEROX IMAGING SYSTEMS
9 Centennial Drive
Peabody, MA 01960
Phone: (800) 248-6550
Fax: (508) 977-2437
Manufactures and distributes adaptive technology devices for persons who are blind, have low vision, or are dyslexic.

Other Resources

Both the Kurzweil Scanner and the Reading Edge devices may be obtained by telephoning Xerox Imaging Systems-Personal Reader Department at 1-800-421-7323. Information about acquiring the Navigator is available by telephoning the manufacturer, Telesensory, at 1-800-227-8418. Zoomtext is compatible with IBM formatted computer systems; information about the device may be obtained by contacting the Ai Squared Corporation at 1-800-362-3612.

NOTES

1. Rybczynski, W. (1985). *Taming the tiger: The struggle to control technology*. New York: Penguin.
2. Zabala, J. S. (1996). SETTing the stage for success with assistive technology. Available online at http://sac.uky.edu/~jszaba0/JoySETT.html.
3. 20 U.S.C.S. 1401 (26).
4. Alliance for Technology Access. (2002). *Computer and Web resources for people with disabilities: A guide to exploring today's assistive technology*. Alameda, CA: Hunter House; and Lesar, S. (1998). Use of assistive technology with young children with disabilities: Current status and training needs. *Journal of Early Intervention, 21*(2), 146–159.
5. Kinney, P., & Blackhurst, A. E. (1987). Technology competencies for teachers of young children with severe handicaps. *Topics in Early Childhood Special Education, 7*(3), 105–115.
6. Angle, B. (2001, February). Technology use with students with learning disabilities compared to other exceptionalities. Poster session presented at the annual meeting of the Learning Disabilities Association of America, New York; Bakken,

J. P., & Whedon, C. K. (2001, February). Teachers' knowledge and perceptions of assistive technologies for students with learning disabilities. Poster session presented at the annual meeting of the Learning Disabilities Association of America, New York; King, T. W. (1999). *Assistive technology: Essential human factors.* Boston: Allyn & Bacon; and Lesar (1998).

7. Technology-Related Assistance for Individuals with Disabilities Act of 1988. Pub. L. 100–407, Title 29, U.S.C. 2201 et seq: U.S. Statutes at Large, 102, 1044–1065, August 19, 1988.

8. Austin, V. L. (2001). Teachers' beliefs about co-teaching. *Remedial and Special Education, 22*(4), 245–255.

9. Bixler, L. L. (1998). Perceptions of co-teachers: An exploration of characteristics and components needed for co-teaching. Doctoral dissertation, University of Oklahoma. *Dissertation Abstracts International, 59-03A,* 0780–1012.

10. Bryant, D. P. (2003). *Assistive technology for people with disabilities.* Boston: Allyn & Bacon; Dede, C. (Ed.). (1998). *Learning with technology.* Alexandria, VA: Association for Supervision and Curriculum Development; and Warger, C. (1998). Integrating assistive technology into the curriculum. ERIC/OSEP Digest E568. ERIC Clearinghouse on Disabilities and Gifted Education, Reston, VA.

11. Bain, B. K., Dooley, K. F., & Leger, D. (1997). Assistive technology: An interdisciplinary approach. In B. K. Bain & D. Leger (Eds.), *Assistive technology: An interdisciplinary approach* (pp. 1–7). New York: Churchill Livingstone; and King (1999).

12. Alliance for Technology Access (2000); Bryant (2003); Elkind, K. (2004, May/June). Choosing assistive technology for teaching reading and writing. *Media and Methods,* 20; and Erickson, V. (2004, March/April). Spotlight on assistive technology. *Media and Methods,* 4.

13. Mates, B. T. (2000). *Adaptive technology for the Internet: Making electronic resources accessible to all.* Chicago: American Library Association.

14. Mates (2000).

15. Raskind, M. H., & Higgins, E. L. (1998). Assistive technology for postsecondary students with learning disabilities: An overview. *Journal of Learning Disabilities, 31,* 27–40.

16. King (1999); and Riviere, A. (1996, Summer). Assistive technology: Meeting the needs of adults with learning disabilities. Washington, DC: National Adult Literacy and Learning Disabilities Center.

17. Parette, P., & McMahan, G. A. (2002). What should we expect of assistive technology? Being sensitive to family goals. *Teaching Exceptional Children, 35*(1), 56–61; and Riviere (1996, Summer).

18. Bryant (2003).

19. Flippo, K. F., Inge, K. J., & Barcus, J. M. (Eds.). (1995). *Assistive technology: A resource for school, work, and community.* Baltimore: Paul H. Brookes Publishing Co.

20. Long, T., Huang, L., Woodbridge, M., Woolverton, M., & Minkel, J. (2003). Integrating assistive technology into an outcome-driven model of service delivery. *Infants and Young Children, 16*(4), 272–283.

21. Inge, K. J., & Shepherd, J. (1995). Assistive technology applications for strategies for school system personnel. In Flippo, Inge, & Barcus (1995), pp. 133–167.

22. King (1999); and Raskind & Higgins (1998).

23. Mates (2000).

24. Carey, A.C., Delsordo, V., & Goldman, A. (2004). Assistive technology for all: Access to alternative financing for minority populations. *Journal of Disability Policy Studies, 14*(4), 194–203; Finlayson, M., & Hammel, J. (2003). Providing alternative financing for assistive technology: Outcomes over twenty months. *Journal of Disability Policy Studies, 14*(2), 109–118, 125; and Mates (2000).

25. Wallace, J.E. (2003). A policy analysis of the assistive technology alternative financing programs in the United States. *Journal of Disability Policy Studies, 14*(2), 74–81.

26. Bryant (2003); Wolfu, K.E., Candela, T., & Johnson, G. (2003, November). Wired to work: A qualitative analysis of assistive technology training for people with visual impairments. *Journal of Visual Impairments and Blindness, 97*(11), 677–694; and Weikle, B., & Hadadian, A. (2003). Can assistive technology help us to not leave any child behind? *Preventing School Failure, 47*(4), 181–186.

27. Parette & McMahan (2002).

28. Young, E.B. (1988). One university's role in supporting special needs locally. *Electronic Learning, 8*(3), 10–12.

29. U.S. Congress. House of Representatives. Committee on Education and the Workforce. (2002). *Assessing the Assistive Technology Act of 1998.* Hearing before the Subcommittee on 21st Century Competitiveness of the Committee on Education and the Workforce. 107th Cong., 2nd sess. (107–152).

30. Bryant (2003); and King (1999); Wolffe, Candela, & Johnson (2003, November); Weikle & Hadadian (2003).

31. Individuals with Disabilities Education Act, 20 U.S.C. 1400 et seq. (1997); and Behrmann, M.M. (1995). Assistive technology training. In Flippo, Inge, & Barcus (1995), pp.211–223.

32. Raskind & Higgins (1998).

33. Bryant (2003).

34. Church, G., & Glennen, S. (1992). *The handbook of assistive technology.* San Diego, CA: Singular Publishing Group.

35. Brett, A., & Provenzo, E.F., Jr. (1995). *Adaptive technology for special human needs.* Albany: State University of New York Press, p.24.

36. Brett & Provenzo (1995), p.24.

CHAPTER 13

Effective Inclusive Schools

Gerald M. Mager and Matt Giugno

EVERYONE SUGARING

You could feel the energy in the fifth grade science classroom. An organized, enthusiastic teacher and twenty-six active ten-year-olds were at work on a project. The topic: maple sugaring. Three of the twenty-six students have disabilities; two of them had been in a self-contained setting the previous year. One of these students had a prior history of aggressive behavior. The other two students had low reading ability and needed ongoing support in the classroom.

How did this work? A teaching assistant was assigned to all three. She was there, but not there. She gave each of the students room, and that allowed a really nice natural incident to occur. One of the students lost his place in the provided notes while the science teacher was talking. A classmate noticed his confusion and, without being prompted, reached over, found the place, and told him in a quiet voice, "We're right here." A very nice, natural moment. No adult needed.

Inclusive classrooms are models of good instruction and positive social interaction. Children and youth—all of them—learn and feel a part of the venue. Adults are challenged to call on their best professional and personal capacities, and in the success they and their students fashion, they come to a deeper appreciation of what it is to teach, what it is to be a teacher. But getting to this end—in spite of how seemingly natural good, inclusive education is—is not easy.

CREATING AN INCLUSIVE CLASSROOM

Teachers who want to teach inclusively face big obstacles to achieving that end. Perhaps the most pervasive and sometimes the most subtle of these obstacles is the tradition that shapes and guides the collective view of what schooling is and what it should be. The traditional "system" of education with which we are familiar was not designed with inclusive practices in mind. In fact, traditional schooling in many ways works against it.

For example, in grouping students for instruction, traditional schooling argues for minimizing the differences among learners as a step toward teaching them more effectively and efficiently. "Ability grouping" and "tracking" are but two expressions of this argument. The assumption is that schooling will generally be conducted in whole-class groups and that students who are alike will more likely benefit from the same instruction. That is, the entire class will address the same content, through the same activities, at the same pace, leading to the same measures of achievement. Inherent in this approach is the assumption that students who seem to be alike in their present achievement all learn pretty much in the same way.

Today, this assumption is being called into question. While educators may not feel ready to explain all the ways in which students learn, it is relatively certain that not all students learn in the same way. Individual differences among learners—including interests, family supports, cultural backgrounds, motivations, learning styles, and so on—are also important. Traditional schooling cannot accommodate differences, let alone value them as a source of richness in the classroom and the society. As parents you will want to be aware of current approaches that support inclusive education for your child. Traditional models of schooling that support segregation of children with disabilities are no longer acceptable.

Other components of traditional schooling are also being looked at with a critical eye. For example, the traditional teacher's role as the "provider of knowledge" is giving way to more dynamic views of that role. Indeed, views of what knowledge, skills, and values are important to learning, the variety of ways students learn, and how learning should be assessed are all emerging from the more static, traditional perspectives. Some would argue that traditional schooling is changing and that as inclusive teaching and schooling become more widely practiced, this barrier is diminishing. And so it would seem. It nonetheless remains a large obstacle.

CREATING NEW VIEWS OF THE CLASSROOM

It is easy to see how tradition comes up short in support of inclusive classrooms and schools. It is less easy to create the "inclusive system." The challenge is to transform, to design, and to invent the classrooms and schools that would better serve all students, of all interests and needs. This is no simple task, for tradition does not support the concept of inclusion, and new models of practice are yet emerging. No ready-made answers are at hand. Rather, in the dynamic environments in which teachers are to create inclusive classrooms, real transformation, real design, and real invention must take place.

Re-creating the Role of Educators

Teachers Must Have a Vision of Inclusive Teaching and Schooling. It may be easy to rail against what we see as the limits of traditional schooling, its schools and its classrooms, but it is much more difficult to develop and communicate a plan of change. And it is a step further to put those ideas into practice. Somehow, we must develop enough of a vision of what inclusive teaching and schooling are to guide subsequent thinking and action. Our vision of inclusion must be articulated so that others can understand, challenge, and support it. This vision must be connected to the daily practices of the classroom and to school policies and practices such that it can shape reality.

Teachers Must Transform Their Views of Student Learning. Educators must become more sophisticated in their understanding of student learning and accept the premise that all students are capable of learning complex material. Learning is in itself inventive, meaning that all students' understanding is in large measure fashioned by them in ways that make sense in their unique construction of understanding.

Teachers Must Transform Their Teaching Roles. Teachers are no longer viewed simply as providers of knowledge. If we accept the notion that learners construct their own understandings, what is the educator's role in this experience to be? How are teachers to help students learn? Teachers must rethink their daily practices to align with these different views of learning and teaching.

Planning an Inclusive Lesson

At the fifth grade planning session, the classroom teacher, the special educator, and the teaching assistant met to discuss the language arts lesson plan for the next day. The classroom teacher described what work he wanted the students to complete during the day. The students had just finished reading a book on the flora and fauna of the woods and were to write two paragraphs on a topic they selected.

Most of the students could handle this assignment with little adult help. For the students with disabilities, some modification of the assignment was necessary. Two had significant reading difficulties, and one would need assistance in spell-checking. They would have the same assignment as their classmates, but would have advance organizers to use in order to give them a little extra time to complete the project.

The special education teacher—the "collaborating teacher," in this school's parlance—outlined two strategies she would employ with the students who have difficulty with reading. The student who has difficulty with spelling would have the teacher assistant as a helper as well as a paired-up classmate who would also provide a "natural support."

Teachers Must Design Teams Who Will Support Their Work with Students. Teachers can no longer be classroom isolates who are solely responsible for the education of their students, provided with little or no assistance, spurred on by little or no challenge, and left to sustain their enthusiasm with little sense of being appreciated. Teachers should work as a team of educators who share responsibility for the education of children and youth, who work together in the classroom, and who together assure that all students achieve their potential. Collaborative teaching—succeeding together—is the mark of an accomplished teacher.

Teachers Must Invent Ways of Productively Engaging Parents and Caregivers. Evidence is strong that the involvement of parents and other responsible adults in the education of children and youth enhances achievement. Yet teachers do not use this tool for promoting student learning very well. Engaging parents and caregivers in the school experience—in classrooms and other venues—is a challenge to the creative genius of teachers. Extending that invention and invitation to the fuller communities in which our students live is the next step.

Creating these transformations, designs, and inventions and pulling them together into a functional whole presents teachers with major challenges. Seldom are there clear markers by which to gauge success. And because the students, the classroom, and the school are dynamic, the transformation, design, and invention must be ongoing. As the context changes, we and the team of educators we lead must be willing to create continually.

Teachers Must Tap into the Resources That Might Inform Practice. Teachers and parents must be voracious, efficient, and discriminating consumers of what knowledge is available. Resources include written descriptions, oral presentations, and informal exchanges, as well as books, videos, and journals. Reports of others who are engaged in similar challenges offer relevant information and perspectives, as well as ways to put that knowledge to work. Consulting these resources may save us from erring and will help us place our efforts in a broader set of professional practices.

About Using the Textbook

Ryan Coulter is in her second year of teaching tenth grade biology. Though she feels that she provides good instruction in class, she knows her students must also read the textbook if they are to learn the content. She wants them to have a deeper understanding of the concepts and processes of biology, and to be able to use that understanding in practical applications. Her classes are geared toward these ends, and the textbook extends the students' opportunity to learn and perform.

But Ryan suspects that many students either don't read or don't know how to read the textbook. Given that the textbook is so important to the students' overall achievement, she decides to investigate her suspicion. She wonders if she could be doing something in class to support the students in their use of this resource.

Ryan selects three learners from each of her classes and invites them to join her for lunch in the classroom on a day when they are available the following week. She includes two students who have been identified as having learning disabilities who she knows struggle with their reading. She offers to buy sub sandwiches of their choice if they will agree to be interviewed by her. They have to promise to be candid and complete in their responses. Altogether, fourteen students agree, and a schedule is set.

Several questions are foremost in Ryan's mind: Do students take the textbook home and read it? If and when they read the textbook, how do they read it—with note taking, outlines, using the box examples, surveying the chapter first? What do they like and dislike about the text? How easy or hard is the language of the text for the students to comprehend?

The following week, Ryan had lunch with four focus groups of students to carry out her inquiry project. She learned, somewhat to her surprise, that most of the students valued the textbook, but that most were unsure when to read it, and few did more than just read silently to themselves when they did use it. One of the students who struggled with reading used the text but had a friend read it with him when that collaboration could be scheduled. The other student who struggled preferred to just take more time. Ryan noticed that several of the students were surprised that other students used strategies to remember what they read. Some students thought they might try these same approaches.

Ryan decided to do three things as a result of her inquiry: (1) alert students about the appropriate sections of the textbook they should read to parallel the class sessions; (2) ask selected students to describe and model their use of the textbook in each class; and (3) have an open discussion about the use of the text with all the students.

Teachers Must Become Students of Their Own Teaching. Because the knowledge educators need to use in their work may not be at hand, they have to know how to generate relevant, context-specific knowledge that can guide their designs and inventions. This is particularly true since what they are doing is creative and dynamic work: what they need to know may need to be generated in the process. Teachers will have to know:

- what the important questions are in the context of their classrooms and schools;
- how to collect data that will allow them to think clearly about those questions;
- how to use the results of their self-study to inform their practice;
- how to communicate their findings to others who should reasonably be interested in them, particularly parents; and

- how they might make their work available to broader professional and lay audiences.

Thus, a significant challenge to creating inclusive classrooms and schools is the creation itself. Teachers must have some vision of what they want to create, they must engage others in the process, and they must have the knowledge, skill, energy, and enthusiasm to carry it out. Through this all, they are creating themselves as inclusive teachers, for they cannot remain apart from the transformation, design, and invention. And clearly, creating or re-creating themselves is no small challenge.

Working in Contexts

The creation of inclusive schools is done in a given context. It is a context that, as has been argued, is typically given to traditional views of teaching and schooling. Teachers are acting to create that context, but because they are also the object of their creation, they are part of the context. The context itself is important. Beyond these challenges, yet another challenge to creating inclusive classrooms and schools is addressing the particulars of the context in which this effort is situated.

Examining Noninclusive Values

The school or community context in which educators teach—the one that they want to make inclusive—may reflect strong noninclusive values. Elements of racism, sexism, or social elitism may be subtly woven into the lives of adults. Disrespect for gay and lesbian people may be overt. Issues of economic privilege, cultural hegemony, and religious intolerance may go unaddressed by those who might make a difference in these matters. Teachers have been known to ignore these matters, considering them beyond the scope of the school's responsibility. Children and youth will undoubtedly adopt values that reflect the same noninclusive stances. In such a context, arguing for the full inclusion of learners who have special needs will present an extra challenge. For where any individual or group is disregarded, that same disregard is more easily directed at others as well.

Securing Administrative and Fiscal Support

More specific to the classroom and school context is the level of administrative support for creating inclusive classrooms and schools. It is clear from research that the overt and sustained endorsement of building administrators is essential to school reform initiatives. If administrators are not themselves the leaders of reform, they should be visible and hearty supporters of those of us who would lead. They should see our initiatives as valuable expressions of professional commitments and capacities. This is not to suggest that they must accept unquestioningly our vision or practices. In fact, to the contrary, they must regularly challenge any initiative to assure that it serves all students in their learning. But given evidence toward these ends, administrators should be ready at hand with human and fiscal resources, as well as moral support. Nonetheless, it remains evident that not all administrators understand or endorse inclusive schooling. Those of us who work with such administrators face the additional challenge of garnering their support. Fortunately, there are resources to help, including those administrators who are among the strongest proponents and leaders of inclusive schooling.

In some schools and school district contexts, established ways of thinking prevail about the delivery of special educational services. For example, special education is seen as a place—a room down the hall—rather than a set of services available for learners. Fiscal resources are allocated to support this arrangement. Teachers in such school districts have to work to change both this view of special education and the funding arrangements that sustain it. Changing the conception of special education to allow for inclusive classroom practices is essentially an educational challenge. Though it is not easy, it is a challenge teachers should be able to take on. Influencing funding is a more difficult contextual challenge, since teachers typically do not involve themselves directly in fiscal policy matters. But again, the challenge is not insurmountable; and again, there are resources that can help budget officers and administrators rethink their present policies.

High Standards for All Learners

Finally, considering the broadest context, it is clear that the education of children with disabilities is taking place at a time and in a society that places a premium on the rhetoric of high standards, high stakes assessments, and accountability. Importantly, these means-ends are espoused for all learners; children and youth with special needs are not automatically being exempted from these outcomes. Their inclusion in these expectations, opportunities, and requirements argues for their inclusion in our regular schooling. At least some recent evidence suggests that many are being successful, presumably with the guidance of teachers and others, in achieving these outcomes. But working to create inclusive classrooms and schools in a societal context, and in schools and classrooms, where all learners, teachers, administrators, parents, and caregivers feel the added pressure of these means-ends, is additionally difficult. While the pressure may spur us all to work, it also may lead us to take fewer risks, and it may sap some of the energy needed for creative initiative. This context is not likely to change soon. Perhaps the challenge, then, is to see how striving toward these means-ends and realizing the vision of inclusive schooling can be merged.

Vision, Knowledge, Commitment, and Courage

It is clear that although inclusive classrooms and schools can succeed in meeting the learning and development needs of all learners, getting from where we have been in practice to fully inclusive policy and practice is not easy. Obstacles and challenges stand in our way. It would be easier not to undertake the effort.

Bringing Selena Back Home to School. In the rush of the moments between classes, with students and teachers wending their way through the halls to their next classes, you would not notice Selena unless you were an outsider. Then you might see her awkward gait, and you might see that she seems more hesitant than the other teens in making her way through the corridor. But most of the people in this typical high school scene just don't notice.

A few minutes later, in her math class, Selena works on her "money poster." She has decided to show what she knows about the equivalences of dollars and dimes and nickels and quarters and pennies by making a poster, just as the other students are doing. Their posters are more about geometry—particular theorems and important people in the history of the field. All the posters will be displayed and talked about at the end of the week.

Selena is in her third year at this inclusive school. Before, she was bused to a special school across the county. She liked the teachers there, but not the long bus ride. None of her neighborhood friends went there. When her guardians and the school administrators and teachers talked with her about her schooling, it became clear that she wanted—and would likely benefit from—a change of schools. The decision was not difficult, but the steps that followed—actually bringing Selena back home to school—were fraught with uncertainty. In retrospect, seeing Selena so much an unremarkable part of the school seems to have confirmed the wisdom of the decision.

Good teachers are driven by an interest in serving their students well. They are willing to go to great lengths to assure student success in the important tasks of learning. This motivation is shared by thousands of teachers, colleague educators, administrators, and the families and communities that send their children and youth to school and support education. Success will breed further success. But taking the first step is itself sometimes the challenge. Three questions can guide teachers on this journey:

1. Where are their students headed in the long run?

2. What are their hopes for their students as they leave school and enter adult life?

3. What do the students and their parents envision for their future?

These are important questions for all students, not just those who have special educational needs. And considering them is the responsibility of all who make up the enterprise.

CREATING SCHOOLS THAT ARE MOST LIKELY TO HELP ALL STUDENTS ACHIEVE LONG-TERM GOALS

Educators' best professional knowledge and personal capacities come into play when they work to create the schools that achieve the ends students envision for themselves, and that teachers envision for them.

Vision, knowledge, and commitment are characteristics that teachers must cultivate in themselves if they are to undertake this journey toward achieving successful schools. We have seen how these qualities play out in creating inclusive classrooms. But courage is also needed. For without the courage to take bold steps where results are uncertain, without the courage to face challenges even when others do not back us up, without the courage to look inside ourselves at what we must also re-create, the other characteristics may go untapped. Vision, knowledge, and commitment may not be enough. Completing this journey will draw on educators' best and most significant professional and personal capacities.

CHANGING THE SYSTEM

As daunting as the challenge is, it is important to realize that we are not undertaking it alone. In fact, if we are to create more-inclusive classrooms and schools that can sustain these practices, then we cannot depend on individual teachers working alone, even with supportive colleagues and families. If we are to achieve the end of transforming schooling as we know it into inclusive schooling as we envision it, then we must change the system. Teachers and parents engaged in this effort can reasonably ask, "What efforts are under way toward this end?" The response is multifaceted, but perhaps the largest coordinated effort has been dubbed "systems change."

Systems Change Projects

Systems change efforts are, indeed, under way across the country. With the support of the United States Department of Education, states have worked to transform the delivery of special educational services from segregated models into systems that integrate all learners, with and without special educational needs. Such systems change projects have been funded for over a decade, and much has been learned from them.

Through systems change projects, state policy makers, school district administrators, parent and community representatives, building administrators, and teachers have worked together to consider the professional and philosophical questions posed by inclusion. Each systems change project was unique, which allowed the projects to learn from one another over the years. It is useful to consider what has been learned, and to see how these projects have brought about changes in policy and practice that have had an impact on classrooms and schools.

Good practice informs and drives policy; policy urges and supports good practice. Without seeing how multiple levels of efforts intertwine to change the system, we could not form a complete picture of this educational reform.

The New York Statewide Systems Change Project

In October 1989, the New York State Education Department's Office for the Education of Children with Handicapping Conditions submitted a proposal titled "Programs for Severely Handicapped Children" to the U.S. Department of Education, Office of Special Education Programs. The New York State Education Department was awarded a five-year grant. This was the beginning of what became a ten-year project developing inclusive options for students with disabilities in the state. Matt Giugno, a co-author of this chapter, participated in the project as a member of the New York State Education Department.

The project planned to establish inclusive special education in various schools around the state and to provide support as these districts, schools, and the teachers and administrators involved designed their programs. Specific emphasis was placed on services to students with more severe disabilities, who historically had been receiving their educational services in self-contained, typically center-based programs. Based on this, the project goal was to develop, implement, and evaluate a systems change process and components of an educational service delivery model that are related to the provision of quality services in integrated environments—neighborhood schools in the local school district.

What the project needed to do was simple: find a number of school districts around the state willing to give this "inclusion stuff" a try.

Bringing People Together. During the 1990–91 and 1991–92 school years, regional conferences open to teachers, administrators, parents, advocates, and community agencies were conducted around the state. This "road show" approach was successful in bringing together hundreds of people who had an interest in inclusive practices. While most of the participants at these sessions were either in favor of or interested in examining this "inclusive educational philosophy," some were outspoken in asserting a belief system that was not committed to inclusion. Some even accused the project of disregarding the needs of, for example, medically fragile students—students on respirators and those who needed full-time nursing care—imagining them placed in typical classrooms without regard to their needs. It was clear that the work of systems change would not be simple.

Themes of Change. Upon examination of school districts that met the entry criteria, it was quickly discovered that without full support at the district level and from building level administrative staff, the project would not be effective.

Staff Development and Attitudes. The challenge was twofold: enlisting the support of teachers not prepared to create inclusive classrooms and schools, and changing the attitudes of teachers who did not want to create inclusive classrooms and schools. It was, in part, a matter of teacher education (or lack thereof) and, in part, a matter of perception. Developing strategies to address these challenges became paramount, as is evident in the following scenario.

CHANGING ONE SCHOOL'S SYSTEM

The fourth visit of the technical assistant (TA) from the systems change project fell on a Friday at noon. A small group of educators and parents had committed themselves to leading the change toward inclusion in this school. They were willing to address the challenges of integrating three new students into the school. Few teachers and students in the school had any prior experience with people with significant disabilities. The system itself was not set up for this. But that made the project all the more worthwhile and important.

The meeting began with a round of comments about "good news and issues" so that everyone had a chance to put their perspectives on the table and be heard. Then the agenda was taken up; some parts of it were already referenced in the comments shared.

The group talked about the experiences the three students were having in the classrooms and school, and whether progress was evident toward the goals that had been set for each student. They talked about supports that were called upon by the teachers and what supports the students still needed, as well as changes in the school that would further facilitate the inclusion of others—schedules, teachers' belief systems, other students' needs for understanding.

The group members challenged and supported one another. They set plans for the next several weeks. The TA participated in but did not lead the discussion. She helped them over hurdles when they seemed to get stuck. As a group, they figured out how to create a tentative system that better served these three students, and prospectively all others as well.

In spite of these challenges—and perhaps because of them—the systems change project began working with teachers, administrators, and parents in over forty schools and districts that wanted to move toward creating inclusive classrooms, schools, and communities. While project interventions were limited—a small grant to fund elements of the project, technical assistance to resolve many how-to questions, and lots of empathy and inspiration to sustain their efforts—the results were often remarkable. Most of the credit, of course, goes to people at the local site who made it work and literally changed the systems. Especially important was that the education provided to all learners was markedly enhanced.

Over the five years of the initial project, each of these sites revealed lessons about successful inclusion, including where errors could easily be made. Learning from their experiences and their perspectives has done much to shape state policy and to suggest practice in other districts across the state. Systems change initiatives—those ideas that were discussed in the earliest meetings, and those practices that were first explored in the volunteer schools—are now becoming institutionalized and accepted as everyday practices.

Precisely because we were learning so much from these efforts, a statewide annual conference was initiated so that others might learn as well. The Inclusive Schools and Communities for Children and Youth Conference, which has been held every spring since 1992, replaced the "road show" presentations as it became clear that the ways in which inclusive teaching and schooling had advanced in the state required a larger, regular venue in which practices and policies, challenges and successes could be shared. The conference now averages over 1,000 participants each year—teachers, parents, administrators, teacher educators, researchers, and policy makers. We learn from each other by bringing together presenters from across the state and around the country who are leaders in systems change and school reform. The conference serves a range of participants, from those who are new to inclusive teaching and schooling, to those who are leaders in practice and policy and research in this field. It is a key vehicle for changing the system in New York State.

Evidence that the system is indeed changing continues to accumulate. The Least Restrictive Environment Policy Paper, originally published by the state education department in 1994, along with its revisions and updates, incorporates many of the best practices for integrating students with disabilities into general education classes. Up to the enactment of IDEA'97, it was the definitive document calling for the development of more integrated options throughout the state, using some of the systems change materials.

Another change in the system followed. When IDEA '97 and the revised Part 300 of the Code of Federal Regulations (1999) were published, new emphasis was placed on the development of "inclusive options." That is, the term "inclusion" became part of the vocabulary of schools. It took its rightful place alongside more common practices for the provision of special educational services, such as mainstreaming and integration. The idea that inclusive education should be part of the continuum of services available to learners with special educational needs had been accepted. This was reaffirmed when IDEA was again reauthorized in November 2004.

What We Learned from the Example of Systems Change 2000

The original five-year grant was extended with the award of a second five-year grant. In developing the second grant, now termed "The New York State Partnership for Statewide Systems Change 2000," the focus was to

- encourage and support those who were trying to include students with emotional disabilities;
- help educators at the secondary level find productive and satisfying ways of including these youth in their classrooms and schools;
- help select colleges from across the state to develop and implement inclusive teacher preparation programs; and
- help current regular and special education teachers engage in quality staff development on this agenda.

CHALLENGES

One of the biggest challenges was successfully integrating students with emotional difficulties into inclusion programs. Few teachers were willing to take on this challenge, and the "system," as we observed it, was ready to leave them out of the regular school experience. We decided to focus our efforts in the primary grades—an age level where we thought we might be most successful. Our hope was that success at this level would show that children with emotional disabilities could be included successfully, and that once they were part of the school experience, they might stay with their peers through subsequent grades. Success might then prompt other educators to include such learners early on in their schooling as well.

Helping Educators at the Secondary Level

While the project had met with considerable success in promoting the inclusion of students at the elementary level, many of these same students were facing new obstacles when entering the middle grades, and particularly when they entered high school. Teachers and educators cited the nature of secondary schooling, more complex organizational structures, and concerns about high stakes testing as sources of potential problems facing students with significant disabilities in classrooms and schools. We knew that if inclusive schooling was to be effective in the long run, students could not be included at the start of their school career and then excluded through the important academic and social experiences of adolescence.

Inclusive Teacher Preparation Programs and Quality Inclusive Staff Development

Teachers had indicated that they were not prepared for inclusive teaching; administrators confirmed this message. Clearly, the system—of which teacher preparation and staff development are key parts—had to be changed in this regard as well.

- The preservice component became known as the Higher Education Task Force on Quality Inclusive Schooling. About twenty institutions joined the effort and have sustained their efforts for the five-year time span. Many of these institutions now offer teacher preparation programs that encourage inclusive practices; some of them lead to dual certifications in regular and special education fields.

- The in-service component was enacted through the existing Special Education Training and Resource Center (SETRC) network that has as its mission the provision of staff development experiences in districts across the state. Our work was to help these staff development providers reorient toward inclusive rather than separate schooling. Through the SETRC network, thousands of currently practicing teachers have been able to access ideas and practices, as well as ongoing support, as they seek to become inclusive teachers.

While each of these initiatives remains a work-in-progress, they have already helped move the system from more traditional policies and practices to those that work to serve all learners.

The RSSCs, the SIG, and the HESC

Though New York's systems change projects, as such, have come to an end, the initiatives supported through these projects have continued, now linked to new New York State initiatives. These build on the successes of the systems change projects and integrate other initiatives that have been generated through policy and practice.

In the summer of 2000, the New York State Education Department established ten Regional School Support Centers (RSSCs), a cooperative undertaking between the Office of Vocational and Educational Services for Individuals with Disabilities (VESID) and the Office of Elementary, Middle, Secondary and Continuing Education (EMSC). The RSSCs are designed to assist schools and districts where it is evident that students are struggling to reach the higher standards that have been set for all New York State students. This initiative recognizes that matters of achievement are not cut along the lines of "special education" and "regular education"; in fact, the challenge of helping all students achieve requires a more integrated approach. The RSSCs are organized to help teachers and administrators in these schools and districts use the many resources at their disposal to understand the root causes of low achievement in their schools and districts, and to develop contextually appropriate responses to those needs.

Collaboration between these two units of the New York State Education Department should in itself be seen as an important change brought about by leaders intent on being sure the educational system addresses the needs of the state's students. But it is also useful to see the structure of the RSSCs as support for changing the systems found in local districts and schools. It empowers teachers and administrators to understand the particular challenges they face in helping students achieve, and encourages them to change instruction, curriculum, and organization in response.

In the summer of 2001, VESID was awarded a five-year State Improvement Grant (SIG) from the federal government. The SIG will allow additional steps to be taken in support of these initiatives. One key component of the SIG will be continued support for changing the teacher preparation programs in the state's many colleges and universities. A Higher Education Support Center (HESC) has been established at Syracuse University, designed, among other things, to sustain the efforts of the Task Force on Quality Inclusive Schooling—over fifty colleges and universities across the state who have formally made two commitments: (1) to develop, implement, study, and improve inclusive teacher preparation programs on their campuses; and (2) to build partnerships with high-need schools and districts through their RSSCs, engaging in both teacher preparation and professional development in those venues. Building a more seamless system—one that links student achievement challenges with the resources and structures of teacher education at all levels—holds great promise for addressing the persistent challenges of education.

Partnering to Change the System. The task force conference room is set up in ten clusters of tables and chairs. Over eighty people are engaged in clusters of various sizes. Over fifty colleges and universities are represented; schools and school districts are represented; Regional School Support Center staff members are there too.

They are building many varied partnerships describing the teacher preparation programs they have developed and the ones they would like to develop. They are thinking about the high-need schools—schools where students struggle to do well academically—in the region. They are discussing how they might put their resources and challenges together to serve better their many ends.

A presenter from VESID displays a chart showing that even some economically poor school districts in the state seem to succeed in helping their students achieve academically. He wonders aloud what we could learn from these educators and their contexts that might inform practice elsewhere.

After the meeting, a professor from one of the colleges reflects that progress is slow: there is much to be done, and it is hard to move so many people and institutions in the same direction at the same time. Indeed, that is true. Building partnerships takes time, at least in part because the partnerships represent real changes to the traditional systems we are used to operating in. But from the new partnerships we are able to fashion will come new systems that will hopefully be more responsive and more effective for all.

In New York State—as in most states, for that matter—as the statutes and regulations raise expectations for all learners, changing the system remains our only hope of serving all learners well. Traditional practices will not do it. New general education diploma requirements are tougher; new special education requirements support the participation of all learners in the general education environment; teacher preparation and staff development requirements are changing in response to various reform initiatives. In all these cases, we see the field moving toward the integration of students with disabilities into general education. For that matter, the field of education is seeking to serve all learners better than it has in the past. Reform in all of these arenas is moving the system to real systems change where all students have a place.

SUMMARY

Knowing that inclusive teaching and schooling can work to support the achievement of all learners gives us hope that the goals teachers set for their own practices can be achieved. Knowing that long-term efforts are under way to change the system in support of inclusive education provides some comfort that gradually the system itself will be a source of support, and that educators and parents are not alone in working toward these goals.

And no easy solution to this challenge is at hand. But, perhaps as good teachers and good schools have always been, we are required to work it out anew each day and each year. Indeed, a premise of inclusive teaching and schooling is that each learner deserves the kind of unique and creative opportunity to learn that fine teachers and schools can provide. In a sense, each learner—and all learners—provide new challenges. Educators can never quite sit back and think that the challenges have been addressed completely. In fact, as students change, as the curriculum changes, and as teachers themselves change, new challenges will emerge, requiring new ways of responding. How can educators and parents keep up with the dynamics?

In the best sense, we must develop "learning communities" focused on inclusive teaching and schooling. We must tap into what knowledge and what perspectives are available in this area of education, and use that knowledge and those perspectives to support, confront, and advance educational practice. Through learning communities, we can begin to change the system right where we touch it: in the classrooms and in the schools where students are taught. And through broader learning communities, we can continually keep abreast of the emerging field of practice and policy.

Tips for Educators and Parents

✎ Identify a conference, a college course, an advocacy group, a literature circle, a speaker, or another good book that addresses the concept and practices of inclusion. Connect with this resource in some fashion. Take notes on what you learn in the process.

✎ Select a Web site and spend some time with it and the links it offers you. Invite another parent or colleague to visit the same Web site and talk about what each of you found of interest there.

✎ Use the World Wide Web as a valuable resource, a "virtual community" of information and ideas.

RESOURCES

To support our efforts, dynamic resources are updated regularly by people and agencies committed to the work of serving all learners well. The following Web sites provide information and commentary that should inform our learning. Each of these Web sites is a dynamic resource for teachers, administrators, parents, and community members as they seek to understand and respond to the opportunity for creating inclusive classrooms and schools and communities and, indeed, re-creating themselves along the way. These Web sites, linked as they are to each other and to yet other sites, already form a type of learning community: broad in context, virtual in medium, and unbound by most traditions. But these sites—and others that are yet to be created—also provide a platform on which we can build local learning communities around the particular opportunities and issues we must address: contextually particular and relevant, face-to-face in medium, and with a vision of how to build on the traditions that might yet serve us well. Within and between these communities—broad and local—we can seriously inform our practices and our deepest thinking about the world we would create.

Center on Human Policy. http://soeweb.syr.edu/thechp

This Web site is the home of the Center on Human Policy, based at Syracuse University. The center works on the national level to ensure the rights of people with disabilities through research, advocacy, information dissemination, training and consultation, and the design of policy related to this field. The center is supported by the work of a wide range of individuals whose backgrounds and personal and professional commitments align with the mission of supporting individuals with disabilities.

Council for Exceptional Children (CEC). www.cec.sped.org

This is the home site for the CEC, the largest professional organization that addresses the needs of students with disabilities (as well as those who are "gifted"). Many resources are available from CEC through this Web site. CEC sponsors an annual "international" conference that attracts nearly 5,000 participants. Studying CEC's activities and the initiatives can put you in the mainstream of service to learners with special needs.

Council of Chief State School Officers (CCSSO). www.ccsso.org

CCSSO is an organization that brings together the executive officers of state education agencies. CCSSO coordinates some activities across the state agencies and serves their projects and interests. Its Web site provides links to each of the individual state agencies, which, in turn, will allow you to tap into the policies and practices related to inclusive education promoted by each of the states.

DRM Guide to Disability Sources on the Internet. www.disabilityresources.org

This Web site serves as a well-organized point of entry to a wide range of information and resources related to disabilities. It includes links to education-related topics, and also goes well beyond education issues and practices. There are links to each of the fifty states and the District of Columbia for resources and agencies more particular to each of those jurisdictions.

Education Development Center, Inc. (EDC). www.ideapractices.org

This Web site is developed and maintained by EDC, a nonprofit organization in Newton, Massachusetts. It offers itself as an interactive resource for service providers and administrators, responding to questions and providing strategies that work in implementing IDEA. Through this Web site, you can link to twenty partner organizations of service providers (ASPIIRE) and seventeen partner organizations of program administrators (ILIAD). A frequently asked questions section is provided under "ideaQUESTS" at this site.

Families and Advocates Partnership for Education (FAPE). www.fape.org

This Web site is the home of FAPE, an organization that seeks to educate families and advocates about IDEA and promising practices that have been developed to implement this legislation. Spanish and English versions are available. Through this Web site you can access materials on cultural diversity and important court cases related to IDEA.

Inclusion Press. www.inclusion.com

This Web site is the home of Inclusion Press International, a small, independent press that promotes inclusion in schools, the workplace, and the community. Through this Web site, you can access a wide range of resources, from books, newsletters, and other text materials to videos and workshops. The Web site also offers an "Inclusion Gallery" which displays various visual materials that can be used for staff development.

National Clearinghouse for Professions in Special Education (NCPSE). www.special-ed-careers.org

This Web site is the home of the NCPSE, whose mission is to support the recruitment and preparation of personnel for special education. Through this Web site, you can access information about careers in this field of practice and tap into a variety of professional resources. An interesting part of the site is a "Featured Professional"—a capsule description of an educator currently practicing, in his or her own words.

National Organization on Disability. www.nod.org

This Web site is the home of the National Organization on Disability, a privately funded effort supporting full and equal participation of all people with disabilities in all aspects of life. Through this Web site, you can access data describing the status of individuals with disabilities in American life as well as analyses of the implications of these data. The organization's newsletters and press releases are also available.

New York Higher Education Support Center for SystemsChange. www.systems change.syr.edu

This Web site is the home of the New York Partnership for Statewide Systems Change 2000, an effort often referred to in this chapter. Through this site, you can link to the Higher Education Task Force on Quality Inclusive Schooling, to the resource list on inclusive practices maintained by the project, and to current activities of the project and the Office of Vocational and Education Services for Individuals with Disabilities (VESID).

OSEP. www.ideapolicy.org

This Web site is one of four linked projects funded by the U.S. Department of Education, Office of Special Education Programs (OSEP). This site, titled The Policymaker Partnership (PMP), is linked to the ILIAD, ASPIIRE, and FAPE Web sites. You can access the home page of the National Association of State Directors of Special Education, Inc. (NASDSE), as well as other Web sites.

Special Education News. www.specialednews.com

This Web site provides general information related to issues of disability. It includes current and archived articles, as well as links to other organizations and resources. You can participate in polls on various issues through the site's interactive component.

TASH. www.tash.org

This Web site is the home for an international association committed to the inclusion of all people in all aspects of society as the norm. It is made up of people with disabilities, their families, and professionals. TASH has local chapters across the country and internationally. An annual conference is held at which members and other interested individuals can learn about the many and varied efforts of those associated with this movement, their successes, and the challenges they face.

U.S. Department of Education (USDE). www.ed.gov

This Web site is the official home of the U.S. Department of Education. It offers a wealth of information about policies, practices, research, and issues in education from across this country. Thus it is a rich general resource for those who are looking at the larger context of teaching and learning. You can access information about inclusion and other approaches to special education through one of its most popular pages, "Disabilities Education (IDEA)." There are links to two other government offices associated with special education: the Office of Special Education and Rehabilitative Services (OSERS) and the Office of Special Education Programs (OSEP). All of these Web sites link with each other and with other related sites.

Part III Bibliography

Alliance for Technology Access. (2002). *Computer and Web resources for people with disabilities: A guide to exploring today's assistive technology.* Alameda, CA: Hunter House.

Andrews, S. E. (1998). Using inclusion literature to promote positive attitudes toward disabilities. *Journal of Adolescent and Adult Literacy, 41,* 420–425.

Angle, B. (2001, February). Technology use with students with learning disabilities compared to other exceptionalities. Poster session presented at the annual meeting of the Learning Disabilities Association of America, New York.

Austin, V. L. (2001). Teachers' beliefs about co-teaching. *Remedial and Special Education, 22*(4), 245–255.

Bain, B. (1993). Section 6A: Assistive technology. In H. Hopkins & H. Smith (Eds.), *Willard and Spackman's occupational therapy* (8th ed.) (pp. 325–340). Philadelphia: J. B. Lippincott.

Bain, B. K., Dooley, K. F., & Leger, D. (1997). Assistive technology: An interdisciplinary approach. In B. K. Bain & D. Leger (Eds.), *Assistive technology: An interdisciplinary approach* (pp. 1–7). New York: Churchill Livingstone.

Bain, B. K., & Leger, D. (Eds.). (1997). *Assistive technology: An interdisciplinary approach.* New York: Churchill Livingstone.

Bakken, J. P., & Whedon, C. K. (2001, February). Teachers' knowledge and perceptions of assistive technologies for students with learning disabilities. Poster session presented at the annual meeting of the Learning Disabilities Association of America, New York.

Bauer, A. M., & Shea, T. M. (2003). *Parents and schools.* Upper Saddle River, NJ: Prentice Hall.

Behrmann, M. M. (1995). Assistive technology training. In K. F. Flippo, K. J. Inge, & J. M. Barcus (Eds.), *Assistive technology: A resource for school, work, and community* (pp. 211–223). Baltimore: Paul H. Brookes Publishing Co.

Biklen, D. (1992). *Schooling Without labels: Parents, educators, and inclusive education.* Philadelphia: Temple University Press.

Bixler, L. L. (1998). Perceptions of co-teachers: An exploration of characteristics and components needed for co-teaching. Doctoral dissertation, University of Oklahoma. *Dissertation Abstracts International, 59*–03A, 0780–1012.

Blanton, L. P., Griffin, C. C., Winn, J. A., & Pugach, M. C. (Eds.). (1997). *Teacher education in transition: Collaborative programs to prepare general and special educators.* Denver: Love Publishing Co.

Bos, C., & Vaughn, S. (1998). *Strategies for teaching students with learning and behavior problems.* (4th ed.). Boston: Allyn & Bacon.

Bowe, F. (2000). *Universal design in education: Teaching nontraditional students.* Westport, CT: Bergen & Garvey.

Brant, R. (Ed.). (1994–1995). The inclusive school. *Educational Leadership, 52*(4).

Brett, A., & Provenzo, E. F., Jr. (1995). *Adaptive technology for special human needs.* Albany: State University of New York Press.

Brooks, R. B. (2004). To touch the hearts and minds of students with learning disabilities: The power of mindsets and expectations. *Learning Disabilities: A Contemporary Journal, 2*(1), 1–8.

Bryant, D. P. (2003). *Assistive technology for people with disabilities.* Boston: Allyn & Bacon.

Carey, A. C., Delsordo, V., & Goldman, A. (2004). Assistive technology for all: Access to alternative financing for minority populations. *Journal of Disability Policy Studies, 14*(4), 194–203.

Christiansen, J., & Vogel, J. R. (1998, November–December). A decision model for grading students with disabilities. *Teaching Exceptional Children, 31*(2), 30–35.

Church, G., & Glennen, S. (1992). *The handbook of assistive technology.* San Diego, CA: Singular Publishing Group.

Couchenour, D., & Chrisman, K. (2004). *Families, schools, and communities: Together for young children.* Clifton Park, NY: Thompson Learning.

Council for Exceptional Children (CEC). (1994). *CEC standards for professional practice in special education.* Reston, VA: CEC.

Dede, C. (Ed.). (1998). *Learning with technology.* Alexandria, VA: Association for Supervision and Curriculum Development.

Dyson, L. L. (2003). Children with learning disabilities within the family context: A comparison with siblings in global self-concept, academic self-perception, and social competence. *Learning Disabilities Research, 18*(1), 1–9.

Elkind, K. (2004, May/June). Choosing assistive technology for teaching reading and writing. *Media and Methods, 20.*

ERIC/OSEP. (1998, Summer). A curriculum every student can use: Design principles for student access. Appendix: A framework for universal design in curriculum development. ERIC/OSEP Topical Brief. http://www.cec.sped.org/osep/appendix.htm.

Erickson, V. (2004, March/April). Spotlight on assistive technology. *Media and Methods, 4.*

Finlayson, M., & Hammel, J. (2003). Providing alternative financing for assistive technology: Outcomes over twenty months. *Journal of Disability Policy Studies, 14*(2), 109–118, 125.

Fischer, D., Sax, C., & Pumpian, I. (1999). *Inclusive high schools: Learning from contemporary contexts.* Baltimore: Paul H. Brookes Publishing Co.

Flippo, K. F., Inge, K. J., & Barcus, J. M. (Eds.). (1995). *Assistive technology: A resource for school, work, and community.* Richmond, VA: Paul H. Brookes.

Forgan, J. W. (2002). Using bibliotherapy to teach problem solving. *Intervention in School and Clinic, 38*(2), 75–82.

Garza, K. (2002) School security moves into the digital age. *THE Journal, 30*(5), 44–46.

Gaustad, J. (1999). The fundamentals of school security. *ERIC Digest Number 132,* 23–27.

Gestwicki, C. (2004). *Home, school, and community relations: A guide to working with families.* Clifton Park, NY: Thompson Learning.

Getskow, V., & Konczal, D. (1996). *Kids with special needs: Information and activities to promote awareness and understanding.* Santa Barbara, CA: Learning Works.

Hanson, M. J., & Lunch, E. W. (2004). *Understanding families: Approaches to diversity disability and risk.* Baltimore: Paul H. Brookes Publishing Co.

Harry, B., & Kalyanpur, M. (1999). *Culture in special education: Building reciprocal family provider relationships.* Baltimore: Paul H. Brookes Publishing Co.

Heubert, J. P., & Hauser, R. M., (Eds.). (1999). *High stakes: Testing for tracking, promotion and graduation.* National Research Council. Washington, DC: National Academy Press.

Inge, K. J., & Shepherd, J. (1995). Assistive technology applications for strategies for school system personnel. In Flippo, K. F., Inge, K. J., & Barcus, J. M. (Eds.), *Assistive technology: A resource for school, work, and community* (133–167). Richmond, VA: Paul H. Brookes.

Jorgensen, C. M., et al. (1998). *Restructuring high schools for all students: Taking inclusion to the next level.* Baltimore: Paul H. Brookes Publishing Co.

Kame'enui, E. J., & Simmons, D. C. (1999). *Toward successful inclusion of students with disabilities: The architecture of instruction.* Vol. 1: *An overview of materials adaptations.* Reston, VA: Council for Exceptional Children.

Kennedy, M. (2002). Balancing security and learning. *American School and University, 74*(6), 8–11.

King, T. W. (1999). *Assistive technology: Essential human factors.* Boston: Allyn & Bacon.

Kinney, P., & Blackhurst, A. E. (1987). Technology competencies for teachers of young children with severe handicaps. *Topics in Early Childhood Special Education, 7*(3), 105–115.

Kluth, P., & Straut, D. (2001). Standards for diverse learners. *Educational Leadership, 59*(1), 43–49.

Lesar, S. (1998). Use of assistive technology with young children with disabilities: Current status and training needs. *Journal of Early Intervention, 21*(2), 146–159.

Long, T., Huang, L., Woodbridge, M., Woolverton, M., & Minkel, J. (2003). Integrating assistive technology into an outcome-driven model of service delivery. *Infants and Young Children, 16*(4), 272–283.

Lupinacci, J. (2002). A safe haven. *American School and University, 74*(6), 8–11.

Marchant, M., Young, Y. K., & West, R. P. (2004). The effects of parental teaching on compliance behavior of children. *Psychology in the Schools, 41*(3), 337–350.

Mates, B. T. (2000). *Adaptive technology for the Internet: Making electronic resources accessible to all.* Chicago: American Library Association.

McNulty, M. A. (2003). Dyslexia and the life course. *Journal of Learning Disabilities, 26*(4), 363–381.

Mercer, C., & Mercer, A. R. (2004). *Teaching students with learning problems.* Upper Saddle River, NJ: Prentice Hall.

Mount, B. (1997). *Person centered planning: Finding directions for change using personal futures planning.* New York: Graphic Futures.

Norwicki, E. A. (2003). A meta-analysis of the social competence of children with learning disabilities compared to classmates of low and average to high achievement. *Learning Disability Quarterly, 26*(3), 171–188.

Parette, P., & McMahan, G. A. (2002). What should we expect of assistive technology? Being sensitive to family goals. *Teaching Exceptional Children, 35*(1), 56–61.

Peterson, K. D. (2002). Positive or negative. *Journal of Staff Development, 23*(3), 21–30.

Phillips, P. (1990). A self-advocacy plan for high school students with learning disabilities: A comparative case study analysis of students', teachers', and parents' perceptions of program effects. *Journal of Learning Disabilities 23,* 466–471.

Raskind, M. H., & Higgins, E. L. (1998). Assistive technology for postsecondary students with learning disabilities: An overview. *Journal of Learning Disabilities, 31,* 27–40.

Riviere, A. (1996, Summer). Assistive technology: Meeting the needs of adults with learning disabilities. Washington, DC: National Adult Literacy and Learning Disabilities Center.

Rybczynski (1985).

Salend, S. J. (1998). *Effective mainstreaming: Creating inclusive classrooms.* Upper Saddle River, NJ: Prentice Hall.

Seligman, M.E.P. (1975). *Helplessness: On development, depression and death.* New York: W. H. Freeman.

Slavin, R. E. (1987). *Cooperative learning: Student teams.* Washington, DC: NEA Professional Library.

Slavin, R. E. & Cooper, R. (1999). Improving intergroup relations: Lessons learned from cooperative learning programs. *Journal of Social Issues, 55*(4), 647–663.

Smith, J. D. (1998). *Inclusion: Schools for all students.* Belmont, CA: Wadsworth Publishing.

Stipek, D. J. (1993). *Motivation to learn: From theory to practice.* (2nd ed.). Boston: Allyn & Bacon.

Stolp, S., & Smith, S. (1994). School culture and climate: The role of the leader. *OSSSC Bulletin* (Eugene: Oregon School Study Council).

Turnbull, R., Turnbull, A., Shank, M., Smith, S., & Leal, D. (2002). *Exceptional lives: Special education in today's schools.* (3rd ed.). Upper Saddle River, NJ: Merrill Prentice Hall.

U.S. Congress. House of Representatives. Committee on Education and the Workforce. (2002). *Assessing the Assistive Technology Act of 1998.* Hearing before the Subcommittee on 21st Century Competitiveness of the Committee on Education and the Workforce. 107th Cong., 2nd sess. (107–52).

U.S. Congress. Office of Technology Assessment (OTA). (1988). Power on! New tools for teaching and learning (OTA-SET-379). Washington, DC: U.S. Government Printing Office.

Van Reusen, A. K., Bos, C. S., Schumaker, J., & Deshler, D. (1987). *The education planning strategy.* Lawrence, KS: Excell Enterprises.

Vaughn, S., Bos, C. S., & Schumm, J. S. (2003). *Teaching mainstreamed, diverse, and at-risk students in the general education classroom.* (3rd ed.). Needham Heights, MA: Allyn & Bacon.

Vernon, D. S., Deshler, D. D., & Schumaker, J. B. (1993). *The teamwork strategy.* Lawrence, KS: Edge Enterprises.

Vernon, D. S., Schumaker, J. B., & Deshler, D. D. (1993). *The SCORE skills: Social skills for cooperative groups.* Lawrence, KS: Edge Enterprises.

Wallace, J. E. (2003). A policy analysis of the assistive technology alternative financing programs in the United States. *Journal of Disability Policy Studies, 14*(2), 74–81.

Warger, C. (1998). Integrating assistive technology into the curriculum. *ERIC/ OSEP Digest E568.* Reston, VA: ERIC Clearinghouse on Disabilities and Gifted Education.

Weikle, B., & Hadadian, A. (2003). Can assistive technology help us to not leave any child behind? *Preventing School Failure, 47*(4), 181–186.

Wolffe, K. E., Candela, T., & Johnson, G. (2003, November). Wired to work: A qualitative analysis of assistive technology training for people with visual impairments. *Journal of Visual Impairments and Blindness, 97*(11), 677–694.

Young, E. B. (1988). One university's role in supporting special needs locally. *Electronic Learning, 8*(3), 10–12.

Zabala, J. S. (1996). SETTing the stage for success with assistive technology. Available online at http://sac.uky.edu/~jszaba0/JoySETT.html.

Glossary
Terminology Demystified

accommodations. Changes in the educational environment that facilitate the student's access to the general education curriculum.

adaptations. Changes to the general education curriculum or to specific lessons and activities that will make it possible for the student with disabilities to learn the basic concepts of the body of knowledge and to meet general education standards.

assistive technology device (ATD). Any item, piece of equipment, or product system, whether acquired commercially off the shelf, modified, or customized, that is used to increase, maintain, or improve functional capabilities of individuals with disabilities.

assistive technology service. Any service that directly assists an individual with a disability in the selection, acquisition, or use of an assistive technology device.

committee on special education (CSE) or multidisciplinary team (MDT). A multidisciplinary team of at least five members, including a special education representative, a school district special education representative, a school physician, a parent of a student with a disability residing in the district, the student's teacher, and other members who may be helpful to the team.

consultant special education teacher. Special educator who works in collaboration with the general education teacher; services may range from consultation to co-teaching.

CSE. *See* committee on special education

functional skill. A skill that is immediately useful to the student in his or her daily life.

goal. General statement of what the student will accomplish in one year.

IDEA. *See* Individuals with Disabilities Education Act

IEP. *See* individualized education plan

inclusion. Students with diverse backgrounds, capabilities, and support requirements participate in general education settings as full members of the learning community. Necessary services and instructional assistance for the students and teacher are provided within the classroom. The general classroom teacher, in collaboration with support professionals, assumes responsibility and accountability for designing meaningful learning experiences that maximize learner strengths and assure the success of all students in achieving curricular learning goals that meet high standards (Standards for Inclusive Teacher Preparation Programs, 2000).

individualized education plan (IEP). Student-centered learning plan, developed by a multidisciplinary team, created to identify the short- and long-term special educational needs of a student and the specific implementation processes and methods necessary to meet those needs.

Individuals with Disabilities Education Act (IDEA). Federal law assuring that all students with disabilities have available to them a free appropriate public education.

least restrictive environment (LRE). Educational setting that allows a student with special needs to be educated to the greatest extent possible with his or her nondisabled peers.

long-term adult outcomes. Long-term goals reflecting the student's needs, preferences, and interests in postsecondary education/training, employment, and community living.

modifications. Changes that will allow a student with special needs to participate in the general education curriculum to the fullest extent possible.

multidisciplinary team (MDT). *See* committee on special education

objective. Measurable, intermediate steps between the student's present level of performance and annual goals.

personalized supports. Materials, technology, and human resources that support access to information, activities, and opportunities.

positive behavioral supports. Proactive and preventive modifications and strategies that enhance the student's socialization and learning in the general education classroom.

related services. Developmental, corrective, and other support services required for a student with disabilities to benefit from education.

transition services. Interagency responsibilities or other linkages that will help the student move from school to adulthood.

Index

About the Editor and Contributors

DIANE SCHWARTZ is the Director of the Special Education and Early Childhood Special Education master's degree programs and Associate Professor in the Department of Counseling, Research, Special Education and Rehabilitation at Hofstra University. She was a founder of the New Interdisciplinary School in Suffolk County, a program for children from birth through age five with disabilities and their families. More recently Dr. Schwartz has been instrumental in developing teacher preparation programs for inclusive education. She has served on the New York State Higher Education Task Force for Quality Inclusive Schooling and is the co-author of *Diverse Populations of Gifted Children: Meeting Their Needs in the Regular Classroom and Beyond*. Dr. Schwartz continues to be actively involved in the education of young children with disabilities and is currently President of the New York State Division for Early Childhood for the Council of Exceptional Children.

VANCE AUSTIN is an Assistant Professor in the special education program at Nyack College. His experience and interests lie in investigating effective inclusive practices both in the United States and Vietnam as well as developing successful approaches for working with students with various types of emotional/behavioral disorders. He also works part-time in a residential treatment program for students with emotional/behavioral disorders in Nyack, New York, where he teaches English and drama. He recently published "Inclusive Practices in Middle Tennessee" in the *Journal of Research on Childhood Education*. He is presently completing a research project on attitudes toward disability and inclusion in Vietnam.

JOAN M. BLACK, Ed.D., is currently serving as the Hudson Region liaison for the New York State Higher Education Task Force on Inclusive Schooling. She was until recently an Associate Professor and Chairperson of the Inclusive Education Programs at Marymount College in Tarrytown, New York. Dr. Black is a language arts consultant and dedicates her professional efforts toward supporting struggling learners in their literacy development.

NANCY L. CLOUD is a Professor at the Feinstein School of Education and Human Development at Rhode Island College and serves as co-coordinator of the graduate program in urban multicultural special education. She authored a chapter on "Responsive Instructional Planning" in *English Language Learners with Special Needs: Identification, Placement, and Instruction,* edited by Alfredo J. Artiles and Alba A. Ortiz (2002).

LAURA G. DOROW, Ed.D., is an Associate Professor of Education at Utica College, Utica, New York, and the Coordinator of Student Teaching and Fieldwork. She serves as Co-Director of the Adapting Curriculum for Student Success (ACSS) project, supported by funding from the U.S. Department of Education. ACSS is a demonstration project to assure that students with disabilities receive a quality higher education program. Dr. Dorow is President of the New York State Association of Teacher Educators.

NANCY DUBETZ is an Associate Professor in the Department of Early Childhood and Childhood Education at Lehman College, City University of New York. She teaches courses in the bilingual extension program and serves as Professional Development School liaison with Public School 291 in the Bronx. Her research focuses on professional development school partnerships and the efforts of practicing bilingual teachers and teacher candidates to meet the needs of English language learners. Her most recent publication is "Improving ESL Instruction in Bilingual Programs Through Inquiry-Based Professional Development," which appeared in *Second Language Teacher Education: International Perspectives,* edited by D. Tedick (2005).

LOIS A. FISCH, Ph.D., is an Associate Professor of Education at Utica College, Utica, New York. She is Director of the Institute for Excellence in Education and Teacher Education Co-Director of the Adapting Curriculum for Student Success (ACSS) project. Supported by funding from the U.S. Department of Education, ACSS is a demonstration project to assure that students with disabilities receive a quality higher education program. She also serves on the Executive Board of the New York Association of Colleges for Teacher Education.

NEIL GAROFANO is an Associate Professor and Chair of the Marymount College Fordham Inclusive Education Program, where he has taught since 1989. Dr. Garofano has maintained a clinical practice in learning disabilities in upstate New York since 1972. He holds an M.A. in both child psychology and learning disabilities as well as an Ed.D. from Teachers College in special education and is a trained Montessori teacher. He began his career in special education in 1969 as Director of Montessori Associates, a school for students with disabilities.

MATT GIUGNO is an Associate Professor in the office of Vocational and Educational Services for Individuals with Disabilities in the New York State Education Department. With Gerald M. Mager, he is Co-director of the New York Higher Education Support Center (HESC) for Systems Change, an effort to promote quality inclusive teacher preparation programs in colleges and universities, and partnerships between those institutions and local high-need schools and districts in the seven regions of the state.

GERALD M. MAGER, Ph.D., is a Professor in Teaching and Leadership Programs in the School of Education at Syracuse University. With Matthew Giugno, he is Co-director of the New York Higher Education Support Center (HESC) for Systems Change, an effort to promote quality inclusive teacher preparation programs in colleges and universities, and partnerships between those institutions and local high-need schools and districts in the seven regions of the state.

LINDA MILCH is the Clinical Director of Long Island Advocacy Center. Ms. Milch received her M.S. in early childhood education at Brooklyn College. She taught in the New York City Public Schools before joining the Advocacy Center in 1990. As an educational advocate, she helps parents of children with disabilities understand and assert their rights and advocate for their children's educational needs. Currently she is an Adjunct Professor in special education at Hofstra University and on the Board of Directors of Long Island Families Together.

DARRA PACE, Ed.D., is an Assistant Professor in the Special Education Program at Hofstra University in Hempstead, New York. Currently, she teaches courses in methods and curriculum for diverse student populations, the nature and needs of individuals with cognitive disabilities, introduction to the exceptional child, and issues in special education. Dr. Pace is Long Island liaison to the New York State Task Force on Systems Change. Her recent publications include articles on co-teaching, developing university public school partnerships, and teaching mathematics to students in an inclusive setting.

WAVERLYN L.J. PETERS is the Director of Pupil Services in the Baldwin School District. Her responsibilities include special education, Section 504, and ADA. She is an Adjunct Professor at Hofstra and Molloy universities and a former regional supervisor for the New York State Education Department.

MELISSA PRICE currently serves as the project coordinator for the New York Higher Education Support Center for Systems Change (HESC) at Syracuse University. HESC is a collaborative project between Syracuse University and the New York State Education Department Office of Vocational and Educational Services for Individuals with Disabilities (VESID). HESC supports New York State institutions of higher education as they work to develop and maintain inclusive teacher preparation programs and serve high-needs schools throughout the state. Melissa is certified in general education (N–6) and special education (3–21) and has served a broad range of students over the years.

BEVERLY RAINFORTH is a licensed physical therapist and special education teacher. Currently she is Professor of Special Education at the State University of New York at Binghamton and chair of the Related Services Committee of TASH. She is author (with Jennifer York) of *Collaborative Teams for Students with Severe Disabilities: Integrating Therapy and Educational Services* (1992), and editor (with Judy Kugelmass) of *Curriculum and Instruction for All Learners: Blending Systematic and Constructivist Approaches in Inclusive Elementary Schools* (2003).

LILLIAN SANABRIA-HERNÁNDEZ is an adjunct professor at Hofstra University. She is certified as a teacher of special education and has worked in the field for over fifteen years. Lillian is the founder and president of Early Success Inc., an early intervention agency dedicated to providing therapeutic services to parents and children. She also has a regular advice column, "En Confianza" of *HOY Newspaper*, which is in circulation in New York, Chicago, and Los Angeles.

GLORIA LODATO WILSON, Ph.D., is an Assistant Professor in the Special Education Program at Hofstra University. She teaches classes in psychoeducational assessment and in learning disabilities, and her current research interests include effective inclusionary practices in co-taught classes and strategic instruction for students with learning difficulties. She is currently the President of the Council for Exceptional Children, Chapter 71. Her recent publications include articles on student perceptions of co-teaching, self-efficacy of students with disabilities, use of technology in Individual Educational Programs, and inclusive techniques.

RALPH ZALMA, Ed.D., is Professor Emeritus in Special Education at Hofstra University, where he served as a professor, coordinator of graduate programs, and department chair for over thirty years. He received his doctorate in special education from Teachers College, Columbia University. He has taught courses to students in education and psychology on the nature and needs of students with neurological impairments, attention deficit hyperactive disorders and learning disabilities; psychoeducational assessment in special education; and professional problems and issues, and was a member of the Center for Teaching Excellence.